1,001 OLD-TIME HOUSEHOLD HINTS

1,001 OLD-TIME HOUSEHOLD HINTS

Timeless Bits *of* Household Wisdom *for* TODAY'S HOME *and* GARDEN

By the Editors of YANKEE MAGAZINE®

Yankee Publishing Staff

President: Jamie Trowbridge
Book Editor: Fern Marshall Bradley
Contributing Writers: Sally Jean Cunningham, Rose R. Kennedy, Dougald MacDonald, Deborah L. Martin, Margaret McVeigh, Kathleen Byrne Meehan, Arden Moore, Donna Shryer
Researchers: Michelle Friedman, Aliza Schiff
Book Designer: Jill Shaffer
Interior Illustrator: Carl Kirkpatrick
Manuscript Review: Kenneth S. Burton Jr., Mary Jane Horton, Sarah Kirby
Copy Editor: Nancy Rutman
Indexer: Nanette Bendyna
Proofreader: Barbara Jatkola

Rodale Inc. Editorial Staff

Editor: Karen Bolesta
Senior Project Editor: Marilyn Hauptly
Cover Designer: Christina Gaugler

Printed in the United States of America on acid-free ♾, recycled paper ♲.

Library of Congress Cataloging-in-Publication Data

1,001 old-time household hints : timeless bits of household wisdom for today's home and garden / by the editors of Yankee Magazine.
p. cm.
Includes bibliogaphical references and index.
ISBN-13 978-0-89909-398-7 paperback
ISBN-10 0-89909-398-1 paperback
1. Home economics. I. Yankee Magazine.
TX158.A145 2005
640—dc22 2005009121

Distributed to the trade by Holtzbrinck Publishers
2 4 6 8 10 9 7 5 3 1 paperback

We inspire and enable people to improve their lives and the world around them
For more of our products **visit rodalestore.com** or call 1-800-848-4735

Contents

INTRODUCTION

Hunting for Treasures from the Past

In the days before television, the Internet, and free how-to classes at Home Depot, most people had few resources for learning how to cook, clean, take care of their health and family, or maintain their homes and gardens. One essential item in old-time households was a household help book, which had a place of honor on the shelf next to the almanac and the family Bible. These books were storehouses of practical advice and instructions, and their titles ranged from the quaint to the surprisingly modern. For example, there's *Housewifery: A Manual and Text Book of Practical Housekeeping,* from 1919. *Cookery and Housekeeping: A Complete System of Household Management for All Who Wish to Live Well at a Moderate Cost* was first published in 1886, while Depression-era families looked for money-saving ideas in the 1936 book called *1000 Helps and Hints for the House and Home.*

These household manuals from the past include a hodgepodge of recommendations, many of them outdated or routine but a surprising number of them highly effective and ingenious—hints and tips that have been lost in our fast-paced, ultramodern society. The trick is in having the time and know-how to find the gems among the thousands of pages of old books and other publications. And that's where our expertise as editors of *Yankee* magazine comes into play.

While researching *1,001 Old-Time Household Hints,* we and our writers scoured stacks of vintage books, magazines, journals, and memoirs, sifting out the humdrum and outmoded to find the very best recipes, how-to instructions, simple projects, and sage advice for everyday living: preparing meals, cleaning, doing laundry, self-care, staying healthy, caring for pets, home repairs, even fashion tips and old-time recommendations for recreation and holiday time.

Here at *Yankee* magazine, it's second nature for us to seek out and appreciate ingenious and useful ideas, because our country's heritage of self-reliance was formed and refined in New England, the home of *Yankee* magazine. For example, we found old-time recommendations for more than a dozen ways to use ordinary bar soap to achieve great cleaning results in the kitchen, bathroom, and more. Plus, there are ingenious suggestions for substitutes for commercial furniture polish to fix blemishes in wooden furniture, beauty secrets of Victorian belles, homemade holiday decorations from the days before Hallmark, and terrific recipes for favorite comfort foods such as baked ham, gingerbread, and hot cocoa. And our team wasn't content just to find great *old-time* ideas. Throughout the book, we added adaptations and improvements to old-time methods that use today's technology and materials. We wanted readers of *1,001 Old-Time Household Hints* to enjoy an unparalleled treasury of the best ideas from both the past and the present.

1,001 Old-Time Household Hints is actually three reference books combined in one. In part one, Your Old-Time Home Handbook, you'll find hundreds of great tips for home cooking and baking, cleaning, decorating, home repairs, crafts, entertaining, and celebrating the holidays. Part two, A Personal and Pet Care Compendium, focuses on remedies for common ailments, staying healthy, beauty and grooming, fashion and etiquette, and pet care. Part three, An Old-Time Gardener's Guide, rounds out the book with advice on vegetable gardening, flower gardening, and indoor gardening. As you browse through this book, you'll come across an eclectic variety of useful, ingenious ideas and projects: how to use sand and ketchup as cleaning helpers; how to turn a plain modern lampshade into a lovely Victorian-style beaded lampshade; how to make *real* sourdough bread the way the pioneers did; how 19th-century women got age spots to fade without fancy cosmetic products; and how to keep a single houseplant thriving for up to 75 years.

Watch for special types of tips that are highlighted throughout the book. For example, "Trash or Treasure" points out the ingenuity of old-timers who knew how to find usefulness and value in the humblest items. You'll discover how to put items such as an old inner tube, a worn tennis ball, and an extra piece of garden lattice to good use around your house and garage. "Old-Fashioned Favorites" flags simple recipes and techniques from the past that will surely become favorites today, such as an excellent recipe for authentic hot cocoa or exquisite ingredients for the soothing bath of a Victorian lady.

1,001 Old-Time Household Hints offers plenty of solid practical advice on every page. But to lighten the mix, we've sprinkled in some of the more amusing and unusual finds that turned up during our research. "Pearls of Wisdom" offers wise and sometimes pointed sayings that still apply to our 21st-century lives. "Old-Time Oddities" describes strange gadgets and gizmos that past generations employed for day-to-day tasks, from a toothbrush made with hog bristles to a bicycle-powered washing machine. "Roughing It" includes descriptions of the rigorous effort needed to complete everyday tasks in olden times—showing us that we sure can't complain that "life is rough." And "Bizarre but True" recounts some of the strange and amusing practices and habits of our forefathers and foremothers, including applying crushed garlic to the feet to cure hoarseness and an old Easter tradition that allowed strangers to (literally) pick one another up in the street.

For those tips in which we wanted to add the extra touch of modern ingenuity and expertise, we consulted a wide range of experts from across North America. You'll see the names of these doctors, researchers, veterinarians, business owners, horticulturists, and consultants throughout the book. We're grateful for the generous and helpful advice from experts such as Norman Rosenthal, M.D., of Rockville, Maryland, an internationally known expert on seasonal affective disorder (SAD). Nationally recognized image development trainer and consultant Susan Fignar, president of Chicago-based Pur-sue Inc., dispensed advice on keeping a modern wardrobe up to snuff as well as the art of shaking hands. And longtime Master Gardeners Carl and Betty Walter, of Hamburg, New York, offered some of their best advice for overwintering bulbs and raising houseplants. The specialized knowledge of these experts and many others adds an extra dimension and new information that builds on the wisdom of the past.

Every generation discovers breakthrough ideas and creates innovations that make daily life easier, more convenient, and more enjoyable. *1,001 Old-Time Household Hints* has skimmed the cream from the ideas of dozens of generations of inventive folks from all across North America and other countries to boot. So put up the footrest on your recliner, grab a cup of coffee, and enjoy venturing through this guide to the ingenuity of your foremothers and forefathers. After all, good ideas never grow old.

The Editors of *Yankee* Magazine

PART ONE

Your Old-Time Home Handbook

Home truly is our castle. It's where we relax, spend time with our families, enjoy crafts and hobbies, and celebrate the holidays. Of course, we do a lot of chores at home, too: cooking, cleaning, laundry, home repairs, and more. Homeowners and homemakers have pursued these same pastimes for generations, and we've gone back to their old-time cookbooks, home maintenance manuals, housekeeper's handbooks, and hobby guides to discover how they managed their households and pursued their family traditions around hearth and home. We've taken their best ideas and added a touch of present-day ingenuity and technology to help you get the best value and greatest satisfaction out of your household routines and activities.

CHAPTER 1

In the Kitchen
Man Does Not Live by Bread Alone

Savory casseroles, delectable sauces and desserts, and fragrant gingerbread cooling on the windowsill—everyone loves genuine home cooking. In this chapter, you'll find a hearty serving of practical ideas for organizing and cleaning your kitchen and its contents, along with dozens of hints from Colonial, pioneer, and Depression-era cookbooks on choosing the best ingredients and serving up flavorful homemade meals. Better still, you'll learn how to apply old-time know-how to modern convenience foods so you can enjoy the best flavor without all the backbreaking labor.

Kitchen Cleaning and Organization

The kitchen is often the most used room in the house, and keeping it clean and neat takes effort, purpose, and a lot of good tips! With fewer modern cleaning and cooking appliances at hand, old-time homemakers needed ingenuity and efficient practices even more than we do now. Read on for some of their best ideas for maintaining the kitchen.

Borax Grease on Kitchen Walls

■ One aspect of the kitchen that hasn't changed much from centuries past is grease—it still has all the same grimy properties, and unless you swear off frying, you're bound to spatter a bit on the walls. Instead of buying a special grease-cutting product that will take up space in your cabinet, make the borax from your laundry room do double duty. Here are instructions for cleaning grease off painted kitchen walls, from the pages of the *Cooking School Text Book; and Housekeeper's Guide to Cookery and Kitchen Management* (1879): "Wash the paint with a piece of clean flannel dipped in hot water, in which borax has been dissolved in the proportion of one tablespoonful to a gallon of water." If any spots still won't budge, says the *Cooking School Text Book,* use a little bit of mild dish-washing liquid dissolved in water (in about the same proportions you'd use to wash dishes) to rub them off. Then wipe the area with a damp rag, rinsing repeatedly, to remove the soap.

A Simple Fly Trap

HAVE FLIES INVADED your kitchen? Try the clever fly trap described in *500 More Things to Make for Farm and Home* (1944), which is made with nothing more than a funnel and a broad-mouthed jar. Put bait, such as a piece of fruit or bread, in the jar, insert a funnel in the mouth, and stand the two upside down on several blocks of wood, so a small gap is formed between the funnel and the surface of the table or floor. Flies will be drawn into the jar by the bait but won't be able to find their way out, like lobsters in a trap. To get rid of the flies, turn the jar and funnel right side up, fill the bottle with water through the funnel, and then remove the funnel and pour the drowned flies down the drain or outside the house.

Removing Grease from Kitchen Wallpaper

■ If your kitchen walls are wallpapered rather than painted, borax won't help clean off grease stains. Instead, try this method adapted from one used by 19th-century homemakers. Plug in your electric iron and heat it to medium. Then cover the grease spot with white cotton rags or a cloth diaper. Unplug the iron and hold the hot iron against the rag, which will absorb the grease. Voilà—no more grease stain! *Caution:* Use this method on paper wall coverings only. Do not use it on wallpapers that contain any form of vinyl or plastic.

Paint Keeps Kitchen Walls Cleaner

■ If you live in an old house with plaster walls, heed the advice of Emily Holt in *The Complete Housekeeper* (1912) the next time you redecorate your kitchen: Choose paint instead of wallpaper or wooden paneling. Paper and wood surfaces absorb dampness and cooking odors, and are difficult to clean. Painted plaster is best. "Grease which volatilizes in a degree from every sort of cooking, and is deposited upon the walls, does not penetrate the painted surface. Hence washing removes it entirely. Indeed, with a well-painted wall, a minimum of care keeps it fresh the year round."

If your home was built after about 1945, it probably has walls made of drywall. If so, choose washable latex paint or wallpaper containing plastic or vinyl so you can wash the walls by wiping them with a cloth dipped in warm water mixed with a mild soap.

Sweeping Secrets for the Kitchen Floor

■ Sweeping a tile or linoleum kitchen floor can be a dust-swirling proposition, particularly if you've had a recent baking spree or beachgoers have descended on you with sandy feet. Instead of struggling to suck up every last grain of flour or sand with the vacuum, do a better job with a plain old broom, using this recommendation from *Housewifery: A Manual and Text Book of Practical Housekeeping* (1919), by Lydia Balderston. She recommends "dustless sweeping" by "moistening the broom and shaking out all the water before sweeping." This technique takes a little experimentation to get right, however, because if the broom is too wet, the dust or grit will get gooey and stick to the floor.

An even better alternative: Use a spray bottle to sprinkle a section of newspaper with water until it's lightly damp and "then tear into bits and scatter over the floor; it need not be over the whole floor, but here and there in small quantities" before sweeping. The damp paper will keep the dust or flour from swirling into the air. You can just sweep the newspaper into the dustpan and throw it away along with the other floor debris.

Flannel Bags Give Brooms a Boost

ANOTHER WAY to enhance a plain old broom for improved performance on kitchen floors: Use a broom bag, as recommended in *Housewifery* (1919). This flannel cloth cover for the head of a broom will pick up dust, flour, and animal hair even in tight corners and under cabinets. Afterward, you wash it and reuse it—no throwaways here. You won't find flannel broom bags for sale at your local discount store, but you can easily make your own. Using worn-out soft flannel sheets or shirts, or those soft yellow dust cloths sold at discount stores and grocery stores, just sew a drawstring bag to fit your broom head. For extra oomph, spray the cloth with electromagnetic "dusting spray" between washes.

Paper-Scrape Your Dishes

■ Even when you're using a miraculous modern dishwasher, it's still a good idea to scrape plates before washing them. Whether you're cleaning your fine china or just want to prolong the life of your everyday dishes, keep in mind this tip from Lydia Balderston in *Housewifery* (1919). "This is usually called scraping the dishes, but it is better if wiping is the process actually employed, because the sharp edges of knives used in scraping harm fine finishes." But instead of dirtying a dish towel or wasting paper towels to wipe dishes, use yesterday's news. "A little wad of paper or the skin of a baked potato makes an excellent wiper," says the author. "A rubber scraper is made for the purpose, but it is only one thing more to keep clean." Particularly before a lavish family meal, be sure to put a section of newspaper beside the trash can and another next to the sink. Remember, this same technique works well if you need to

TRASH OR TREASURE

New Uses for Old Soap

FROM *Be an Artist at the Gas Range* (1935) comes this method for washing dishes that "saves soap and besides produces quicker action." Instead of buying expensive dish-washing liquids, try putting one or two teaspoons of soap or soap powder into a small bowl. (You can even use small leftover pieces of bar soap.) "Fill this with about one cup of hot water. Now you have a concentrated soap mixture, which will instantly remove any grease. Rinse in running hot water and dish washing will be made as easy as it is possible to make it."

Another use for old pieces of bar soap is cleaning metal stovetop coffeepots or teakettles. These vessels often become stained—coffeepot stains result from coffee sediment, and teakettles develop calcium rings when tap water is left in them for days. To combat sour stovetop pots, use this easy tip from M. B. Bosson in *Aunt Mena's Recipe Book* (1888), which will keep your pots sparkling and your tea and coffee tasting their best: "To brighten the inside of a coffee or teapot, fill with water, add a small piece of soap and let it boil on the stove for about 45 minutes." Avoid heavily perfumed soaps. Ivory Soap is one good choice for this task. Be sure to rinse the pot thoroughly afterward, and don't try this method for glass pots or carafes.

remove food debris from one of today's highly sensitive nonstick-finish pots or pans, too.

Dish Towels Aren't Just for Drying Dishes

■ When you wash delicate glass and china, follow advice from Emily Holt, author of *The Complete Housekeeper* (1912), and put a folded dish towel in the bottom of the dishpan or sink before you start to wash. "The use of it is to save breakage, both in turning about or by accidental dropping."

A Sticky Situation

■ Sometimes two drinking glasses soaking in a sink full of dishwater will stick together as if they were glued. When you try to pull them apart, you risk breaking the glasses and cutting yourself. Here's a quick trick from *1001 Entirely New Household Hints* (1937) for unsticking two glasses: Pour cold water into the inside glass and then run warm water from a tap over the outer one. The glasses will quickly and easily separate.

Save Suds, Save Time

■ Whether you wash dishes for a small family or a large one, tricks that improve efficiency—and leave dishes and utensils squeaky clean without damaging them —are always welcome. Here are some tips from the days before electric dishwashers, from Lydia Balderston, author of *Housewifery* (1919).

Soaking makes it simple. "Most people dislike to wash the pots and pans; but if they are put to soak the minute they are emptied, with a little soap powder or dissolved [baking] soda to cut the grease, with cold water for the egg and milk dishes, and hot water for the greasy and sugary dishes, it will be found that they have cleaned themselves to such an extent that their washing is no harder than that of china."

Group and conquer. "Grouping the dishes at the beginning means that the same group or pile is now ready to be put away without further sorting."

Hot-rinse plates. "If the rinse (for plates and other ceramic dishes) is very hot, and the dishes are placed in the [drying] rack, they will dry while the heavier dishes are being washed."

No knives allowed. "The knives are usually separated and washed by themselves because they are heavy and are likely to scratch the silver forks and spoons."

A Cleaner Grater

■ Certain foods, such as hard cheese, can be tough to clean from a grater without ripping up your sponge (or your fingers). To speed cleaning of graters, *1000 Helps and Hints for the House and Home* (1936), by Mabel Zirbes, suggests grating a raw potato through the cheesy area of the implement. The potato will clean off easily, leaving the grater ready to rinse.

Cooking School Trick for Clean Copper

■ Copper cookware promotes even heating and is the darling of gourmets and professional chefs. If you're lucky enough to have a vintage pot or pricey gourmet pan with copper on the bottom, try this easy, natural, and fume-free method of getting it clean, provided by Juliet Corson, author of the *Cooking School Text Book; and Housekeepers' Guide to Cookery and Kitchen Management* (1879): "One of the best chefs belonging to the New York Cooking School always had the coppers cleaned with the following mixture . . . equal parts of salt, fine sand, and flour, made into a thick paste with milk or buttermilk." The chef would rub on this mixture by hand, wash it off with clean, cold water, and use a soft towel to dry the copper pot thoroughly. Make sure you use the sterilized sand you have on hand for crafts or indoor gardening, not builder's sand.

Even if you own the stainless-steel-lined copper sauté pans, tell everyone in your household not to send the pans through the dishwasher, says Sarah Job, an assistant manager at the Williams-Sonoma gourmet cookware store in Knoxville, Tennessee. "Any dish or pan that is even part copper requires hand-washing with a soft sponge and mild soap, not dishwasher detergent," she says. Other abrasives to avoid with copper: steel wool, ordinary scouring powder, and sponges with a rough nylon surface.

There are also foods to avoid cooking in an unlined copper pot—anything acidic involving tomatoes, citrus, vinegar, and the like. When these ingredients make contact with unlined copper, salts are formed that can contaminate the food and make diners ill.

If you do have an unlined copper bowl or saucepan, pull it out when you want to whip egg whites, cook polenta, or caramelize sugar. "When the whites react with the copper, it makes them fluffier and they stay more stable," says Sarah. Polenta reacts to unlined copper by becoming creamier, and sugar cooked to the caramel stage is less likely to recrystallize.

Suds Are the Secret for Aluminum

■ Cleaning messy aluminum pots and pans has been a problem for generations. *Be an Artist at the Gas Range,* a 1935 gas-company advertisement, recommends this method: "Rub plenty of soap on your dishcloth. Put a little water in the pan to be cleaned—about a tablespoon, no more. Now rub your cloth on a bar of cleanser or sprinkle on the cloth a *very little* cleanser and very lightly rub around the pan to be cleaned. That lubricates the grit in the cleanser and stops its scratching. Rub the pan very lightly with plenty of suds and you will have bright, clean pots and pans." Be sure to choose a mild household cleanser that does not contain chlorine bleach.

To remove burned food from an aluminum pot or pan, *1000 Helps and Hints for the House and Home* (1936), by Mabel Zirbes, suggests filling the pot with cold water and adding a couple of splashes of vinegar. Bring the water to a slow boil and allow it to boil for 5 to 10 minutes. Remove the pot from the heat and allow it to cool partway. The remaining burned gunk now should be easy to clean.

Cleaning the Toaster Is a "Crumby" Job

■ "A soft pastry-brush will reach the most difficult corners of an electric toaster and brush out the most elusive crums," according to *The Butterick Book of Recipes and Household Helps* (1927). Bill Meehan, of Haddonfield, New Jersey, a leading collector of pre–World War II percolators and toasters, agrees. "Methods used to clean most modern electric toasters today are the same as they were in the 1920s. Start by unplugging the toaster. Then open the bottom crumb hatch and gently dust it out with a small, clean, soft paintbrush. If the toaster's exterior is plastic, wipe it with a damp, soft cloth. Use plastic polish if you need to remove scratches from the plastic. To clean chrome-plated appliances, use chrome polish, like you would use for the trim on a car." Bill notes that by 1940, most American homes included an electric toaster, which could be bought at Sears or Montgomery Ward for, believe it or not, about 79 cents.

The Art of Cleaning an Electric Percolator

■ Many people still love their coffee perked in an electric percolator. But cleaning an electric percolator can be tricky. To do the job right, follow these directions from the 1936 brochure *How to Care for Your New Royal Rochester Percolator* when you clean your vintage or modern percolator: "It is best always to clean any coffee-maker immediately after using it. Rinse with scalding hot water and dry thoroughly, leaving it open to the air, if possible, before putting it away.

Never wet the lower part of the coffeemaker. The heating unit and electrical connections are in the lower part and should be kept dry always. Do not use strong cleaners. The majority of strong cleaners are alkaline, very corrosive, and ultimately their use results in permanent damage. For cleaning use only baking soda—about one tablespoon to four cups of water. Attach the cord for twenty minutes and rinse thoroughly."

Percolator collector Bill Meehan, of Haddonfield, New Jersey, believes that electric percolators make the smoothest, mellowest coffee. "The number-one secret to success when cleaning your percolator is to rinse it thoroughly with water, dry it thoroughly with a paper or cloth towel, and let all the parts and the inside of the pot air-dry completely before putting them away." Bill notes that a percolator will need only occasional cleaning with baking soda if it is simply rinsed and dried properly. The best way to ensure this is to let it dry overnight. Also, never use steel wool or any abrasive inside or outside your coffeemaker, because it will destroy its appearance and remove the protective interior finish.

Rice Deodorizes a Spice Mill

WHEN YOU USE a coffee or spice mill, a food processor, or a mortar and pestle to grind strongly flavored spices, such as those used for curries or hot Mexican food, the taste and odor may taint the next thing you put in the mill. "To clean [a mill] after grinding strong spices, grind a handful of rice through it," advises Mabel Zirbes in *1000 Helps and Hints for the House and Home* (1936). "Any flavor will be removed."

No More Fishy Frying Pans

■ Nutritionists encourage us all to eat more fish, but few people have enough pans to dedicate one solely to cooking fish. That makes it all the more important to make sure you get a fish pan clean—no one wants to ruin expensive ingredients or waste time by imparting a fishy odor to their vegetable stir-fry or sautéed chicken dish.

To rid a pan of fish odor, try this technique from Juliet Corson in the *Cooking School Text Book* (1879): "If you are obliged to use the same gridiron for broiling steak that has been used for fish, wash it thoroughly with hot water, soap, and [baking] soda, rinse it in clean, hot water, heat it over the fire, rub it thoroughly with clean brown paper, and then with an onion cut in two pieces."

Think you've succeeded in cleaning a "fishy dish"? Try this test, says Juliet Corson: "When about to use a fish kettle, set it over the fire [stove burner] empty to heat; if it is not perfectly clean, an odor will be perceptible." On a modern stovetop, low heat will be fine for a 1-minute test. If it's a baking pan, try a few minutes in a 300°F oven to reveal any lurking odors of fish.

Nix Food Odors with Mustard

■ To remove strong odors from glass jars and bottles, try this tip from *2,000 Useful Facts about Food* (1941): "Pour a solution of water and dry mustard [start with 1 tablespoon mustard in 1 quart warm water] into them and let stand for several hours or use a dilute chlorine solution [a few drops of chlorine bleach per quart of water] then rinse in hot water." After either treatment, run the jars and bottles through your dishwasher, and they should be clean and odor-free, ready for reuse.

Clever Cooking Hints

It's amazing how easily tips and hints developed by cooks more than a half-century (or even a century!) ago take care of common cooking troubles, from the quest to dress up the same old soups to the battle to prevent home-fried food from turning out too greasy. Follow these foolproof methods to produce your own consistently delicious dishes.

Souped-Up Soup Suggestions

■ Canned soup is a handy fallback for days when you're too rushed to cook, and with a little old-time knowledge, you can add simple but special touches that will turn a plain meal into dining pleasure. Borrow these serving suggestions for soups from the *Woman's Institute Library of Cookery* (1928) to enhance canned or take-out soups—without cracking veal knuckles or stewing oxtails like homemakers of yore.

Cream the competition. Fancy up the flavor and appearance of any hot or cold soup by stirring a little mashed pimiento into plain whipped cream and placing a dollop on each serving.

Bake some no-fuss pastry strips. "A very appetizing addition to soup may be made by cutting pastry into narrow strips and then baking these strips in the oven until they are brown . . . and serving in place of crackers, croutons, or bread sticks." Don't fuss with mixing pastry from scratch, though. Just add refrigerated piecrust or packaged crust mix to your shopping list, and this treat will take only minutes to prepare!

Serve supercrisp crackers. Packaged crackers are a classic accompaniment for soup, but don't serve them plain in the wrapper. To add extra crispness, "crackers should always be heated before they are served. Their flavor can be improved by toasting them until they are light brown in color." *Tip:* Spread crackers on a baking sheet and toast in a 250°F oven, just as you would heat corn taco shells.

Whisk Away Soup "Skin"

■ A congealed layer on the surface of a cream soup or chowder is a turnoff, and this practical tip from *New Delineator Recipes* (1929) will help you avoid the problem: "If a cream soup or a milk soup is beaten just before serving, the froth protects it against skin formation." Here's the perfect time to use that handheld blender contraption or dig out Mom's old manual eggbeater. For chunky chowders, use a wire whisk instead.

A Splash of Vinegar for Easy Stirring

■ Stirring together the ingredients for a big bowl of pasta or tuna salad can literally be a pain if you have arthritis. Ease the task with a hint from the *Amaizo Cook Book* (1926) for any type of salad with a mayonnaise base. Before you mix the ingredients together, thin the mayonnaise by adding a splash of white vinegar or lemon juice (½ teaspoon per ½ cup of mayonnaise). Try it—you'll find that the stirring is much easier. And the small addition of tart liquid won't affect the overall flavor of the dish.

Avoid Deep-Fried Fat Overload

■ Chicken tenders, cheese-stuffed jalapeños, ravioli, even battered pickles—deep-fried appetizers are all the rage at restaurants and sports bars. But you don't need to go out when you have a hankering for one of these newfangled taste treats. You can easily make deep-fried appetizers at home (and at quite a cost saving), but you'll need some old-fashioned advice to get the best results and to preserve your digestion. "Allowing the food to soak up quantities of fat during the frying is neither economical nor conducive to a digestible dish," write home economists in the *Woman's Institute Library of Cookery* (1928). To avoid this, the authors advise dipping your favorite treat into a liquid that contains some protein—such as a beaten egg or an egg-milk mixture—before you pop it into the fryer. Protein coagulates quickly in hot fat, forming a barrier that will prevent the fat from soaking into the food. Your treats will taste better and be better for you.

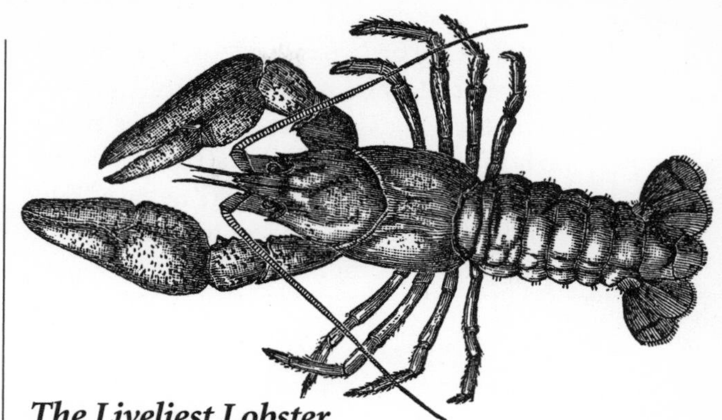

The Liveliest Lobster Proves the Tastiest

■ When you treat yourself to lobster, go all out for the best taste and most substantial portion by following this advice from Juliet Corson's *Every-Day Cookery, Table Talk and Hints for the Laundry* (1884): "Lobsters and crabs should be chosen by their brightness of color, lively movements, and great weight in proportion to their size." Oh, yes, and take a few extra minutes to have the clerk at the seafood market hold up your top choices and see how they act: "When lobsters are fresh, the tail will flap quickly back against the body when they are lifted up."

That's not just a fishwives' tale, says Fern Giard, who owns a lobster wharf and distributorship in Harpswell, Maine. "The lobster that picks up its tail and claws is strong and healthy." An even better test: "If you hold the live lobster and feel it vibrate . . . A growling lobster will taste the best."

Fern doesn't recommend buying any lobster that's already living in a tank, however. "There are too many in the space and they use that water for a bathroom, so they start getting weak and unhealthy really fast. They're just not worth the money." His recommendation if you don't live near lobster fishers is mail order from a reputable supplier such as Cook's Lobster House, in Bailey Island, Maine. "They air-mail pretty much right from the dock," he says. "The lobster is fresh—it never hits a tank."

☞ OLD-TIME ODDITIES ☜

A Fish Boiler

GRILLED FISH is a popular (and tasty) choice today, but in the days before gas grills, boiling was a common method for preparing fish. Cooks could even use a special fish boiler especially designed for the task. Here's how the *Woman's Institute Library of Cookery* (1928) describes a fish boiler: "A utensil in which fish can be boiled or steamed . . . This fish boiler, as it is called, is a long, narrow, deep pan with a cover and a rack on which the fish is placed. Attached to each end of the rack is an upright strip, or handle, that permits the rack containing the fish to be lifted out of the pan and the fish thus removed without breaking. To assist further in holding the fish together . . . a piece of gauze or cheesecloth may be wrapped around the fish before it is put into the pan."

If you can't cook a live lobster right away, don't feed or water it, Fern says. "A live lobster can survive in the cold at the very bottom of your refrigerator for as much as 48 hours. It will just lie there and wait to be cooked." Store the live lobster in an open container, and keep it just a little moist with a seawater-dampened towel or newspaper. Do not immerse lobsters in water or place them on ice in an airtight container—they will suffocate.

Cooking School Shellfish Tips

■ To be the most humane and to save time when you cook the lobster, make sure your water is at a rapid boil and contains a handful of salt—and put the lobster in headfirst, as recommended by Juliet Corson in the *Cooking School Text Book* (1879): "This contact with the boiling water kills them instantly." The same holds true for any other shellfish.

Bored with Bran? Start Waffling!

■ If eating bran cereal to add fiber to your diet is becoming monotonous, transform the bran into a breakfast, brunch, or light supper treat. That's right, make plain old bran into tasty hot waffles, using the recipe the Kellogg's All-Bran folks published in *219 New Ways to a Man's Heart* (1929), a bonus from the publishers of *True Story* magazine.

Sift 1½ cups flour, 4 teaspoons baking powder, and 1 tablespoon sugar. In a separate bowl, beat 2 egg yolks and combine with 1¼ cups milk. Add ⅓ cup melted shortening and ¾ cup Kellogg's All-Bran cereal. Stir in the dry mixture half a cup at a time, just until mixed. Add 2 stiffly beaten egg whites. Pour the batter into a hot waffle iron and bake.

By the way, these waffles freeze just as well as any other kind and can be reheated in the toaster or toaster oven.

Easy-Bake Bacon and Eggs

▪ Bacon and eggs are an unbeatable breakfast combination, and making them doesn't have to be a matter of spattering grease and frying pans. Instead, try this convenient, quick combination adapted from *New Delineator Recipes* (1929): Curl one slice of just-cooked bacon around the inside of each cup in a six-muffin tin. Break an egg inside each bacon ring, season with salt and pepper, and bake at 400°F until set but not hard—about 8 minutes. "Remove carefully from the dish so that the egg will remain fastened to the bacon. Arrange on a platter and garnish with parsley."

These bacon-and-egg rings can also become a better-tasting—and less expensive—alternative to fast food breakfast sandwiches. And there's no waiting in the drive-thru while you waste precious gasoline! Just tuck one of the rings into a home-baked biscuit, adding some grated cheese if you'd like. If you want less fat in the dish, spray the muffin tins with fat-free cooking spray. Using the slices from a package of store-bought precooked bacon work best for this dish—unlike crispy home-cooked bacon, precooked bacon is flexible and will bend in a circle easily.

The Better Boiled Egg

▪ Boiled eggs are an ideal high-protein breakfast option and the mainstay ingredient for any number of tasty salads and creamed dishes. If things haven't improved at your house since the authors of *The Dominion Home Cookbook* (1868) lamented that "the boiling of an egg is a very simple operation, but is frequently ill-performed," take heed. Here's how to get the best results whether you're anticipating decorating Easter eggs, planning to wow them with a platter of Grandma's deviled eggs, or craving a traditional chef's salad:

Soft-cooking. "Put the egg into a pan of hot water [just ready to] boil." When you put in the egg, use a pot holder to lift the pan from the heat by its handle, and hold the pan above the heat source for an instant or two. "This will allow the air to escape from the shell, and so the egg will not be cracked in boiling. Set the pan on the fire again and boil for three minutes or more if the egg be quite fresh, or two minutes and a half if the egg has been kept any time."

Hard-cooking. "Eggs to be used hard for salads and other dishes should be put into cold water, and boiled for a quarter of an hour after the water comes to the boil. In this case, the shells should not be taken off till the eggs are cold."

PEARLS OF WISDOM

"There is a vast difference
between the savage and
the civilised man,
but it is never apparent
to their wives until
after breakfast."

HELEN ROWLAND,
A Guide to Men (1922)

Meat Mastery

Roasts, chops, and other meat dishes were the centerpiece of the dinner table in many American homes until briefly falling from favor in the 1980s and 1990s. But with a new emphasis on high-protein diets and the wide availability of lean cuts of beef, pork, and white-meat poultry, preparing meaty meals is in vogue again. Look to the advice of past generations for preparing meats that are sure to please.

Easy Homemade Gravy

■ Lots of recipes instruct the cook to flour meat—sometimes before browning, sometimes before adding to a stew pot. But just about any cookbook from the early years of the 20th century will remind you of an important extra step that's often overlooked these days: Flour the bottom of the roasting pan before placing the meat in there (or on a rack in there) to roast. That will make the drippings thicker if you're serving the meat *au jus*, and it will eliminate the step of browning the flour separately if you're making gravy.

When your roast is fully cooked, remove the pan from the oven and transfer the roast to a cutting board or serving platter. If you're going to use the drippings for *jus*, pour them into a gravy boat or serving pitcher.

If you want to make gravy, put the roasting pan (with the drippings still in it) on your stovetop. Turn the heat on low and stir even more flour into the drippings until they have the consistency of heavy cream. Continue stirring constantly as you add enough water, milk, stock, or beer to make one cup of gravy. Add salt, pepper, or dried herbs to taste.

Low-Grease Sausage Strategy

■ Trendy gourmet recipes explain how to make your own lean, spicy sausage patties at home. But you can reduce the fat in any type of sausage patties—homemade or store-bought—if you cook them in accordance with this recommendation from Mrs. M. F. Walling, a contributor to *The Woman Suffrage Cook Book* (1886): "Put them in a baking tin in the oven [375°F], turning frequently as when frying. Brown them well. They are less greasy than if fried, and are more delicate in every way." Thankfully, there's a modern convenience item—not invented in Mrs. Walling's time—that will reduce by half or more the time required to clean the baking pan: aluminum foil. Just line the pan before you put in the patties. Also consider putting the sausages on the top half of a broiler pan with drainage holes, so the grease can drain into the bottom half of the pan. Spray the top with cooking spray first, and line the bottom with foil for quick cleanup.

Season Meat Loaf... With a Pickle!

■ It may seem as if 21st-century cooks have the corner on flavorful ethnic dishes, but check out this tip from *My Meat Recipes*, a pamphlet published in

1926 by the National Live Stock and Meat Board: To lend meat loaf what the pamphlet calls a "Creole" touch, season your ordinary recipe for 1½ pounds of meat with the typical chopped onion (1 small) and green pepper (1 large), and then add 2 chopped dill pickles!

The Untouched Meat Loaf

■ Making meat loaf can be a messy business. Most people wash their hands and stick them directly in the mixture of ground meat, eggs, bread crumbs, and seasonings to form the mix into a loaf shape. To keep the meat loaf sanitary and your hands clean, use this tip from the late Margaret E. Blecha, of Ridley Park, Pennsylvania. "My grandma used to actually make a meat loaf without touching it," says Margaret's granddaughter, Kathy Byrne. "After mixing her ingredients in a bowl with a fork, she would turn the whole business out onto a large piece of waxed paper. Wearing a plastic baggie on each hand like mittens, she would skillfully form the loaf and lift it into a pan. Grandma made the best-tasting—and cleanest—meat loaf around!"

Tender Ham with Fancy Topping

■ A luscious baked or boiled ham is a simple way to serve lots of guests—and the leftovers put prepackaged cold cuts to shame for flavorful, fresh sandwiches. Look to the past for tips on baking a ham to its tender, tasty best and presenting it with delectable garnishes. The guidelines given by Annabella Hill in *Mrs. Hill's New Cook Book* (1872) go far beyond the scanty directions available on most ham labels or in modern cookbooks, and work whether you're boiling or baking. (If you're cooking a canned or precooked ham with the skin on, though, you won't have any drippings to work with.)

Put down that fork. "Avoid piercing the meat [during cooking]; this makes unsightly marks and lets out the juices."

Cook cabbage separately. After you remove the meat from the pan, "cabbage, greens, beans, etc., may be boiled in the broth (or in water flavored with a tablespoon or so of the drippings). It is not proper to boil cabbage, or any kind of greens, with the ham, as they impart a disagreeable taste to the meat."

BIZARRE BUT TRUE

Don't Mock the Turtle Chef

DOUBTLESS this was a serious topic to Anna Ella Carrol, a contributor to *The Woman Suffrage Cook Book* (1886), but as most modern-day cooks need not rely on turtle soup for nourishment, her instructions for cooking terrapin take on a comic air: "Decidedly the terrapin has to be killed before cooking, and the killing is often no easy matter. The head must be cut off, and, as the sight is particularly acute, the cook must exercise great ingenuity in concealing the deadly weapon."

Dress it up. "After being skinned, hams may be ornamented in different ways. Brush over the top with the beaten yolks of eggs; sift over fine cracker or bread crumbs evenly; bake half an hour in a moderate [350°F] oven."

Try an Irish coating. "Or, cover with a thin coat of (boiled) Irish potatoes, rubbed through a colander [or grater]. Set it for a few minutes in the oven."

California Mock Duck

ROAST DUCK is a treat, just as it was in 1926, when the National Live Stock and Meat Board published *My Meat Recipes,* but fresh duck is not always easy to find at your local grocery store. Here's a substitute that uses regular flank steak instead for a delicious "mock duck" dish. This recipe was submitted by Dorothy Rodkey, of Blue Rapids High School, in Kansas.

1 ½ pounds soft bread crumbs
1 egg, lightly beaten
1 cup chopped prunes
½ teaspoon salt
⅛ teaspoon pepper
1 teaspoon lemon juice
1 ½ pounds flank steak
Small pieces of suet or slices of raw bacon

In a small bowl, combine the bread crumbs, egg, prunes, salt, pepper, and lemon juice. Pound the steak to tenderize it, and then brown it quickly on both sides in a hot skillet. Place the bread crumb mixture in the center of the steak. Roll it up and tie it with twine. Lay pieces of suet or bacon over the top, place it in a roasting pan, and cover with hot water. Bake at 375°F for 1 hour, or until the juices run clear. Thicken the liquid for gravy.

Five Innovative Meals from Old-Time Cooks

In the 1920s, take-out food and eating out at a restaurant on a weekday were virtually unheard-of, so cooks were interested in any novel way to vary their typical meat and potatoes. These delicious ideas from *My Meat Recipes* (1926) might inspire you to cook an economical meal at home tonight—you certainly won't find the same dish at any fast food restaurant.

1. "Cook a pot roast with one cup of currants."

2. "Lamb or mutton may be roasted on a bed of tart apples."

3. "Cheese melted [into] creamed chipped beef is a good addition."

4. "An oyster placed in the center of each sausage cake is a surprise dish."

5. "Serve fried oysters with beef pot roast and use the oyster liquor [the liquid in which the oysters were packed] for making the gravy."

Warm the Water for Tender Meat

To make savory homemade meat dishes, remember the age-old chemistry of H_2O. A lot hinges on water temperature when you make roasts or soups, claims the *Presbyterian Cook Book* (1873). When you pour water (or marinades or sauces that contain water) over the top of a roast before cooking, be sure the liquid is boiling. If you're going to boil fresh meat, such as chicken for chicken salad, bring the water to a boil before adding the meat. On contact with boiling water, the outer part of the meat "contracts and the internal juices are preserved," notes the book.

But for soup, the reverse is true. That's because cold water draws juices from the meat into the stock, which is what you want. So start stock in icy water.

Flour Power for Baked Ham

■ When you fix ham only once a year for the holidays, it's hard to get it right. Here's a little-known, old-fashioned way to keep the juices in the meat and prevent the ham from burning: Cook it in a "blanket" of flour. This technique comes from *My Meat Recipes* (1926). Stud a 10-pound cured ham (already skinned) with ¼ cup whole cloves and then cover with 1 cup sugar. Make a very stiff dough using 4 cups flour and as much cider or water as needed. Roll the dough to a ½-inch thickness and spread it over the meat. Bake the ham at 325°F for about 5 hours. "When done," the authors remark, "remove the crust, and you will be delighted with the results."

The Very Best Veggies

For fresh ways to get your three to five servings of fruits and veggies per day, go back to the future. Whether it's a Colonial side dish meant to wow the wigs at a formal dinner or a Victorian tactic for tender potatoes, our forefathers knew how to make tasty vegetables—and they knew how to pick 'em, from garden or grocer. Take their advice, and you've nothing to lose but your dull dinnertime routine.

More Minty Peas, Please

■ Here's a simple way to add flavor to green peas without adding fat. When you steam or boil them, "put them in with a

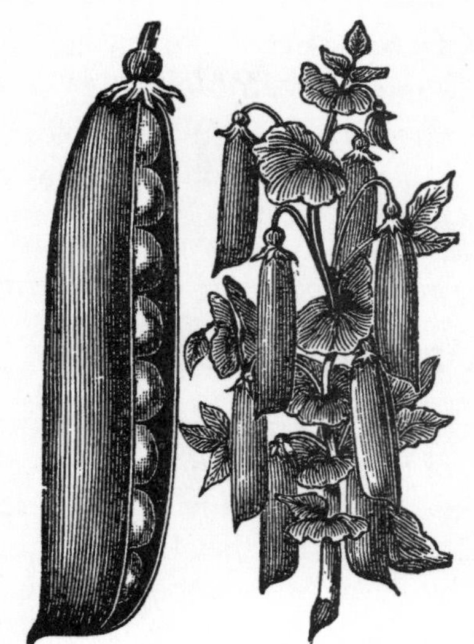

few leaves of mint," suggests Amelia Simmons in *American Cookery* (1798). If you don't have fresh spearmint or peppermint handy, try ½ teaspoon dried mint leaves, but tie the dried leaves in cheesecloth or enclose them in a tea ball before plunging them into the cooking water—you don't want dry chips of mint in your tender peas.

Scrape Corn Kernels with a Spoon

■ When you want to make fresh corn fritters, succotash, or chowder, scraping the kernels from the cob is a necessary evil. To extract as much of the kernel as possible, minimize the milky mess, and completely avoid cutting your finger, don't use a knife for this task, advises *The Dominion Home Cookbook* (1868). Instead, the task is "most expeditiously done" by "passing the blade of an iron spoon, slightly inclined to the cob, down the rows." In our day, a stainless-steel soup or slotted spoon does the trick—or try the edge of a grapefruit spoon for smaller kernels.

How Green Was My Cooked Vegetable?

■ Bright green cooked vegetables just taste better, and it's not difficult to preserve that appetizing hue when you cook beans, asparagus, broccoli, peas, or even brussels sprouts, according to Juliet Corson in *Every-Day Cookery, Table Talk and Hints for the Laundry* (1884). "The green vegetables should be washed in cold water as soon as they are tender, and allowed to stand in cold water until just before using, when they are to be heated quickly and served at once; treated in this way their color is perfectly preserved." The tastiest way to reheat (and still keep that nice green color) is to bring a tablespoon or so of water to a boil in a saucepan, add the drained vegetables, cover, and boil for a minute or so until they're heated through, says Bonnie Sheeley, a Cooperative Extension home economist in Knox County, Tennessee.

Care for Carrot Pudding?

TODAY'S NUTRITIONISTS rave about carrots and the powers of beta-carotene. Old-time cooks may not have known the scientific basis for carrots' nutritional bonanza, but they knew that carrots had delectable flavor when properly prepared. The recipe recommended by D. Petre in *Her Book* (1705) is almost like a carrot quiche, and it's versatile enough to include in a variety of meals. Use it for one of your main dishes at brunch or a light supper, as a side dish for a full dinner, or as your contribution to a potluck meal. Here's the basic recipe, with a few amendments made for the modern palate—and a few specifics where D. Petre gave only generalities.

Preheat the oven to 400°F. Coat a 13-by-9-inch glass or ceramic baking dish with butter or cooking spray. In a large mixing bowl, combine 1 quart whole milk, 6 to 8 lightly beaten eggs, 1 pound cleaned grated carrots, 1 stick of melted butter or margarine, ¼ cup packed brown sugar, ½ teaspoon salt, 1 teaspoon ground nutmeg, and ¾ cup flour. Mix well and pour into the baking dish. Bake at 400°F for about 30 minutes; then reduce the heat to 350°F and bake for 30 minutes longer. Serve with brown sugar to each diner's taste.

How the Pickiest Pick Produce

■ Of course, today's supermarkets have already narrowed your fresh fruit and vegetable choices for you—and you don't have to worry about such nuisances as weevils or borers in the produce on most grocery shelves. Just about anything you buy will be uniform and good quality—but there are ways to choose the tastiest of what's available, whether from your garden, a farmers' market, or the grocer's shelves. Here are words of wisdom from Amelia Simmons, author of *American Cookery* (1798), that still hold true in this day of hybrid technology and flash-frozen products.

Use the ruler for carrots. When you want big chunks of carrot for stew or need grated carrot for cakes or muffins, you can't rely on those convenient prepeeled baby carrots; you need bigger roots. If you rarely buy full-size carrots, remember that they're not all created equal. Be sure to choose carrots that are "middling siz'd, that is, a foot long and two inches thick at the top end." Their flavor and sweetness is "better than overgrown ones," but they're large enough to work with easily.

See red for slaw. If you've got a food processor and want to try your hand at home-shredding cabbage for slaw, try red Savoy cabbage. The reddest of the small, tight heads are best for slaw, claims Amelia Simmons. But don't try to cook any leftover cabbage, she warns. "It will not boil well, comes out black or blue, and tinges other things with which it is boiled."

Pick the pudgy parsley. Whether you're making a selection from your own herb garden or the produce section, look for "the thickest and branchiest" parsley for the fullest flavor. "The best-tasting parsley is always growing vigorously and getting enough water, so it won't be straggly or yellow," says Rose Marie Nichols McGee, co-owner of Nichols Garden Nursery, in Albany, Oregon. "And if you're picking parsley from your garden or a window box, you should pick from the center, but not just because it's thickest there." Picking parsley from the center on a regular basis prevents the plant from bolting (producing a seedstalk). Plants that bolt may have an off flavor, Rose Marie explains.

My watermelon is like a red, red rose. In *American Cookery* (1798), Amelia Simmons advises readers to choose red-cored watermelons, since they are "highest flavored." And this is easy to do these days, since grocery stores and farmers' markets often sell cut halves and slices of watermelon—you don't have to wait to get home and cut your melon open to see what you've got. As for selecting the best uncut melon, Leslie Coleman, director of communications for the National Watermelon Promotion Board, suggests that there is a more reliable method than the proverbial thump. "Select a firm, symmetrical watermelon that is free of bruises, cuts, and dents. Turn the melon over. If the underside is yellow and the rind has an overall healthy sheen, the watermelon is probably ripe. Select melons that are heavy for their size."

☞ OLD-TIME ODDITIES ☜

Get a Handle on a Watermelon

"WE FEEL very sure that when a thing is needed, it will be supplied by some inventor," wrote *The American Agriculturist* in 1878. A case in point: the watermelon handle. "No one article in the market is more unmanageable than a watermelon," the journal explained. The solution was a basswood handle, two lengths of twine, and two wooden "beckets" (rings) to adjust the twine for different sizes of melons.

Towel Trick for Best Boiled Potatoes

■ Simple boiled potatoes can be a grand, uncomplicated side dish—not to mention a wonderful source of vitamin A and a good alternative to fatty fries. Thing is, whether you're boiling chunks of peeled Idaho or whole baby blue or 'Yukon Gold', you'll want the potatoes to be mealy and moist, not watery. So do as they did in the 19th century and throw in the towel—or should we say throw *on* the towel? Here's the trick, as described by Juliet Corson in *Every-Day Cookery, Table Talk and Hints for the Laundry* (1884): When the potatoes are tender enough to be pierced with a fork, remove from the heat completely, drain, and return to the pan (still removed from the stove). Cover the pan with a dry, clean dish towel folded over several times, and the potatoes "may be kept hot and mealy for hours. It is the water soaking into the softened substance of the interior of the potato after it is cooked that makes it watery." Add your favorite seasonings or toppings right before serving.

"If the boiled potatoes are wanted for the table directly they are tender," adds the author, "drain them; put the cover again on the sauce-pan in which they were boiled, and shake them about (over medium heat) for a couple of minutes." If you have a glass-top range and aren't supposed to shake pans around on the surface, try wearing oven mitts and lifting the pan off the heat for a few seconds to shake it, then putting it back on the eye for a few seconds to reheat.

Once you're done with the moisture removal, and after completely removing the pan from the heat, potatoes should be sent to the table covered with a folded napkin. Don't re-cover the pan, or "the steam condensing on the inside of the cover will fall back upon the potatoes and make them watery."

BIZARRE BUT TRUE

Cabbage Cocktail?

EVEN THOUGH it was the time of the Great Depression, this appetizer recipe from *The Service Cook Book* (1933), published exclusively for the F. W. Woolworth Co., still seems a bit, well, odd. The authors would have you tantalize the tastebuds before meals with Sauerkraut Cocktail: Combine ½ cup shredded fresh tomatoes, 1 cup sauerkraut, a few drops of meat sauce, ½ tablespoon lemon juice, and ½ cup sauerkraut juice. Chill and serve in small cocktail glasses.

Old Cranberries Can't Jump

You stocked up on fresh cranberries in November and December, and several months hence, you're wondering whether those berries in the crisper are still fresh enough to use. Use a tip from post–Civil War days—when growers still picked each cranberry by hand—to sort the good from the bad. Drop any suspicious berry onto a hard surface from a height of at least 2 feet. If the berry bounces, it's still good; if not, out to the compost with it.

Luscious Leftovers

Since their families ate almost all meals at home, old-time cooks were experts at gussying up leftovers to become another delicious dish the next day, and just as adept at substituting one ingredient for another in a pinch. Pair their ideas with today's modern convenience foods for supertasty, clever dishes.

Four Rules for Great Leftovers

Think that cooking a roast, whole turkey, or whole chicken takes too much effort? Think again! Overall, preparing a large cut of meat is a time-saver, because leftover meat is a great starting point for quick-and-easy meals—as long as you know how to use it well.

Tap into old-time know-how from the days when all good home cooks knew how to make the best of leftovers, and you'll soon be creating your own simple recipes for tasty leftovers. Just follow four simple guidelines from *New Delineator Recipes* (1929). You can use a homemade sauce or rely on the modern advantage of convenient and delicious canned and prepackaged soups and sauce mixes.

1. Cut or shape the leftover meat into pieces of uniform size—bite size is usually best.

2. Since the meat has already been cooked, choose a gentle way to reheat it. First cook potatoes or a grain that you'll serve with the meat, and then mix the meat into the hot accompaniment. Heat through before serving.

3. Along the same lines, if you're going to serve the meat in a sauce, cook the sauce thoroughly, and then stir in the meat. Let it heat gently until the meat reaches serving temperature.

4. To figure out how much sauce to make, start by deciding on the approximate amount (in cups) of meat and vegetables you plan to serve. Prepare half that amount of sauce.

A New Look at Homemade Hash

As a comfort food for a chilly night, you can't beat hash—plus it's a great way to use up leftover roast or cold potatoes, and easily mastered by ordinary cooks. If you pair modern innovation with old-time know-how, you can make your hash even more delicious and nutritious—and go easier on the dishwasher to boot.

The basics. If you're rusty on how to make hash, try this simple recipe from the *Metropolitan Life Cook Book* (circa 1930): Chop 1 to 2 cups leftover meat and cube an equal portion of cold, cooked potato. Sprinkle with 1 teaspoon minced celery or onion and ¼ teaspoon black pepper. Melt butter in a frying pan (1 tablespoon for each cup of hash mixture), spread the meat and potatoes evenly over the bottom of the pan, and moisten with milk, meat stock, or leftover gravy (a few tablespoons should suffice). Then cook slowly (over medium-low to medium heat) for 20 minutes, until the meat and potatoes are browned on the bottom. Shake the pan occasionally to prevent sticking.

Opt for the oven. If you don't have time to hover over a pan, try a convenient oven hash. The *Metropolitan Life Cook Book* also notes, "The hash may be put in a buttered pan and baked in the oven," at 350°F for about 30 minutes. To make double sure the baked hash won't stick to the bottom of the pan, use cooking spray before melting the butter in the pan.

Coffee Bread Pudding

THESE DAYS, this recipe might be called Mocha Pudding Supreme, but when it was published in the F. W. Woolworth Co.'s *Service Cook Book* (1933), this pudding was noted as a practical way to make good use of leftover bread and coffee. Today, you can use it to be trendy, or just to be sensible.

- 1 cup strong black coffee
- 1½ cups milk
- 1 cup soft bread crumbs
- 2 eggs, separated
- ½ cup sugar
- ½ teaspoon vanilla
- Few grains salt
- ⅛ teaspoon baking soda
- Cream

Combine the coffee and milk and scald—heat the mixture in a pan or the top half of a double boiler on the stove, stirring constantly, until tiny bubbles form all the way around the edge of the pan (don't boil the mixture). Pour the scalded liquid over the crumbs and let stand until they have absorbed most of the liquid and the mixture is cool. Beat the egg yolks, sugar, vanilla, and salt until creamy, and add to the coffee mixture. Add the baking soda (dissolved in 1 tablespoon warm water). Whip the egg whites until stiff and fold into the batter. Transfer to an oiled pudding pan or dish and set in a pan of warm water. Bake at 350°F for 40 minutes, or until a knife when inserted comes out clean. Cool slightly and serve with whipped cream.

Talk turkey. "I use these really great old-time recipes with lower-fat turkey leftovers," says Amy Witsil, chief cook and bottle washer for a family of five in Chapel Hill, North Carolina. "I up the amount of gravy to about a quarter cup, since the meat is lower-fat, and I add a bit more onion and sometimes a teaspoon of minced jalapeño to make the turkey hash superflavorful."

Over-easy hash omelets. Here's a remarkably simple but effective suggestion for making a plate of hash look more appetizing, courtesy of the *Woman's Institute Library of Cookery* (1928): "Before serving, fold over as for an omelet and serve on a platter garnished with parsley."

Try a Little Coffee in Your Jelly

■ A light, summery, and distinctive dessert will always be within reach if you keep a packet or two of unflavored gelatin in the cupboard (its expiration date is usually years after the purchase date). The only other thing you'll need is that morning's coffee to create this favorite dish from post–World War I Florida described in *Cross Creek Cookery* (1942), by novelist Marjorie Kinnan Rawlings. She calls it Coffee Jelly, though our generation would probably call it Coffee Jell-O. To make this treat, dissolve 1 tablespoon plain gelatin (one envelope of Knox brand) in 2 tablespoons cold coffee, then add the gelatin-coffee mixture to ½ cup reboiled hot coffee and stir. Finish off by stirring 1½ cups additional cold coffee into the gelatin mixture. Pour in a bowl or mold and chill until set. Mrs. Rawlings recommends adding about a tablespoon of sugar to the "jelly" when you add the boiled coffee and serving it with unsweetened cream.

And as a denizen of the modern world, you can improve on her idea—just try making it with your favorite flavored brew (coffee, that is, not cappuccino or flavored creamers).

Rice Is Nice with Pineapple

▪ Love rice pudding? No need to bake, boil, or buy tiny plastic cups of the stuff when you can easily stir up a plentiful batch. This Rice and Pineapple Pudding, adapted from novelist Marjorie Kinnan Rawlings's *Cross Creek Cookery* (1942), offers calcium, fruit, and grains, but who cares? Mostly it's delicious and simple. To make it, use a fork to mix 1 cup chilled, boiled rice with ¼ cup granulated sugar, ⅛ teaspoon salt, and ½ teaspoon vanilla. Stir in one chilled 10-ounce can of crushed pineapple in natural juices (drain the juice and reserve it for another use). Fold in 1 cup whipped cream, lightly and quickly. Put the pudding in the refrigerator for a few minutes, and then dish it into sherbet glasses. And if you replace the whipped cream with vanilla yogurt, you've got a dish suitable for breakfast or to jazz up your brown bag lunch.

Custom Spices and Sauces

You won't find any "five-alarm" spices on an old-time menu. Cooks of yesteryear based their reputations on special sauces and an even hand with seasonings, and many of their ideas taste just as good on modern meat and vegetable dishes. A major advantage of making your own sauces and spice mixes is convenience: You'll always have just the right type of mixes on hand when you want to cook. And it doesn't hurt that homemade mixes cost much less than ready-made gourmet brands.

Old-Time Secret for Gourmet Mustard

▪ Flavored mustards like caper mustard and horseradish mustard are tempting to try, but if you don't like the flavor you pick off the gourmet store shelf, you've wasted your money. Instead, test exotic mustard blends in small batches you make yourself, using a technique that was commonplace on old-time American homesteads.

In *The Kentucky Housewife* (1839), Mrs. Lettice Bryan recommends making mustard by combining a little salt with some dry mustard (½ teaspoon salt per tablespoon of mustard) and stirring in boiling water a bit at a time until the mixture has a smooth consistency. The *Housewife* notes that some people use vinegar in place of water, while those who prefer mild mustard substitute milk and sugar for the water and salt.

Rob Stanford, a modern-day chef at the Tampa Yacht Club, in Florida, recommends that those experimenting with dry mustard concoctions use Colman's brand, available at any supermarket.

"That way you'll have it available for ordinary recipes that call for dry mustard, like deviled eggs and Welsh rarebit," he says. "You can't use those superhot Asian mustard powders for everyday cooking."

Mix and match any of these additions to a homemade mustard: prepared or dry horseradish; toasted whole (or crushed) mustard seeds; balsamic, flavored, or rice wine vinegar in place of apple cider vinegar or white vinegar; a little brown sugar, honey, or molasses; sour cream in place of some or all of the milk; or ample amounts of cracked black peppercorns. You can even add a spoonful of jelly or preserves for a fancy-flavored relish.

ROUGHING IT

How Did Cooks Ever Ketchup?

NEXT TIME you grab a handful of condiment packets at the nearest fast food joint, pause a few seconds to appreciate what our 19th-century counterparts endured to make the sauce they called Lemon Catchup, as recorded in *The Kentucky Housewife* (1839), by Mrs. Lettice Bryan.

"Mix together two ounces of grated horseradish, two of mustard seed, half an ounce of nutmegs, half an ounce of mace, half an ounce of black pepper, a quarter of an ounce of cayenne pepper, and a quarter of an ounce of cloves. Beat them very fine in a mortar, and put it in a stew-pan with one dozen lemons, which have been sliced and divested of seeds, a large handful of salt, and three pints of good vinegar. Cover the pan, and boil it for fifteen or twenty minutes; then put it in a jar, cover it, and let it stand for four weeks, stirring it occasionally; after which strain it, put it in small bottles, and cork them tight. A very little of this catchup . . . gives an agreeable flavor to fish and other sauces."

Dry Rub Dresses Up Routine Roast

Dry spice rubs are all the rage for Cajun steaks and tenderloins. Way back in 1926, a contributor to *My Meat Recipes* was touting a dry rub for pork roast. It isn't superhot or spicy, but it *is* tasty—and even a novice cook can turn out a well-browned, melt-in-your-mouth roast from this recipe, using cuts far less expensive than tenderloins. Here's the recommended procedure: Choose a lean roasting piece of pork, such as the shoulder or a cut of fresh ham. Preheat the oven to 425°F. Make several deep incisions in the meat. Mix 1 tablespoon salt, ½ teaspoon paprika, 1 tablespoon dry mustard, 1 tablespoon flour, and 1 teaspoon Tabasco sauce. Rub the mix into the incisions and let stand for 10 minutes. Place the roast in the oven at 425°F. While the meat is roasting, chop 1 sweet pepper fine and add to a pint of boiling water. When the meat is nicely browned, pour the pepper mixture over the top. Reduce the heat to 350°F and bake slowly for 40 minutes. Baste every 15 minutes.

Grind Herbs in Marble

Homegrown herbs make the best sauces, and old-time cooks used only a marble or brass mortar and pestle—not a wooden one—for grinding their dried herbs. They knew that the essential oils from the herbs would penetrate the porous surface of a wooden mortar, muddying the flavors of the herbs.

Concoct a Special Soup Mix

Gourmet Bean Soup Mix may sound like something exotic, but it's surprisingly easy to make yourself. You'll enjoy the simple task, and homemade soup spice mix is a great addition to add to homemade gift baskets.

This spice concoction hails from Colonial times and was later published in *The Cook's Oracle* (1829), by Dr. Kitchiner. "Pound together in a marble mortar half an ounce each of dried mint and sage, [1 teaspoon] of celery-seed, and [¼ teaspoon] of Cayenne pepper; rub them through a fine sieve," recommends the doctor. This amount will make enough to flavor one potful of soup, so multiply the recipe by four or more if you want to make enough for gift-giving. To simplify the process, use a coffee mill to grind the spices, or buy them already ground.

To make a pot of savory bean soup, combine 2 cans navy or pea beans with 8 cups water or soup stock. Add ½ cup chopped onions, 1 cup chopped celery, ½ cup chopped carrots, and the spice mix. Allow the mixture to simmer for about an hour.

Don't Let Your Spices Expire

If you have spices that sit unused in the cabinet from one Thanksgiving pie to the next, try this delicious old-time spice blend for everyday cooking, courtesy of Mrs. Lettice Bryan in *The Kentucky Housewife* (1839). "Take an ounce [1 tablespoon] of black pepper, one of white pepper, one of cinnamon, one and a half of [ground] ginger, half an ounce of red pepper, half a one of nutmegs, [1 teaspoon ground] mace and two dozen cloves. Mix them all together, and grind or pound them till they are very fine. Bottle and cork it securely. It will keep its strength, and will be found a very convenient article—nice for flavoring fresh meat gravies, &c." Of course, you can buy cloves and peppercorns already ground, or use an electric coffee grinder to grind whole ones.

"Dry spices lose much of their flavor after a few months, so you really should replace them at least once a year," says Volena Askew, supervisor of Adult Home Economics for Knox County, Tennessee, schools. "If you make this mix and keep it next to the stove, you'll remember to use it before the spices expire. You can also toss in a teaspoon or two of ground sage, if you have it on hand, or use ground thyme in place of the ginger."

OLD-TIME HUMOR

"England has forty-two religions and only two sauces."

VOLTAIRE (1694–1778)

No More Soggy Sandwich

Picnic packers the world over know that one way to keep sandwich fillings from making bread soggy is to butter the insides of the bread slices before adding

❦ OLD-FASHIONED FAVORITES ❦

Hot and Heart-Warming Cocoa

PREPACKAGED hot chocolate mix is convenient, but old-fashioned cocoa is lots tastier than instant, and making cocoa from scratch doesn't have to take extra effort. The ingredients are simple: sugar, water, and powdered cocoa (which you can also use to make homemade brownies). Best of all, old-fashioned hot cocoa is made with calcium-rich real milk, and you can decide what ratio of flavor to fat you want by using any variety from fat-free to whole. Here's the basic recipe from the *Metropolitan Life Cook Book* (circa 1930): "The general rule for cocoa is 2 teaspoons cocoa, ¼ cup cold water, 1 teaspoon sugar, and ¾ cup milk for each cup cocoa desired. Cook the water and cocoa together until thick; add the sugar; stir until dissolved; add milk and boil a minute."

Note: If you'd like, heat the cocoa and water together in the microwave for about 30 seconds on high. After you add the milk, however, transfer the cocoa to a small saucepan on the stove, where you can readily see when the milk starts to boil (you don't want to overcook your cocoa).

anything else. You can use that strategy to add flavor while subtracting a condiment with a tip from the *Presbyterian Cook Book* (1873): Mix dry mustard into the softened butter before spreading. Though the cookbook suggests 1 tablespoon mustard per ½ pound of butter, our modern palates would probably prefer 1 tablespoon per ¼ pound stick of butter. This tip works every bit as well with softened low-fat margarine, too.

Worry-Free Egg-Based Dressing

■ Nothing matches homemade salad dressings, but toppings such as Caesar dressing that involve raw egg can be dangerous, because raw eggs are a prime source of harmful bacteria. Instead of taking a chance on a raw-egg dressing, take a page from *Practical Vegetarian Cookery* (1897) and make a cooked homemade dressing. Here are two to try.

Aunt Susan's Salad Dressing. "Beat together one level teaspoonful of (dry) mustard, one heaping teaspoon of sugar, one dessertspoonful [tablespoon] of melted butter, one half teaspoon of salt and the yolk of one egg; add one cupful of milk and cook in double boiler until it thickens; stirring all the while. When thick add lemon juice or vinegar to taste."

Salad Cream. "Heat one half cupful of vinegar and one half cupful of sugar. When very hot, add one half cupful of sour cream into which the yolks of two eggs have been beaten. Stir well, remove from the fire, and then chill before using. Very nice on cabbage slaw."

If you follow the recipe precisely, Aunt Susan's Salad Dressing would definitely reach the temperature needed to kill unsafe bacteria—160°F—says Libby

Hull, a nutritionist with the Clemson University Extension program, in South Carolina. "But you would want to test the Salad Cream to make sure it reached 160°F both before you added the sour cream and afterward." Modern cooks also have access to three products that would remove any guesswork. "You could use fresh eggs that are marketed as 'pasteurized in the shell,' Egg Beaters, or any frozen egg product," Libby says. "There would be no question about the safety of the dressing."

Jelly Works Jolly Well for Glaze

■ Hankering for a sweet fruit sauce to finish off, say, ham steaks or chicken stir-fry? Don't rush to the store to buy a jar of ready-made glaze or sweet-and-sour sauce. All you need is that jar of jelly in your refrigerator and this shortcut from *New Delineator Recipes* (1929): Melt ¾ cup grape or currant jelly in 1 cup boiling water, and then mix it with the juice of 1 lemon. Voilà!

This glaze also works well if you're baking fruit. *New Delineator* authors particularly recommend it for Bananas *en Casserole,* itself a quick substitute for Bananas Foster without the flambé or the rum. Here's the recipe: "Peel six small bananas. Remove the coarse threads and divide in quarters, cutting first crosswise and then lengthwise. Place in a greased casserole dish and pour over them [the hot jelly sauce from recipe above]. Cover the casserole and bake [at 400° to 450°F] until the bananas are tender. The cover may be removed at the last moment and the bananas sprinkled with granulated sugar and allowed to brown slightly. Serve with game, mutton, or beef."

Better Baking Tips

Do you love rich, frosted desserts? The old-time tips and recipes on the following pages will help you bake incomparable sweet treats, along with lighter biscuits and quick breads loaded with moist fruit that are the equal of any dessert served in a fancy restaurant. Plus, you can revive some wonderful cake and cookie recipes, while taking advantage of the time savings of using today's quick mixes.

"Grate" Tip for Delicious Gingerbread

■ Hot gingerbread is a wholesome treat, but there's no need for you to prepare it from scratch (and mess with gooey molasses) when there are so many good boxed mixes for gingerbread available. Add a special touch to your boxed-mix gingerbread with this ingredient from a gingerbread recipe in *The Rumford Modern Methods of Cooking* (circa 1930), by Sarah Splint: Just add the grated rind of one orange to the batter before baking.

Easy Egg Substitute

■ Ran out of eggs in the middle of baking? Take this tip from Sarah Splint in *The Rumford Modern Methods of Cooking* (circa 1930). For cakes and quick breads, you can use one egg fewer than the recipe calls for as long as you add 1 teaspoon of baking powder in its place.

OLD-FASHIONED FAVORITES

Start the Sourdough Tradition

PIONEERS CROSSING the plains loved sourdough bread not because of its tangy flavor, but because it was the one way they could enjoy eating leavened bread far from civilization's comforts. Families would carry a batch of starter and pass a portion to other folks they met on the trail. The tradition is still alive today, with some folks who claim to be baking with part of a batch of sourdough starter that's been alive for more than 100 years!

Using real sourdough starter is one of the secrets of fancy artisan bakers (who sell their loaves for at least $4 each). You can enjoy the same delicious bread yourself by making your own sourdough starter. It takes a little patience to get started, because sourdough "sponge" requires time for the potatoes to ferment. You can use your starter with any recipe for sourdough bread or pancakes.

You will need:

Unpeeled medium potatoes
Sugar
Wheat flour
Earthenware crock with cover, or glass jar (such as a canning jar)

Step 1. Make "potato water" by boiling 2 potatoes in water to cover until they literally fall apart. Lift the skins out and mash the potatoes until they are a thick puree. Let the puree cool; then add enough water to make 2 cups of thick potato water.

Step 2. Add 2 tablespoons sugar and 2 cups flour to the potato water. Beat until smooth and creamy.

Step 3. Pour the mixture into the crock or jar, cover it, and set it aside in a warm place to ferment. As the process gets going, your mix should begin to form tiny bubbles and start to smell like sourdough. In about 2 weeks, the starter should be ready to use. At that point, unlike the pioneers, you can store it in the refrigerator.

Step 4. Each time you use some starter, replenish it with equal amounts of flour and thick potato water plus 2 tablespoons sugar for each 2 cups of the flour–potato water mixture. Beat the starter until it's smooth and creamy again, and let it ferment in a warm place for about 1 week.

Step 5. If you use the starter only occasionally, you still need to feed it with potato water and flour every 2 to 3 weeks and let it ferment for a week so that the yeast won't die. If the starter looks thin and watery and starts to smell bad, throw it away and start a new batch from scratch.

■ If you come up with a starter that produces distinctively delicious breads, give it a name (such as "Mary Jo's Super Sourdough Starter") and hand it out to friends and family in quart-size resealable plastic bags with directions for keeping the starter going and a recipe attached. You can find one great sourdough recipe source at pastrywiz.com.

Forgotten Secrets for Superior Baked Goods

▪ We have a love affair with muffins and quick breads, and a glance at old-time cookbooks shows that the obsession dates back nearly a century. *Any One Can Bake* (1927), from the folks at the Royal Baking Powder Company, reveals these forgotten tips for better quick breads that are just as useful today, whether you're starting from scratch or enhancing a boxed mix with dried fruit.

Rely on flour power. Recipes for fruit breads commonly call for dried fruit to be lightly floured before adding it to the batter (in order to keep it from sinking to the bottom during baking). But *Any One Can Bake* points out that you should not use *extra* flour to coat raisins, dates, currants, or prunes—take the quantity of flour you'll need from the flour you've measured out for the batter. Otherwise, your bread will turn out too heavy.

Make them pleasingly plump. "If fruit is put in oven [at about 300°F] for a few minutes just before flouring and adding to a cake batter, it will be less likely to sink during the baking. Raisins are plumper and more juicy if heated for three minutes."

Plump up nuts, too. The same simple procedure—a few minutes in a 300°F oven before adding to your favorite recipes—keeps nuts from making their way to the bottom of the batter during baking.

Bake In Some Peanutty Protein

▪ Here's a Depression-era recipe for a quick bread that has peanut butter right in the batter, so it's perfect for an energizing, take-to-work breakfast or lunch. Coat one large or two small oblong loaf pans with cooking spray or vegetable shortening. Sift 2 cups flour, 4 teaspoons baking powder, 1 teaspoon salt, and ⅓ cup sugar together into a bowl. Add ½ cup peanut butter and mix it in. Add 1½ cups milk and beat thoroughly. Pour the batter into the pan or pans and smooth the top(s). Bake at 350°F for about 1 hour, or until a toothpick inserted into the center comes out clean.

Oatmeal Pie Replaces Dozens of Cookies

▪ When you've got the taste for oatmeal cookies but not enough time to fill cookie sheets, settle for the taste without the fuss by baking an oatmeal pie. This recipe comes courtesy of the Shakers, who were one of the first "communal living" groups established in the late 1700s and prominent in the United States in the mid-19th century.

Mix together ¾ cup granulated sugar, ¾ cup corn syrup, and 6 tablespoons softened butter. Fold in 2 slightly beaten eggs. Add 1 teaspoon vanilla extract and stir in ¾ cup quick rolled oats (uncooked). Pour into an unbaked pie shell and bake at 350°F for 30 to 35 minutes.

Quick Cake Toppings

▪ If you've got an, ahem, "naked" cake, you can cover it with a delicious frosting without lots of fussing with whipped butter and the like. No need to rush out and buy a tub of premixed frosting—with all its artificial gunk—either. Instead, try one of these fresh but simple cake toppings, depending on what ingredients you have on hand.

Translating Tablespoons

You can follow any recipe with confidence and without a lot of fuss if you know how to translate cups to pounds and back again—no matter how your ingredients are packaged and labeled. For example, if that snazzy bed-and-breakfast recipe calls for 3 ounces of cocoa and all you have is a 1-pound box, you can get accurate results without a math degree by using this old-fashioned chart and a newfangled calculator. This vintage table is courtesy of the Royal Baking Powder Company's pamphlet *Any One Can Bake* (1927).

MATERIAL	CUPS PER LB.	TBS. PER OZ.
Wheat flour (sifted)	4	4
Corn meal	3	3
Rice	2	2
Granulated sugar	2	2
Confectioners' sugar	3¼	3
Cornstarch	3	3
Gelatin	—	3
Cocoa	3½	4
Raisins	2⅔	1½
Currants	2⅔	1½
Dates	2½	—
Prunes	2½	—
Almonds (chopped)	3⅕	2¼
Walnuts (chopped)	3½	2⅔
Butter	2	2
Lard	2	2
Honey	1⅓	1
Salt	—	2
Molasses	1⅓	1½

Strawberry delight. "Crush ten strawberries with a little sugar and a few drops lemon juice and let stand until juicy. Mix in gradually three cups of confectioner's sugar. Spread between layers and on top of cake." —*Any One Can Bake* (1927). If you're using frozen strawberries, let them thaw in the refrigerator first, without draining.

Wake me up when it's iced. "Mix 1 cup brown sugar, 1 teaspoon butter, 3 teaspoons hot coffee and ½ teaspoon vanilla to a smooth paste and spread on the cake while warm." —Sarah Splint, *The Rumford Modern Methods of Cooking* (circa 1930).

Give a Lift with Lemon Sauce

▪ No time for making fancy dessert at the end of a long day? Or—let's face it—most any day? Get a luscious lemon taste and a sweet treat that only looks time-consuming when you top store-bought day-old pound cake or vanilla ice cream with a homemade lemon sauce. In the 1920s' days of full-time moms (and perhaps even a family cook), this sauce might have been merely a finishing touch to a lavish made-from-scratch confection. In our time-pressured era, you can make the sauce in 7 minutes flat from ingredients you probably have on hand. Here's how: Boil 1 cup sugar and ⅓ cup water for 5 minutes, or until syrupy. Add 1 tablespoon butter and 4 teaspoons lemon juice.

CHAPTER 2

Housecleaning
Cleanliness Is Next to Godliness

OKAY, LET'S ADMIT IT. Some of us really do like to clean! Rather than viewing housecleaning and laundry as endless hours of drudgery, we see these activities as a domestic art. Many old-time homemakers also took pleasure in keeping their homes fresh and sparkling clean. This chapter brings you some of their best techniques, such as how to clean windows without streaks, make a magic polishing pad that will restore the shine to wooden floors and furniture, and use sour milk to remove stains.

Super Tips for Specialized Cleaning

SOME CLEANING TASKS require just the right cleaning product or technique. Whether it be making windows shine, waxing wooden furniture, or polishing the brass, old-time homemakers took pride in knowing which procedure would achieve the desired result. Many old-fashioned methods still work fine today. But to avoid possible damage to your belongings, be sure to test these tips on a small, inconspicuous area of fabric or furniture before you embark on a large-scale cleaning effort.

Drip-Free Window Washing

■ "When windows are washed with a long-handled scrubbing brush or broom, there is often great discomfort arising from the suds and water running down the brush handle and upon the hands and clothing of the operator," writes B. B. Halsted in *Household Conveniences* (1884). How to avoid getting soaked? Cut a ring of "stout leather" to fit around the brush handle, about a foot or so below the head of the brush or broom. With this gizmo in place, the sudsy water should deflect onto the ground and not up your sleeve. A simpler solution today would be to cut out the bottom of a bleach bottle or similarly sized plastic jug, cut a small hole in the center, and push the plastic disk onto the handle.

PEARLS OF WISDOM

"The following remark we consider worth fifty dollars . . . The best way to clean a house, is to keep it clean by a daily attention to small things, and never allow it to get into such a state of dirtiness and disorder as to require great and periodical cleanings, which turn comfort out of doors."

The Old Farmer's Almanack (1855)

Window Washer's Secret

■ Here's an old trick from experienced window washers, recommended by *Short Cuts to Better Housekeeping* (1949). When you're drying windows after washing them, always use vertical strokes on the outside and horizontal strokes on the inside. That way, if you leave any streaks, you can tell at a glance whether they are outside or inside the window. To beat the streak, do what modern-day window

washer Kim Carpenter, of Longmont, Colorado, does. Use a professional-grade squeegee with a smooth rubber edge. Crumpled newspaper also works fine, but avoid the color sections, which don't dry as well. Kim recommends washing windows in the evening, or when they're in the shade or the day is cloudy, because glass that dries too quickly is more vulnerable to streaking.

Wall-Cleaning Wisdom

■ Painted walls are easy to clean, according to *The Good Housekeeper, or The Way to Live Well, and to Be Well While We Live* (1841). We can use the same method today as author Sarah Josepha Hale recommended in the mid-19th century. Begin by adding a little washing soda, sodium carbonate, or soda ash (see "The Scoop on Sodas" on page 33) to a pail of water to soften the water; start with 1 tablespoon. (This step may not be necessary if you live in an area that already has soft water.) Then wash the paint with a flannel rag and a mild soap such as Ivory Liquid diluted in the softened water. Wipe off the soap with a rag dunked in clear water and wipe dry with a clean linen cloth.

Wallpapered walls are a cinch to clean as well, notes *The Good Housekeeper*. First lightly sweep off all of the dust. Then rub the paper with stale bread. "Cut the crust off very thick and wipe straight down from the top then begin at the top again and so on." (When finished, spread the crusts and any usable leftover bread outside for the birds and squirrels.) This cleaning technique may or may not be effective on modern vinyl wallpapers. Try it on a small area first, and judge the results for yourself.

Make the Best of Snow

Old-time New Englanders swear that the best way to clean wool rugs or blankets is with snow—it doesn't make a big mess or require chemicals that could strip the wool of its natural oils, and it turns a cleaning chore into a game kids will enjoy. (Do not try this technique on any rug that is marked "dry clean only.") On a cold, clear day (25°F or colder), with at least several inches of fresh powder snow, take the rug outside and leave it for a couple of hours until it has frozen. Lay the stiff carpet in the snow and whack the exposed surface with a broom. Shake the rug out, turn it over on a fresh patch of snow, and beat the other side. If you wait for a cold, dry day, the rug will barely become wet when you clean it this way, but before returning it to the house, brush off any visible snow. Then leave it outside for another hour or so to let sublimation—the cold-weather process whereby snow or ice transforms directly from solid to vapor—do its work. By nightfall, the rug should be clean and dry (but don't return the rug to its place until it is completely dry).

Damage Control for Grease Spills

"If grease is spilled on a wooden floor, pour cold water over it at once," recommends *1001 Entirely New Household Hints* (1937). That way the grease will congeal before it has time to penetrate the wood, where it will be difficult to remove. Use as little water as possible—it's not a good idea to drench a wood floor with water.

Quicker Picker-Upper

The Housewife's Receipt-Book (1837) offers this cleaning tip: "When you sweep a room, throw a little wet sand all over it, and that will gather up all the dust." This old trick works particularly well for cleaning concrete floors in a barn or garage—the grains of sand attract and hold oil, dust, and other mess. An even better version of this method today is to sprinkle cat litter to absorb oil and other fluids before you sweep. This method is not advisable for linoleum or wooden floors, as it may scratch the finish.

Shoe Polish Shines Furniture

For many generations, fathers have been teaching their sons how to polish their shoes. What you may not know is that while the men were making their shoes shine, mothers were teaching their daughters how to use shoe polish to

The Scoop on Sodas

Soda ash is the active ingredient in washing soda. Its chemical name is sodium carbonate. Soda ash is more basic and less acidic than sodium bicarbonate, which we commonly call baking soda.

beautify wooden furniture. Shoe polish is actually a wax—the same kind of wax you use on your furniture, but with some coloring added. Shoe polish makes an excellent touch-up for covering nicks and scuffs on your furniture. Got a scratch on your mahogany table leg? Rub a bit of "shell cordovan" or another reddish brown shoe polish on the scratch, and it will disappear permanently. Try light or medium brown polish on oak or walnut furniture.

Warm Polish Works Best

■ When it's time to polish the furniture, keep in mind that warm furniture polish penetrates the pores of wood faster and more thoroughly than cold polish, notes *Short Cuts to Better Housekeeping* (1949). If you keep your furniture polish and other cleaning products on a shelf in a cold garage, pantry, or basement, bring the polish into the house and let it warm to room temperature before you start shining up the furniture.

Restore Wood with Old-Fashioned Wax

ARE YOU FED UP with dull finishes and scratches on your wooden furniture? The old-fashioned—and highly effective—way to perk up drab, marred furniture is to wax it. Classic furniture wax products, such as Butcher's Bowling Alley Wax, fill tiny scratches in wooden furniture. They can help you to restore shine and protect the piece from future wear. You can use this type of wax today the same way it was used in the late 1800s. (Check the instructions from your furniture manufacturer, though, to make sure that they don't advise against this type of restoration technique.)

You will need:

- Murphy Oil Soap or other mild soap
- Superfine (0000) steel wool (available at hardware stores)
- One container paste furniture wax
- 3 or 4 clean, soft cloths

Step 1. Gently wash the wood surface with a solution of mild soap and water and allow it to dry.

Step 2. Dampen a piece of steel wool and rub it on the surface of the wax so that a small amount of wax adheres to the steel wool. (If 0000 steel wool is not available, use a soft cloth. Do not use any other type of steel wool.) Now rub the wax over a small area of the surface using small circular motions.

Step 3. Let the wax sit for 5 to 10 minutes, until it hazes over. Then gently wipe off the excess wax with a cloth. You should not be able to streak the surface of the wood after wiping.

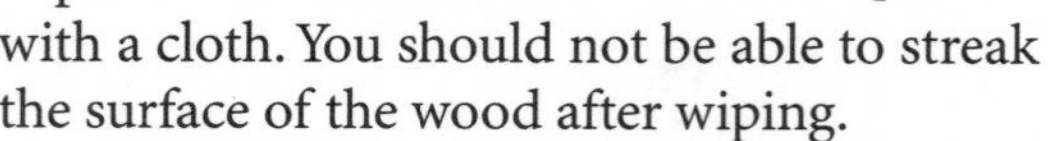

Step 4. Buff the surface again with a new clean cloth. Don't wait too long, or the wax will be more difficult to remove.

Step 5. Apply another coat and repeat Steps 3 and 4.

■ The best way to keep waxed furniture shiny is to clean it with a feather duster or a damp rag. Don't apply furniture polish over the wax.

Dustless Dusters

■ Premoistened wipes for dusting wooden tabletops aren't such a newfangled product as we might think. In 1920, author Winnifred Shaw Fales wrote about a technique for making wipes in *The Household Dictionary*. However, her method involved a lengthy process and at least one ingredient that few of us have on hand—typewriter oil. An easy and inexpensive way to make your own dustless dusters is to use cheesecloth and lemon oil (available at hardware stores and some grocery stores). Pour ¼ cup lemon oil into 1 pint hot water in a bucket. Soak four or five pieces of cheesecloth (about 10 inches by 10 inches each) in the mixture. Wring out the cheesecloth squares until they feel almost dry. Hang them in a cool, dry spot for 24 hours. Now you have your own premoistened tabletop wipes. There are no special storage needs. When the wipes become dirty, machine-wash them and re-treat them with the lemon oil solution as before.

Easy Wicker Wipe Downs

■ The woven patterns of wicker furniture are beautiful, but those intricately woven reeds can be a challenge to clean. Here are two time-tested ways to clean wicker furniture from *The Complete Housekeeper* (1903), by Emily Holt (updated a bit with modern conveniences).

The first method works for wicker furniture that has a natural finish. On a breezy, sunny day, gather rags, a scrub brush, a bucket, and borax. Mix 1 gallon warm water and ¼ cup borax in the bucket. Move the wicker furniture outdoors. Dust off the wicker, and then use the brush to scrub the wicker with the borax solution. Use your garden hose to rinse the furniture. Let it dry in the sun; then take it back indoors.

Varnished or painted wicker furniture needs a different cleaning approach—sans water. "Rub very dirty places with a swab of tripoli [a form of limestone] as big as the end of the thumb, dipped as lightly as possible in boiled linseed-oil," instructs *The Complete Housekeeper.* Although this method would work, it's quite messy. Instead, use a clean, soft paintbrush and a spray bottle of furniture polish. Spray the bristles lightly with the polish and swiftly swirl the brush in all the crevices in the wicker. Use a paper towel to wipe the bristles clean periodically. Respray the bristles with more polish after wiping. Continue until every dust-trapping crevice in your wicker furniture is clean.

A Tune-Up for Cane Chairs

HAVE YOU EVER NOTICED that the seats of cane chairs tend to become saggy and loose? This easy method from the *Receipt Book* (circa 1840) of New Jersey homemaker Mary Anna Clement will allow you to both clean and tighten your cane chairs. Turn the chair upside down and wash the cane seat thoroughly with soap and water and a soft cloth. Let it air-dry, and it will be as clean and firm as new.

Freeze Away Candle Wax

When you need to remove candle wax from woodwork, head for the freezer first. You'll need a few ice cubes, because the best way to remove wax is by chilling it, notes *Short Cuts to Better Housekeeping* (1949). Put the ice cubes in a plastic bag, and hold the bag against the wax. Once frozen, the wax will be easier to break up and chip off. Wipe the residue with a cloth moistened with mineral spirits (paint thinner). Many sources recommend warming candle wax to wipe it off, but this may only drive the wax deeper into the pores of the wood. *Caution:* Use mineral spirits with care, because it is a flammable substance. Be sure the area where you're working is well-ventilated.

Old-Time Cleaners for Piano Keys

Whether your piano has ivory or plastic keys, avoid harsh cleaning solutions and aggressive scrubbing. Instead, clean the keys with a soft cloth dampened with rubbing alcohol or cologne, recommends *Marion Harland's Complete Cook Book: A Practical and Exhaustive Manual of Cookery and Housekeeping, Containing Thousands of Carefully Proved Recipes* (1903). Or try this tip from *1001 Entirely New Household Hints* (1937) for ivory keys: Wash piano keys with warm milk. Several applications may be necessary if the keys have yellowed.

Lemon Remedies Rust on Marble

For those homeowners lucky enough to have a marble mantelpiece or tabletop, the problem of rust stains from metal plant holders, candlesticks, and decorative ironwork may be familiar. To remove such stains, rub them with lemon juice, recommends Mrs. Henry Ward Beecher in *All Around the House; or, How to Make Homes Happy* (1878). Test the lemon juice on a small area of the marble first. Since lemon juice is a mild acid, it could etch the marble.

Spring Showers Freshen Feather Pillows

Victorian homemakers knew how to make the most of a spring rain. In *Aunt Mena's Recipe Book* (1888), M. B. Bosson suggests a way to freshen and lighten feather pillows: Leave them outside in a drenching spring rain. Afterward, set the pillows in the sun and turn them regularly until they are perfectly dry. (Damp pillows can become moldy or mildewed.)

Eggs and Wine Do *Mix*

Red-wine decanters are awkward to clean after the party's over. To restore these glass vessels to a brilliant, clear luster, pound eggshells small and put the crushed eggshells and some water into the decanter, writes Mrs. William Parkes in *Domestic Duties (Or Instructions to Young Married Ladies)*, published in 1828. Shake and swirl the shells vigorously to clean out all of the nooks and crannies.

Guide to Old-Time Cleaning Ingredients

MOST 21ST-CENTURY READERS will have a hard time making sense of 19th-century instructions such as this recipe for cleaning marble, from *The Household Cyclopedia of General Information* (1881), by Henry Hartshorne: "Take verdigris and pumice-stone, well powdered, with lime newly slaked. Mix with soap lees [sediments], to the consistence of putty. Put it in a woolen rag, and rub the stains well . . . Or, cover the stains with fuller's earth or plaster of Paris, and when dry brush it off." Here's a guide to some of the most common old-time cleaning substances, many of which are still available today, though they often are used for purposes other than cleaning. If you want to use any of these old-time products, be sure you read the product label thoroughly and follow all instructions for safe use.

OLD-TIME NAME	WHAT IS IT?	COMMON OLD-TIME USES	WHAT TO USE TODAY
Black lead	Graphite	Polishing iron grates and stoves	Williams Stove Polish made with graphite is still available
Bluing (Blueing)	Very finely powdered blue iron suspended in liquid	Whitening yellowed fabric in laundry	Mrs. Stewart's Bluing or household bleach
Fuller's earth	Natural form of absorbent clay, originally used by "fullers," or textile workers, to remove oils from sheep's wool	Cleaning, absorption of fluids, cosmetics, cat litter	Still available; cat litter is the best substitute for an absorbent
Hartshorn powder	Ground or flaked deer antlers —an early source of ammonia	Cleaning, leavening of bread	Household ammonia
Muriatic acid	Dilute hydrochloric acid	Cleaning masonry and swimming pools	Found in many toilet bowl cleaners; still sold for masonry, pool cleaning
Slaked lime	Calcium hydroxide, or lime to which water has been added (its "thirst" slaked)	Mortar, cements, paints, household cleaners	Still found in toilet-bowl and pool cleaners
Tripoli	Powder of silica, also known as *rottenstone*	Fine abrasive polish	Still sold as a fine-furniture polish
Verdigris	Green deposit that forms on copper, brass, or bronze	Painting, decoration, cleaning	Not used today
Verjuice	An acidic medieval condiment, made from the unfermented juice of semiripe grapes	Cleaning and spot removal, condiment	Still sold as a condiment; vinegar is the best substitute for cleaning
Whiting	Powdered chalk (calcium carbonate)	Scouring, polishing	Still the principal ingredient in Bon Ami and other powdered cleansers

Standing in Soda Shines Silver Flatware

Polishing silver flatware can be an awful job. Here's an easy, old-time way from "the Mystery Chef," author of *Be an Artist at the Gas Range* (1935), to keep your silver knives, forks, and spoons shining. "All you have to do is stand them in a bright and clean aluminum pot—don't use an old, tarnished pot—into which you have poured some boiling water, or very hot water, and a heaping teaspoon of baking or washing soda. Put the silver in—let it stand a minute—take it out, and you will find the tarnish all gone. Then, just rinse and dry thoroughly." Test this technique on one piece of your silver first to make sure that the treatment doesn't harm the finish. Do not use hot water on silver pieces that have a lacquer coating.

BIZARRE BUT TRUE

Wash Your Phone?

"WASH AND BOIL the mouthpiece of the telephone occasionally," says *1000 Helps and Hints for the House and Home* (1936). This sounds like oddball advice, but, on reflection, maybe it's not such a bad idea—just think of all the germs that must get lodged in your phone and passed from sick people to healthy ones as the family passes around the phone. Most phones today don't have a handy screw-off mouthpiece, and you'd likely fry the electronic innards if you tried to wash a phone, let alone boil it. But a weekly swipe with a household disinfectant would be a good call.

Lemon and Ketchup Clean Brass

Old-time homemakers and military men were often faced with discolored brass objects in need of a good cleaning. A method from Mary Anna Clement's handwritten *Receipt Book* (circa 1840) was to rub the discolored brass with a cut lemon and then wash with a weak solution of ammonia and water. To make this cleaning solution, try adding a few drops of ammonia to 1 quart water. *Caution:* Do not allow the ammonia to drip directly on the brass or on your skin.

Former U.S. Marine Corps second lieutenant William H. Carroll, of Haddonfield, New Jersey, says that a great way to clean brass or any metal that oxidizes is by covering it with ketchup. "When I was a U.S. Marine, we used ketchup to clean everything from brass buckles to lieutenant's bars. Just lay the pieces side by side without letting them touch each other. Paint on a good layer of ketchup and let them sit overnight. Then rinse with warm water and dry thoroughly for a nice shine." Bill notes that he recently used ketchup to clean dingy brass hinges and doorknobs from a door he was repainting, letting the hardware sit in a coating of ketchup for a few days before rinsing it and rehanging the door. "The door looked like new!" Bill says.

Greet Guests with a Shiny Brass Plate

Way back when, the design of the entranceway to a home was almost as important as the living room or parlor. Front doors were made of beautiful wood, flanked by sidelight windows, and adorned with brass knobs, knockers, and doorplates. What goes around comes around, and highly stylish entries are again the rage.

If you want to keep your entry looking its best, you'll want to shine up the brass accessories from time to time. To do this without smearing brass cleaner all over your beautiful front door, try this trick from *The Household Dictionary* (1920), by Winnifred Shaw Fales: Cut a protective shield to fit around the brass accessory. For example, if your door has a brass doorplate, take a piece of heavy cardboard and trace the doorplate on it. Use an X-Acto knife to cut through the cardboard, forming an opening the exact size of the plate. Slip the shield around the plate while you clean, and you'll have no worries about getting brass cleaner on the surrounding woodwork. You can make a shield to fit around a doorknob or knocker, too. Once you cut the opening in the middle of the shield, make a cut from the outer edge of the shield to the edge of the opening. That will allow you to slip the shield in place around the base of the doorknob or handle.

If you clean your brass accessories regularly and don't want to fuss with cutting new shields each time, make aluminum shields by cutting them from an aluminum pie tin or baking pan. Store the aluminum shields with your brass cleaner so they're handy whenever you need them.

Old-Fashioned Soap Cleans Showers and More

WASH YOUR SHOWER STALL and clean up paintbrushes after a big painting job with a laundry product that your great-grandmothers used: Fels-Naptha Bar Soap. To use this heavy-duty laundry bar soap to clean your shower, wet the bar and rub it with a nonabrasive scouring sponge. Scrub down shower walls and rinse clean. To clean paintbrushes, work up a good lather on a bar of Fels-Naptha and drag the bristles across the bar. Then rinse the brushes out well.

Weekly Bleach for Tip-Top Toilets

Grandmothers kept toilets clean with old-fashioned laundry bleach. Pour ¼ cup bleach into the toilet, being careful not to splash the bleach on your clothes, skin, or rug, and let it sit for at least 15 minutes (be sure the bathroom is well ventilated). Bleach does double duty: It kills the germs that discolor and foul your toilet, making it sparkling clean in the process. Scrub the inside of the bowl with an ordinary toilet brush before flushing away the bleach. This method has been used every week—usually on Saturday mornings—for generations.

If your bowl still isn't looking clean enough, perhaps because of old, deeply

☞ OLD-TIME ODDITIES ☜

The Soap Saver

WHEN YOUR BAR SOAP reduces to a tiny slippery chip, you throw it away, right? Wrong! Old-time homemakers designed a device called a *soap saver* that allows for bar soap frugality. This small wire basket opens and closes to hold small pieces of soap and has an attached handle so the user can lower the basket of soap slivers into water, swish it around, and create suds. If your house is plagued with odds and ends of leftover bar soap, you can still find soap savers today; see Resources on page 349 for suppliers.

set stains, try a scouring powder treatment. Flush the toilet a few times to be sure all the bleach is flushed away; then sprinkle your favorite scouring powder in the bowl. Some of these contain bleach, too. If your scouring powder has bleach, let it sit 5 to 10 minutes before scrubbing. If not, scrub right away. Flush. Repeat if necessary. *Caution:* Be sure your bathroom is well ventilated whenever you use bleach or cleaning products that contain bleach.

Flush Away Hard-Water Stains

■ Follow the lead of an old-time recipe for cleaning marble published in *Godey's Lady's Book* (May 1872) to eliminate hard-water stains in your bathroom. The magazine recommended cleaning stained marble with a mix of two parts common soda (baking soda), one part pumice stone, and one part finely powdered chalk, all blended with water. Leaping forward into the 21st century, we can simplify this recipe and use a pumice stone alone to quickly rub out stubborn hard-water stains in porcelain tubs, sinks, or toilet bowls (you'll want to wear rubber gloves while you work). The process is usually harmless for bathroom fixtures—after all, a pumice stone can be used on your feet. If you're concerned about scratching the finish, test the pumice stone by rubbing it on a stain in an inconspicuous spot. Look for pumice stones in the foot care aisle of any grocery store or drugstore.

Scouring Powder Still Brings Out the Shine

■ Despite all of the expensive newfangled products available, many folks consider ordinary scouring powder the best cleaner to use for tubs and sinks. Wetting the surface with a little water before sprinkling on the powder will make it stick better. *Caution:* Scouring powder may scratch or dull certain surfaces, such as ceramic, fiberglass, and polished stone. Read the package directions carefully before using. Helen Wagner, of Abington, Pennsylvania, recalls that her sister, Ethel Engle, always relied on worn-out terry cloth washcloths and towels for scrubbing bathrooms. Laundered after every use, old terry cloth items will last a long time before they finally disintegrate.

If your tub and sink have chrome- or nickel-plated fixtures, avoid using scouring powder on them, as it will eventually wear away the finish. Instead, use automobile chrome polish, which is sold in most hardware and auto parts stores. Apply it with a cotton rag, such as an old T-shirt. It will not only shine your nickel or chrome plating right up but also leave behind a protective film, keeping the fixtures shiny much longer than any scouring powder can.

Clever Cleaning Tools

Before you begin any cleaning project, it's important to have the right tools on hand. What are you cleaning? What is the object made of? Is it fragile or sturdy? What type of dirt do you face? Is it dust, grease, dirt, or some sort of stain? You'll need different tools to tackle various cleaning tasks. From brooms to polishing pads, here are some old-time tools you can use today to make your home sparkle.

An Inventory of Timeless Tools

Homemakers at the turn of the 20th century knew what was needed to make a home really clean. You may find these tools equally useful.

- Scrub brushes (a large one for cleaning floors and smaller ones for cleaning windowsills and hard-to-reach surfaces)
- Dustpan and brush
- Clean paintbrushes—one large, one small (for dusting small, fragile objects)
- Large, stiff broom (for use indoors and out)
- Soft broom (for wooden floors)
- Clean mop
- Plenty of old washcloths
- Wash-leathers (chamois for drying glass to prevent streaking)
- Swabs (a modern-day swab is a cotton ball on a stick; use it to clean cracks and crevices around windows, in bathrooms, and the like)
- Rubbing flannels (soft cotton flannel for dusting and polishing)
- Rubbing pad
- Lightweight buckets
- Steel wool (superfine for delicate jobs like removing hardened bird droppings from windows, and rougher grades to clean screens and aluminum storm doors)

All Brooms Are Not Created Equal

When it comes to brooms, the latest newfangled product probably *isn't* the best. For superior sweeping, choose a type of broom invented more than two centuries ago: a broomcorn broom. "Broomcorn is a type of sorghum—a big grass—that looks like corn but produces

TRASH OR TREASURE

Reuse a Busted Broom

What to do with a broken broom handle? Whittle the end to a sharp point and use it as a handy and back-friendly tool for planting spring bulbs, suggests *1000 Helps and Hints for the House and Home* (1936).

no ears. It's been used since the mid-1700s for making brooms. Just the 'brush' on top of the plant is used," says Samuel E. Moyer, Ph.D., "The Jersey Jerry Broomsquire" (who is also a professor emeritus of biology at Burlington County College, in New Jersey, and a sorghum geneticist). "A broomcorn broom can sweep fine particles. And while dirt clings to a plastic or synthetic broom, a natural broomcorn broom is self-cleaning. Dirt doesn't cling to it. It's like magic!"

Some old-time sources recommend soaking brooms in sudsy water or boiling them to keep the straw supple, but Dr. Moyer says those are old wives' tales. A broomcorn broom needs no washing or soaking, but when not in use, it's best stored in a dry place, off the bristles. Hang the broom from a hook or turn it upside down so that it rests on its handle.

Benjamin Franklin is credited with promoting the planting of broomcorn in America, and Dr. Moyer and other broomsquires are still making these vintage brooms. There are different types of broomcorn brooms, including kitchen brooms with softer bristles (so floors won't suffer scratches) and outside brooms with rattan added for extra stiffness. To purchase handmade broomcorn brooms, see Resources on page 349.

Fire Up a Feather Duster

When you picture old-time maids or housekeepers, you probably imagine them armed with a feather duster. That's because professional housekeepers really did use feather dusters! Feather dusters are still a smart cleaning choice, because they work well to remove dust from just about everything. Feathers don't transfer static electricity, and they attract and hold dust. After you finish dusting, you can easily freshen your feather duster by shaking it outside your house or inside a paper bag. Feathers are particularly good for cleaning glass, houseplants, paintings, and other delicate items that need a gentle touch. According to M. B. Bosson in *Aunt Mena's Recipe Book* (1888), "The wings of turkey, geese, and chickens are good to wash and clean windows as they have no dust as cloth." For suppliers of feather dusters, see Resources on page 349.

Make Dusting Miniblinds a Minitask

If you think that dusting miniblinds is a modern-day dilemma, consider these harsh words from author E. C. Gardner in *The House That Jill Built, After Jack's Had Proved a Failure* (1896): "If [the] blinds are made of open slats, many housekeepers despise them as being no better than small cabinets maliciously contrived to accumulate dust." Yes, the problem of dusty blinds is an old one, but fortunately, there's a modern tool for easy blind-cleaning: a tricket. This nifty tool resembles a pair of tongs with a small squeegee or sponge on the inside of each tong. Visit your local hardware store or cleaning supply shop, and ask if they sell trickets, or see Resources on page 349 for suppliers. This handy tool helps you quickly clean both sides of your blinds at once. A tricket costs about $20, but that's far less expensive than hiring a professional cleaner.

Make a Magic Wood-Restoring Pad

IF YOUR HOME has real wooden paneling, you need a restoring pad. Old-time homemakers considered a restoring pad, also called a *French polishing pad,* the essential tool for restoring damaged wood finishes on walls and furniture. You can make your own, and according to housekeeping expert Emily Holt, author of *The Complete Housekeeper* (1912), "such a pad will last a lifetime, growing better all the while."

To use the pad, first remove all wax from the damaged wood surface. Saturate the pad with boiled linseed oil (available at hardware stores; don't boil it yourself). Wring out the excess oil and apply about ¼ teaspoon shellac to the pad. Then scrub hard at the damaged surface. Don't stop, or your pad may stick.

Antiques collector Bill Meehan, of Haddonfield, New Jersey, has used this method. "As you rub, your magic pad will force shellac into the scratches and scuffs of your furniture, leaving a gorgeous shine," Bill says.

You will need:

- Penknife or router
- Block of wood (pine is a good choice)
- 1 one-inch-wide strip of soft wash-leather or sheepskin chamois
- Small hammer and small tacks
- 3 pieces of soft wash-leather, each slightly larger than the wooden block
- 2 pieces of thick, cotton flannel, the same size as the leather
- Needle and strong thread

Step 1. Use the penknife or router to hollow out the two upper edges of the wood block so it fits comfortably in your hand. (You can also ask to have this done for you at the lumberyard.)

Step 2. At the midpoint of the hollows, fasten the strip of wash-leather with tacks, so that you can comfortably slip your hand under the strip to hold the pad securely.

Step 3. Cover the face, sides, and upper surfaces of the pad with a layer of wash-leather, using tacks to secure it. Leave the hollows where you'll grip the block exposed.

Step 4. Sew a layer of flannel to the leather, fitting it snugly as you work.

Step 5. Continue sewing alternate layers of wash-leather and flannel to the block, until you've attached five layers (the final layer should be leather). Be certain all tacks are covered so that they won't scratch surfaces.

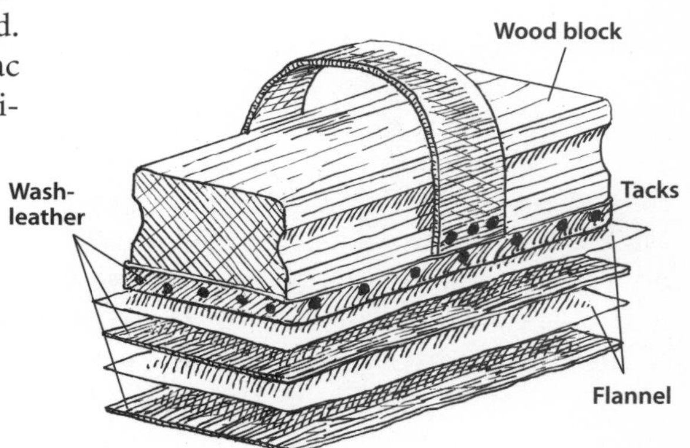

■ "Store your magic pad in an airtight bag when you're done," Bill says. "Don't clean it! To use it again, just apply fresh coatings of boiled linseed oil and a bit of shellac." (Be careful not to overuse linseed oil, though, or you may end up with a gummy surface on your walls or furniture.)

Clean Crannies with a Toothbrush

■ Use a small, soft-bristled brush that's been dipped or sprayed in furniture polish to reach into small cracks, nooks, and corners in furniture, suggests *1001 Entirely New Household Hints* (1937). An old soft toothbrush is ideal for this.

The Minisqueegee

■ Professional window cleaners use rubber squeegees to wipe windows without leaving streaks. But what if you're trying to clean small windows like those in fancy doors, appliances, or cupboards? *1001 Entirely New Household Hints* (1937) has an answer: Use a soft, clean rubber spatula or bowl scraper as a minisqueegee for wiping off tiny windows. Choose the cleanest, newest, and straightest spatula in your kitchen.

On both small windows and big ones, professional cleaners say, the key to proper squeegee use is to dry one area on the top or side of the window, then start the squeegee in that dry area and drag it across the wet surface. Starting on a wet part of the pane promotes streaks.

OLD-FASHIONED FAVORITES

Clean Rugs Better with a Beater

Before carpet sweepers and electric vacuum cleaners, old-time homemakers regularly used rug beaters to clean smaller area rugs. Haddonfield, New Jersey, homemaker Adele B. Carroll says, "My grandmother always used to beat small rugs with a rug beater. I still have her rug beater! Mine is made of wood. She would hang the rugs over the clothesline in the backyard in Philadelphia and beat the dirt out of them." One advantage of using a rug beater is that, unlike a vacuum cleaner, it can clean both the top surface and the underside of a rug. Rug beaters are still available today. You may find a vintage one at a yard sale or antique shop, or look for them in stores that sell reproduction "country" items.

Laundry Day Secrets

Traditionally, Monday was laundry day. With leftovers from Sunday available for the evening meal, old-time homemakers spent every Monday pretreating stains and soaking, boiling, rinsing, wringing, hanging, and folding clothes. We still spend a lot of time doing laundry. To speed the job along and improve results, try these old-fashioned laundry tips, including a novel way to iron a tablecloth and a method for removing tea stains from linen with sugar. Keep in mind that homemade products aren't as uniform or predictable as commercial products, though, so test out these tips on an inconspicuous spot on a garment to be sure the technique doesn't harm the garment.

Vanquish Extra Suds with Vinegar

■ When you've put too much soap in your washing machine and you see excess suds, use good old-fashioned vinegar to save the day. Pour in ¼ cup vinegar and watch to see whether the suds subside. If necessary, add a second ¼ cup to solve the problem.

Use Bluing for Laundry and More

■ Keeping the laundry white and bright has long been the laundress's goal. Bluing has been the answer for more than a century. "When I was a little girl, my mother always had a piece of old-fashioned bluing in a lump about the size of a walnut that looked like chalk, and she kept it in an old piece of sheeting that was tied at the top," explains Dianne Snodgrass, vice president and chairman of collections for the Historical Society of Haddonfield, New Jersey. "She would swish it around in the washing water. Today, I just use a few drops of Mrs. Stewart's Bluing."

Several brands of laundry bluing are available, and you can use any of them for a variety of purposes besides brightening laundry. Some suggestions:

- Whitening dingy white hair on yourself or your pet
- Reducing algae growth in birdbaths, fishponds, and fountains
- Brightening swimming pool water
- Easing the discomfort of an ant bite or bee sting
- Coloring white carnations blue

Refer to product directions before using bluing for any purpose.

Potato Cleaner for Soiled Silk

■ How do you clean delicate silks? *Cookery and Housekeeping: A Complete System of Household Management for All Who Wish to Live Well at a Moderate Cost* (1886) recommends sponging soiled silk with water in which potatoes have been boiled and to which ammonia has been added—try 1 tablespoon ammonia in 1 quart potato water. Fold the garment while it is damp and press with a cool iron.

OLD-TIME ODDITIES

Wash Day Play?

"HERE IS A WAY of making play of wash day," writes Rolfe Cobleigh in *Handy Farm Devices and How to Make Them* (1909). The book describes a man who rigged an old bicycle frame to his hand-cranked washing machine via a belt, so the machine could be run by pedaling. Perhaps because cycling was still considered risqué for women, or maybe just because he was chivalrous, this man didn't even expect his wife to do the wash. "He can read the paper while he washes, and he does not lose much time from field work either."

It's interesting to note that a similar practice has long outlived the hand-powered washer. How many millions of people have ridden a stationary bike for exercise while a load of wash tumbles nearby in the automatic washer and dryer?

Getting Rid of Gum

■ Chewing gum can make a nasty, hard-to-clean mess on clothing or upholstery. To get the gum out, *Short Cuts to Better Housekeeping* (1949) recommends freezing it. If the gum is stuck to a garment, place the item in your refrigerator or freezer to chill the gum and harden it

ROUGHING IT

Let the Wash Simmer Overnight

DOING THE LAUNDRY was one of the most tedious, backbreaking tasks for early-19th-century homemakers. Here's a description of how laundry was done back then, taken from the handwritten *Hartel Family Receipt Book* (circa 1810), that will make you want to kiss your modern Whirlpool! "To wash clothes, the night before washing day put the clothes to soak in water placed on a hot stove in a suitable vessel of soap, cut small, one ounce Bor-Ax and two quarts water. Let these simmer until the fire goes out in the morning. The mixture will be solid. In the morning have the wash kettle nearly filled with cold water. Put in about one fourth of the mixture. Wring out the clothes. Put them in the kettle. Make it boiling hot. Take them out. Put them in clean cold water. Rinse well in two waters. Then hang them out." Whew!

thoroughly. Gum on upholstery can be chilled with an ice cube in a plastic bag. Once it's cold, the gum can be cracked and scraped off with a dull knife.

Iron Away Candle Wax Woes

■ That romantic candlelight dinner for two was wonderful, but now your tablecloth is a waxy mess. To rescue the cloth, try a trick using your electric iron, as described in *The Butterick Book of Recipes and Household Helps* (1927). First use a dull knife to scrape off as much excess wax as you can. Then place the stained area of the tablecloth between two absorbent white cotton rags and press the area with an iron set on low heat. This should get rid of the rest of the wax. If the tablecloth still has a stain, try washing it with clear water, or if the tablecloth is white cotton or linen, soak it in a dilute bleach solution.

10 Stain Removal Basics

■ We've all been there—red wine spills on the tablecloth; tomato sauce spatters onto a favorite blouse. Stains have been a challenge to those who do the laundry for as long as there have been clothes. Remembering some basic rules can help. Here are 10 good suggestions from *The Butterick Book of Recipes and Household Helps* (1927).

1. "Each stain demands individual attention. Patience is essential."

2. "Do not use strong chemicals. If the stain disappears instantly it is likely that your cloth will do likewise in time. Method is more important than the chemical you use."

3. "Follow directions carefully and be ready to make more than one effort."

4. "Cover only a small section [a few square inches] at a time."

5. "Either place a thick pad of old toweling under the stained material to absorb the remover and stain or stretch the soiled fabric over a bowl into which hot water can be poured."

6. "When in doubt use cold water. It will not injure the fabric." (Unless the fabric is not a washable fabric.)

7. "Water stains can be removed by steaming."

8. Always try to identify the cause of the stain and "then determine which remover will be most effective without injuring either texture or color of fabric."

9. "Work toward the center of the stain to avoid rings and continue light strokes until spot dries."

10. "If one method fails, try another."

TRASH OR TREASURE

Sour Milk Stops Stains

DON'T THROW that sour milk down the drain! According to M. B. Bosson, author of *Aunt Mena's Recipe Book* (1888), sour milk is just the ticket for cleaning ink stains out of cloth. Soak the fabric in the sour milk overnight and then wash it with soap. Sour milk also removes tomato stains, says *1001 Entirely New Household Hints* (1937).

Here's another milky tip: Buttermilk removes mildew from cloth. Soak the cloth in the buttermilk and then spread it on the grass in the sun. After the cloth dries, wash normally, and the mildew should be gone.

Sugar Takes Out Tea Stains

After a tea or dessert party, you may find your fine linen tablecloth covered with troublesome tea stains. New Jersey homemaker Mary Anna Clement offered a helpful tip for removing tea stains from linens in her handwritten *Receipt Book* (1840): "Take tea stains out of linen tablecloths by immersing in a strong solution of sugar and water for a few minutes and then rinsing in soft water." To make the strong sugar water solution, use 1 quart water and keep adding sugar to it until the sugar no longer dissolves completely.

Stain Removal for Chocolate Lovers

If you love chocolate (doesn't everyone?), you've probably had occasion to deal with chocolate-stained clothing. Getting rid of chocolate stains can be tough, but first try washing the fabric in cold water and soap, says *The Butterick Book of Recipes and Household Helps* (1927). If that doesn't work, the book recommends this method instead: "Cover [the stain] with borax and wash in cold water, following if necessary with boiling water." If you decide to try this method, test a small area of the fabric first, says retired textile designer and engineer William H. Carroll, of Haddonfield, New Jersey. "Boiling water may be too harsh for some fabrics. Also, hot water should flow through the fabric from back to face, as well as through the stain and out into the sink."

Line-Drying, The Right Way

▪ Two short clotheslines can provide more space for drying clothes than one long clothesline. It works, if you try this trick from *The Butterick Book of Recipes and Household Helps* (1927): "String two lines about two and one-half feet apart [and] hang clothes with one corner on one line and the other corner on the other line. In this manner two lines will accommodate many more clothes."

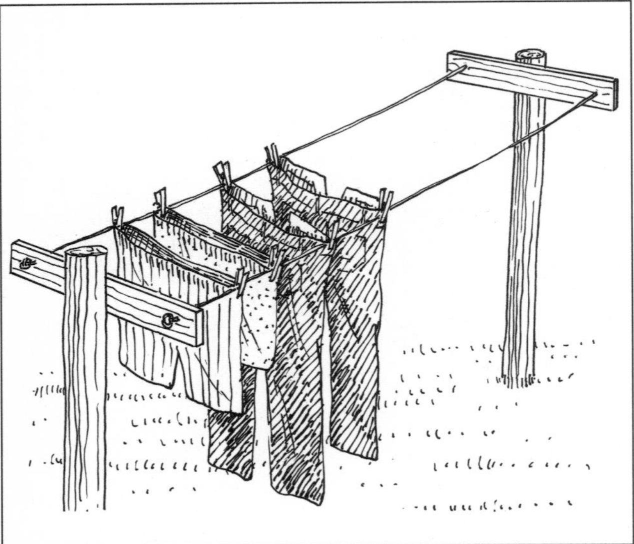

Dry more clothes in less space by hanging them between two clotheslines.

To use this tip today, think about what types of clothing or linens you hang out on the line most often. Then set the distance between the two lines based on the length of those items.

Hang Linens with Care

▪ According to Emily Holt in *The Complete Housekeeper* (1912), "It is nearly as essential to hang out things properly as to wash them well. If big things, such as table and bed linen, dry out of shape, stretching and pulling them straight wears them more than use. Hang sheets, tablecloths, towels, and napkins evenly across the line, ends down . . . All washable things should be so hung out that the weight while wet—which is thrice the weight dry—comes upon the lengthwise threads." Retired textile designer William H. Carroll, of Haddonfield, New Jersey, confirms this: "It's best to resist the temptation to hang a tablecloth or sheets by the shorter side to maximize clothesline space. By hanging it lengthwise, there will be less shrinking."

Drying Sweaters Can Be a Breeze

▪ Many sweaters can't be dried in an electric dryer, nor can you hang them on a clothesline for fear they will stretch. Instead, dry wool, washable silk, and cotton sweaters on a window screen, suggests *The Butterick Book of Recipes and Household Helps* (1927). "Cover the screen with some thin cloth to protect the sweater, then lay the garment flat on the cloth and pat it into shape. Place the screen on two chairs near the stove or register [heating vent], if possible, being sure that there is a free circulation of air around the screen." Another option is to set up the screen outside in the shade on a warm, breezy day. Avoid exposure to direct sunlight, which might cause a sweater to shrink or fade.

Clothes Hanger Drying Rack

▪ When you're washing small items such as fine lingerie or hose, it can be tough to find enough space in the laundry room

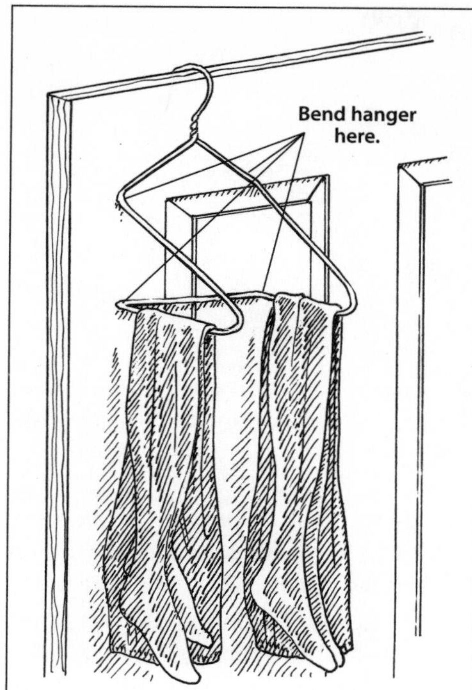

Adapt a clothes hanger to serve as a drying rack for small, delicate items.

to air-dry them. Here's a neat trick from *Short Cuts to Better Housekeeping* (1949) for making temporary drying racks. Bend a clothes hanger so it forms two "wings" that project backward when you hook the hanger over the top of a door. Drape the items to be dried over the lower wire of the wings.

Basket Cloths Keep Clean Clothes Cleaner

■ Have you ever tossed your freshly washed and dried clothes into your laundry basket, only to discover later that they have picked up dirt from the bottom of the basket? Emily Holt offers an easy solution to this problem in *The Complete Housekeeper* (1912): "Keep a clean cloth thrice as big as the basket to go in the bottom of it, and another smaller one, to tuck over the top. To insure the clothes being clean, provide two of each [size cloth], and see to it that the spare one is washed every week." The top cloth is useful if you don't have time to fold your clothes right after you remove them from the dryer or clothesline. The covering prevents the clean clothes from picking up dust or odors while they're sitting in the basket.

Sheets That Last Twice As Long

■ Have you ever noticed that sheets tend to wear out in the middle first? Thrifty Victorian homemakers had a remedy for just this problem. They called it *turning the sheets.* When the center of your cotton sheet starts to thin from washing and wear, cut it down the middle lengthwise, turn the cut edges to the outside, and rejoin the two halves. (You'll have to add a new hem to the cut edges.) Now the worn portion will be along the edges, and the center will be strong. If you think you'd be bothered by a seam down the middle of your sheet, use worn sheets to make pillowcases instead.

Sunbath Solves Scorch Marks

■ Accidentally scorching a shirt or trousers while ironing is just as annoying to us as it was to old-time homemakers. They solved the problem by hanging the scorched clothing outside so that the scorch mark was directly in the sun. Try this the next time you scorch a garment. With luck, the sun will cause the mark to fade away.

A Mending Basket Makes Good Sense

A well-stocked mending basket is just as useful today as it was for old-time homemakers. Do as they did and make mending part of your weekly laundry ritual. The time you invest in assembling a mending kit will be paid back many times over by the time and money you save on scrounging for mending materials—or, worse, throwing out a garment just because it needs a simple repair. As M. B. Bosson proclaims in *Aunt Mena's Recipe Book* (1888), "by having all these arranged in pockets or pouches in one basket, endless time and trouble in searching may be saved."

- A large basket or plastic container with a lid
- Several grades of white cotton thread
- Several grades of black cotton and silk thread
- Variety of threads in different colors
- Needles of various sizes
- Buttons (keep them in a jar in the basket)
- Hooks and eyes
- Small pieces of fabric for patching
- Measuring tape
- Thimble
- Small and large scissors
- Pincushion with pins

Rolled Tablecloths Resist Wrinkles

Company's due in 20 minutes, and your best tablecloth is full of creases! To avoid this crisis in the future, try this tip described by Emily Holt in *The Complete Housekeeper* (1912) for storing tablecloths wrinkle-free. Find a sturdy card-

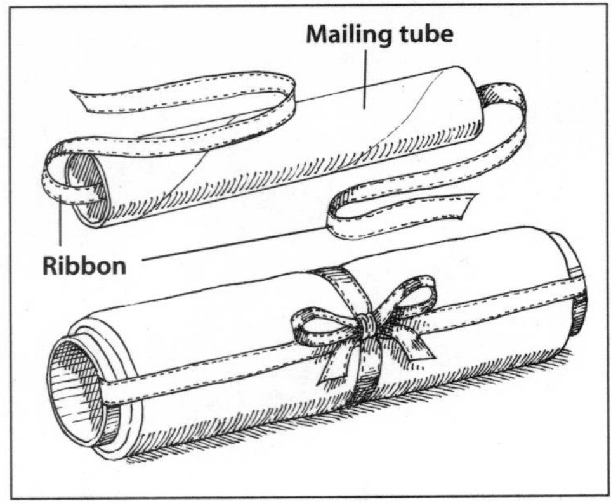

Roll a folded tablecloth around a mailing tube and tie it with ribbon for smooth storage.

board tube a little longer than half the width of your tablecloth. Depending on the size of your cloth, you can try a poster mailing tube or a large wrapping paper tube. Attach a narrow ribbon to the inside of the tube so a yard hangs out of each end. Iron your tablecloth and fold it in half once lengthwise. Lay the tube along one short end of the tablecloth and roll the cloth around the tube, keeping it straight and smooth. Bring the two ends of the ribbon together and tie them snugly to secure the outer edge of the tablecloth. Then wrap the ends around the tube and tie them together again on the other side. "Thus the cloth keeps its unmarred smoothness, yet is easy to handle, and easier to store in the closet," Emily Holt writes.

Helpful Homemade Cleaning Solutions

The next time you're at the supermarket, walk down the cleaning supply aisle. There's an amazing array of products available, but many are rather expensive—especially if you won't be using them often. Save money and simplify your cleaning routines by using the following cleaning solutions and product suggestions that have stood the test of time. Whenever you use a homemade cleaning solution, though, test the solution on an inconspicuous spot first to be sure that it's effective and doesn't damage the surface.

Three New Uses for an Old-Time Laundry Booster

Borax is a favorite for use as a laundry booster, but that's not the only cleaning use for this natural mineral compound (composed of sodium, boron, oxygen, and water), which has been mined in Death Valley, California, since the late 1800s. Try these cleaning techniques with your borax laundry booster.

1. To give fine china a dazzling shine, rinse the pieces in a sink full of warm water and ½ cup borax. Hand-painted designs will not fade. Finish the job by rinsing again in clear water.

2. To remove wet carpet spills and stains, start by soaking up excess wetness with paper towels, a sponge, or a cloth. Then sprinkle borax over the area. Let the area air-dry and then vacuum. (Always test first for colorfastness on an inconspicuous area of the carpet.)

3. To deodorize a garbage can or trash can, wash it with a solution of warm water and borax (about ½ cup in a bucket of warm water). After the can has dried, sprinkle borax in the bottom. Add another shake of borax when the can is half full to prevent new odor problems.

Natural Cleaning with Murphy

You can make a great natural bathroom cleanser by combining a venerable old-time cleaning substance—baking soda—with an old-time commercial cleaning product—Murphy Oil Soap. (Invented back in 1905, Murphy Oil Soap is a biodegradable, phosphate-free vegetable oil soap.) Sprinkle baking soda on porcelain bathroom fixtures as you

OLD-FASHIONED FAVORITES

Eye of Newt, Gall of Bullock

BILE FROM THE GALL BLADDER of an ox was among the most highly touted ingredients in 19th-century cleaning recipes. *What I Know (Hints on the Daily Duties of a Housekeeper)*, written by Elizabeth Nicholson in 1856, suggests mixing 1 pint of gall in 3 gallons warm water to use for scouring carpets. *Cookery and Housekeeping* (1886) gives a recipe for ox-gall soap that was supposed to be excellent for delicate fabrics: Take 1 pint gall, cut it into 10 pounds common bar soap, and add 1 pint boiling water; when cold, cut the soap into bars.

It's unlikely many people today would pour ox gall into their washing machines for the delicate cycle, but the brown, ropy, translucent liquid is still available. Artists use it as a wetting agent to increase the flow of watercolor paints on a canvas, and also in marbling, the printing of stonelike patterns on paper or fabric.

Gussy Up That Rabbit Cage

NOTHING BEATS old-fashioned white vinegar as a natural cleaner and disinfectant. Vinegar cuts through grease and makes mirrors and glass shine. It's also the best thing to use for cleaning a rabbit's cage. Don a pair of disposable gloves, pour vinegar straight onto paper towels, wipe down the cage, and then throw out the soiled gloves and paper towels. Rinse the cage thoroughly with water.

would a cleanser. Rub with a wet rag. Add a little Murphy Oil Soap to the rag and rub again. Rinse well. To clean the toilet, shake baking soda inside the toilet bowl. Add a few drops of Murphy Oil Soap. Scrub with a toilet brush.

Another Murphy Oil cleaning trick is to don an old pair of white cotton gym socks on your hands like mittens and spray the mitts with Murphy Oil Soap. Then start cleaning, two-handed! You'll finish your cleaning in half the time and exercise your arms to boot. This method is good for dusting furniture, mantels, tabletops, cabinets, miniblinds, and even ceiling fans.

Unusual Uses for Ivory Soap

■ In 1927, to promote its hot-selling soap, Procter & Gamble produced a short book called *Unusual Uses of Ivory Soap*, filled with 68 suggestions and recipes for Ivory Soap cakes and Ivory Flakes. Some of these suggestions may still be useful today. Before you try these suggestions on a large scale, though, sample them on a small area. Surfaces of items such as furniture and tile may be different than they were back in the 1920s, and these formulas may not be effective for today's surfaces.

Kill insects. "Soak the roots [of plants] occasionally with Ivory suds. If the leaves or stems are attacked, spray them with the same solution."

Remove finger marks from furniture. Mix 1 quart water, 1 tablespoon Ivory Flakes, and 1 tablespoon salad oil as a cleaner.

Polish silver. Blend 1 tablespoon Ivory Flakes, 1 cup water, ½ cup whiting (chalk), and 1 teaspoon glycerin.

Clean tiles. Make a paste of 1 small package of Ivory Flakes, ¼ pound whiting (chalk or Bon Ami), and 1 ounce ammonia. "Excellent for old or disfigured hearths or tile bathrooms."

Prevent candle drips. Wet your hands and rub a cake of soap until a thick, dry lather is formed. Roll the candle in this until it is coated. (Don't touch the wick with this lather.) The candle will burn without smoking, will not smell, will not drip, and will last longer. Or so says Procter & Gamble.

Keep edges from fraying. Dampen material, rub it with soap, and allow it to dry before cutting buttonholes.

Brush your teeth? "Many folks like to use just plain Ivory Soap suds for scrubbing the teeth," the pamphlet claims. Wouldn't that be called *washing your mouth out with soap*?

Lavender Air Freshener

"IN THE MIDDLE AGES, the laundress was called the *lavender*," says Lorraine Kiefer, herbal expert and owner of Triple Oaks Nursery, in Franklinville, New Jersey. The name reflected the use of lavender to scent linen and laundry. "If you sprinkle lavender on your carpet or couch before vacuuming, it will be a beautiful air freshener," Lorraine adds. "If you sprinkle lavender oil on furniture, under cushions, or on carpets, it will rid your home of that doggy smell. And cats will refuse to sit in a spot sprayed with lavender oil."

Here is a homespun lavender recipe based on one in the handwritten *Hartel Family Receipt Book* (1810) that you can still use today to keep your home smelling lovely. Dab this mixture on a cotton ball or a piece of cloth to scent drawers, closets, and rooms. You can adjust the quantities of herbs and spices in this mixture to your liking.

2 teaspoons lavender flowers
½ teaspoon mace
½ teaspoon cinnamon
¼ teaspoon cloves
¼ teaspoon saffron
¼ teaspoon nutmeg
1 pint spirits (rubbing alcohol)
2 teaspoons camphor oil

Combine all the ingredients except the camphor oil and let the mixture stand in a glass jar (it may be covered, but leave it unsealed so the alcohol can evaporate) for 10 days in a moderately warm place. Strain the mixture through cheesecloth and add the camphor oil, following the directions on the camphor packaging closely. Dip cotton balls and/or cloth into the mixture to make lovely sachets. When the sachets lose their scent, make up a new batch.

Lavender has even more uses, Lorraine notes. "Lavender is wonderful when added to a bath, too. Put some lavender into an old clean sock with some Epsom salts or baking soda and add to a tub of warm water for a wonderful bath."

Disinfect with Lavender Tea

▪ If you're looking for a natural way to fight household germs, try lavender. In ancient Rome, people added lavender to the water at public baths not only for its relaxing qualities but also to help keep the water germ-free. *Note:* Lavender doesn't have the concentrated germ-fighting power of modern commercial products.

"I learned a great way to use lavender for my own home from the late Bertha Reppert, a wonderful author and owner of the Rosemary House, in Mechanicsburg, Pennsylvania," says Jane Irvin-Klotz, of North Wales, Pennsylvania, an herbal expert and member of the Herb Gatherers Club of Pennsylvania. "You can make lavender water [also called *lavender tea*] and store it in a clean recycled or new spray bottle to clean your countertops and doorknobs. It's also great for cleaning out plastic ice chests. Lavender water in a spray bottle is a good idea for teachers, too. Sprayed in the air, it will disinfect the classroom and calm the students at the same time."

1 cup fresh or ½ cup dried lavender flowers
Sheer cloth bag or cheesecloth
Glass container (one that can withstand boiling water)
1-pint sterilized plastic or glass spray bottle

Put the flowers in the bag or tie them in a square of cheesecloth. Place the bag or cheesecloth in the glass container. Boil 1 pint clean tap or bottled water. Pour into the glass container. Cover the container and let it cool. Remove the bag or cloth containing the lavender flowers from the container, gently squeezing the excess moisture into the container. Pour the lavender water into the spray bottle and store it out of the sunlight in a cool place.

An alternative method is to add a few drops of essential oil of lavender to 1 pint distilled water. Start with 3 to 5 drops and increase the amount if you would like a stronger lavender scent. Lavender tea will keep for about 4 to 6 weeks. Don't use the tea if a dark ring shows in the bottle or if there is a dark scum on top of the water. It's best to label the bottle with the date you made the batch and update the label every time you make a fresh batch.

Good Cologne Water Fights Odors

▪ One technique that turn-of-the-century homemakers used to combat offensive odors was sprinkling cologne water (essential oils mixed in water or alcohol) on a cloth to sweeten a drawer or closet. This still works today. A homespun recipe for "good cologne water" from the handwritten *Receipt Book* (1899) of New Jersey homemaker Anna E. Nicholson, suggests using oils of lavender, bergamot, lemon, orange, and flower water. For directions for making cologne water (also known as *eau de toilette* or *toilet water*), see "Blend Your Own Vintage Scent" on page 203. Keep in mind that in some cases, masking odors is only a temporary solution. For odors due to sources such as mildew, you'll eventually need to find and treat the source of the odor.

CHAPTER 3

Home Decorating
Our Home Is Our Castle

When it comes to giving your home a royal decorating makeover, you don't have to spend a king's ransom to do it. In this chapter, you'll find a wealth of decorating ideas inspired by old-fashioned know-how, both homespun and highly elegant. And as the saying goes, everything old is new again. Grandma's doilies, old-time baker's racks, and antique music cabinets can all serve a purpose in our very modern homes. Plus, you'll find excellent advice on painting, wallpapering, and accessorizing your living room, dining room, family room, and bedrooms. So take a walk through these hints from yesteryear—you'll soon be making dull rooms a thing of the past!

Fine Furnishing and Accent Ideas

Decorating your home depends greatly on your personal style and taste. But you can use the old-time tips that follow as general guidelines to help you choose window treatments, select fine furniture, and display your favorite knickknacks and art objects.

Classic Glass for Your Windows

▪ Add sparkle to a room by using leaded glass as a window accent. Victorian decorators couldn't get enough of decorative panels filled with pieces of stained or beveled glass soldered together with lead. These exquisite panels depicted still lifes, landscapes, animals, or even scenes of human drama reminiscent of stained-glass windows in churches. Decorators used them to embellish many areas throughout the house—door transoms or windows, for example. An 1875 advertisement for Tilghman's Sand Blast Works in New York that hawked "plain and colored embossed glass for windows" even offered to reproduce any design a customer wanted to submit.

Today, some antique stores and salvage yards sell vintage leaded-glass panels, usually framed in wood or lead, at reasonable prices. Or look for a modern-day leaded-glass artisan in your area and buy directly from the source.

If the panel has not been professionally modified for hanging, suspend it from a pair of thin picture-hanging wires wrapped around the entire length of the panel at each side, discreetly overlapping a line of lead, not glass. Determine the level at which you want the panel to hang, and measure the distance from the top of the panel to the top of your window frame. Also measure the height of the panel itself. Cut two pieces of wire, each equal in length to the distance from panel to window frame, plus twice the height of the panel, plus 6 inches. Wrap a wire around each side of the panel, leaving one end of the wire shorter than the other. Twist the short end of the wire around the long end to secure the panel tightly so it can't slip out. Then install hooks at the top of your window frame and attach the long ends of the wires to the hooks. Stained glass will reflect colorfully on nearby objects; colorless beveled glass will shimmer like diamonds. Your vintage window panel will dress up your window and become a focal point of the entire room.

Go Dutch Treat on Curtains

HIGH-TECH "top down, bottom up" shades are versatile, offering privacy but still allowing natural light into a room. They can be quite pricey, however, and they aren't easy to install in all window styles. An inexpensive alternative that offers the same benefits is traditional double or Dutch-style curtains. In *How to Furnish Old American Houses* (1949), coauthors Henry Williams and Ottalie Williams note that these plain café-style curtains cover the full length of a window in two tiers (four panels). Each tier is hung on its own rod. Keep the bottom tier closed for privacy, but pull the top tier open to let in light. Or make Dutch curtains out of sheer material that prevents people outside from looking in but still allows light to come through. There's nothing pricey *or* high-tech about buying or making these simple curtains.

Treat Your Windows Grandly

■ Your windows may be of modest proportions, but that doesn't mean they can't put on some grand airs, the way tall windows did in 19th-century Federal and Victorian houses. JoAnn Marra, an apparel designer and design consultant from West Bay Shore, New York, furnished her average-size condo windows with curtains extending to the floor to give the illusion of height to her 8-foot ceilings, as well as her windows. You can enhance the illusion by adding a romantic top treatment called a *window scarf*—a plain rectangle of fabric, sometimes with fringe trim, draped over curtain tieback hardware or over the length of a decorative curtain rod (the finials at each end of the rod help secure the scarf). Position the scarf so that the highest points of its drape barely overlap the top of the window. You can find hardware and finished window scarves at most discount stores and home centers, as well as at smaller specialty retailers and in catalogs.

Homespun for Colonial Curtains

■ If you're partial to Colonial style—whatever the architectural style of your home—you can add a Colonial feeling to a room by making curtains out of homespun. This simple, coarse cotton fabric typically has a blue or brown checked or plaid pattern on a cream background. To further evoke a Colonial spirit, hem curtains at sill length and set them into the window reveal (the window equivalent of a doorjamb) instead of fastening them to the window frame or the wall, recommend coauthors Henry Williams and Ottalie Williams in *How to Furnish Old American Houses* (1949). The bonus is a neater appearance and more exposure for a window's rich wood trim.

Making curtains can be as simple as measuring the height and width of your window's reveal and buying a piece of homespun that is about double the width and about 4 inches longer than the height of the reveal. Cut the fabric in half to make two panels. For each panel, turn under ½ inch of fabric along the sides and bottom. Turn under again ½ to ¾ inch; then sew simple hems. Along the top of each curtain, turn down ½ inch of fabric, then turn down the fabric again about 2 inches and sew a hem. Then create a curtain rod sleeve by sewing an extra seam, leaving 1 inch of fabric above the sleeve to serve as a ruffle. Hang the curtains using special socket brackets and custom-cut metal or wooden rods (available at fabric stores or stores that sell ready-made curtains). Or use tension sockets, which don't require any hardware to hang. Add to the homey, homespun look by making coordinating seat-cushion covers or throw pillows.

Furniture for the Ages

■ It's not easy to find the kind of well-made wooden furniture that prevailed long ago, and few of us can afford to purchase those precious antiques that have survived. Even so, we'd do well to arm ourselves with some old-time expertise before embarking on a furniture-buying expedition. "The first advice I give to someone buying furniture is to understand the types of materials used to make furniture," says Ed McDonough, a furniture maker and writer from Walpole, Massachusetts. "The second bit of advice is to understand how the furniture was crafted." Here are a few tips on features that make for good—and not-so-good—purchases, from furniture experts of the past and present.

Know the hard (and soft) facts. Hardwoods, such as oak, teak, maple, and cherry, are generally more resistant to scratches and dings than softwoods like pine. Russell Kettell writes in *The Pine Furniture of Early New England* (1929) that lightweight pine is suitable for small portable pieces like footstools or benches, as well as chair seats. But avoid chairs made entirely of pine because their joints will loosen over time.

Look under the table. Tom Sippel, a custom wooden furniture maker from Cummington, Massachusetts, advises that you can uncover a multitude of sins if you look *under*—as well as *at*—prospective furniture acquisitions, such as wooden tables and chairs. "Hardware to brace cracked or unstable pieces is one warning sign of trouble," Tom says.

PEARLS OF WISDOM

"We would gladly see the money now expended in the trashy, half-made articles of furniture, merely because the uncomfortable shapes of some of them are said to be the latest style, laid out for those which are truly strong and comfortable, and, for this reason, elegant."

GEORGE WOODWARD, *Woodward's Cottages and Farm Houses* (1867)

Check the construction. In the *Furniture Treasury (Mostly of American Origin),* Volume III (1933), author Wallace Nutting advises readers to judge furniture by how it is put together, or "its joints." Look for the old-time technique of mortise-and-tenon instead of simple dowel construction in joined parts such as chair legs and cross-braces. Another standard of quality in furniture is the dovetailing of drawers in chests of all kinds.

Don't forget the finish. "From a durability perspective, the amount of finish applied to the piece is equally important as the type of finish," Ed McDonough says. Ed recommends a topcoat of durable lacquer, varnish, or polyurethane for items that will receive a lot of day-to-day use.

Tom Sippel, on the other hand, warns that some heavy-handed finishes not only can hide the beauty of a wood's natural grain but also can mask imperfections in the wood—irregularities that might eventually surface if you decide to refinish the piece. "Maple furniture that is factory made is often finished with an orange-brown toning agent that totally covers up the grain," he notes with some disapproval.

Display Art in an Old-Time Style

Decorating your home with art isn't limited to hanging pictures, as Victorian women knew well. They often displayed small art objects in tiers on console tables. These tables are typically long, narrow wooden tables on long legs positioned behind a sofa or against a wall. But any tabletop will lend itself to your favorite small pieces, spaced closely in tiered rows, with the tallest objects in the back. A tiered pantry organizer that discount stores or home centers carry could add to this effect; a simple board on blocks also works. Either way, drape a linen napkin or embroidered runner over the organizer or board to add a dressy finishing touch.

Soft Treatments for Hard Surfaces

GIVE YOUR DINING ROOM or living room a storybook look King Arthur himself would feel at home in. Portieres, or doorway curtains, were used in drafty castles to insulate areas where kings, queens, and knights lived. Fast-forward to the 1800s, and decorative portieres of rich tapestry or jacquard were in vogue not only for interior entryways but also as wall hangings.

Take a page from these stories to add real romance to your walls, perhaps over the buffet or behind your sofa. It's easy to make a wall hanging by hand or machine, using a scenic tapestry-style throw blanket, available from discount stores and online catalogs. All you need to do is attach a sleeve to insert a hanging rod.

You will need:

- Throw blanket
- Plain, sturdy woven fabric (cotton or synthetic) 4 to 5 inches wide and long enough to extend almost the full width of the throw
- Thread
- Sewing machine (optional)
- Decorative wooden or metal hanging rod at least 4 inches longer than the width of the throw
- Straight pins
- 2 rod brackets and screws

Step 1. Measure the blanket's width (as you'll hang it on the wall). Cut the woven fabric to this length or about 1 inch shorter.

Step 2. Fold the woven fabric in half lengthwise and sew a seam about ¼ inch wide along the long edge.

Step 3. Turn the fabric *outside in* so the raw edges of the seam do not show.

Step 4. Slip the rod into the fabric sleeve and use straight pins to mark a second seam on the opposite long side. Allow enough space to easily slip the rod through. Remove the rod and sew the seam.

Step 5. Using an overcast stitch, sew the raw edges of the short ends together to prevent fraying, except for the actual rod sleeve portion (there, simply overcast each layer of fabric).

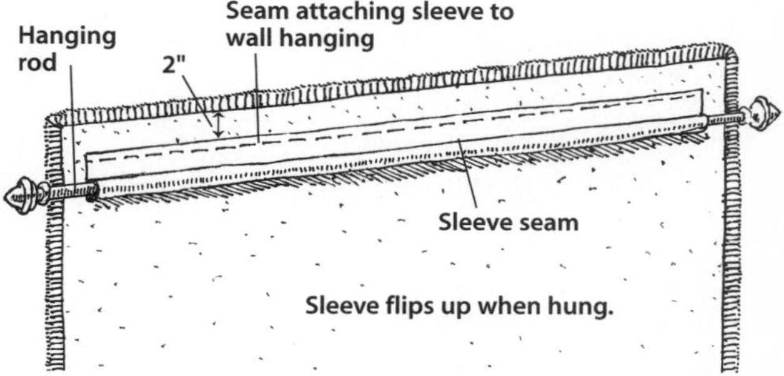

Step 6. Using a blending thread color, sew the fabric sleeve to the back of the throw, about 1½ to 2 inches down from the throw's top edge (the sleeve must not extend above the top edge when it is flipped up for hanging). The stitching should run through the sleeve fabric about ½ inch away from the side opposite the rod sleeve.

Step 7. Position the brackets on the wall so that the left and right sides of the throw just cover them. If you have plaster walls, drill pilot holes for wall anchors to secure the bracket screws.

Step 8. Insert the rod through the sleeve and hang it by placing it in the brackets.

Classic Picture-Hanging Hints

▪ Victorians, being the great art collectors that they were, introduced interesting innovations for hanging pictures that still work well today. Try some of these techniques for displaying your favorite pictures.

Picture rails mean no nails. Make picture hanging a nail-free proposition with picture rails, strips of wall molding originally designed to safeguard plaster walls. Pictures were hung from wires or braided cords hooked to this high-perch molding. Hooks and braided cords with steel wire cores are still available at stores and through mail-order suppliers that specialize in reproduction hardware and accessories. But before you go shopping for picture rail molding, look up at your own walls: Since picture rails didn't fall out of use until around 1940, you may have them and not be aware of it!

Art from all angles. If you want to hang pictures high on the wall, do what Victorian art mavens did: Tilt them out slightly for better viewing below. Hang ones that are more on eye level flush with the wall.

Cluster, not clutter. One way to avoid having your treasured framed photos and pictures look like so much "stuff" is to group them for an artful effect. Create your own pattern by hanging the pictures close together on the wall, the Victorian way. Maintaining a neat square or rectangular outside perimeter is particularly impressive.

OLD-FASHIONED FAVORITES

Hello, Doily

GET REACQUAINTED with your grandmother's all-but-forgotten doilies in that dusty attic chest: These little decorative lace or embroidered mats are great furniture protectors, and they're also a charming ornament that brings old-time gentility to your home. In *Homes and Their Decoration* (1903), Lillie French writes that for the luncheon table, "a square of old church lace on the bare board"—a doily—is the only cloth your table needs. Doilies are also great for dressing up your buffet or masking not-so-perfect finishes on end tables and coffee tables.

Featuring Your Favorite Colors

▪ You don't have to paint an entire room—or even a single wall—to introduce rich color into a room. Author Bernard Jakway points out in *The Principles of Interior Decoration* (1923), "It is a common mistake to assume that the stimulating or satisfying power of a favorite color depends upon the area of the surfaces over which it is distributed . . . A single ruby-red porcelain bowl against a cream or gray-green wall will have more power to satisfy a real craving for red than will a room done in crimson rugs, walls, and hangings." Following this line of thinking, try these tactics to introduce or bring out a favorite color.

A couch of many colors. If your couch is a neutral taupe, sage, or navy blue, layer it with colors. Try a richly hued chenille or plush thermal throw blanket, throw pillows, or standard pillows covered with show-off quality pillowcases or tailored pillow shams.

Line up your collections. Pick a shelf in your family room, clear off as much space as you need, and display some beautiful kitchenware, such as green Depression glass, as a colorful group.

Picture this. A wall of framed family photographs offers a great spot for color. Just paint every frame in your favorite color (provided the frames aren't expensive, custom-made items, of course). Take the photographs out of the frames before you paint them. It's a fast job, and the results can be sensational.

No-Crater Picture Hanging

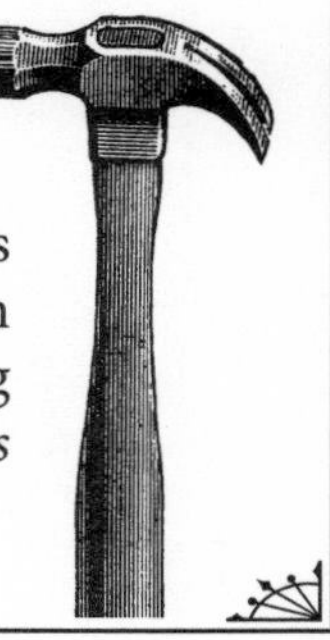

DRIVING A NAIL to hang a picture in an old plaster wall can leave a big divot in the wall as the plaster crumbles around the nail. To avoid this problem, dip the nail in hot water from the tap for a few minutes before driving it, recommends *1000 Helps and Hints for the House and Home* (1936).

Give Bookcases a Built-In Look

Built-in bookcases have long been a classic feature of traditional homes, be they Colonial, Federal, or Victorian. But you can give any tall bookcase some of the same appeal, says Kathleen Butler, a retiree from Kearny, New Jersey. "Painting the bookcase to blend in with the walls is the key," Kathleen says, adding that it's easier to pull off this built-in effect if the bookcase is fairly shallow and you apply a trim color that echoes that of your walls. She undertook her own experiment with two inexpensive, unfinished pine bookcases positioned on each side of her sofa. Her walls were a flat-finish antique white, and her cornice moldings and window frames were medium gray-green in a satin finish. To echo this combination, she painted all surfaces of the bookcase a closely matched flat white (first using a wood primer to prevent the pine knots from bleeding through), except for the thin front edges of the frame and of the shelves, which she trimmed in the same green paint used for the moldings. "The effect was amazing!" Kathleen says. If you want to try this with a bookcase that is already finished, keep in mind that you may first have to sand it down to bare wood before painting.

WALLS, CEILINGS, AND FLOORS

MOST ROOMS are a basic box: four walls, a floor, and a ceiling. Your challenge is to decorate this box so it becomes unboxy. It's a classic interior design challenge, and we've mixed old-time know-how with modern technology to bring you great ideas about wall paints that help make a chilly room feel warmer, area rugs that laugh at dirt, and even a way to put a ceiling to work.

Tone Sets the Mood

Before you become engrossed in comparing paint chips and samples to select a color for a redecorating project, think about how you want people to feel in the room you're redoing. In *The Principles of Interior Decoration* (1923), Bernard Jakway explains: "We will lower the tone of the walls in rooms where a marked effect of tranquillity is aimed at, and raise it in rooms where a marked effect of gayety and animation is desired." You can think of "tone" as a paint's intensity. For example, pastel robin's egg blue has a lower tone, while deep royal or navy blue has a high tone. You can apply this theory to any color you'd like. Simply look for paint chips that include three or four tones of the same color. And following this theory, you might choose a pale shade for the tranquil bedroom and a high tone for the family rec room.

OLD-TIME HUMOR

Rugged Individualism

JOSEPH McVEIGH, of Rosedale, New York, recalls that a poor but independent-minded farmer neighbor back in Ireland made the following retort (circa 1925) to visitors aghast at his cottage's untidiness: "We keep this house for our own accommodation!"

Color-Code Your House

Learning about color therapy also will help you decide what color to paint your dining room or bedroom. For example, red is a superb color for the dining room, since it's said to encourage the appetite, but in the bedroom, it's more likely to promote midnight refrigerator raids. During the 19th century, rich, strong colors were popular in every room, but interior designers such as Robert Edis eventually moved to milder palettes, explaining that "bold patterns might be likely to fix themselves upon a tired brain, suggesting all kinds of weird forms." To put your brain in a soothing place, here's a quick look at the seven basic colors and how you might react physiologically and emotionally to each.

Red. Gives energy, passion, courage; reportedly stimulates the appetite and promotes sociable feelings.

Orange. The color of happiness and stability; possibly decreases inhibitions, increases confidence, and aids digestion.

Yellow. Uplifting and energizing; may increase awareness, stimulate interest, and promote clarity of thought.

Green. Calming and comforting; thought to help relax muscles, nerves, and thoughts, inducing a sense of harmony.

Blue. A relaxing, soothing color that's said to be ideal for those suffering from insomnia, stress, or nightmares; there is some evidence that blue reduces blood pressure and dispels hunger.

Indigo (deep blue). Stimulates insight, mysticism, and understanding; may strengthen intuition, boost imagination, and encourage dream activity.

Purple. Promotes beauty, creativity, and fertility; reportedly helps with weight loss, enhances artistic talent, and improves self-assurance.

Color Consultant from Above

■ Another way to decide on the color scheme for a room is to consult the sun. According to Candace Wheeler in *Principles of Home Decoration* (1903), sun exposure should be a key factor in color choice. For a room with northern exposure, use yellow and other warm tones in the spectrum, but for a sun-filled space, cool it down with green or blue.

Sold on Bold

■ "Plain, flat tints give apparent size to small rooms," writes Candace Wheeler in *Principles of Home Decoration, with Practical Examples* (1903). We might put it this way: Light colors tend to make a room appear larger. It's a classic principle that does hold true, but styles today often break that tradition. Bold colors are in! But it can be unnerving to paint a room a rich green or red when you're used to living among off-white and pastel walls. To help build your courage, test a strong color first by painting a small patch on one wall. Don't buy a gallon of paint in order to make your test, though, or even a quart. Many paint manufacturers and stores now offer small paint packets, mixed to the color of your choice, providing enough paint to cover about 2 square feet of wall. The packets cost about $2 apiece. After completing your test patch, observe how it looks at different times of day and in various kinds of light. What does it look like with bright natural sunlight versus 60-watt lightbulbs at night? After 48 hours, whether the room is small or big, let your instincts tell you whether that room is the right place for a splash of bold color. And if the color pleases you, who cares if it makes the room appear a bit smaller. Remember, a small room can also be a cozy, warm, and inviting room.

PEARLS OF WISDOM

"The first impression of a room depends upon the walls. In fact, rooms are good or bad, agreeable or ugly in exact accordance with the wall-quality and treatment. No richness of floor-covering, draperies, or furniture can minimize their influence."

CANDACE WHEELER,
Principles of Home Decoration (1903)

Say It with Style

■ Stenciling a favorite saying on the wall of your living room, dining room, or bedroom is an old-time idea that's new again. "If one wishes to mount a favourite motto or question on the walls, where it may give constant suggestion or pleasure—or even be a help to thoughtful and conscientious living—there can be no better fashion than the style of the old illuminated missals . . . the words running on scrolls which are half unrolled and half hidden, and showing a conventionalized background of fruit and flowers," writes Candace Wheeler in *Principles of Home Decoration* (1903). Today, we would probably skip the half-unrolled-scroll effect and pick instead a short

Getting Acquainted with Wall Paints

"To paint the side walls of a room is to many a laborious and expensive job; but when one is acquainted with the work, it does not seem to be so great a task, and therefore we will endeavor to tell just how to begin and how to finish a wall." This is how Franklin Gardner begins a chapter in *Everybody's Paint Book* (1884), followed by page after page of detailed instructions. Fortunately, the modern house paint industry has revolutionized the art of painting interior walls, making the job easy and inexpensive. Here are a few recent innovations in house paints.

R-value paint. If a room leans toward the chilly side, especially if this room has an outside wall and you're certain the chill isn't due to window drafts, select a paint, primer, or paint additive with an R-value—the measure of insulation's resistance to heat dissipation, which serves to keep a home warmer in the winter and cooler in the summer. The higher the R-value, the more effective the insulation. These paint products, tinted to any desired color, cost more than traditional wall paints, but they're far less expensive than tearing down a wall in order to beef up insulation.

Paint for humid rooms. For the bathroom, basement, kitchen, and any other room exposed to lots of moisture or humidity, try a wall paint guaranteed to be mildew-proof and blister-proof.

Paint that covers cracks. Several new paints on the market fill hairline wall cracks as you apply them, which will significantly reduce preparation time before painting.

Easy-to-clean paint. Ceramic paints are latex wall paints that contain tiny round ceramic particles called *microspheres,* which block anything from penetrating the painted surface. This means that stains remain on the wall surface and wipe off easily.

cherished phrase, or three to four inspirational words. For example, "Live, Love, Laugh" for the bedroom; "Eat, Drink & Be Merry" in the dining room. If you're nervous about painting the words yourself, hire someone with a flair for calligraphy. Another take on this concept is to frame a piece of sheet music of a song that touches your heart, such as a meaningful piece that was played at your wedding or the theme song from a poignant movie. Slightly more expensive but ultrafast: Visit almost any home store and buy ready-to-hang letters, which are available in a range of sizes, painted or unfinished. To maintain her perspective, Chicago freelance copywriter Donna Shryer says, "I used these letters to spell out a saying on the wall near my desk that helps me maintain my perspective when life seems a little too crazy." Donna's motto? She spelled out "WHATEVER."

Choose Wallpaper without Going Mad

Addressing the wallpaper selection process, Mary Northend laments in *The Art of Home Decoration* (1921), "The problem confronting the buyer is which shall constitute the chosen few, how to pick the gold from the dross [inferior material], and even more confusing, how to recognize it among the mass?" Almost one hundred years later, nothing has changed! However, there *are* ways to head off wallpaper overdose and pinpoint that one wonderful sample. Here are a few pointers.

Make a plan. Start by deciding whether your goal is to significantly brighten up the room, blend with existing colors, or accentuate one particular color. Then, decide whether you want to cover all wall surfaces, one select wall, or just the area below a chair rail. Generally speaking, if you plan to paper a large proportion of the wall area, stick with neutral colors and/or patterns.

Collect samples. Gather swatches of fabric, such as a small carpet scrap (or snip a few threads from a hidden spot and tape them to an index card), an arm cover from an upholstered chair, a throw pillow, or curtain tiebacks.

Set a timer. Before you enter the wallpaper shop, set a time limit for browsing. Looking through too many books at one sitting is inviting frustration!

Ask for guidance. A salesperson can explain how the store's sample books are organized. The books may be divided into groups, such as Contemporary, Traditional, Metallic, Stripes, and other categories. Understanding this organization process is like the difference between jumping in an ocean and sticking your toe in a puddle.

Work systematically. Lay your fabric samples on a table, open your first book, and flip through quickly. Keep the swatches in your line of vision so that complementary color palettes will catch your eye. Bookmark pages that work

OLD-FASHIONED FAVORITES

Glaze Away Wallpaper Woes

To improve a potentially beautiful wallpaper that is too bold or too bland, add a glaze. It's an old technique that was also used to soften wallpapers with "glaring designs," states Candace Wheeler in *Principles of Home Decoration* (1903). Back in the author's day, glazing was accomplished by covering "the whole surface with a kalsomine or chalk-wash, of some agreeable tint." Chalkwashing has evolved into an elegant faux finish called *glazing*. The process produces a rich antique quality. It can tone down colors, make washed-out paper appear to be intentionally faded, or turn a mistake into an asset.

Your best bet is to call in a professional when it comes to glazing wallpaper, since different papers require different kinds of preparation for glazing, such as sealing the paper with a water-based varnish. As for the glazing process itself, it usually involves applying a water-based stain with a rag, which creates a dimensional, soft, blended layer over the wallpaper without concealing the paper's pattern and color.

colorwise. You'll consider specific designs and patterns later.

Make cuts. Review the bookmarked pages and accept or reject individual patterns.

Live with it overnight. Once your selection is down to 10 or fewer samples (this may take several days), ask the salesperson about the store's take-home policy. Most shops allow you to check out sample books at least overnight for free.

Cheaper Wallpaper Isn't Always Cheaper

Believe it or not, expensive wallpaper can be more cost-effective than cheap wallpaper. How can this be? It's just as Ethel Seal explains in *Furnishing the Little House* (1924): "When any one compromises on a moderate-priced paper and then 'a little border to take away that bare look,' I always feel tempted to request them to count up the cost of both paper and border, to prove that the whole has come to a total sum that would have bought the really fine paper they would have felt an extravagance in the first place." It's still true today. If you've chosen an economically priced wallpaper and border for a room of your house, be sure you do the math before you buy. Total the price of the paper and border and the cost to have both hung, and compare that to the cost of a "dream wallpaper" that you think you can't afford. Often, you'll find that the cost of the dream wallpaper comes out to less than the cheaper-paper-and-border combination.

Cover Up Passé Paneling

Wooden paneling that is "fine in proportion and finish," such as is recommended by Mary Josephine Quinn in *Planning and Furnishing the Home: Practical and Economical Suggestions for the Homemaker* (1914), is a beautiful feature of vintage homes. But many homeowners today struggle to decide what to do about walls covered by faux wood and wood veneer paneling, which was highly popular in the 1950s through 1970s. Although it was an affordable alternative to real wooden paneling, old faux and veneer paneling looks dated at best and shabby at worst. The good news is that you can update an unattractively paneled room without too much wear and tear on your back or budget. Don't rip out the paneling; instead, coat it with a stain-killing bonding primer—several brands are available. Choose water-based latex versions if easy cleanup is a high priority; oil-based versions serve better for high-humidity areas. Both types provide a surface that accepts wallpaper or paint, and sometimes even glass, Formica, or ceramic tile.

The Subtleties of Ceiling Color

Some interior designers consider the ceiling a "fifth wall"—an opportunity for bold, off-the-wall color options. But the general consensus remains as interior designer Helen Gloag states in *Simple Furnishing and Arrangement* (1921): "No ceiling should be dead white in colour, and the blue tone dear to the heart of the ordinary painter and decorator is a depressing hue and one to avoid. A little raw sienna or umber should be mixed with the white distemper [paint], producing in the ceiling a slightly warm shade." Avoid stark white ceilings, because they're too harsh. And you probably don't want dark colors, because ceilings are seen in a shadow, which will darken a dark color even more.

If you have a yen for some sort of color, buy ceiling paint several shades lighter than the wall shade. To visualize the shade you need, find that original paint chip for your wall color. One paint chip often includes three to four tones of the same color. For a ceiling, you want the palest version of the color available. In do-it-yourself mode, mix your wall color into white paint using a ratio of 25 percent color to 75 percent white.

Crown Your Ceiling

■ With some do-it-yourself determination, you can give even the plainest walls and ceilings regal stature by installing crown moldings, which are available in many shapes and styles at lumberyards and millwork shops. As coauthor of *The Decoration of Houses* (1902), socialite novelist Edith Wharton describes how fancy plasterwork cornices—the precursors of milled moldings—could fool the eye by softening the angles between wall and ceiling, greatly increasing the "apparent height" of low-ceilinged rooms. You can pull off the same trick by installing milled molding and painting it. Paint-grade pine or fir moldings made from short pieces that are "finger joined" together are among the more reasonably priced. Lumberyards can cut the moldings to your specified lengths. Or if your budget allows, you can buy ready-to-paint, highly decorative moldings made from high-density polymers from home improvement stores.

You'll need finishing nails, Spackle, paint, and an inexpensive miter box and saw to cut the corners of the moldings to fit. But for your first step, pick up a home

☞ BIZARRE BUT TRUE ☜

Sensible or Superstitious?

ONE INTRIGUING FEATURE of some older Colonial homes is the "funeral door." This door to the porch or yard was so dubbed because it was often used instead of the main entrance for carrying coffins in and out of a house. The funeral door provided the direct egress from the area commonly used for viewing the dead: the family parlor. Today, such doors would probably be viewed as a challenge rather than a convenience to home decorators trying to squeeze in a suite of furniture. In Colonial times, however, they spared pallbearers the logistical difficulties of turning tight corners into hallways and colliding with pieces of furniture. The funeral door may also have served an altogether different purpose: Some superstitious types maintained it spared the household the bad luck incurred by carrying a corpse out the front door.

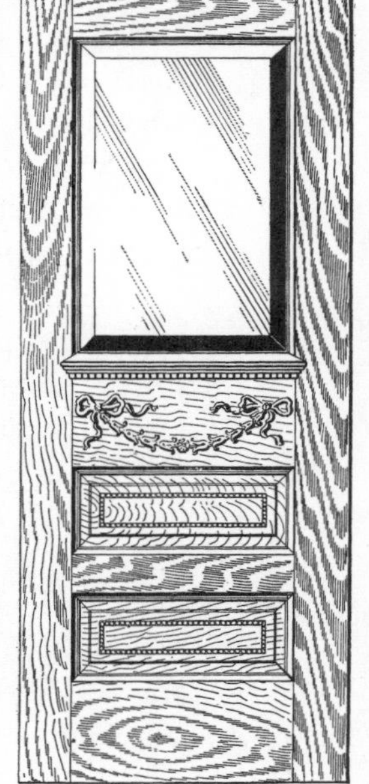

projects book or attend a molding-installation how-to session at a local home improvement store. That way you'll discover all you need to know before you start—including the estimated installation time based on your level of expertise.

Small Rugs Fit Large Rooms Best

■ A large area rug may not be the best choice for your large living room or family room. In the words of *Godey's Lady's Book* (June 1855), "Let the carpet be made in about three pieces, in order that it may be frequently taken up and beaten or shaken, and the floor scrubbed clean." This old-time advice certainly makes sense, and there are other reasons to choose a group of small rugs for a big room rather than one mammoth floor covering, as well.

◆ Smaller area rugs, such as 4 feet by 6 feet or 5 feet by 8 feet, create the illusion of intimate living spaces.

◆ Small rugs are more manageable if you like to roll up and store your area rugs or substitute lighter floor mats for wool rugs during the summer months.

◆ Since small rugs are so easy to clean, using them can be smarter than laying a large rug or installing wall-to-wall carpet. Efficient and frequent cleaning significantly reduces the risk that molds and mildews—which can create allergy problems—will develop.

◆ With the increased popularity of area rugs, you can now find them in a variety of shapes, such as square and round. These not only make an instant design statement but also make it easy to find a rug of the precise size and shape you need.

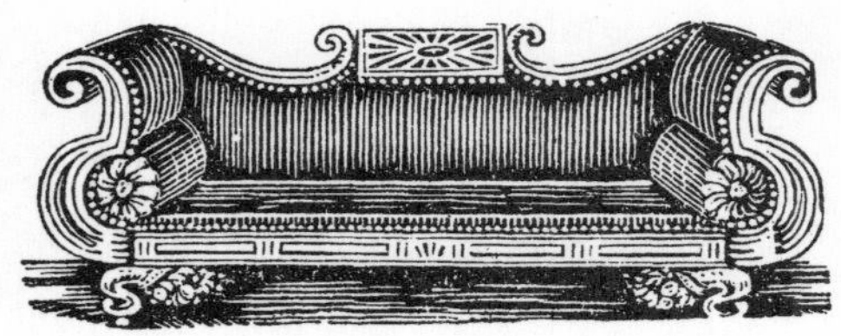

Lively Ideas for Living Rooms

Home decorators over the centuries have done a lot of deliberating over that high-profile room once known as the *parlor* but that we now call the *living room.* The challenge then, as it is now, was finding ways to blend comfort with good taste. Here you'll find plenty of old-fashioned parlor tricks, from livening up a room with lamps to hiding your soot-covered hearth with an easy-to-make fire screen.

Romantic Lighting for Modern Living Rooms

■ Your living room can have that soft, romantic ambience that was the hallmark of bygone eras. In *How to Furnish Old American Houses* (1949), coauthors Henry Williams and Ottalie Williams note a long succession of lighting innovations since the austere 1600s, when colonists "made wooden 'candles' out of pitch pine slivers or soaked rushes in fat and called them rushlights." Lighting became increasingly sophisticated, from Colonial lanterns to curvy Victorian shades and Tiffany-style stained glass—all great options for seeing your living room in a whole new light. Better still, many of these can be found at seemingly old-fashioned prices. Here are some enlightening examples.

Switch to fancy shades. Try replacing the standard white shades on your table lamps with some period styles, such as shades with beaded or twisted-cord fringe. Or splurge on a classic Tiffany-style stained-glass lamp, with its stylistic bronze base.

Use floor lamps in tight spaces. Floor lamps are great space-savers, squeezing in next to an easy chair or recliner where a side table can't.

Add accent lamps. Small table lamps are ideal for accentuating occasional furniture or livening up an otherwise dark corner. They're also a great alternative to an art light, highlighting a special painting or print from a table below instead of from overhead. Add some magic with a Colonial-style electrified lantern of pierced tin, with its characteristic rays of light shooting out through its tiny perforations.

Soften the room with sconces. Add some soft lighting by mounting sconces on both sides of your fireplace mantel, or to frame any area of your wall. Eighteenth-century-style electric candle sconces with mirror reflectors have made a comeback recently. You can even find some quick plug-in types in catalogs or at stores that specialize in moderate-priced period furniture and accessories.

Rustic Seating without Big Spending

For a low-cost, uniquely rustic suite of furniture, try chairs made from simple oak barrels. In *The Architecture of Country Houses* (1850), architect Andrew Jackson Downing describes these home-made seats called *barrel-chairs:* "These chairs are easily made by sawing off a portion of the barrel—nailing on a few boards, to form the seat, and leaving part of the staves a little higher than the others, to form the back or arms." But save yourself the sawing by selecting a reasonably priced version that's preconstructed from recycled oak barrels; online garden supply companies market them for indoor as well as outdoor use (see Resources on page 349). You can leave

☞ OLD-TIME ODDITIES ☜

The Tête-à-Tête

During Queen Victoria's long reign—64 years—her subjects and American contemporaries alike had plenty of time to devise all manner of curious style and tradition. Take the tête-à-tête, for instance: Victorian "party animals" loved to indulge in gossip and other intimacies, and indulge they did. The tête-à-tête, an often S-shaped sofa for two, was made just for that purpose. Gossipers sat facing in opposite directions, but the sofa's contour also allowed them to face each other with a minimum of neck turning as they whispered across the armrest/seat back divide. Another design benefit: a combined 360-degree range for spotting gossip fodder!

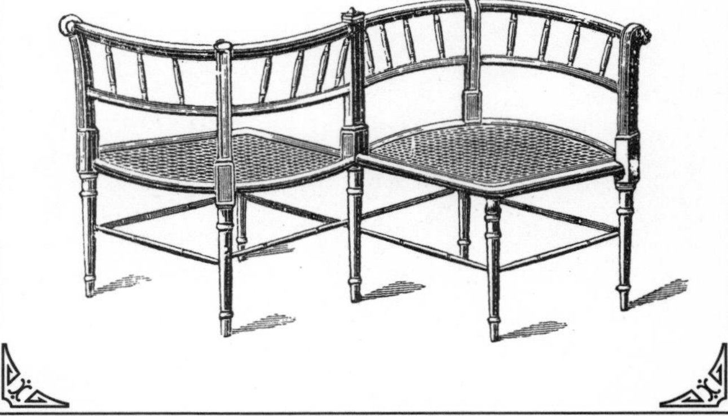

them natural or lacquer them. Or you can fashion seat and back cushions from canvas stuffed with "any cheap material and covered with chintz." Add finishing touches of a shirred skirt and contrasting piping to the upholstered version, and nobody would ever guess your chair's humble beginnings! Throw in a coffee table by buying a half barrel and topping it with a circular piece of clear or tinted glass, which is available from custom glass and mirror companies.

Space-Saving Table

Old-fashioned three-legged, tilt-top tables can be as serviceable for you as they were in Colonial times. In *The Quest of the Quaint* (1927), Virginia Robie praises this sort of table, with its tilting mechanism and often "a raised edge to prevent cups from slipping off," as "a treasure indeed!" Besides tea for two, you can use a tilt-top table to hold appetizers when entertaining, or as a fireside gaming table. It can be ready for service at a moment's notice. When not needed, tilt it flush with the wall. The top will add an ornamental effect without eating up valuable space, especially if embellished with that style table's signature "piecrust" edge or hand-painted floral design. Tilt tables are sold in specialty furniture catalogs. Watch for them at antique stores, too.

From Kneaded Dough to Knickknacks

Thinking of giving your old, canister-crammed kitchen baker's rack the heave-ho? Maybe it has a fancier future in your living room as an étagère. The Victorians loved these freestanding, French-inspired shelving units for displaying figurines and other dainty pieces of porcelain. In its day, the étagère was usually made of elaborately carved wood, but a wrought iron or other metal baker's rack with shelves and work surface can be converted into a charming étagère-like display case. Mildred Karl, an active widow from Mount Kisco, New York, agrees. "I was planning to get rid of that rack because it was too big for my little kitchen," Mildred says. "Then, as I browsed a furniture store for a curio cabinet to hold all my knickknacks, I passed a baker's rack similar to mine and stopped dead in my tracks!" Now her baker's rack elegantly holds her large collection in her living room.

OLD-TIME ODDITIES

Self-Fanning Rocker

BENJAMIN FRANKLIN: What *didn't* this quirky patriot do? We're all familiar with the Franklin stove and the lightning rod. Not as well known, perhaps, is that Benjamin Franklin is widely credited with the invention of the rocking chair. His self-fanning rocker is particularly intriguing, as *Rocking Chairs by Ben Franklin: They Soothed a Century* (1940), by Edmund Boots, relates: "His ultimate model, the comfort of his final years, was a great rocker with a wide arm for reading and writing and fly-fan attachment operated by the rocking motion."

When you set up a baker's rack as a display case, try hanging a fancy framed mirror from the backboard to further reflect a traditional étagère. If the shelf surface isn't solid, safeguard small treasures by lining each shelf with a stiff material, such as cardboard (use shirt packaging or the backs of legal pads, for instance). Then cover the liners with old-fashioned cloth runners and add your collection.

Try a Trio of Mirrors

Nothing looks more charming over the mantel than one of the old gold-leafed mirrors "in three parts" popular in the late 1700s and early 1800s—unless, perhaps, it's a *trio* of mirrors. In the *Furniture Treasury,* Volume III (1933), Wallace Nutting notes that the overall effect of these classically framed Chippendale mantel mirrors "is rich rather than tawdry, because the carving is delicately done and . . . covered with gold leaf." Your trio needn't be gilt framed, or identical, for that matter—in fact, it's more interesting if it's not. The adaptation is improved by mixing shapes, as well as frame colors and motifs. One possible arrangement: a rectangular mirror in a stained or painted wooden frame bookended by two round or diamond-shaped mirrors of similar height, perhaps in frames of gilt wood or even metal. If the frames have a set of hangers, one on each side, you can create a dramatic effect by hanging all three mirrors using decorative chains. Otherwise, you can adapt wooden frames for this treatment by attaching screw eyes to both sides of the back. Add small S-hooks to both ends of the chains and attach each end to a screw eye. Finally, hang each mirror by its chain from a decorative hanger attached securely to the wall. You'll find the chains and hardware in picture-framing stores, as well as at most hardware stores. As for your "looking glasses," seek them out at your local thrift shop to really make the arrangement unique.

OLD-FASHIONED FAVORITES

Simple, Sturdy, and Fragrant Hooks

OLD APPLE or cherry branches make some of the best wood for fires. But if you're pruning or taking down a dead tree, heed a lesson from old-time farmers and save the crotches of the branches for superdurable, pleasant-smelling hooks and brackets. In days past, people carved branch crotches into hooks for carrying buckets and cans of maple sap, milk, and the like. For use in your home today, try sawing one side of a tree crotch so it fits flush against a wall for a simple hook, shelf bracket, or coat rack.

Cooking Crane Might Come in Handy

Give your fireplace a piece of history that's both decorative and dependable in a pinch: an iron cooking crane. Sound far-fetched for this day and age? Not if you own an electric stove and microwave, and your electricity—not to mention your heat—suddenly goes off one evening during a blizzard. You can buy a reproduction version of this impressive-looking, centuries-old device, often made of heavy wrought iron and used for suspending food-laden kettles and pots over the fire. Its pivoting action makes it easy to swing out from the fire to attach or detach pots and stir when needed. In 1924, Wallace Nutting, author

Fancied Up and Fire-Free

After the long, dreary winter is finally over, banish that view of the soot-covered fireplace with an item that was a standard fixture in 19th-century drawing rooms: a fire screen. *The Architecture of Country Houses* (1850), by Andrew Jackson Downing, notes that fire screens were very popular both because they were decorative and because they shielded people from too much direct heat from a fire. You can easily assemble your own —purely decorative—three-panel wooden fire screen with less than $20 worth of supplies from any home improvement or hardware store.

Arching the top of the panels is a nice effect, but you'll need a jigsaw to cut the arches. Make circular paper templates using a large compass or any circular object, such as a bowl rim, that is the width of each panel or less (less makes for an even fancier effect, with the arch set in slightly from both ends of each panel). Draw a line across the center of each circle. Position the templates so the top of each circle is aligned with the center of each panel's top edge and your pencil lines are parallel with the top edges of the panels. Then trace the arch pattern onto the plywood with pencil, down to the half-circle lines, and cut away the excess plywood with the jigsaw.

You will need:

- 2- × 4-foot piece of ½-inch plywood (if possible, have the store cut it into three 2-foot-high pieces of equal width)
- Tape measure
- Pencil
- Workbench clamps
- Safety glasses
- Circular saw or handsaw (if plywood is not precut)
- Jigsaw (optional)
- Fine-grade sandpaper
- Tack cloth
- Wood primer
- 1½-inch paintbrush
- Satin-finish latex paint
- Large sheets of plain or graph paper
- Tracing paper and carbon paper (optional)
- Semigloss latex paint (or acrylic craft paint) in one or more colors
- Artist's paintbrush
- Four 1- to 1½-inch-long simple brass cabinet hinges with screws
- Drill
- Screwdriver

of *Furniture of the Pilgrim Century (of American Origin)*, noted that cooking cranes became indispensable to New England wives of the 1600s: "The hanging of the crane symbolized the setting up of the household." Crowding around the fire for light, warmth, and conversation while cooking may be an experience you'll remember long after the lights go back on. You can always substitute a candle lantern or a hanging pot of silk flowers for the cooking pot. Mail-order catalogs specializing in old-time ironworks are promising places to search for cooking cranes, which should come with instructions for attaching them securely to the sidewalls of fireplace interiors (see Resources on page 349).

Step 1. If the plywood hasn't been precut, use the tape measure to measure its length, then divide by three. Draw dividing lines in pencil for three panels. If the plywood has been precut, skip to Step 3.

Step 2. Clamp the plywood to a worktable. Wearing safety glasses, saw the plywood into three equal panels. Mark and cut arches with a jigsaw as described above, if desired.

Step 3. Sand the panels and clean them thoroughly with tack cloth.

Step 4. Working in a sawdust-free, ventilated area, apply the primer using the 1½-inch brush.

Step 5. Paint the panels, front and back, with satin-finish paint. Apply at least two coats, following the paint can's directions for adequate drying time between coats.

Step 6. Work out the graphic design you want on paper, color-coding each area for future reference.

Step 7. After the panels have dried for 24 hours, copy your design outline onto the panels (you may want to use tracing paper and carbon paper to transfer the outline to the panels).

Step 8. Using your color codes as a reference, apply one semigloss or craft paint color at a time with the artist's paintbrush until your design is complete.

Step 9. After they've dried, lay the panels facedown next to each other. Place two well-spaced hinges between each side panel and the center panel and mark the locations of the screw holes with the pencil. Remove the hinges and drill pilot holes; then attach the hinges with the screws.

Delightful Dining Rooms

Do you save your dining room for special occasions or eat there every day? Either way, you can pick up some unique decorating hints from old-timers who applied their ingenuity to enhance the scene of their household meals. Find out how to make distinctive centerpieces, choose the most practical and attractive floor coverings, and more. You'll soon be creating a room you'll not only want to feast in but also feast your eyes upon!

The Desk That Came to Dinner

■ Don't fire your secretary just because its office skills seem a tad outdated. Keep it working and earning its keep—in the dining room. This stately drop-leaf desk has always gone the distance to be accommodating, especially when topped by a bookcase. *Old Furniture: Designs Selected from the Best Examples* (1883) includes examples of this longtime fixture of American households that dates back to the 1700s. However, its sweet little drop-leaf writing surface may seem ill suited to the modern-day office, with its space-hogging computer. Transform your heirloom into a compact combination sideboard/china closet. A secretary desk is ideal for dining rooms where space is too snug for a traditional sideboard or china cabinet, which Maggie McVeigh of Katonah, New York, discovered when she acquired hers. "When I inherited the secretary, I sent it directly to the dining room," Maggie says. She knew that the desk drawers would offer storage space for tablecloths, linen napkins, and place mats, and the bookcase above was a natural to display small pieces of glassware. Interior drawers and pigeonhole compartments can handle an assortment of serving items, such as your good flatware or drink stirrers. "What's more," Maggie says, "for those times when company is coming, I'm glad to have the extra surface that the drop leaf provides for serving."

Distinctive Centerpieces Anyone Can Make

■ Centerpieces are inspiring examples of old-time creativity. Every period of history offers clever centerpiece concoctions, some extremely elaborate and some quite simple. All manner of porcelain, glass, silver, or other material has sometimes been able to stand on its own merits, without the help of fruit or flowers, when it comes to making a centerpiece. Let your imagination take you to any room of the house for source materials. Here are a few ideas from tables past.

Invite a plant to the party. Select one of your prettier houseplants and wrap the pot in a linen napkin or piece of lace, secured with French wired ribbon tied in a bow. Surround the plant with an eclectic assortment of figurines for an old-fashioned, whimsical touch.

Mix up the mood. Create a "footed" bowl with these kitchen essentials: your mixing bowls, particularly if they have flat rims and an old-fashioned look. Invert the smallest bowl and place the largest faceup on top of it. Fill the top bowl with floating flower buds or scented candles.

Update a Victorian classic. Create your own epergne, an elaborate centerpiece for flowers that the Victorians loved. Theirs usually had a trio of trumpet-shaped glass vases connected to a single base; yours can be as easy as clustering a trio of champagne flutes filled with roses or hydrangeas.

The Removable Feast

■ Add and remove extra serving space in your dining room in a snap with a modern-day version of the "moving sideboard." These three-tiered tabletop shelves supported by footed brackets come highly recommended by Andrew Jackson Downing in *The Architecture of Country Houses* (1850) "for receiving dishes, holding dessert, etc., when there is not room for a large sideboard." Today, the serving piece we call a *plate stand* is just as versatile. Typically, a plate stand is a round, three-tiered open metal frame that supports dinner plates under their rims. It is usually about 16 to 20 inches high and is designed to be placed on a table or sideboard. Scaled-down models are sized for dessert plates. Use your plate stand to stack plates until they're needed on the dinner table. These devices are also great for stretching buffet space—put a single plate on each tier and fill it with an assortment of appetizers, muffins, desserts, or candy. Afterward, your little "sideboard" can be tucked into a corner until needed again.

Classy Crumb Catchers

■ You can protect your dining room carpet from food or wine stains and just plain wear and tear with a dining area standby that dates back to the early 1800s: the "crumb cloth." This floorcloth was placed under the table and chairs, and the advice of the day was to take it up after the meal and shake it outside. Fortunately, we don't have to include that in our daily chores anymore—a vacuum cleaner can handle the job. But apart from any protective benefits, putting a patterned area rug under your table and chairs can add liveliness to a room with solid wall-to-wall carpeting, particularly in the dreary winter months. Writer Washington Irving used one; visitors to Sunnyside, his Hudson Valley home dating back to the mid-1800s, can't miss his dining room's crumb cloth of vivid red baize (felt).

Pick Plain Dishes

■ Just because a purchase is highly convenient doesn't mean it can't be elegant. So save some time and know you're still in the best of taste when purchasing china or an everyday dinner service by following this venerable advice from

Juliet Corson in *Every-Day Cookery, Table Talk and Hints for the Laundry* (1884): "Unless a person is rich enough to at once replace broken dishes belonging to decorated sets, plain white dishes are most desirable; they are in perfect taste, and with a snowy cloth, and clean glassware, they set a table nicely." You'll save time if you need to replace a broken or lost piece of china, because it's easier to find a white piece than one that will match a hard-to-find decorated set. Since you can replace as you break or lose an item, you'll be able to enjoy a full set more often, and you'll never need to "retire" or replace a partial set of china because it's lost too many pieces.

Setting Rug Sizes for Dining Rooms

Ever since civilized folks began eating in formal dining rooms, homemakers have faced the dilemma of how to hide crumbs between cleanups. Laura Thornborough addresses the quandary in *Interior Decorating for Everybody* (1925): "Rugs with small designs are best in dining rooms and halls, and do not show crumbs and dust and dirt as much as plain rugs." If you're wondering what size rug with a "small design" to choose for your dining room, use this simple mathematical equation: Measure the length and width of your dining room table and add 4 feet to each measurement. Then round up to the nearest standard rug measurement. Measure the table without the extra leaves that you use only on occasion. If you don't like the look of the rug when you extend your table fully, then roll up the rug on those occasions and store it behind a bedroom door for the night. This makes after-party cleanup a little easier, too.

Practical Floor Covers from the Past

■ Rediscover the appeal of a venerable forerunner of linoleum for protecting your wooden floors—oilcloth. In the late 1700s and early 1800s, oilcloth often graced dining rooms over, or in lieu of, carpeting, because of its durability and waterproof quality. Linoleum displaced it long ago, but today oilcloth is once again in style on the bare wooden floors of discriminating home decorators, who savor its history, classic look, and water-resistance. This historic floorcloth had a base of heavy canvas—which could be plain, stenciled, or printed in repeating geometric patterns using wooden blocks—treated with several coats of oil-based paint and some varnish. Contemporary artisan Natalie Browne-Gutnik, of Bayside, Wisconsin, uses the term *floorcloth,* not *oilcloth,* to describe her craft because she uses acrylics instead of oil-based paints. "The dry time of oil paints is eleven months, and the dry time for acrylic or latex paints is three months," she notes. Floorcloths are available custom made by individual artisans or through Internet sites of specialty suppliers (see Resources on page 349).

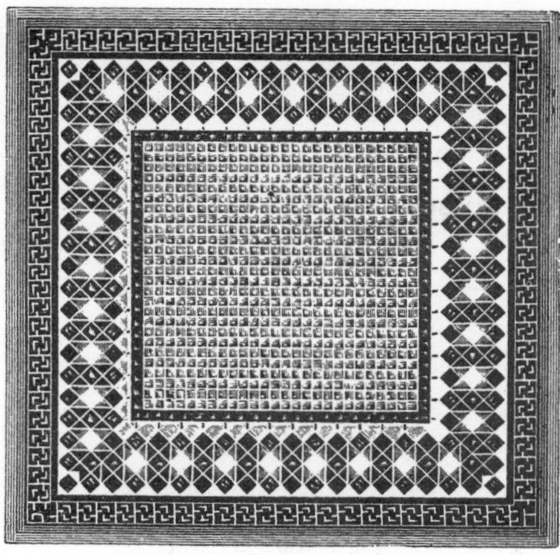

Accessorize with Today's Oilcloth

■ One type of oilcloth isn't used for floors or painted with oil-based paint. It's the type well suited to whipping up some wipe-clean dining room accessories. Over the decades, the raw materials used to make this shiny, somewhat stiff waterproof fabric have changed; more recently it is a vinyl film bonded with woven cotton mesh for a new level of fade-resistance and durability. Available at fabric and hardware stores in solids, florals, ginghams, and other patterns, oilcloth is a great choice for home decorating projects. "It's a product that people are very happy to have available again," says Cardie Molina, an importer of oilcloth since 1995 who lives in Los Angeles. She notes that U.S. oilcloth production ended in the 1960s, after which the market was flooded with poor imitations. Today's oilcloth fabric comes close to the genuine oldie. "It's even still printed with the old rotogravure roller technique," says Cardie.

In addition to a standard tablecloth, you might use oilcloth to make place mats, seat cushions, and curtains—even window shades. When sewing oilcloth, use a size 14 needle and a long stitch. If you're using a sewing machine, spraying the fabric with silicone will add temporary glide for the process.

Even if you're not skilled at sewing, you can make oilcloth place mats for your table. Buy a pair of scissors that produce a decorative edge, such as scallops, and with just a few cuts, you can create fancy-edged place mats that won't fray.

Fabulous Family Rooms

Unknown a couple of generations ago, the family room is now the most-used room in many homes. Because a family room's decor is usually designed around entertainment, decorating dictates for 19th-century music rooms often apply—when you use a creative approach. A closer look at this old-time space supplies some remarkably modern ideas for creating a friendly family room, from where to place the television and how to organize CDs to how to create a restful ambience that promotes fun and togetherness.

A Worry-Free Family Room

■ "A too formal treatment places a sort of restraint on the quiet and ease of the room," writes Charles Edward Hooper in *The Country House: A Practical Manual of the Planning and Construction of the American Country Home and Its Surroundings* (1905), referring to the music room. In Mr. Hooper's music room, there would have been a piano and possibly a harp, along with comfy furniture. A century of technological advancement later, Mr. Hooper's opinion still holds true for decorating family rooms. Here are a few tips to ensure an informal, peaceful, and worry-free room.

Wear and tear no more. Select fabrics that can withstand a gentle rubdown with spray-on upholstery cleaner (available in your grocery store's cleaning supply aisle). To give you more time between scrubbings, look for earth-toned fabrics, because these shades won't show dirt as easily. For instance, look for a rich, bark-colored, completely washable, nearly indestructible Ultrasuede. The nap and tone hide dirt; the fabric's appearance exudes luxury. Or if you strongly favor more colorful upholstered furniture, ask the salesperson whether the fabric has been pretreated with a chemical that resists stains, such as Scotchgard.

On again, off again. Another furniture option is removable, machine-washable slipcovers. If the budget allows, buy two covers, so you don't have to wash the dirty one ASAP. If the budget is tight, purchase slipcovers only for the cushions, since this is where grape jelly tends to land. And remember, it's stylish to swathe cushions in a fabric that's different from but coordinates with your couch fabric. If slipcovers aren't for you, keep a king-size sheet on hand to throw over a couch as needed.

Pick washable paint. Generally speaking, the best choice when painting your family room is a satin or semigloss finish, since a flatter finish is more difficult to clean. However, new types of paint being developed may challenge this rule, so ask the salesperson at a local paint store to show you the most-washable selections.

Start at the bottom. A real or faux wooden floor and area rugs are best in the family room. It comes down to fast, easy cleanup! For rugs, look for plaids, florals, paisleys, or oriental patterns. Small patterns are less overpowering and make the scattered cookie crumbs more tolerable until cleanup time.

Circular makes sense. When selecting end tables or coffee tables, opt for round or oval shapes whenever possible. Tables with glass tops and sharp corners can be dangerous when children are romping.

Preserve open space. If you have children or you're caring for an older loved one, keep the room's layout as open as possible. Aim for at least 36 inches of walking space between furniture pieces to significantly cut the risk of trip-ups.

Everything in Its Place

■ To control family room clutter, first toss the junk. If you think there is no junk in your family room, look again. As Ethel Seal notes in *Furnishing the Little House* (circa 1924), it's easy to overlook expendable items: "We are used to it, we don't see it, and we continue to dust and cherish meaningless objects that are honestly fit subjects for the nearest rum-

mage; though it were more kindly to throw them away." After you've gotten rid of the unneeded stuff, it's time to organize what's left.

The magazine basket. For magazines, pick up a wicker basket and place this basket near the sofa. Larger baskets tend to be less expensive at craft stores. And remember: No one needs more than one basketful of magazines. If your basket overflows, recycle older issues.

The remote control bowl. For remote controls, go to the housewares department in your favorite home store and buy a low, wide, brightly colored bowl—the sort you might put fruit in. When the remote is in your hand, the bowl becomes a pretty coffee table accent piece; when the remote is in the bowl, it's nearly impossible to miss!

The toy collector. A good home for toys is a laundry basket, one with cutouts on all sides so the kids can see what's on the bottom. You can find a wealth of attractive laundry baskets to choose from, in great colors and with circles or random geometric patterns cut out of the plastic sides.

The Family Room Bulletin Board

The common bulletin board has long been given uncommon value when it comes to family matters, as described by Lillian Moller Gilbreth, a pioneer in ergonomics, in *The Home-Maker and Her Job* (1927): "The bulletin board . . . not only makes the home-maker's planning easy, but gives stability to the home life, eliminates suspense, and contributes surprisingly to efficiency." And in today's homes, the family room really is the best

Spread the Music

In *The Healthful House* (1917), Lionel Robertson and T. C. O'Donnell write: "Your home may be elaborate enough to afford a music room. If so, let the music by all means overflow into the living room." While most of us have a family room with a CD player rather than a full-fledged music room, we would still enjoy having music overflow into the living room, dining room, kitchen, and more. One way to do that is to install remote speakers in all rooms. An ideal time to do this is during a remodeling project, so if you are planning one that will require opening up existing walls, ask your contractor about installing speakers throughout the house. (Be sure to bring up the subject while the project is still in the planning stage.) That way, your investment in one CD player can fill the whole house with music.

place for a bulletin board. The family room is a great place to display your children's or grandchildren's artwork. There's no danger it will be splashed by stray sauce or juice, as it might be when hung on the refrigerator door. Also, a family room art display is available for you and your guests to enjoy while you relax on the couch or easy chairs. Also, make this bulletin board the designated spot for phone messages, eliminating the proverbial question as to whether a message is best left on the kitchen counter, on the dining room table, or beside the phone.

☞ BIZARRE BUT TRUE ☜

The More Things Change, the More They Stay the Same

THE FAMILY ROOM is often home to the family computer. If children ever use your home computer, you're probably concerned about which Web sites they visit. This seems like a modern concern that past generations didn't have to worry about, but in a way, they did! Media content has been a concern ever since mass media began. For our grandparents (or great-grandparents), the influence that potentially corrupted youth back then was—*radio*. A 1931 article in *The Journal of Home Economics* notes: "We may call our radio programs by any name we wish—advertising, entertainment, formal instruction—they are all education. They affect our attitudes, influence our speech, and help to determine our purposes and ideals. The individual parent becomes powerless and is forced to exercise whatever control may be necessary through common action, through legislative regulation, and an active, informed public sentiment."

Antique Cabinets Hold Modern Music

There's something so elegant about using an antique for its intended purpose, but with a contemporary twist. For example, old music cabinets are still available in antique shops, or perhaps you have one in your attic. This piece of furniture was designed for home music rooms and held sheet music. As Alice Kellogg describes in *Home Furnishing, Practical and Artistic* (1905), "The keeping of music in orderly fashion away from the dust can be achieved only with a cabinet having doors, a point that, in some music cabinets, is overlooked." Today, these antiques make wonderful CD holders, keeping your treasured music orderly, dust-free, and always within reach. You can stack CDs directly on the cabinet shelves or, for additional order, place appropriately sized CD organizers on the shelves. If you go this second route, you don't need to spend much money—a simple rectangular box with CD-size cubbyholes is fine. When you close the cabinet doors, no one will see a thing.

Oversized TVs Don't Always Fit

Since the size of televisions is ever on the increase, it's important to know how much space you need between TV and sofa for optimal viewing. Ignoring these numbers violates some vintage—but still applicable—advice from Bernard Jakway in *The Principles of Interior Decoration* (1923): "A decorative idea or material or process or object is good only when, in a given situation, it fits its purpose. Otherwise it is bad." Buying a television that's too large to watch comfortably definitely diminishes its purpose of providing an enjoyable viewing experience. So before you buy that giant-screen TV, decide where you will position it in relation to the sofa or recliners that you'll sit on while viewing. Measure the distance between these two objects, and use these guidelines to see how big a screen you should buy:

- 8 feet: 25- or 27-inch television
- 10 feet: 32-inch television
- 11 feet: 35- or 36-inch television
- 12 to 15 feet: 50- or 60-inch big-screen television

In Search of Better Televisions

The piano was the focal point in a 19th-century music room, but not always to the homeowner's pleasure, seeming to "hang just where it has been for years, an ugly, clumsy monstrosity, a jarring note wherever it goes." That's how Charles Edward Hooper describes the grand piano's appearance in *The Country House* (1905). Do his words remind you of our modern-day attitude toward the television set? For the past generation, the solution was to tuck the TV inside an armoire, but another approach is to invest in a new slim television. These new TVs offer a great viewing experience and take up considerably less space than a big, boxy TV. Before you buy a new TV, though, it pays to understand 21st-century TV lingo.

DTV. An abbreviation for *digital television.* Many satellite systems and all DVDs use digital signals.

Flat-panel screen. Traditional TVs have curved screens. Flat-panel TVs reduce glare from windows or lamps and lessen distortion of images.

HDTV. This stands for *high-definition television.* HDTV is high-resolution digital television (see DTV) combined with sophisticated sound capabilities.

LCD. A type of screen with fluorescent backlight and liquid crystals. One nice feature of these wide-screen, flat-panel TVs is that they are extremely thin, as slim as 4 inches, and may be put on a stand or mounted flush against the wall.

Plasma. These wide-screen, flat-panel TVs use sealed cells of gas to create the picture. The plasma set is also as thin as 4 inches and may be put on a stand or mounted flush against the wall.

Surround sound. This involves a system of up to six speakers placed strategically around the room. Sound comes

Primitive Television

THE WONDERS of television were first demonstrated on a large scale in 1939 at the New York World's Fair and at the Golden Gate International Exposition in San Francisco. The American public was amazed and delighted at these "larger than life" boxes, available for purchase at the World's Fair's RCA Pavilion. For a mere $200, you could buy a "normal size" 5-inch screen; for $600, you could splurge on a "big screen," which measured a whopping 12 inches.

from beside, in front of, and in back of you for a realistic effect.

Wide screen. Unlike traditional TVs, which have square screens, wide-screen sets have rectangular screens. This format allows you to view DVDs just as you would in a theater.

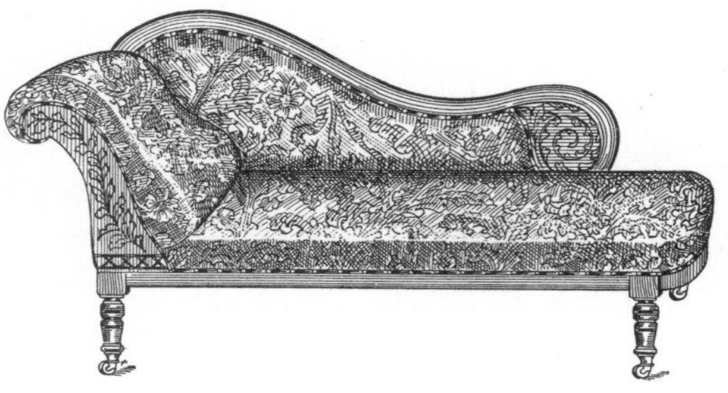

Beautiful Bedrooms

The bedroom is where we rev up each morning and calm down each night, so the bedroom's decor must be both invigorating and soothing. The bedroom is also where we spend a lot of "me" time, making a few personal luxuries mandatory. Comforting boudoirs were once the norm, and now, thankfully, they're back. If you're looking for ways to make your bedroom more welcoming—an inviting color palette, appealing linens, and personal photographs that recall cheerful memories—read on to see how homemakers and decorators created cozy bedrooms way back when.

On Vacation . . . In Your Bedroom!

Your bedroom is your private refuge. In *Principles of Home Decoration* (1903), author Candace Wheeler explains that the bedroom is "in a certain sense the home of the individual occupant, almost the shell of his or her mind." One way to be sure you'll feel happy and at home in your bedroom is to let memories of a favorite vacation spot be your guide to selecting bedroom colors, furniture style, and fabrics. Only you can decide what that beloved vacation place might be, but here are some examples of how a vacation dream vision might translate into a bedroom's color palette. If you love vacationing at an inn with an ocean view, include airy blues, greens, taupe, and white in your color scheme. Skiing enthusiasts can evoke the atmosphere of a rustic ski lodge by using rich browns, oranges, burgundy, and ivory. And if you were in heaven in the five-star hotel room you stayed at during your last getaway, this probably means choosing a neutral color plan, plumped with luxurious fabrics and rich textures.

Bedrooms Are for Lounging

When furnishing your bedroom, try to keep a desk out of the decor equation. Do you really want to connect bill paying with peaceful slumber? As *Godey's Lady's Book* (May 1884) succinctly explains: "The bedroom is a place to lounge in at ease." Playing off this notion, you do want a CD player or radio in the bedroom, so you can drift off to soothing music at night or churn up your energy level in the morning. Other modern inventions also help to make a bedroom the ideal lounging spot.

- An air purifier, especially for people with allergies, allows you to sleep peacefully instead of sniffle.
- In the winter, a room humidifier helps loosen mucus and phlegm so you don't wake up in the middle of the night feeling parched, and also helps prevent dry, itchy "winter" skin.

◆ An electric space heater is a winter luxury as well. It's a tough trick to relax while you're changing clothes, reading, or watching TV if the room is so cold that you're shivering. For safety reasons, choose a space heater that remains cool to the touch and shuts off automatically if toppled over. Use it to warm the bedroom during the evening until you're ready to go to sleep, and again during your morning wake-up routine. Using a space heater in your bedroom is also an economical choice if you set your house's main thermostat at a low temperature from evening through morning.

A Simple, Practical Nightstand

■ Most of us have a nightstand, but many of us keep it so cluttered it can barely do its job. What exactly is the nightstand's function? As Agnes Wright explains in *Interior Decoration for Modern Needs* (1917): "[Every bed] should have a nightstand with a light. Nothing is more inconvenient than to have no place but the floor to lay a book, a bottle or a tray or a glass of water. However simple the table, it is a requisite."

With these words in mind, the first order of business is to evaluate the lamp on your nightstand. Does it take up too much space? If so, get rid of it and buy one that really fits your nightstand. Select one that takes a halogen lightbulb, if possible. These bulbs cost a bit more than traditional bulbs, but they last up to three times longer, produce up to 50 percent more light for the same amount of energy, and offer the brightest light for easier reading. Next, buy yourself a proper carafe for those midnight sips of fresh water. Inexpensive modern carafes

TRASH OR TREASURE

A Sentimental Pillow Cover

In the 1800s, thrifty pioneer women never threw anything away if they could help it, including old clothes. In *The American Frugal Housewife* (1831), Lydia Maria Child advises readers, "After old coats, pantaloons, etc. . . . are no longer capable of being converted into garments, cut them into strips, and employ the leisure moments of children, or domestics, in sewing and braiding them for door-mats." We don't need to be quite so frugal with old clothes, but *Frugal Housewife* serves as a superb springboard for a home decorating project with sentimental overtones: Turn old but treasured clothing into a throw pillow to toss on the bed or a comfortable chair. With a minimal amount of sewing knowledge, you can make a pillow from the body of a baby's cardigan, fabric from a wedding dress that cannot take one more redesign, or a christening gown that is no longer heirloom quality but still holds treasured memories.

usually include a small glass. Turn the empty glass upside down and it becomes the carafe's lid. Add a box of tissues and an alarm clock. All that's left is to set out one or two personal items, such as photos in tiny frames (3 inches square) to keep loved ones always nearby.

Untraditional Headboard Ideas

▪ Wooden headboards are beautiful, but they aren't affordable for everyone or a match to every kind of decor. If a traditional headboard isn't in your budget or to your taste, go for a creative approach instead. *Be Your Own Decorator* (1922) author Emily Burbank advises readers with "absurdly high" wooden headboards to cut them down to a size that approaches the "standard of to-day." We don't suggest taking a saw to your wooden headboard, but here are some modern alternatives you may want to try.

It's all material. Visit a local art supply store and purchase four stretcher bars (used to make a painter's canvas). Assemble the bars to create a headboard frame of the desired size. Lay a piece of fabric on the floor (wrong side up) and place the assembled stretcher bars face-down on top of the fabric. Wrap the fabric around the bars and staple it to the back of the bars with a staple gun. Then hang your "canvas" as you would any framed picture, on the wall where the headboard would go. Use fabric that matches your drapes or a flat sheet that coordinates with your bedspread.

An idea with depth. Cut a piece of common garden lattice to the height and width of your desired headboard (use a circular saw or ask a friend who has a saw to cut the lattice for you). Nail or glue 1-inch half-round mitered molding to the lattice front to create a finished frame. To hang, secure picture hooks (available in a home store's frame department or any hardware store) to the back of your lattice headboard and hang as you would any picture. Paint the wall at the head of your bed one color and the lattice a contrasting or complementary color. Bold colors look great!

Faster than fast. Place a decorative screen flat against the wall at the head of your bed and push the bed against the screen to hold it in place. Try a screen made from bamboo and then carry out the theme with coordinating natural woven shades.

A room with a view. Use a window framed with an attractive window treatment as your headboard. If the window is narrower than your bed, visually stretch the window to the size of a traditional headboard by hanging curtains on a rod that measures the same width as, or a smidge wider than, your bed. When closed, the curtains themselves are your "headboard." When the curtains are open, the window, framed with color, serves the same role.

Set Up a Five-Star Guest Room

▪ For most Americans, the den, library, or home office pinch-hits as the guest room when relatives or friends pay a visit. To help visitors enjoy their stay in your guest abode, heed the advice of Mabel Kittredge in *The Home and Its Management: A Handbook in Homemaking* (1917): "A guest room must suggest welcome. It must not only be comfortable but must show that the homemaker has given her own thought to it and not left it entirely to servants." A few simple touches can transform any room into an inviting guest room. Start by buying a quality sofa bed. If you have a sofa bed already that isn't terribly comfortable, buy a feather bed to place on top of the mattress—your guests will love you for it! Make sure you have sheets that fit the mattress properly. Go a step further by choosing sheets and guest towels that coordinate with the colors of your on-again, off-again guest room. Put away the usual clutter on the end table and outfit it as a nightstand (see "A Simple, Practical Nightstand" on page 83 for instructions). And finally, provide a place for your guests to put their clothing—some open space in the closet or a coat rack in the corner. Other special touches: a full-length mirror behind the door, current magazines on the nightstand, a small radio, and travel-size toiletries placed in a pretty basket.

The Ultimate Guest Test

AFTER FINISHING your home's guest room, whether it's a designated space or a room that serves double duty, pack a suitcase and "travel" to this room. In other words, spend a night in your own guest room. Can it stand up to this worthy advice from Mary Northend in *The Art of Home Decoration* (1921)? "The greatest thought should be expended on its furnishing, for the wants of the transient guest are many and varied, and the hostess' fair repute for hospitality frequently rests upon nothing more momentous than her . . . evidence of solicitude."

To test your thoughtfulness, ask yourself the following questions. Does the mattress crinkle with every move? How do your neck and back feel next morning? Was there enough closet and/or drawer space to unpack, and were there any empty hangers for your clothes? After climbing into bed, did you discover that the only light is in the ceiling and its switch across the room? Did you have to step over the pet's squeaker toys to reach the bed? Come morning, mentally write your own guest room review, and then address what needs to be addressed.

Three Easy Bedroom Makeovers

Sprucing up the living room or den with seasonal touches is often part of cherished family traditions, but decorating bedrooms is often an afterthought—or forgotten altogether. Bedrooms are important personal space, though, and there's great satisfaction in making simple seasonal changes in your boudoir. As Agnes Wright explains in *Interior Decoration for Modern Needs* (1917), "The heavy dark wool curtains that closed us in from the blustering winds of February do not allure us on July 5th. The dotted Swiss with green edgings that refreshed us on an August dog day send shivers through us in November."

There's no need for a complete room makeover, but consider these three quick ways to fit your bedroom with seasonal charm as well as purpose. You can change the decor in one afternoon's work (like spring-cleaning) or as ideas strike you.

1. As summer draws near, swap your down comforter and tapestry duvet for a cool cotton chenille or matelasse (quilted without heavy batting) bedspread and lightweight, open-weave cotton blanket. In the time it takes to zip a zipper, you can exchange rich forest green and navy decorative pillow shams for mint green and sky blue ones. Other possibilities include changing the tablecloth on your nightstand and swapping out wool rugs for jute.

2. Change your bedroom window treatment by replacing heavy fabric panels with sheers. Or install miniblinds, and hang insulated curtains during winter months. Simply remove the curtains, letting the miniblinds go au naturel, when the weather turns warm.

3. Rearrange the furniture. This task may require a son or grandson's strong arm, but moving the bed can bring a breath of fresh air—literally. For example, during the cold months, place the bed near a heating duct. In the summer, move the bed near a window, so you can catch a summer night's breeze.

CHAPTER 4

Home Repair and Maintenance
For Want of a Nail

With the high cost of even minor home fix-ups, it's no wonder that do-it-yourself repairs are popular. In years gone by, doing it yourself was more than a money-saving hobby; it was a basic fact of daily life. Until the mid-19th century, 90 percent of Americans lived in rural areas, and folks were much less likely to call a plumber or carpenter than they are today. Although some of the materials and methods used in home maintenance have changed, many ingenious solutions to everyday problems live on. From getting the most out of your tools to simple fixes for plumbing problems, Great-Great-Grandfather often knew best.

Simple Fix-Ups

Clever home maintenance tips aren't the unique brainchild of television programs or building supply megastores. Before TV, the practical experience of everyday people provided plenty of wise solutions to common household problems such as disguising scratches on wooden furniture, fixing a creaky floorboard, and unsticking a stubborn door.

Garlic and Glue for Loose Brass

▪ If a brass inlay in a piece of furniture has come loose, an old-time method offers the best fix. Use a natural fish or hide glue to bond brass to wood. Available from specialty woodworking shops, these glues dry slowly and bond well to metal, says woodworker Keith Gotschall, of Salida, Colorado. Pull up the loose inlay just enough so you can see under it, making sure not to kink the metal. (An assistant or prop can hold up the metal strip while you work.) To achieve the best bond, Keith recommends this old-timer's trick: Rub the glue side of the brass with a clove of garlic, which seems to etch tiny grooves in the metal and create more surface area to which the glue can bond. Apply a bead of fish or hide glue and press the inlay into place. Clamp or weight the repair for at least 48 hours.

Extinguish Those Scorch Marks

■ Americans don't smoke as much as they used to, but cigarette burns on wooden furniture are still a problem in many homes. Here's how folks used to cover up scorch marks in the days when smoke wreathed most living rooms. Make a paste of cigarette or wood ashes and linseed oil, and rub the paste on the burn mark in the direction of the wood grain. Wipe off the residue using a soft rag moistened with linseed oil.

Natural Scratch Solutions

■ An old-time solution for scratches in dark woods such as cherry or mahogany is to rub iodine into the cut, according to *Short Cuts to Better Housekeeping* (1949). Scratches in furniture made from "nut" woods, such as walnut or pecan, can be fixed naturally with a chunk of the nut in question. To mend a scratched walnut table, for example, break open a walnut and rub pieces of the nut meat into the scratch, pressing the oil from the nut into the groove. Buff with a clean cloth. For other woods—or in cases where these natural fix-ups don't work adequately—head to a furniture or home improvement store and ask for touch-up pens or crayons for wooden furniture. Find the crayon that matches your wood as closely as possible, color in the scratch, and buff the area with a soft cloth.

Give Your Cabinets a Boost

■ The doors of old cabinets and sideboards, especially in older houses, often begin to stick. Sometimes the cabinets or the floor underneath them has sagged and come out of true. When that's the case, a little boost is all they need. Lift each corner of the cabinet a quarter-inch or so and then test the door. If lifting a corner frees up the door, shim the leg on that corner with a bit of wood or cardboard between the foot and the floor.

☞ BIZARRE BUT TRUE ☜

The Mail Trolley

CONVENTIONAL WISDOM has it that Americans of prior generations were much fitter than they are today. People walked to work, to shops, and to school, but they still appreciated laborsaving devices. *Handy Farm Devices and How to Make Them* (1909), by Rolfe Cobleigh, features one oddball example: a miniature cable car for the mail. The book recommends suspending a mailbox from pulleys attached to a series of wires or ropes that would run between the house and a post by the road. The householder who couldn't be bothered to walk out to the mailbox could simply pull the box to and from the road to post mail and collect deliveries.

Board Trick for Sticky Doors

WOODEN DOORS that stick when you open or close them are annoying, but most people think it's too much trouble to remove the door and plane down the offending edge. Back in 1927, *Better Homes and Gardens* magazine offered a much simpler solution for doors that stick, and this method will still work today.

You will need:

- 2 boards, any width, cut about ½ inch longer than half the width of the door
- 2 rags or pieces of cardboard
- Step stool (optional)

Step 1. Place one end of each board against the doorjamb (the upright piece of wood on the inside of the door frame) on opposite sides of the door at floor level. Put rags or cardboard between the boards and the doorjamb so you won't mar the finish.

Step 2. Bring the other ends of the boards together, so that the boards form a shallow V. Now press down on the boards at the point of the V so that the boards press out against the doorjamb. This pressure will cause the door frame to spread slightly.

Step 3. Repeat Steps 1 and 2 on the upper half of the doorjamb, as high as you can comfortably maneuver the two boards (or stand on a step stool to reach the very top).

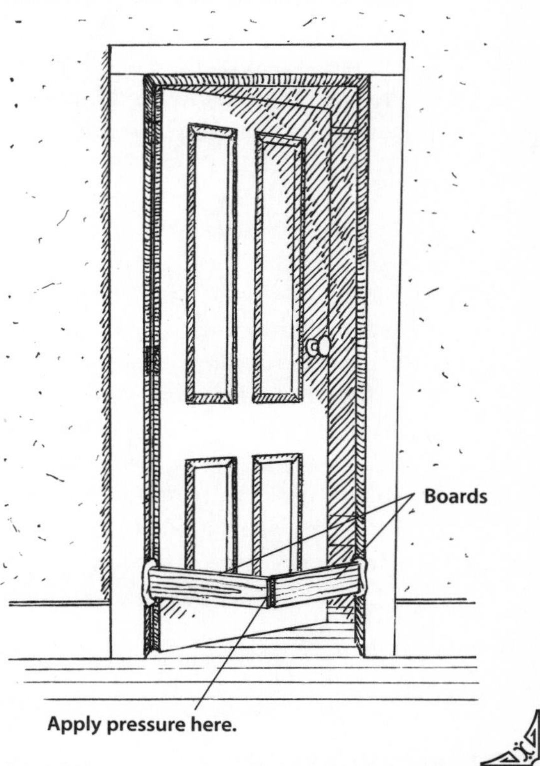

Nice Legs on That Table!

■ When a table or desk leg became wobbly, old-timers relied on a thin piece of old cloth to restore a tight fit. To try this old-time shimming technique, first unscrew or remove the loose leg. Cut a 1-inch-wide strip of cloth and drape it over the joint where it fits into the table. Now replace the leg and its cloth shim back into the table and trim away any cloth that shows. For tightening table legs in this way, modern carpenters often use a piece of panty hose instead of cloth.

The Right Way to Remove a Door

■ There's a right way and a wrong way to remove an interior door (which you may need to do in order to paint or to install trim or new hinges). In *First Aid for the Ailing House* (1934), author Roger

Whitman describes the right way: Open the door about one-third of the way. Prop up the door with a book or two to take weight off the hinges. Remove the pin from the bottom hinge first, then the middle hinge (if there is one), and then the top. A gentle tap against the head of the pin with a hammer and screwdriver should be enough to loosen it from the hinge. When it's time to rehang the door, replace the pins in the hinges in reverse order, propping up the underside before starting.

De-Spook a Door

■ Rub a piece of soap on the hinges of a creaking door, and it will instantly be silenced, recommends *The American Practical Cookery Book: Housekeeping Made Easy, Pleasant, and Economical in All Its Departments* (1859). Soap will quiet a squeak in the short term, but using paraffin (candle wax) is a better solution. Soap tends to attract moisture and will cause metal hinges to rust. Paraffin provides excellent lubrication without making a mess or risking corrosion. To fix a creaky hinge on a modern interior door, it's best to remove the pins from the hinges and then rub paraffin on the pins. This method will leave less potentially damaging residue on the hinges than applying oil or other modern lubricants. The same solution, by the way, works well for unsticking dresser drawers and windows—simply rub a piece of candle or paraffin along the tracks they slide in.

Sift and Shim to Silence Creaks

■ Fixing a squeaky floorboard or stair can be easy—if you can reach the plank from below. First, though, try sifting a bit of talcum powder into the cracks between the squeaking boards, recommend coauthors William Hennessey and William Atkin in the *Encyclopedia of Home Care and Repair* (1948). Sometimes this will silence minor creaks. If it doesn't, you need to stop the board from moving.

With stairs, creaking results when a tread (the horizontal board) separates from a riser (the vertical panel) and the weight of a person drives the tread down. You can stop this shimmy and the creak that accompanies it by locating the creaky stair from underneath and gently tapping a thin wedge, such as the narrow end of a wooden shingle, into the space between the tread and the top of the riser. You can also do this from above on stairs that don't have an exposed undersection, but it usually requires removing a strip of molding between riser and tread, and it might mean repainting or replacing carpet. In such cases, it's often better to hire a professional for the task.

Use Toothpaste before Brushing

There's no need to buy a new can of Spackle just to fill two or three nail holes in a wall before painting. An old-time solution is to spread a dab of non-gel toothpaste into each hole, says woodworker Keith Gotschall, of Salida, Colorado. The paste hardens like Spackle and holds a coat of paint just fine.

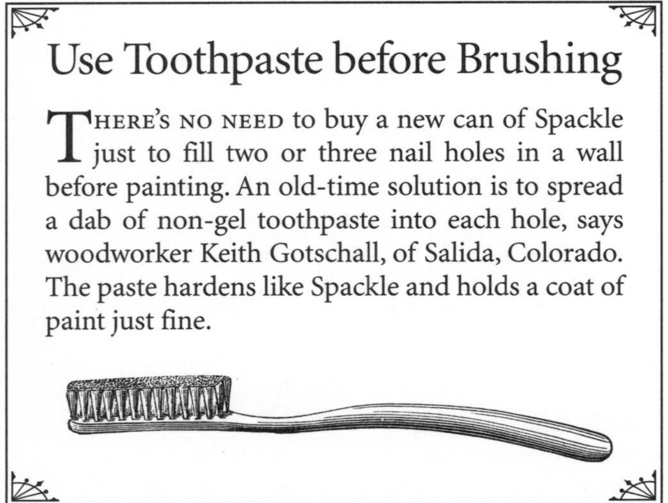

If you have a creaky floor located above a basement that doesn't have a drop ceiling, you can use the same technique to stop the creak. Go down to your basement and then ask a helper to walk around on the floor above. Once you locate the precise source of the creak, tap the shim between the board and the joist (the horizontal beam supporting the floor) or between the subfloor and joist—tap only enough to eliminate the squeak. Add a bit of wood glue to this shim so it won't shift.

Make Hay While the Paint Dries

■ Here's an old-time trick for ridding freshly painted rooms of that chemical smell. Soak a few handfuls of dry hay in water, shake off the excess, and place the hay in shallow pans in the newly painted room. Keep dampening the hay when it dries out; the moist hay will absorb the paint fumes.

Pull Windows, Not Back Muscles

■ Save your back from the strain of prying open a swollen window sash by installing old-time sash pulls. These simple but attractive little pieces of window hardware, when installed in pairs at the bottom of a double-hung wooden window, greatly reduce the effort involved in raising and lowering the sash, especially during periods of high humidity or for windows in awkward locations, such as behind a sofa. Use plain finger-hook styles to suggest a Colonial mood; if your decor has more-Victorian leanings, outfit your double-hungs with more ornate, cast-iron versions. You'll find lots of variety in styles and finishes at hardware stores as well as in mail-order catalogs. The only tools you'll need to install sash pulls are a pencil to mark the screw positions and a screwdriver to drive in the screws. (It's a good idea, though, to use a portable electric or hand drill to predrill the screw holes, especially if your window frames are made of hardwood.)

Brew Up a Fresher Room

A ROOM OR HOUSE with a fireplace that's been unused for months (in a vacation home, for example) often will develop a sooty odor as a result of drafts blowing through the house, even when the damper has been shut. *The Old Farmer's Almanack* for 1914 has this advice: Crumple old newspapers, put them in the fireplace, and sprinkle ground coffee over the papers. Then light the pile and let it burn. The coffee aroma will clear that sooty smell.

Help Heat Registers Avoid a Chill

■ The heat registers in hallway floors of older houses with forced-air heating are often ineffective, especially those near stairways or doors, because even the slight draft from an opening door or cold air descending the stairs can counteract the warm draft from the registers. The solution? In *The Care of a House* (1903), Theodore Clark recommends placing a chest or other piece of furniture over such registers so that they will be sheltered from cold air currents. The furniture should be open at the bottom to allow warm air to escape and heat the room, but not so open that cold drafts can penetrate—a clearance of around 6 inches is ideal.

Stop Smoke Signals inside Your House

Smoke may billow out of your fireplace into the room when you first light a fire, but as long as the smoke diminishes quickly, there may be a simple solution. According to Theodore Clark in *The Care of a House; a Volume of Suggestions to Householders, Housekeepers, Landlords, Tenants, Trustees, and Others, for the Economical and Efficient Care of Dwelling-Houses* (1903), the problem may simply be dampness in the chimney—a damp, cold, seldom-used flue doesn't provide sufficient draft to pull smoke up the chimney. Here's what to try: Set up your wood fire in the fireplace, but before you light it, burn a wad of newspapers, which should quickly warm the chimney. For the next several days, make a fire each day, starting the fire with fast-burning paper and small kindling so that it lights quickly. Burn one normal load of dry wood (the fire should last a couple of hours). This routine should remove any dampness from the mortar and bricks. If this doesn't solve the problem and your fireplace is consistently smoky, consult a professional chimney sweep. Your chimney may need cleaning, or the cap at the top of the chimney may require alteration to change the draft.

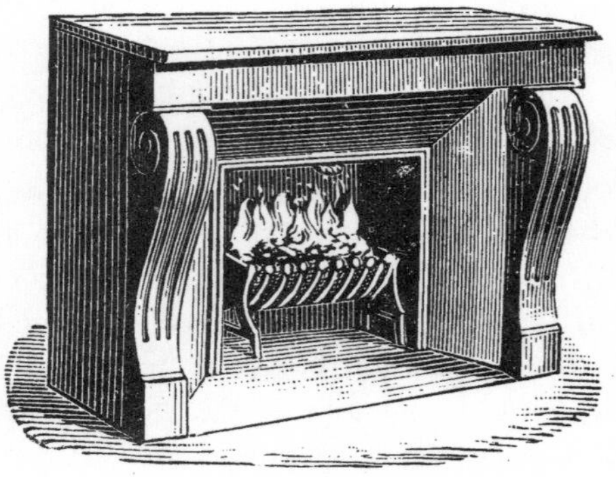

Get a Grip on Grout Problems

Sometimes mildew leaves stains on grout that won't come off, even when you use a strong cleaner. On closer inspection, you may find that bits of the grout have disappeared, too. This calls for a more drastic solution, especially since missing grout can lead to a leaking shower.

The modern approach is to call a contractor and spend thousands on new tile, but old-time homeowners knew better. According to home repair expert Ted Barron, of Philadelphia, the first step in addressing grout problems is to visit a hardware store to pick up a plastic putty knife or a tool called a *tile float,* some phosphoric acid, and fresh grout in whatever color matches the existing grout.

Use the phosphoric acid to scrub away the stains, following the directions on the label, including all safety precautions. You'll probably be directed to dilute the acid with water. Remember to always add acid to water, rather than water to acid. Apply with a sponge using a scrubbing motion. Let the acid solution sit for a minute or two, but don't allow it to dry. Rinse thoroughly to remove all the acid. Mix up a bit of grout according to the instructions on the package. Use the putty knife or tile float to force the grout between the tiles. As the grout begins to set, wipe away any haze on the tile and smooth the grout with a damp sponge. After the grout dries completely, buff the area with terry cloth. "I've done this many times, and the results were great," says Ted. "Give it a day or two to dry, and you will have a brand-new tile floor or shower the rival of any a professional tile setter could make."

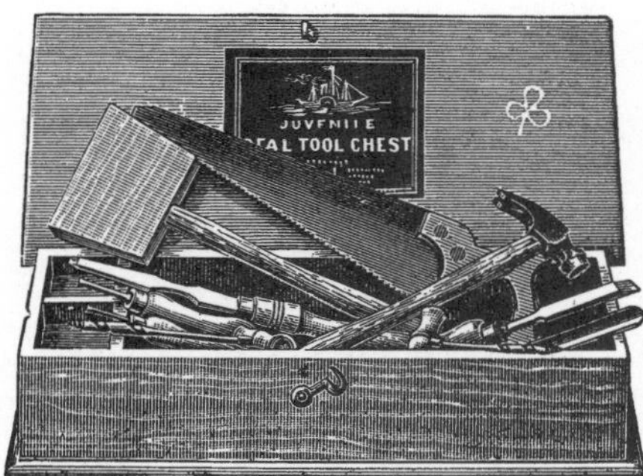

Using Tools Wisely

"It is poor economy to buy cheap tools," advises Rolfe Cobleigh in *Handy Farm Devices and How to Make Them* (1909). On the other hand, *Farm Conveniences and How to Make Them* (1900) warns, "If tools can be well taken care of, it will pay to buy those made of the best steel and finished in the best manner; but in common hands, and with common care, such are of little advantage." In other words, you want to buy the best tools you can afford, but also be sure to use and care for them properly so they'll last a lifetime. Here are some of the ways the old-timers practiced what they preached.

A Basic Tool Collection

What tools should the average homeowner have on hand? The list recommended to farmers in the *Illustrated Annual Register of Rural Affairs* (1863) at the time of the Civil War is very similar to the basic selection of tools needed in a toolbox today.

- Hammer
- Saw
- Augers
- Brace and bits
- Gimlets
- Screwdriver
- Wrench
- Two planes
- Chisels
- Mallet
- Files and rasp
- Saw set
- Trowel
- Box with compartments for different sizes of nails, screws, nuts, bolts, and the like

For a modern toolbox, substitute a cordless electric drill and bits for the augers, brace and bits, and gimlets (small boring tools) on the list above. Since few amateurs sharpen their own saws today, the saw set (a device for correcting the angle on saw teeth) probably isn't necessary. Otherwise, the recommendations are sound—add a tape measure, a Phillips-head screwdriver, standard pliers, vise-grip pliers, a hacksaw, a level, and perhaps a stud finder, and you'll be set for most household repairs.

Instant Mallet

If you have an old crutch or cane with a removable rubber tip, take the tip off and store it in your toolbox. Slipped over the head of a hammer, the rubber tip temporarily transforms a steel hammer to a softer-topped mallet, suggests *380 Things to Make for Farm and Home* (1941).

The Handy Companion: A Toolbox

THE PLAIN PINE TOOLBOX accompanied our great-grandparents whenever they left the shop to tackle a household chore. Today, you can buy a sturdy metal toolbox anywhere. But "building your own toolbox connects you to your roots and helps you practice the proper techniques for using all the tools in the box," says designer Jeanie Stiles, of East Hampton, New York. Jeanie and her husband, David, display many of their designs at www.stilesdesigns.com and www.treehouse-books.com. They've created this simple, old-fashioned toolbox that nearly anyone can build.

You will need:

- Carpenter's wood glue, such as Titebond II
- Drill with 3/32-inch twist drill bit
- 1 pound 2-inch galvanized finishing nails
- 42½-inch clear pine 1 × 10
- Handsaw or circular saw
- 37-inch clear pine 1 × 4
- Electric or hand jigsaw
- 20-inch clear pine 1 × 2

Step 1. Cut the 1 × 10 into three pieces: two at 12 inches (for the end pieces) and one at 18½ inches (for the bottom).

Step 2. Cut the 1 × 4 into two pieces, each exactly 18½ inches (for the sides).

Step 3. On each of the end pieces, measure in 2⅞ inches from each top corner and make marks. Then measure up from the bottom two corners 4½ inches and make marks. Connect the bottom marks to the top marks with pencil lines and cut along the lines with the jigsaw.

Step 4. Using the jigsaw, cut a notch in the middle of the top of each end piece, about ¾ inch wide. Make this notch *slightly* smaller than the width of the 1 × 2, which will become the toolbox handle. Use a file or rough sandpaper to gradually increase the width of the notch until the handle fits snugly into it. Do not hammer the handle into the notches, or you could split the wood.

Step 5. Glue the handle into the notches, and then drill 3/32-inch-diameter pilot holes ½ inch down from the top corner edges of each end piece. Nail through the pilot holes to lock the handle in place.

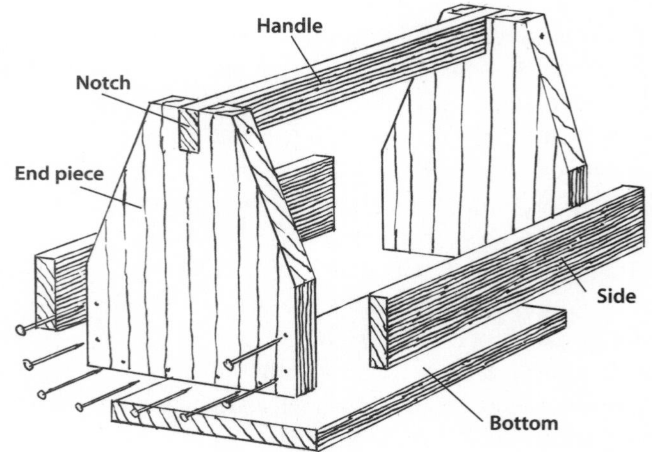

Step 6. Glue and nail the side pieces to the end pieces and then the bottom to the side assembly, forming a simple box.

Try a Handle Switch

■ "It is dangerous to use files and other tanged tools that do not have handles," opines *Better Homes and Gardens* magazine (October 1926). What to do? The magazine suggests making handles for small tools from old paintbrushes. Clamp the brush's wooden handle in a vise and saw it off just in back of the bristles. Drill a hole into the sawed-off face that's a bit smaller in diameter than the tang of the tool, and push the tang into the wood for a protective handle.

Hot Tip for Rusted Screws

■ Farmers used to soak rusty screws and bolts with kerosene before trying to remove them. A better solution today is to spray the screw with WD-40 or a Teflon-based lubricant such as Tri-Flow. However, any lubricant is of limited use for a screw stuck in wood, because the lubricant can't penetrate to the screw without damaging the wood. In that case, try a variation on a trick from *The National Farmer's & Housekeeper's Cyclopedia* (1888), by Frank Lupton, who recommends heating a poker in a fire until it's red-hot and then touching it to the top of the screw for a minute or so. A large nail heated with a propane torch or over the flame of a gas stove may do the trick; hold the nail with pliers to keep from burning yourself. And here's a tip from *380 Things to Make for Farm and Home* (1941) for getting more leverage out of your screwdriver when you work on loosening the screw: Push down on the screwdriver with one hand and the weight of your chest, while using pliers or a wrench in your other hand to turn the screwdriver near its head.

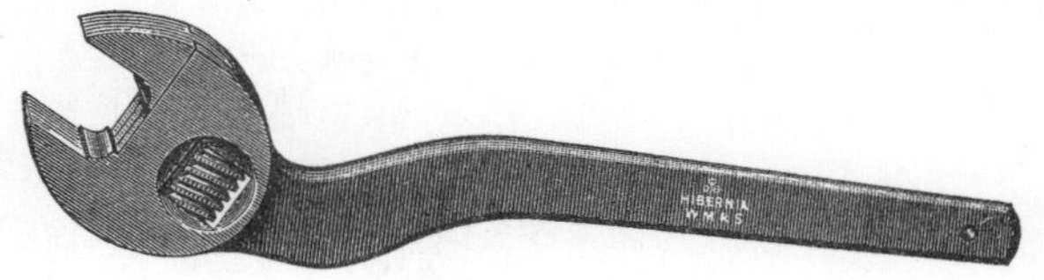

Two Bolts to Start One Nut

■ It can be extremely tricky to thread a nut onto a bolt that's in a cramped space just out of reach. *380 Things to Make for Farm and Home* (1941) proposes a simple, ingenious solution. Grab another bolt of the same size and thread the nut onto it a couple of turns. You may want to secure the nut with a bit of putty or clay. Now, hold this bolt between your fingers. Using the bolt as an extension of your hand, you'll be able to position the nut on the target bolt and start threading it.

The Nuts and Bolts of Cold-Weather Work

■ "Always avoid putting a warm nut on a cold screw," recommends the *Illustrated Annual Register of Rural Affairs* from

Never Lose a Nut Again

"A SMALL MAGNET is just the thing to locate small, misplaced articles of metal in the shop," notes the September 1926 edition of *Better Homes and Gardens*. "You can move the magnet through a mass of shavings on the bench and it will faithfully find tiny screws, etc." Keep a magnet on a string to retrieve metal parts that drop behind a workbench.

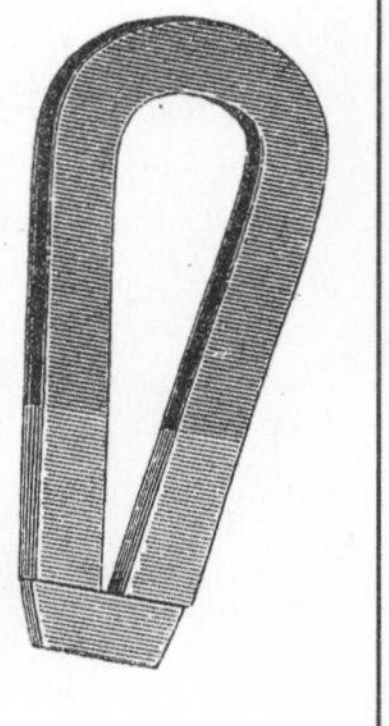

1863. Why? Because a nut held too long in a warm hand or pocket, tightened down on a bolt in winter, will contract as it cools and grip far tighter than planned. If you must work in the cold, let the nuts cool first before tightening them down.

Four Ways to Attack a Stuck Bolt

The simplest way to cut off a stuck bolt is with a hacksaw or chisel. But that usually renders the bolt hole useless. It's better to try to remove a bolt whole. First, try the same steps as with a rusted screw: Lubricate the bolt and nut, and try heating the nut before loosening it. If this approach doesn't work, *380 Things to Make for Farm and Home* (1941) recommends these methods for gaining leverage on a bolt.

1. Wrap tape around the threads protruding below the nut, then grip the bolt with a wrench or pliers and attempt to loosen the nut. Don't squeeze too hard, or you'll bend the threads and defeat your purpose.

2. If it's a roundheaded bolt, use a hacksaw to saw a slot in the bolt head in which a screwdriver can be inserted. Using a screwdriver at one end and a wrench or pliers at the other end (which you've wrapped with tape) may loosen the nut.

3. Use a hacksaw to cut off the sides of the round head on a bolt so you can grip it with a wrench.

4. Use a hacksaw to cut a slot for a screwdriver in the end of the bolt that protrudes below the nut.

A Plug Helps with Pulling Nails

Every handyperson knows that removing stubborn nails with a hammer requires more leverage from the hammer. To improve the levering capacity of their hammers, 19th-century carpenters often mounted their hammer heads a little lower on the handle so a bit of the handle protruded from the top to lever against. But these days, most hammers aren't adjustable. They have a one-piece steel shank and head, or the heads are firmly attached to the handles with resin. So here's a simple trick to emulate the old-time method: Find a ¾-inch rounded hardwood plug (the kind used to fill screw holes in wood) and glue it to the top of your hammer with epoxy, as if it were an extension of the handle. You

A Third Hand for Your Pliers

OPENING a pair of pliers can be awkward when you're working in a tight space, especially for repeated movements. The next time you face this situation, try this elegant solution from *380 Things to Make for Farm and Home* (1941). Keep a short length of stiff rubber hose (about 6 inches) in your toolbox, and when you find yourself in a tight fix, bend the hose so one end fits over each handle of the pliers. The springiness in the hose will open the pliers each time you ease off the handles. Voilà! Self-opening pliers!

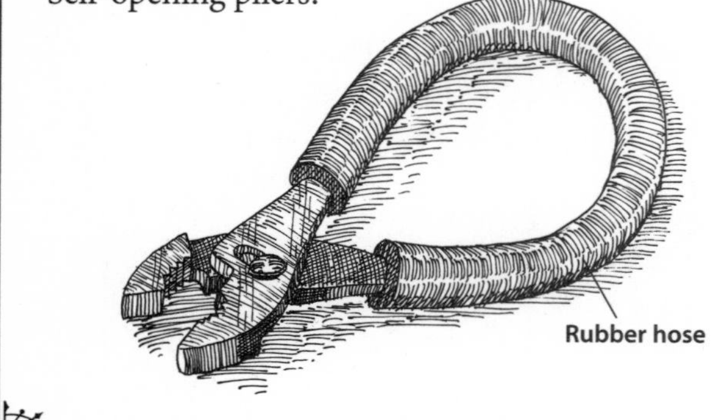

Simple Leveling Strategies

Before the invention of the modern carpenter's level, with its bubbles trapped in liquid, builders improvised other ways to keep things on the level. Knowing some of their tricks can help when you don't own a level or have one handy for a job. A straightedge and plumb bob—a weight hanging from a string—work for making quick measurements, notes an issue of *The American Agriculturist* from the 1880s. A plumb bob hanging parallel to the vertical arm of a carpenter's square assured the user that the horizontal arm was level. You can use the same trick in your home. Say you're hanging a picture and you want to be sure it's straight. Place a straightedge across the top of the picture frame. Tie a simple weight (such as a metal washer) to one end of a piece of string, and tie the other end to the straightedge. Let the weighted string hang alongside the picture. If the string and the picture frame are parallel, the top of the picture is level—and it's much easier to eyeball the string and frame than to gauge whether the picture is parallel to a wall or ceiling that is several feet away.

Handy Farm Devices and How to Make Them (1909), by Rolfe Cobleigh, shows how to improvise a spirit level by filling a small, straight-sided bottle with water so that only a bubble of air remains inside. Use duct tape to attach this bottle on its side to the middle of a perfectly straight, narrow board. Center the bubble in the bottle, and you've got a level surface. To be double sure, turn the device 180 degrees and recheck the reading.

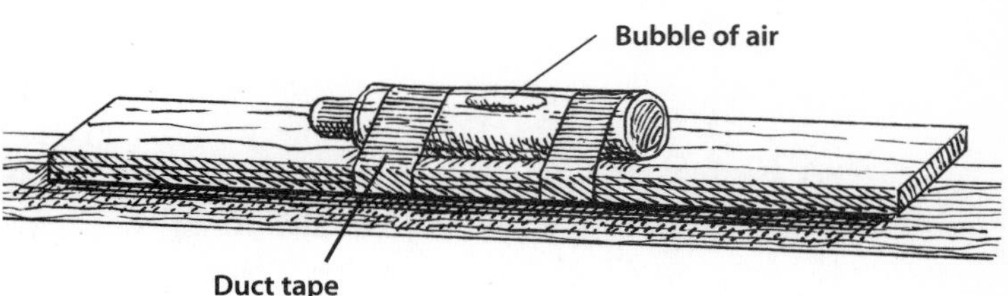

may think that this little round knob looks silly—until you start ripping out nails with ease. *Caution:* That cute little rounded plug can create dents in finished surfaces. To prevent this, place a rag or some other type of padding between the plug and the surface.

Beeswax for Easy Nailing

■ Nails will drive more easily into hardwoods, and without bending, if they are lubricated. In the *National Farmer's & Housekeeper's Cyclopedia* (1888), author Frank Lupton advises that nails should be dipped in lard for easy driving. Carpenters of old were said to carry a lump of lard or tallow on one of their boots for nail-dipping. *Practical Housekeeping* magazine (1883) recommends soap as a nail lubricant. This is certainly more convenient to carry in your nail bag than a lump of lard, but beeswax is an even better option, because soap can attract moisture, which could eventually cause

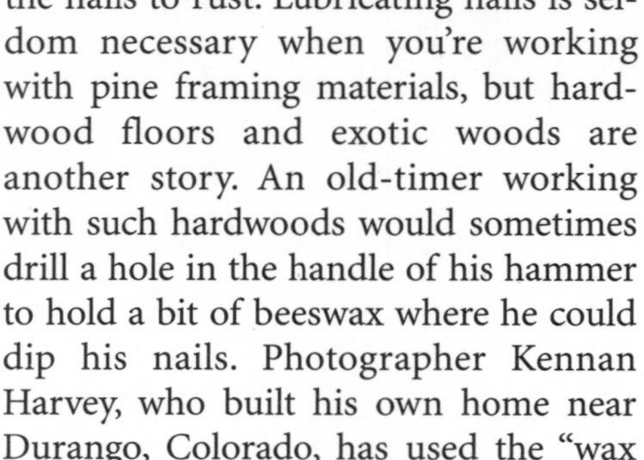

the nails to rust. Lubricating nails is seldom necessary when you're working with pine framing materials, but hardwood floors and exotic woods are another story. An old-timer working with such hardwoods would sometimes drill a hole in the handle of his hammer to hold a bit of beeswax where he could dip his nails. Photographer Kennan Harvey, who built his own home near Durango, Colorado, has used the "wax trick" to lube screws for use in hardwood, even after he has drilled pilot holes for the screws.

A Better Hang-Up

■ Here's a simple idea from *500 More Things to Make for Farm and Home* (1944) for hanging brooms, rakes, and other tools in the garage or shop—and one that's much more secure than the hooks and spring-loaded gizmos commonly sold today. Take a common strap hinge—the kind used to hold fence gates and the like—and drill a 1- to 1¼-inch hole in the middle of one side of the hinge. The easiest way to do this is to drill small holes (around ⅛ inch) with an electric drill and twist bit so they form a ring about 1 inch in diameter. Punch out the center of the ring with a cold chisel and file off the rough edges with a round file. Or, even easier, take your hinge to a machine shop, where they'll do the job in seconds for you, at minimal cost.

Nail or screw the other end of the hinge to the wall or a stud, about 4 feet off the floor. Push your tool handle up through the hole in the hinge—friction and the weight of the tool will hold it in place when you let go.

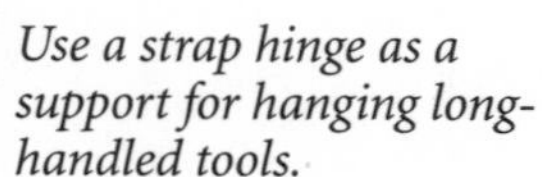

Use a strap hinge as a support for hanging long-handled tools.

Let Your Shovel Be a Lever

■ "In order to work with a shovel . . . that part of the labor which requires the exercise of the most muscular force should be performed with the tool operating like a lever," notes *The Register of Rural Affairs* (1867). This is still excellent advice, and here's how to put it in practice. First, use your whole body to push the shovel into the dirt or snow to be lifted. Drive the tool forward by rocking your body onto a bent knee. To lift the load, brace the shovel's handle over your bent knee. Lift with your upper hand, thereby using your leg as a fulcrum. This is a subtle adjustment in shoveling technique, but it adds up to a lot of saved energy over hours of work.

Four Nifty Ladder Fix-Ups

■ Among the *380 Things to Make for Farm and Home* (1941) are improvements for a wooden ladder that you can also use to enhance modern aluminum ladders or stepladders—with just a few minor adjustments in materials. (For example, you'll use screws, bolts, or glue to make attachments instead of nails.) If nothing else, these ideas will give you a checklist of things to look for in a new

ladder—some models come with these old-fashioned improvements already incorporated.

1. Add a shoe cleaner. Mount a small corner brace (an L-shaped strip of thin metal) to one side rail of the ladder, below the bottom step, and use it to scrape mud off your boots before you climb up. Be sure to attach this brace where you won't trip on it.

2. Cover the top. To keep your ladder from scraping the paint on your house, cover the tops of the side rails with a pair of old gloves or thick socks before using the ladder.

3. Install a paint tin. Mount a metal pie tin to the top of your stepladder to hold a paint can—this will keep the can from sliding off the ladder and will contain spills. The same tin makes a good place to store nails, nuts, and bolts while you work. A metal cake pan will work for this task, too, and offers the advantage of straight sides.

4. Drill holes for tools. Use an ordinary electric drill to create a few large holes in the top piece of a stepladder. Use these holes to slot screwdrivers, awls, and wrenches while you work, saving you countless trips back to the ground or floor.

☞ TRASH OR TREASURE ☜

Four Good Uses for an Old Hose

A COMMON GARDEN HOSE that develops leaks shouldn't be consigned to the trash heap. Here are a few ways suggested in *380 Things to Make for Farm and Home* (1941) and *500 More Things to Make for Farm and Home* (1944) to put short pieces of hose to good use.

1. Replace the top rung of a ladder with a length of chain covered by hose. This will keep the ladder from slipping sideways when it is leaned against a tree, a pole, or the corner of a building.

2. To prevent bruising the bottom of your foot when you use a shovel, pad the top edge of the blade with a short length of hose. Cut the hose to the appropriate length to slip over the top of the shovel blade, on the side where you normally push with your foot.

3. Pad the wire handle of a pail with hose. Most buckets now come with a plastic sleeve around the wire, but these break and sometimes are difficult to grip easily.

4. Pad an ax handle with a half-round of hose. Cut a 6-inch length of hose and then slice it in half. Glue this bit of hose to the side of your ax handle, just below the head. The padding will help preserve your ax handle when errant blows smack the chopping block.

Spick-and-Span Tools

■ "To clean dirt and rust from scissors, pliers, and other tools, dip them in ordinary ammonia for a few minutes," suggests *Better Homes and Gardens* magazine (February 1930). "This will loosen the dirt and rust and make them work like new." Afterward, rinse the tools in clear water and dry them. When using ammonia, follow all precautions listed on the container label.

Tools Go Better with Coke

■ Ever since cola drinks were invented in the late 1800s, mechanics have kept them on hand for more than quenching their thirst—they use cola to clean their tools. New Jersey textile designer and engineer William H. Carroll has had a lot of experience working with gummed-up tools. Bill says, "Soak in Coke! When tools and mechanical items get gummed up with oil and grease, soak them overnight in a bath of Coca-Cola. It will cut the grease and make them shine."

Let There Be (More) Light

■ When you can't see your way to the workbench in your garage, don't reach for a higher-wattage lightbulb; just clean the bulbs you're already using. Dust, dirt, and greasy film often accumulate on bulbs in the garage, basement, and closets. *The Old Farmer's Almanack* for 1939 claims that as much as 40 percent of the light from bulbs is lost when dust accumulates. ("Why pay full price and then get only 60 percent of the value?" the editor asks.) The *Almanack* recommends washing lightbulbs in the fall as the days grow shorter. Remove the bulbs from their fixtures and wipe them with a damp cloth; allow them to dry thoroughly before replacing them and switching on the light. This is also a good time to shake out the dead flies and clean the dust and dirt from globes and other fixtures.

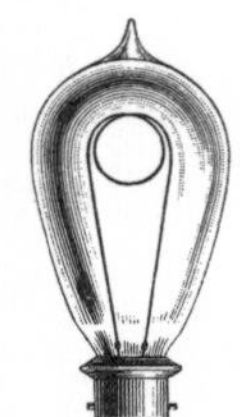

The Well-Sanded Tool

■ *Farm Conveniences and How to Make Them* (1900) recommends cleaning iron and steel tools with dry sand and a corncob, or scraping them with a piece of soft iron. The same principles apply today, but for small tools, you'll find a ball of steel wool more convenient to use than a corncob. For larger tools, such as shovels or hoes, a bucket of dry sand in the garage or toolshed provides a convenient cleaning device. Before hanging up your tools, plunge them into the sand a couple of times to clean off dirt or snow.

☞ TRASH OR TREASURE ☜

Reuse an Old Inner Tube

DON'T THROW AWAY old bicycle inner tubes—they're handy in many ways. For instance, according to *380 Things to Make for Farm and Home* (1941), you can use an inner tube to hang up a coiled hose or rope. First, drive a sturdy nail into a wall or stud in a garage or shed. Loop one side of the inner tube over the nail and the other side through the coil of hose or rope and back up over the nail. (For a permanent fixture, you can nail the tube to the wall.) An inner tube also serves as a flexible and versatile clamp for binding pieces of wood after they've been glued.

A Tool Rack for the Garage

"LAY DOWN THIS LAW . . . Whoever uses a tool shall, when his or her work is done, return the tool to the tool-house and place it where it was found." Thus instructs *Farm Conveniences and How to Make Them* (1900). Anyone who has a garage or shed with exposed stud framing can try a storage system similar to one described in *Farm Conveniences* for shovels, rakes, axes, pry bars, and other heavy tools.

You will need:

- Measuring tape
- Handsaw or table saw
- 6-foot pine 1 × 4
- Hammer
- Sixty 2-inch nails (approximate)
- One 2 × 4 pine stud

Step 1. Select three studs along one wall of your garage or shed. Measure across the studs at floor level, from the outside of the stud on the left to the outside of the one on the right. Saw a piece of 1 × 4 to this length (it should be about 33½ inches).

Step 2. Nail the 1 × 4 across the bottom of the three studs.

Step 3. Cut the 2 × 4 into short blocks, each 3⅝ inches long.

Step 4. Tap these 2 × 4 blocks behind the 1 × 4 so they fit snugly, forming roughly equal gaps between the studs. (Sand off the end of each block if it doesn't fit.)

Step 5. Tack the blocks into place by hammering two nails through the 1 × 4 and partway into each block.

Step 6. Measure up from the floor along one of the outer studs and mark a point at 36 inches. Mark the same height on the center stud. Measure across the pair of studs at this point and cut the remaining 1 × 4 into two pieces of this length.

Step 7. Nail one of the 1 × 4 pieces across the two studs at your 36-inch mark.

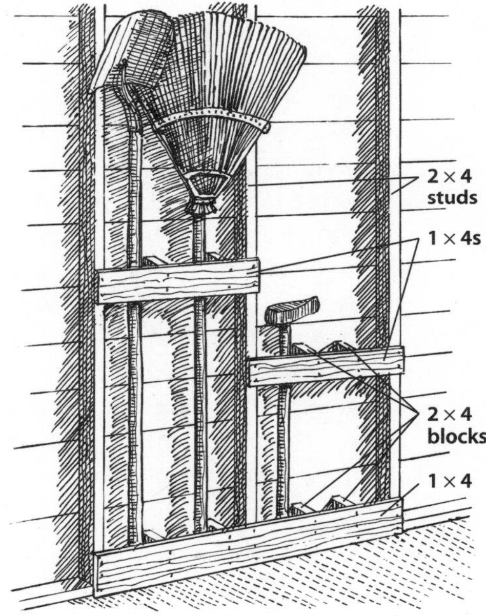

Step 8. Insert more blocks behind this 1 × 4, each exactly above a block that you inserted at floor level. Tack the blocks in place.

Step 9. Test the tools you'd like to store by inserting them behind the 1 × 4s, handle-side down, one in each gap. Adjust the spacing of the blocks as needed. Once the positioning is set, nail the blocks firmly into place.

Step 10. Repeat Steps 8 through 11 with the remaining piece of 1 × 4. Fasten the 1 × 4 across the other pair of studs, choosing a different height to secure shorter tools.

The Proper Grip for a File

■ When using a file on metal—to sharpen tools, for instance—it's tricky to maintain the proper angle on the file and thus the proper edge on the tool. According to *Farm Conveniences and How to Make Them* (1900), this is because many people don't know how to hold a file. The tendency is to grip both ends tightly and drag the file aggressively across a tool. But people tend to oversteer with the hand holding the end of the file opposite the tang, and as a result, the file rocks and rounds the edge of the tool instead of sharpening it. To guide a file properly, grasp the tanged end in your palm with the thumb and fingers wrapped around the tang, and hold the other end lightly between your thumb and forefinger.

To file underneath a tool or other object that is clamped in a vise, grasp the tanged end the same way as above and merely guide the other end of the file by resting it on your fingertips.

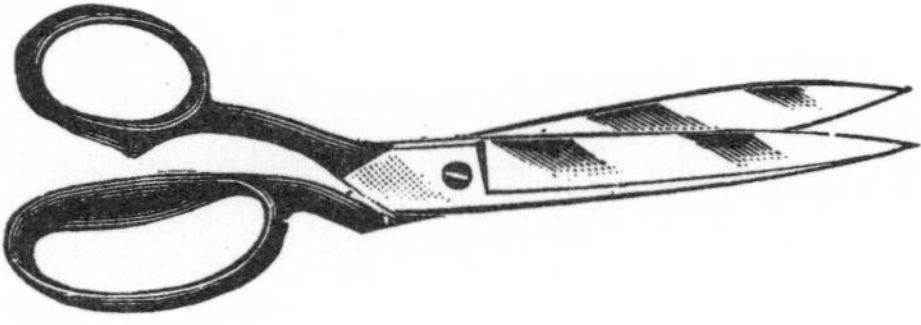

Bottle-Cutting Sharpens Scissors

■ You can sharpen scissors by "passing the blades over glass jars," claims Rolfe Cobleigh in *Handy Farm Devices and How to Make Them* (1909). To do this, simulate "cutting" the neck of a jar or bottle a few times with the scissors, using gentle but steady pressure. Ohio-based knife- and tool-sharpening expert Steve Bottorff explains that "'cutting' a steel rod is the basis of a lot of scissor sharpeners—a glass bottleneck would work the same." However, Steve cautions, don't overdo it. "Too many cuts, and the blades will cut into each other, a far worse condition that takes a lot of grinding to correct." Fifteen to 20 gentle cuts on a bottle is plenty.

Red-Flag Your Tools

■ When you're working outside the house, it's easy to lose small tools among your flowerbeds, shrubs, and tall grass. To keep hand tools from disappearing, *The Register of Rural Affairs* (1858) recommends painting their handles bright red. A more convenient modern solution would be to wrap a couple of bands of red electrical tape around the handles where it won't interfere with your grip. This would also help identify your tools if they should happen to fall into the hands of the neighborhood borrow-it-all.

Helpful Hints for Outdoor Chores

Roofs and windows bear the brunt of harsh weather, and knowing how to care for them has long been an essential duty of the homeowner. Whether the task at hand is removing snow from a roof or repairing loose windowpanes, we can benefit from the experience of generations before us.

All-Important Vent Pipe Covers

■ Anytime you're doing roofing work, remember this important advice from the June 1929 edition of *Better Homes and Gardens*. (And it wouldn't hurt, either, to offer this friendly reminder to professional roofers who work on your house.) Make sure all of the vent pipes that come through your roof are covered before any work begins—the covers will stop bits of shingle, roofing felt, and other debris from accidentally dropping into a vent and causing a nasty clog in the works below.

Old-Time Tool for Clearing Snowy Roofs

Heavy snow piling up on a house or barn roof can be dangerous, warns *The American Agriculturist* (1875). However, the journal adds, it is not "safe or agreeable to stand upon the roof of a shed and shovel snow while a north-easter is blowing." Amen to that. Instead, *The American Agriculturist* offers this plan for a roof scraper. You'll need a board 8 to 12 inches wide and 5 or 6 feet long, and some rope. (Two pieces of ⅜-inch clothesline about 100 feet long should be plenty for most houses.) Drill a hole through the center of the board at each end. Thread a piece of clothesline about 4 feet through one of the holes, knotting it on both sides of the hole. Thread the remaining piece of clothesline through the other hole in the opposite direction, knotting it on both sides of the hole. Now tie the short end of each clothesline to the long end of the other clothesline so that they form a diamond shape. Tie a small weight to the long end of one of the clotheslines and throw the weight up and over the roof. Then position yourself and a partner on opposite sides of the house. One person pulls the board up to the peak, and then the other pulls it down to scrape the snow off the roof. This will work best with soft, powdery snow, and it will take some practice before the board flies right. If you can't get the hang of the board for clearing snow, go the modern route. Buy a roof rake, a broad rake with rounded tines and an extendable handle, available for about $50 at home centers or hardware stores.

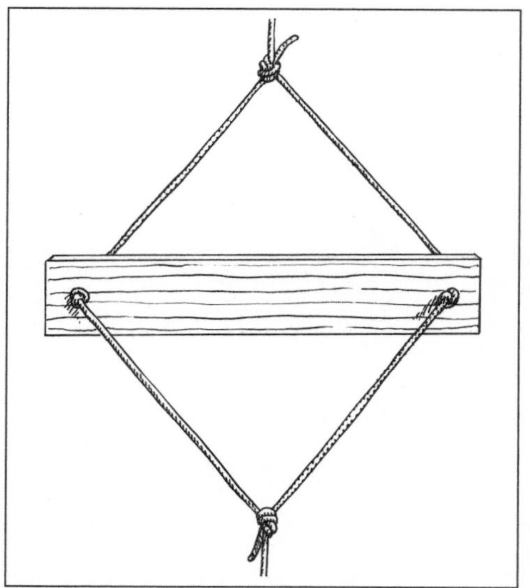

Tie long ropes to a board to create an old-fashioned tool for pulling snow off a roof.

☞ OLD-TIME ODDITIES ☜

The Zax

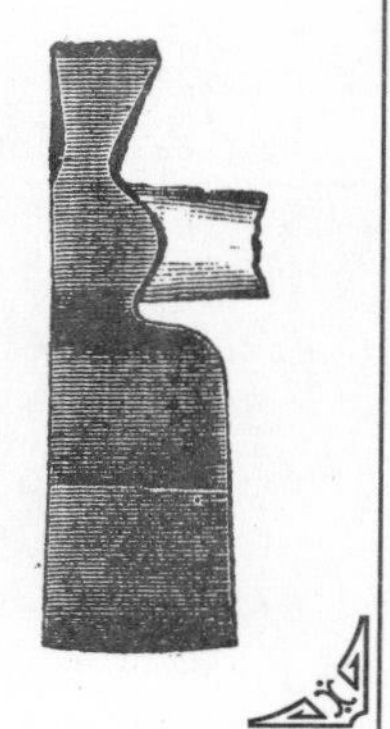

In addition to being a fantastic Scrabble word, the zax was an essential tool for early American slate workers. This heavy, short-handled, long-bladed ax was used to cut and shape roofing slates. A sharp prong opposite the blade was used to hew holes in the slates for fastening to roofs.

Essential Knots for Everyday Use

"IT IS AS EASY, indeed more easy, to make a neat, firm knot, easy to untie, as one clumsy, insecure, and readily jammed," instructs Henry Hartshorne in *The Household Cyclopedia of General Information* (1881). Here are four secure and useful knots from that book, plus one more recent innovation—the trucker's hitch. Every homeowner should learn to tie these basic knots.

Bowline. Try this very strong, easily untied knot whenever you need a loop at the end of a rope. Sample use: fastening a line to a grommet in a tarp.

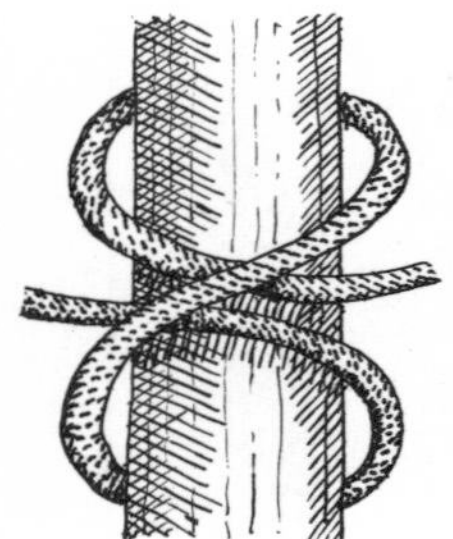

Bowline

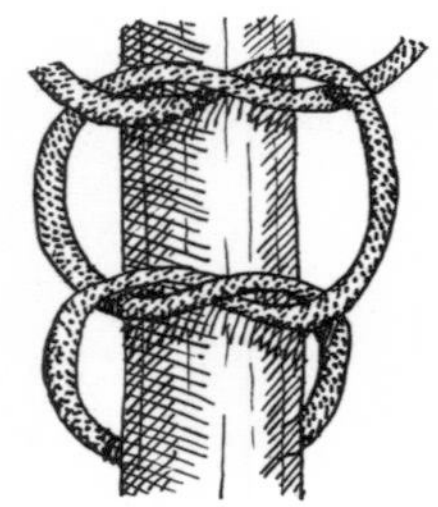

Single half-hitch

Single half-hitch. Simple to tie and undo, this workhorse (also known as the slip knot) is an easy way to tie a rope to a post, tree, table leg, or any other fixed object. Sample use: tying a dog leash to a tree.

Clove hitch. For extra security when attaching a rope to a post or tree, use a clove hitch. Its tension is easy to adjust after it has been tied. Sample use: securing a line on a boat when there's no cleat.

Clove hitch

Reefing knot

Reefing knot. Better known today as the *square knot,* a reefing knot is the standard knot for joining two lengths of rope. Sample use: tying a cord around the top of a bag or bundle.

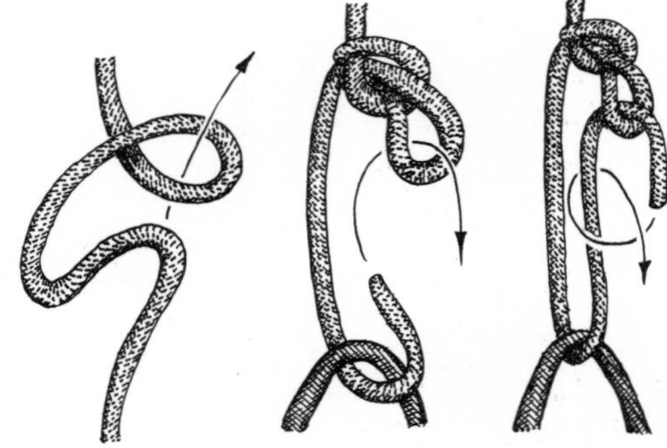

Trucker's hitch

Trucker's hitch. This clever knot can be used to secure a rope when it's already taut. After forming the loop, thread the free end of the line through a fixture and back up through the loop. Sample use: securing a Christmas tree to the roof of your car.

You Say Potato, I Say Hand Warmer

Here's a handy idea from the pioneer days that's even better due to modern technology. In the late 1800s, people compelled to travel in the extreme cold might slip a few baked potatoes into their layers of clothing before setting out on a long sleigh ride. The potatoes retained heat for a long time, and at the end of the journey, they provided a simple meal for the hungry travelers.

The same technique works today, only better. If you're heading out on a super-cold day to shovel snow, haul some firewood, or even just walk the dog, slip a few hot bakers into an inside pocket to generate a little heat or to warm your hands. Use the modern convenience of aluminum foil to wrap your taters, so you won't come home with bits of baked potato stuck in the corners of your pockets. Once home, peel off the foil, and stick the taters in the microwave to boost their heat before you set off outside again. Or if you're ready to stay inside, dress the potatoes with your favorite toppings and dig in. *Caution:* Never put a baked potato directly on exposed skin.

Choose Spirits for Softening Putty

■ Before changing a broken pane in a wooden-framed window, you have to remove the putty or glazing compound that seals the edges of the pane. This may just peel away, but if it doesn't, you must chip off the hardened putty with a knife or soften it with a torch or a soldering iron. Either method can damage the wooden frame or crack an unbroken window. *The Register of Rural Affairs* (1857) recommends moistening hardened putty with muriatic acid, which is a diluted solution of hydrochloric acid. Although muriatic acid is still available (it's used for cleaning masonry and concrete), for safety's sake, home-repair experts today recommend using mineral spirits instead. This liquid is not quite as effective for removing hardened putty, but it won't remove your flesh, either!

☞ OLD-TIME ODDITIES ☜

One Man on a Two-Man Saw

A TWO-MAN CROSSCUT SAW was the state of the art for woodcutting until the invention of the chain saw in the early 20th century. But what if you were working alone on a woodlot? In 1894, *The Rural New Yorker* offered an ingenious solution: a simple 8-foot-tall wooden tripod, to which a fourth piece of wood was bolted at the apex so it could swing freely like a pendulum. The lower end of this free-swinging piece was bolted to the far side of a saw. "We believe that we could do better work with this than with a partner who persisted in 'riding the saw'," the journal opined.

Prevent Window Putty Problems

■ "When putty cracks and falls, it is usually because it has been applied against bare wood, which in absorbing the oil leaves the putty brittle and crumbling," explains Roger Whitman in *First Aid for the Ailing House* (1934). The solution? Before applying putty to a window, seal it with a coat of linseed oil or thin paint.

A Window-Tacking System

■ If you have storm windows and screens that must be changed with the seasons, you need a system for keeping track of which window goes with which frame. In *First Aid for the Ailing House* (1934), Roger Whitman offers this simple solution: "At a 5-and-10 or a hardware store, large-head tacks marked with numbers can be had in pairs." Put one tack in the storm window or screen and its pair in the window frame. If you can't find numbered tacks, write numbers on tacks yourself with a fine-tipped permanent marker. Place any fasteners you remove from a window in a small resealable plastic bag, number the bag to match the window, and tack the bag to the window.

Sensible Plumbing Advice

In earliest America, plumbing problems didn't exist—because neither did indoor plumbing! Of course, this created its own set of problems, but considering the high expense of plumbing repairs, some frustrated homeowners might long for the simplicity of the chamber pot. Fortunately, home plumbing is less complicated than you might think, and many of the solutions developed around the turn of the last century still come in handy today.

Thaw Frozen Pipes Properly

■ In *The Complete Servant; Being a Practical Guide to the Peculiar Duties and Business of All Descriptions of Servants* (1825), authors Samuel and Sarah Adams recommend covering water pipes with bands of hay or straw, tightly twisted around the pipes, to protect them from freezing. Pretty much the same advice applies today: Secure fiberglass insulation with duct tape around exposed pipes, such as those in the cellar or in exterior walls leading to outdoor spigots. Make sure warm air can reach such pipes on exceptionally cold nights—often it pays to open utility closet or cellar doors to allow warm air to circulate through cold spaces.

If you discover that a pipe has frozen but not yet burst, first turn off the main water supply. Then, instructs Theodore Clark in *The Care of a House* (1903), open all of the faucets connected to the pipe and apply heat at the end of the pipe that's nearest the faucets. Although a propane blowtorch is effective, it creates the risk of fire or scorched woodwork. *The Care of a House* suggests soaking rags in boiling water and draping them around the pipe. A neater solution is to direct a stream of hot air from a hair dryer at the pipe. In any case, gradually move the heat source along the pipe as the ice inside melts. Carefully turn on the water supply after thawing, standing by to shut off the water immediately and call a plumber if a crack is revealed.

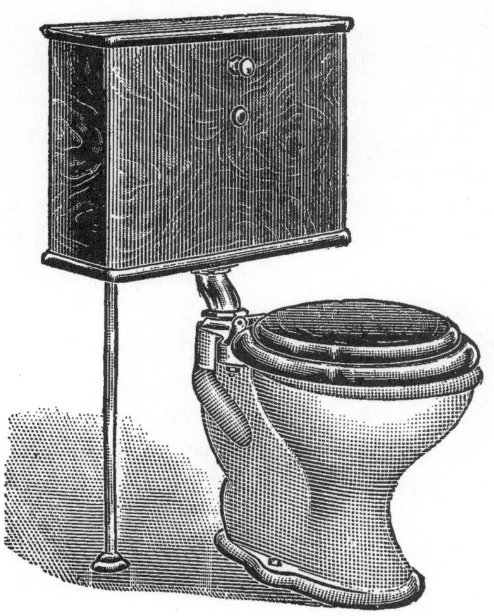

Solutions for Toilet Troubles

▪ The basic mechanical design of the flush toilet is the same today as it was in 1931, when *The American Home Book of Repairs; The Care and Repair of the Home,* by Vincent Phelan, offered advice for the diagnosis and repair of common toilet problems. Try these steps before calling the plumber.

Dealing with a clogged toilet. The "plumber's friend," or plunger, still resides in most bathroom closets and is still the best emergency tool for unclogging a toilet or drain.

Stopping that trickling water sound. Usually this is caused by water trickling into the overflow pipe because the float that controls the water valve is not positioned properly. On older toilets, this can be fixed by bending the wire that holds the float so it sits a little lower and thus causes the valve to stop sooner as the tank fills. Newer toilets have one-piece float and valve assemblies, and each is adjusted differently, usually by moving a plastic or wire clip alongside the float.

Correcting the water level in the tank. If a toilet tank doesn't refill enough after flushing, the problem may be that the float in the tank is positioned too low. Adjust the wire or clips holding the float so it sits a little higher and allows more water to enter the tank before shutting the valve.

Fixing a toilet that runs too long. The most common cause is a worn or improperly positioned rubber flap or ball covering the outflow at the bottom of the toilet tank. Turn off the water supply to the toilet by shutting the valve on the pipe behind the fixture, and then flush the toilet to drain the tank. Clean the flap or ball and the seat it fits into. Make sure the guide wire and guide arm are straight

☞ TRASH OR TREASURE ☜

Tennis Balls to the Rescue

WHEN THE DRAIN is clogged and you don't have a plumber's helper (plunger) on hand, a tennis ball may save the day. "If there is no plunger in the house, cut an old tennis ball in halves," instructs *1001 Entirely New Household Hints* (1937). "Place one half over the drain, and use in the same manner as an ordinary plunger, pressing firmly with the fingers several times." You'll need a vise and a sharp, serrated knife or saw to cut a tennis ball in half, and this will work only with drains smaller than a tennis ball's diameter. But, if nothing else, you'll end up with a good chew toy for a dog.

and the flap seats properly in the drain; if not, adjust it to fit. If the flap or ball is worn or damaged, it can be replaced easily by disconnecting it, taking it to a hardware store, purchasing a new piece of the same model, and reinstalling it exactly as you removed it.

If these simple techniques don't solve your plumbing problems, it's time to call the plumber.

Fill Traps to Stop Sewer Gas

Sewer gas has a nasty odor that no one wants lingering in the air around the house. If you smell sewer gas in your house, however, don't rush to call the plumber. Instead, try recharging the traps in drainpipes throughout your house, recommends Roger Whitman in *First Aid for the Ailing House* (1934). The traps are U-shaped bends in the drainpipes leading to the sewer, and these traps are normally full of water. If the water escapes, the gas can penetrate the house. This problem may arise when pipes crack or joints loosen, and in that case an emergency call to the plumber *is* necessary. However, the traps for cellar drains and little-used sinks may go dry simply from evaporation because they are not recharged often enough. It's a good idea to open all the sink faucets in your house periodically and to pour some water down the drain in cellars, especially in houses that have been shut for a while.

A Makeshift Pipe Wrench

When you need to disconnect some plumbing, the friction of rope around a pipe makes a quick-and-dirty substitute for a pipe wrench, according to Rolfe Cobleigh in *Handy Farm Devices and How to Make Them* (1909). Take a 3- or 4-foot length of 3/8-inch or 1/2-inch rope and place one end along the pipe. Then wrap the rope around the pipe so that it overlaps and covers the end you started with. Keep the coils close together, and be sure to wrap in the direction you want to turn the pipe. When you've got about a foot of rope left, knot a loop in the free end. Now thread a crowbar or another length of pipe through the loop and use this lever as a simple wrench—the friction of the rope against the pipe will keep it from slipping.

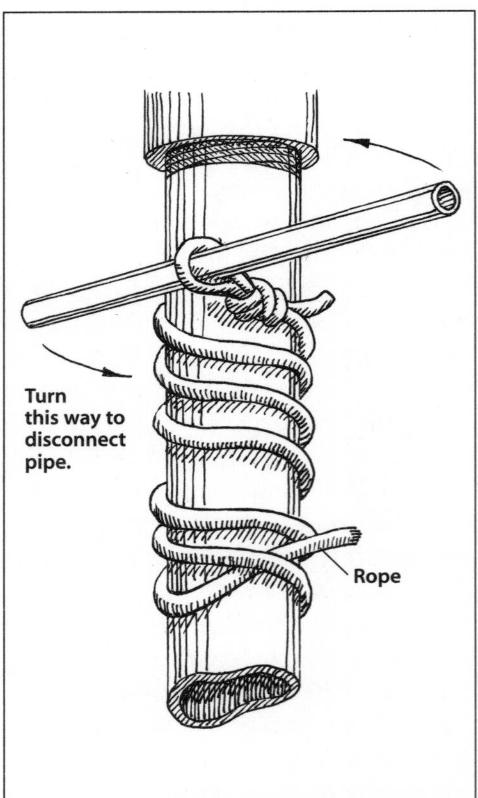

Improvise a pipe wrench by wrapping a pipe with rope and using a metal bar as a lever.

Household Safety

Before modern consumer protection laws and building codes, the home was a dangerous place. Faced with asbestos insulation and lead paint, chimney fires and rickety ladders, it's no wonder our ancestors came up with ingenious ways to safeguard their hearth and home.

Trip-Proof Cellar Stairs

■ Dark cellar stairs are dangerous traps for the unwary. Though most cellars are better lighted today than they were in the past, it still makes sense to follow this advice from Rolfe Cobleigh in *Handy Farm Devices and How to Make Them* (1909): Slap a coat of white paint or whitewash on both the tread and the riser of the bottom step. That way, you can see it clearly, even in dim light, and avoid painful accidents.

Of Mice and Matches

■ Matches are no longer the everyday necessity they were in the days before pilot lights, electric appliances, and butane lighters. But most people still keep matches around the house, so it's important not to forget a piece of basic safety advice that every 19th-century housekeeper knew: Mice and matches shouldn't mix. If mice invade the match supply, they often carry the matches back to their nests, which are full of dry wood shavings and bits of paper. The mice may gnaw on the match heads, and it's believed that many fires start this way, even today. Always keep matches in a covered jar or metal box with a tight lid, where they will be out of the way of children and safe from rodents.

Fix Feet on Old Ladders

■ Old wooden ladders can be useful for outdoor fix-ups, but risky to use if they have worn feet. Take a safety tip from *The Register of Rural Affairs* (1868) and saw off the rounded feet so they form a wedge—sharper if you always place the ladder on the ground; duller if you sometimes use it on indoor flooring or

OLD-TIME ODDITIES

Roof-Fire Alarm

Roof fires ignited by cinders from the chimney were a serious danger in older homes. In *Handy Farm Devices and How to Make Them* (1909), Rolfe Cobleigh offers a novel plan for a roof-fire alarm. A string was stretched tight between two rafters so that it ran in front of the chimney in the attic, right below the roof. From this string dangled a long cord with a weight attached to it. The weight was suspended an inch or two above a button on the mantelpiece in the room below, and if a fire burned through the roof near the cord, the weight would drop onto the button and ring an electric doorbell. The technology is archaic, but roof fires are still serious business—be sure to clean your chimney annually.

concrete. Some old-time farmers shod their ladders with iron straps nailed to the feet for more traction and durability.

Pants on Fire!

■ What should you do if your clothes suddenly catch fire? The advice given by Samuel and Sarah Adams in *The Complete Servant* (1825) is about the same as that promoted today: Don't run—lie down immediately. This is because "flame ascends and accumulates in intensity during its ascent . . . The fatal consequences of this accident arise from the ascent of the flame to the throat, head, and sensitive organs, an effect which cannot take place if the body is instantly placed in a horizontal position." Once prone, a person alight should roll across the floor or ground to smother the fire. Never run, because the rush of air will only fan the flames. Fire departments today summarize this old-fashioned advice with the modern mantra "Stop, Drop, and Roll."

CHAPTER 5

Crafts, Hobbies, and Amusements
All Work and No Play

Old-timers worked hard, and during their limited leisure time, they really knew how to enjoy themselves with simple, ingenious pastimes. They made ornaments and art from colorful can labels and watercolored shells, toys from walnuts and dry corn, and simple games to play by the fireside. When you need a break from high-tech entertainment, go back to a simpler era to try your hand at wholesome pastimes and crafts, from tying together a toy birch bark canoe to playing a rousing round of blindman's wand with no more than a group of friends, a stick, and a blindfold.

Use Nature's Bounty for Handmade Crafts

In old-time America, from early native settlements to the end of the Victorian era, artists and crafters worked with natural materials because that's all they had, lovingly producing beautiful handiwork, from frames to folk art dolls. Today, you can follow their lead or use modern methods to create your own rustic beauty with supplies that literally grow on trees—or litter the beaches.

Spice Up Life with Pomander Balls

■ Freshen the air of your house naturally with a historical handicraft that dates back to the 13th century: a pomander ball. A pomander is a clove-studded piece of fruit. It will last for years, and unlike those car freshener pine trees or air freshener sticks, a pomander is an attractive decoration suitable for the most formal room in your house. Try these old-time ideas for making pomanders and using them in ways you might not have thought of.

Back to basics. If you've never made a pomander ball, the basic strategy is to stud an apple or orange all over with whole cloves, which then scent the air as the fruit dries.

Don't punish your fingers! You can puncture and prick your fingers a thousand times if you try to pound cloves into a piece of fruit using only your hand. Instead, use a fork, nail, or ice pick to make tiny holes in the fruit first. Make a few test holes and push cloves into them to be sure the tool you're using produces holes of suitable size. Also, wrap your thumb well with adhesive tape and use that protected thumb to push the whole cloves into the fruit.

Spice it up. A basic clove pomander is fine, or you can dip your pomander in additional spices. One idea: Place the clove-studded pomander in a bag with 1 tablespoon ground cinnamon and ¾ teaspoon orris root. Orris root, which is available wherever potpourri supplies are sold, speeds drying and helps preserve the pomander. Allspice or pumpkin spice would make other good alternatives to the cinnamon. Gently shake so that the spices cover the ball, shake off the excess, and then place the pomander on a rack indoors to air-dry, which will take about 2 weeks. Every other day, if you think of it, shake on more spices to enhance the fragrance.

Wait to decorate. If you'd like to decorate your pomander with some Victorian-style ribbons or with Christmas ribbon to turn it into a Christmas ornament, wait until after the pomander has completely dried.

Hang in there. Victorians hung pomander balls from curtains, in closets, above doorways, and on Christmas trees. You can choose any of the above places, or consider placing one under the seat of your car or arranging three or four in a bowl as a simple, sweet-smelling centerpiece for your dining room table.

Go ahead, be crabby. Back in the days when oranges were a hard-to-find novelty, pomanders were usually made from apples. But today you can choose oranges, limes, or lemons—all will work well. Or to make tiny pomanders that are perfect for dangling from a houseplant or decorating a Victorian-style tabletop Christmas tree, try starting with crab apples or kumquats. You'll need only 10 to 12 cloves to cover one of these small fruits, which also make lovely scented decorations for wrapped Christmas packages.

Pining for Rustic Craft Materials

■ A picture frame covered with pinecone scales looks earthy and attractive, and it's even simpler for us to make than it was in the late 1800s, when the craft first had its heyday. Crafters back then had to make their own frames; you can just pick up a plain frame from the craft store—cardboard, plywood, or pine, as you choose. You can complete this rustic folk art project in less than an hour. All you do is hot-glue the pinecone scales on the front surface of the frame, starting with the

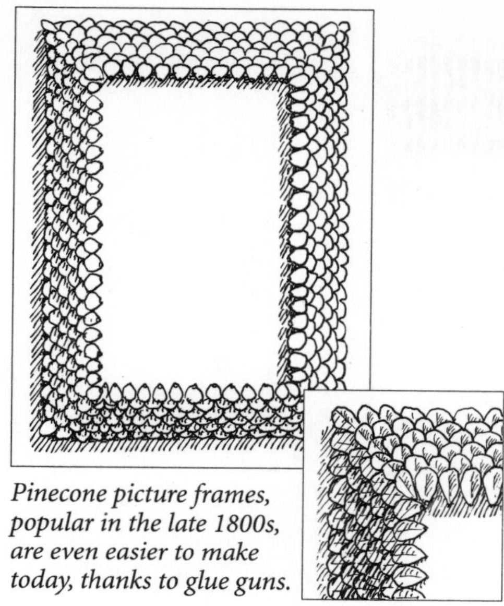

Pinecone picture frames, popular in the late 1800s, are even easier to make today, thanks to glue guns.

outside rim and overlapping them until you reach the center.

First, though, you have to stockpile some pine scales. Use the scales from sturdy cones, such as those from red pine, black pine, and scrub pine, or larger (but softer) scales from white pine. Use a craft knife to carefully cut each scale from the stalk of the cone. Don't discard that little cluster left at the top of the cone when the scales are gone, advise Mrs. C. S. Jones and Henry Williams in *Household Elegancies: Suggestions in Household Art and Tasteful Home Decorations* (1875). "Keep it entire, as it is frequently of great use, looking like a little carved rose, which is a very beautiful addition in some parts of the work."

Natural Ornaments—String 'Em Up

■ What was child's play in another era—chains made from seedpods and other natural materials—becomes a relaxing way to make folk art and rustic ornaments in ours. The technique for making nature chains hasn't changed much from the one described by Elizabeth Sage and Anna Cooley in *Occupations for Little Fingers: A Manual for Grade Teachers, Mothers and Settlement Workers* (1905): "Very attractive chains can be made by the little people from materials which they have gathered . . . using a large needle and rather coarse thread." Natural materials suitable for making chains include:

- Rose hips from wild or domestic rosebushes
- Red ears of corn, dried and shelled
- Dried squash or pumpkin seeds
- Small nuts, horse chestnuts, or acorns
- Maple wings
- Dried sweet gum seedpods
- Dried butterfly-weed pods
- Tulip tree seedpods
- Red chile peppers, dried or fresh
- Tiny pinecones from Scotch pine or hemlock

Gather materials and string them as suits your fancy. You could use chains made from the smaller seeds to wrap around an all-season dry wreath or centerpiece, and the larger materials to garland a mirror or the mantel, says Tom Russell, who designs quilts and craft projects for HGTV, a cable television channel. "Use a crewel or tapestry needle and cotton twine or even heavy gauge fishing line to string. Only the nuts should require any predrilling." Tom notes an advantage to crafting with natural materials: "If you don't like what you have or it gets worn looking, you can throw it away and start over with no qualms."

Shell Out Gorgeous Boxes

WHETHER YOU LIVE near the sea or are just returning from a seaside vacation, making shell artwork is a fine way to display your finds and your artistic style. You can make inexpensive imitations of exquisite designer jewelry boxes and vanity boxes without a huge time commitment. Buy plain wooden boxes at a craft store, or see if you can pick up a heavy cardboard or even light wooden cigar box from your local cigar shop.

You will need:

- Seashells of various sizes and shapes
- White paraffin wax
- Household glue
- Old cooking pan or an empty, clean bimetal can
- Heat mitts
- Small aluminum pie tin
- Wooden or cardboard box

Step 1. Spread out your shells. "Assort your shells according to size and color," instructs author Levina Urbino in *Art Recreations* (1860). Be sure you have plenty of small shells and a handful of uncooked white rice on hand to fill smaller spaces. "The more rice and other small shells you have, the better."

Step 2. Put two parts wax and one part glue in the pan or can. Heat the pan directly on the stove over low heat or put the can into a pan of simmering water to heat.

Step 3. Once the wax has melted, don the heat mitts and carefully pour the hot mix into the pie tin. Allow the mix to cool a bit before handling.

Step 4. Decorate the box. One popular pattern is a rose. Dip the lower ends of several shells of similar size and shape in the hot wax mixture and lay them in a circle. Use smaller shells to build up the layers of "rose petals." "Care must be taken to form the shells into perfect circles, and to take up wax enough to make them adhere to the cover. Shells of different form, say more oblong, can be used for leaves . . . After arranging such figures as you like with the shells you have, fill up the spaces with the very small ones." When you're done, "varnish with a very little copal varnish [shellac or clear spray sealant], using great care."

Dry Seaweed for All Seasons

■ "The sea shore is an inexhaustible source of pleasure and instruction," notes Levina Urbino in *Art Recreations* (1860). The ocean is also an inexhaustible supply of seaweed, and dried seaweed can become a beautiful addition to craft projects. You can use it for pressed-flower bookmarks, in shadowboxes of beach memories, as a border behind a glass-front picture frame, or in place of sphagnum moss in a dried-flower wreath or flower arrangement.

To press seaweed, you'll use a simple press made out of two pieces of plywood (each about 18 inches square), heavy-duty paper towels, and two pieces of muslin (or muslin shop rags). Also gather a large pan, a piece of craft paper, some vegetable oil, and a brick or large book. Spread three layers of paper towels on one of the pieces of plywood.

Now, it's time to visit the beach and collect a bunch of seaweed. Bring the seaweed to your work area. Put the seaweed in the pan and cover it with fresh water. Cut the craft paper to size so you can slip it into the pan. Brush vegetable oil on the paper, and then slip the paper into the pan underneath the seaweed. Use a nut pick or seam ripper to spread out the seaweed. "Great care, patience, and delicacy of handling are necessary in this process, for much of the beauty of the specimen depends upon preserving the minute thread-like fibers of the weed," Levina Urbino writes. "Trace out each thread, separating them all, and giving them such a position on the paper as will show the plant to the best advantage."

Once you're satisfied with the way the seaweed looks, carefully lift the craft paper (with the seaweed on it) out of the pan. Hold the paper on a slant to allow the excess water to run off. Lay the craft paper on top of the paper towels. Cover the seaweed with a piece of muslin. Top that with paper towels, then another piece of muslin, and more paper towels. Lay the other piece of plywood on top of the stack. Weight it down with a brick or large book.

BIZARRE BUT TRUE

Fish Scales and Gold Thread

In the Victorian era, freshwater pearls and other shell ornaments imported from Asia were extraordinarily popular. However, they were also expensive, so women of the day tried any number of make-at-home knockoffs. The one described by Levina Urbino in *Art Recreations* (1860) may stretch the idea a little too far: "Take the shining scales from a carp, or any other fish—the larger the scales, the better," it recommends, and soak them in saltwater overnight. Next, dry the scales beneath a weighted board for a day or two until they're pressed dry and hard. These "jewels" of the sea are to be sewn in patterns on "rich, dark-colored silk velvet [drawn] tightly in an embroidery frame"—with gold thread, no less!

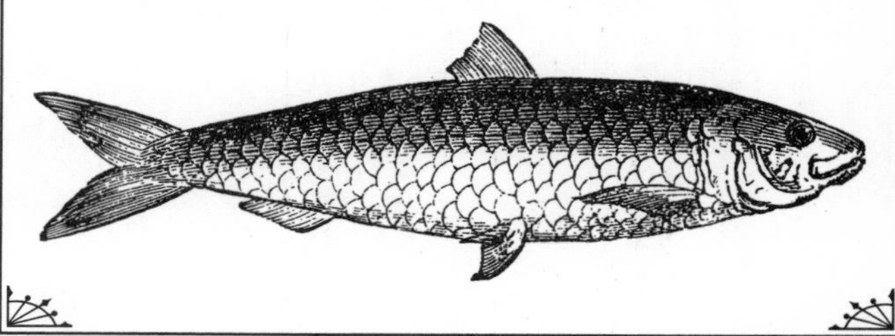

☞ ROUGHING IT ☜

Taking Crafts by the Horns

IT'S HARD TO IMAGINE our foremothers in their petticoats, cheerfully following this advice for creating a cornucopia from *Household Elegancies* (1875), by Mrs. C. S. Jones and Henry Williams. The instructions begin with a call to "procure a large horn, those long, curiously-shaped ones of the Texan oxen are novel and commodious, and quite a curiosity; but curled ram's horns are still prettier . . . The size or form is a matter of taste, and a variety can be had at the slaughterhouses." Next, our old-fashioned crafter was to proceed "with a piece of glass, held in a gloved hand, for fear of accident . . . to scrape the entire horn perfectly smooth. Mark any appropriate design upon certain parts of it, with a small camel's-hair brush, dipped in tallow, and a little beeswax melted together; then place in strong vinegar or acid for a short time, or until the surface not painted is destroyed, when upon carefully scraping off the tallow, etc., and wiping with a cloth dipped in turpentine, the figures will be found raised upon the surface." To finish this dainty project, she would "fasten two brass rings to the extreme ends, in which insert a brass chain. Fill the horn with earth, in which plant trailing vines or creepers, or fill it with dried flowers and leaves."

Allow the seaweed to dry in the press, checking for dryness after 1 week. When the seaweed is dry, carefully remove it from the craft paper and use it for the decoration of your choice.

Ornaments and Artwork

THE ARTISTIC SPIRIT has been alive since the time of cave paintings. Even though our early American counterparts didn't have such niceties as aerosol spray varnish or X-Acto knives, they did have a flair for making appealing and stylish decorative items. Check out the following painting and artwork tips from a mish-mash of historical sources—they still apply, no matter what type of art you dabble in.

Canny Sources for Decoupage Images

■ Crafters who enjoy decoupage can skip a trip to the craft store when they need botanical images for their projects. Instead, they should use source materials that crafters have relied on since the Pony Express and the Crimean War—catalogs and labels from canned goods. Cut images from "colored plates [illustrations] in flower and fruit catalogues," suggest Mrs. C. S. Jones and Henry Williams in *Household Elegancies* (1875). "And even the fruit and flowers upon fruit-cans, tastefully arranged, may be formed into many beautiful designs." To top decorative boxes or the cover for a homemade garden journal, arrange colorful cutout flowers artfully in pictures of oriental vases cut from home decor catalogs.

Press, Don't Burn, Vintage Ribbons

▪ Ribbon-decorated frames and lampshades will look more authentically Victorian if you use vintage ribbons. But those antique-store ribbons you found will probably need straightening before you can use them to decorate a frame or lampshade. This can be tough, since the ribbons are delicate and prone to scorching under the iron.

Here's a World War I–era method outlined in *The Complete Dressmaker, with Simple Directions for Home Millinery* (1916). This technique does the trick whether you're straightening vintage ribbons or ordinary cloth ribbons that got smashed in your shopping bag on the way home from the craft store: "Sponge the ribbon with a mixture of one third [rubbing] alcohol to two thirds water; when partly dry iron it under a cloth." For the best results with the least effort, while you're at it, make sure your ironing motion is "from edge to edge, not through the center of the ribbon." In other words, move the iron perpendicular to the length of the ribbon, not parallel to it.

Chamois Secret for Faux Finish

▪ "Faux painting" seems trendy and different to us today, but *Art Recreations* (1860), by Levina Urbino, provides instructions for imitation finishes that are surprisingly like faux painting techniques. To produce a fancy "ground glass" look on an inexpensive glass bud vase, "coat the vase thinly over with white paint and dab it with a delicate piece of chamois leather rolled up into a small

Ribbons Dress Up Scrapbook Pages

To lend a romantic touch to a modern scrapbook page, try adapting a craft technique from the mid-1800s—a portrait ribbon. A portrait ribbon is a piece of flat ribbon with a pretty bow at the top used to hang photos or small pictures on a wall. To adapt this for a scrapbook, "use double-stick tape or archival glue to attach a photo to a piece of satin ribbon that is an inch or two longer than the photo," explains Anna Griffin, a veteran scrapbooker who owns Decorative Papers in Atlanta. "Then attach the ribbon to the scrapbook and top it with a tiny satin bow." The technique naturally lends itself to sepia prints, wedding photos, and those fun dress-up shots from your trip to a Wild West vacation spot.

ball." Prefer an artificial alabaster look? Try the same technique, but coat the vase a little more thickly with the paint.

Just a Thimbleful of Paint

■ In the 18th and 19th centuries, many women received no academic education, but women of means sure learned how to paint. Even among the wealthiest, though, oil paint was a luxury—and very messy. To avoid waste and stay clean at the same time, women would dab a bit of paint into a metal thimble, which wouldn't tip over on a flat surface, and dip their paintbrush into the thimble as they painted. Several thimbles made a makeshift palette for those who didn't paint often. Another advantage of using small quantities of paint in thimbles: There was no danger of colors running together.

The same technique is still worthwhile today for tubes of acrylic or oil paint—particularly to avoid accidentally cross-mixing the last bit of a tube of paint that you need to complete a project in a particular color.

BIZARRE BUT TRUE

Clean Your Ribbons with Gin

CRAFTERS in the early 20th century used ribbons to festoon just about anything—hats, baskets, pillows, mirrors, and lamps. They sometimes reworked these ribbons from castoffs, but the used ribbons could be tough to clean, "especially white, cream, or light fancy ribbons," notes *The Complete Dressmaker* (1916). For the real stubborn candidates, the book recommends an "old-fashioned but excellent method"—raiding the liquor cabinet! "To half a pint of gin add a tablespoonful of soft soap and a teaspoonful of honey. Lay the ribbon on a clean table and scrub well on both sides with a large nailbrush dipped in the mixture." This does work, though it's a lot of trouble compared to hand-washing with today's detergents formulated for fine washables.

Create Cotton Ball Clouds

■ Whether you're using acrylic or oil paint to create a landscape scene on canvas or a metal tray, it's tough to get the clouds to look fluffy. In *Art Recreations* (1860), Levina Urbino offers a neat trick: Do your best with a paintbrush and then dab the paint with a cotton ball. And don't stop there—use the same technique when painting fluffy sheep, downy chicks . . . you get the picture.

Pummel Wood Smooth with Pumice

■ If your project is too delicate for an electric sander—a light wooden frame or varnished jewelry box, for example—consider using what Victorian ladies employed when they needed to smooth light, fancy wood. They'd pull out a pumice stone. You'll find that a pumice stone is much easier to grip than sandpaper and doesn't put so much pressure on the wood that you run the danger of splitting it or sanding the surface away entirely.

Put Your Stamp on Sturdy Homemade Stencils

THE CENTURIES-OLD ART of stenciling is still hot, and you can buy stencils at any paint or craft store. But there's an advantage of making your own: control. With a homemade stencil like the one described in *The Good Housekeeping Manual of Home Handicraft* (1908), you can reproduce most any pattern you like.

You will need:

- Thin cardboard or manila paper
- Your hand-drawn or electronically produced stencil design
- Carbon paper
- Thumbtacks
- Stylus
- Pine board or smooth-sanded plywood
- Craft knife
- Waxed paper
- Iron

Step 1. Cut the cardboard or manila paper to size—at least 2 inches larger on all sides than the sheet with your design on it. This will be your stencil board, and the outer edges will be your "margin . . . to facilitate handling and to avoid staining the hands or material," as recommended by *The Good Housekeeping Manual.*

Step 2. Lay your design on the stencil board, slip a sheet of carbon paper between the design and the board, and secure it with thumbtacks.

Step 3. Use the stylus to trace the lines of the design.

Step 4. Remove the design and the carbon paper and fasten the stencil to the pine board or plywood with tacks.

Step 5. Holding the craft knife firmly, cut through all the lines of the design on the stencil. Remove the stencil from the board.

Step 6. Cover one side of the stencil with waxed paper and quickly run an iron set on medium heat (no steam) over it until the waxed paper adheres to the stencil. Do the same with the other side; then trim any excess waxed paper to fit. The waxed paper coating will prevent colors from blurring when you work with the stencil.

Stenciling Secrets

■ Try these tips from *The Good Housekeeping Manual of Home Handicraft* (1908) for making and using homemade stencils:

◆ Unbleached muslin is a good choice for your first stenciling project.

◆ If the design is one with a repeat, allow for the repeat as often as you wish—but keep in mind it's "easier and quicker to lift and transfer the stencil than to cut a very long pattern."

◆ Paint your first stencil in one color—deep blue is a good choice. Once you have more experience, you can move to a more elaborate color scheme.

◆ If you're using several colors while applying a stencil, save time and possible mistakes by having a separate brush available for each color.

◆ Drive pins through the stencil into the fabric underneath, "a wise precaution against both blurring and stained fingers."

Revive Spatterwork in Style

SPATTERWORK wall decorations were popular in Victorian times. Victorians used India ink for spatterwork, but you can substitute regular acrylic paint. The results are very appealing. Frame your decoration and hang it in your home, or give it as a gift.

You will need:

- Leaves
- Waxed paper
- Newspaper
- Wooden board
- High-quality drawing paper
- Pushpins
- Straight pins
- Acrylic paint
- Saucer or paper cup
- Soft toothbrush
- 4- to 6-inch-long, ½-inch-diameter stick
- Thin paintbrush

Step 1. Place the leaves you've collected between two pieces of waxed paper and place them between the pages of a book. Put the book under a heavy weight to press them perfectly flat. Press them overnight.

Step 2. The following day, cover your work surface entirely with newspaper. Lay the board on your work surface and fasten the drawing paper to the board, using a pushpin in each corner.

Step 3. Place pressed leaves in a circle on your drawing paper, using straight pins to secure the leaves.

Step 4. Pour some acrylic paint into the saucer or paper cup. Dip the toothbrush bristles into the paint, shaking off any excess. Your goal here is to collect enough paint to create a spatter, but not so much that paint drips off the brush.

Step 5. Hold the brush perpendicular to and directly over the leaves and paper, at least 6 inches above them. Pass the stick over the bristles from bottom to top, very gently. The bristles will send out a fine spray of paint.

Step 6. Repeat this process until the paper is deeply shaded at the leaf edges and blends off to nothing at the paper's edge. Aim for the darkest shade around the lower leaves.

Step 7. Take the pins out of one or two leaves at the bottom and remove the leaves; then carefully spatter the edges of the leaves that were under the ones taken off. Continue taking off leaves, going from the bottom upward and spattering each edge as it is exposed.

Step 8. After you've removed all the leaves, use the paintbrush to sketch in the veins of the leaves, using light, feathery strokes.

Step 9. Allow your spatter picture to dry for at least 48 hours.

Sharp Tips for Needlework

Whether you ply a needle as a creative outlet or to make designer-look home decor for a fraction of the boutique price, all types of tips from the olden days can speed or sweeten your experience. In those days, even the youngest ladies swapped knitting and cross-stitch tips the way we swap bread machine recipes and good Web site finds.

Shear Sense Soothes Hands

■ Avoid hand strain when cutting fabric by learning the difference between shears and scissors. These two types of fabric-cutting tools serve different purposes, so choose based on this advice from Rosamond Cook in *Essentials of Sewing* (1924): "Shears are used for heavy cutting and are distinguished by the length, which is always over six inches, and by the handles, which are . . . arranged so that all of the hand can be used and the strain of cutting distributed. One handle is round to fit the thumb and the other is

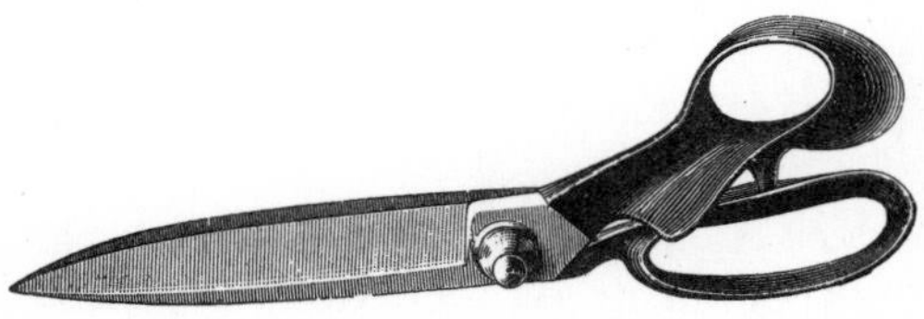

oblong in order to admit two or more fingers." The rims of the handles are also shaped so you can grasp them firmly without discomfort—important when you're cutting through two thicknesses of denim, for example. Buy the best shears you can afford, and keep the blades sharp so you don't waste time or fabric hacking away at patterns.

In the 1920s, sewing scissors were used only for light work, such as trimming edges or cutting short lengths that you can hold in your hand. "Since they

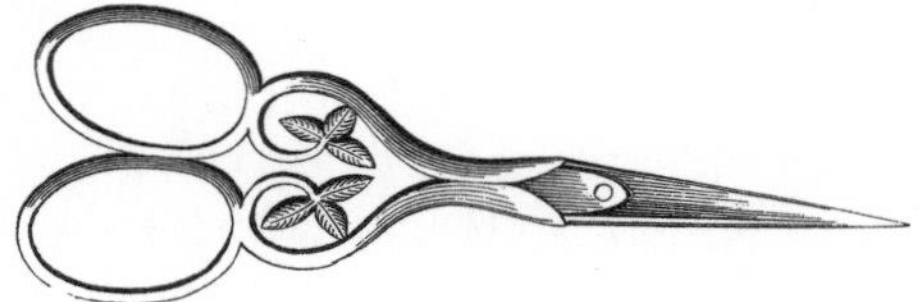

are not used for heavy work they have round handles," says the book. "They are usually provided with sharp points to aid in snipping threads or corners." If you try to use scissors when you should be using shears, you'll know it, either because your hand starts to hurt, or because the cut edge of the fabric will be choppy.

A Smooth Idea for Cutting Fabric

■ Second to sharp shears, fabric weights are your most important tool to ensure that you cut pattern pieces smoothly (which in turn makes sewing accurate seams easier). Instead of holding the pinned pattern and fabric down with your hands, "when your material is laid out smoothly on the table for cutting, it should be held in place by four round iron weights weighing one or two pounds," writes *The New Dressmaker* (1921). In that day, weights from the kitchen scale were recommended. In ours, empty cold cream jars, mint tins, or peanut tins filled with coins or nails will do the trick.

Keep a Band on the Hand

Every seamstress needs to corral that cloth tape measure before returning it to the sewing box—or wrangle with a tangled mass the next time around. The obvious choice for keeping a cloth tape measure under control is to fold it in even lengths and secure it with a small rubber band. Make it easier to remember to replace the rubber band by slipping the band on your little finger while the tape measure is in use, advises author Rosamond Cook in *Essentials of Sewing* (1924). That way, "it will be in safe keeping until the work is put away."

A New Way to "Stitch" a Button

ONE-OF-A-KIND BUTTONS are easy to make if you enjoy embroidery. All you need are embroidery floss and buttons covered in cloth. To decorate covered buttons with embroidery, follow this advice from Mary Picken in *Principles of Tailoring* (1933): "Almost any of the embroidery-stitches—the cross-, satin-, and seed-stitches, French knots, and many others—may be used in ornamenting buttons. Usually those stitches which will produce a flat, tailored effect are the ones that are preferred." Here's another helpful hint: Be sure you secure the thread by catching the material at the center of the back side at every stitch that crosses the underside of the button.

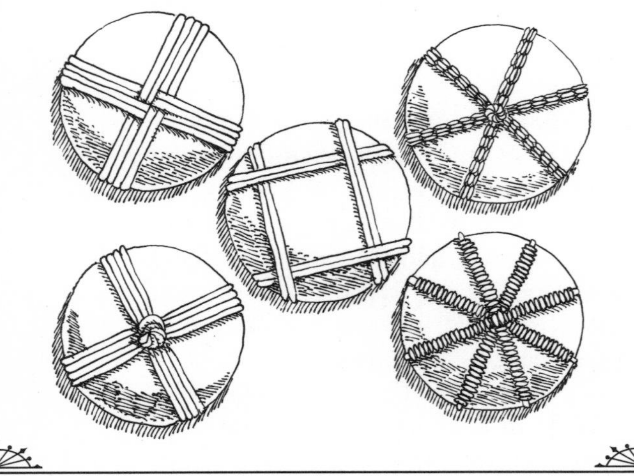

Keep Rust Away from Pins and Needles

Anyone who so much as hems pants needs a good pincushion, "both for convenience and for neatness," states Rosamond Cook in *Essentials of Sewing* (1924). It's easy enough to make a pincushion by stitching up a little pouch and stuffing it with fabric scraps, but mind what you put in the cushion. "Other materials for the stuffing and covering may be used, but . . . wool is better as it prevents the pins and needles from rusting." This is particularly important because many pins and needles are still made of steel. Your fingers tend to sweat when you ply a needle, and because it is naturally water-repellent, wool prevents moisture from corroding the steel.

A Thimble That's Nimble

Thimbles aren't just for collectors. The simple addition of a couple of thimbles can make any type of needlework more pleasant. "A thimble protects your fingertips when you sew," explains Madge Mounger, an adult education sewing instructor from Kingston, Tennessee. "The indentations in the thimble catch the eye of the needle and hold it stable, which is particularly helpful for preventing painful needle punctures. If you've tried a thimble before and it felt awkward, it may have been the wrong fit. Here's how to correct that, according to Rosamond Cook in *Essentials of Sewing* (1924): "The thimble is worn on the third finger of the hand and should be large enough to cover the finger nearly to the first joint. This length allows perfect freedom of the joint and provides a little air space at the end of the finger which acts as a cushion." Thimble sizes aren't reliable—they vary too widely, says the book, and this may be even more true now that so many are manufactured overseas. Instead, "try them on until one is found that will fit the finger comfortably."

While you're trying on thimbles, or even if you're just dusting off a thimble that's been in the family sewing box for decades, make sure that the edges on the thimble's indentations are "perfectly smooth or the material will become roughened or frayed."

Band Together for High-Impact Embroidery

▪ If you want a big splash of color or design on a cloth craft item but don't want to fool with tedious, tiny stitches, try a simple form of old-fashioned embroidery. *The Complete Dressmaker* (1916) describes this technique as particularly attractive and easy. Essentially, you mark a bold line or simple curved pattern on the cloth, then hold together several strands of embroidery floss and stitch it to the line with another single strand of embroidery floss, using an overcast stitch at ⅛-inch intervals. "The several strands are raised between the overcasting stitches, making a fancy braid or cord effect." This technique is great to liven up a pillow cover or tote bag, especially if you have several bits of leftover embroidery floss you'd like to use up.

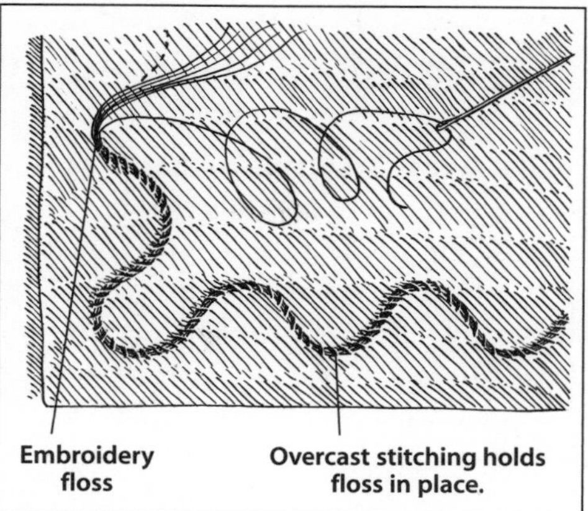

Use an old-fashioned embroidery technique to add a lively accent to cloth pillow covers, tote bags, or tablecloths.

Sewing—Less Strain, More Gain

▪ Ergonomics seems like a trendy new science, but it's really not a recent idea. Back in the 1920s, top sewing instructors were concerned about the sewing housewife's work stress. Following their advice can help you minimize fatigue after a bout of sewing. According to *The New Dressmaker* (1921), the table you use for sewing "should have a smooth, hard, even surface and should be of comfortable height, so you can sit with your feet under it as you would sit at a writing-table." And romantic notions of fireplaces and cushioned chairs should be firmly set aside. "Never sew with your work on your lap. It makes you sit in a fatiguing position, strains your eyes and back, and stretches and crumples your work. Lay your sewing on the table, letting the table support its weight."

Make a No-Loom Heirloom Rug

OLD-TIMERS MADE "rag" or braided rugs out of necessity, but today they're one of the easiest, most enjoyable folk art projects available to the casual crafter. According to Florence Buchanan, author of *Home Crafts of Yesterday and Today* (1917), "The work requires no special tools or equipment. Just a large coarse needle and some very strong thread are all that is needed." Braided rugs make perfect throw rugs for a porch, family room, or mountain cabin. Making home-braided rugs is also a wonderful way to reduce clutter—it transforms that pile of scratchy, worn wool blankets and velveteen curtains you'll never use again into a beautiful and practical part of your home decor. Best of all, making a braided rug is a soothing, pleasantly paced hobby you can do in front of the television or the fire.

You will need:

- Sewing shears or a rotary cutter
- Heavier wool and velvet scraps from old upholstery, curtains, coats, blankets, or dresses
- Sewing machine (optional)
- Large darning needle
- Carpet thread

Step 1. Use the sewing shears or rotary cutter to cut the scraps of material into 1-inch-wide strips. You can cut on the bias or straight; straight cuts are preferable because the strips will have less stretch. However, if the material ravels readily, cut it on the bias. *Note:* If you're using velveteen, cut the strips 1½ inches wide and fold them through the center, "so that the cotton back will not show and the rug will be reversible."

Step 2. Cut the ends of each strip on the diagonal.

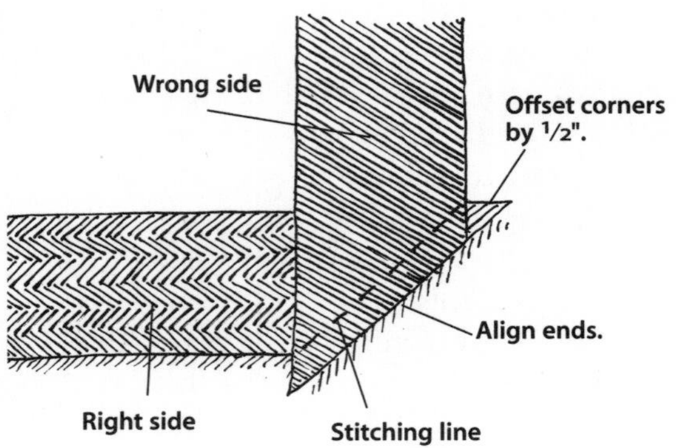

Step 3. Sew strips together to create super-long strips (20 feet long or more). To do this, position the end of one strip at 90 degrees to the end of another strip. The right sides of the fabric should be facing one another. Line up the diagonal edges. Sew a ½-inch seam along the diagonal edge. Using a sewing machine for this step will save you lots of time.

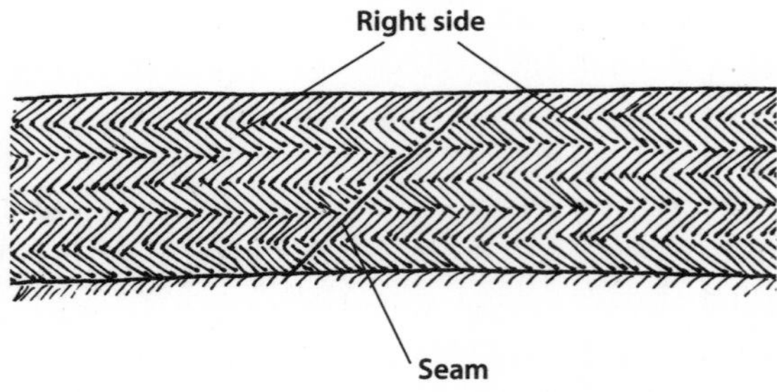

Step 4. Trim the seam and open it flat.

Step 5. Repeat Steps 3 and 4, adding a new strip to the end of the strip you sewed previously, to create a superlong strip (20 feet long or longer).

Step 6. Make two more superlong strips.

Step 7. Roll each superlong strip into a ball.

Step 8. Now it's time to braid the strips. To get started, tie the free ends of the superlong strip fabric strips together and loop them over a doorknob or handle. Braid the strips as you would hair, keeping the material taut but not too tight. When you finish braiding, remove the braid from the doorknob. Cut off the knot close to where the braid begins.

Step 9. Cut the loose ends at both ends of the braid even, fold them under, and hand-stitch.

Step 10. On a flat surface, start coiling one end of the braid to form the center of the rug first. Wind it several times, experimenting with shape (you can make a round rug or an elliptical rug).

Step 11. Once you've settled on a shape, begin sewing the braid together. Use a large darning needle to guide the carpet thread through the braids. Knot the end of the thread and poke the needle end between the braid folds. Make several small, inconspicuous stitches to secure the thread. Then insert the threaded tip through every other braid fold, alternating side to side. The action is similar to lacing shoes. Slip the needle between the strands of the braids without puncturing the fabric.

Step 12. Make another braid and add it to the enlarging rug. Continue making and adding braids until the rug is as big as you want it. For the final braid, braid the strands very tightly near the end to make a thin strip that you can tack closely against the edge of the rug. Also add some extra stitches at the center of the rug to firmly secure the ends of the braid at the very center of the rug.

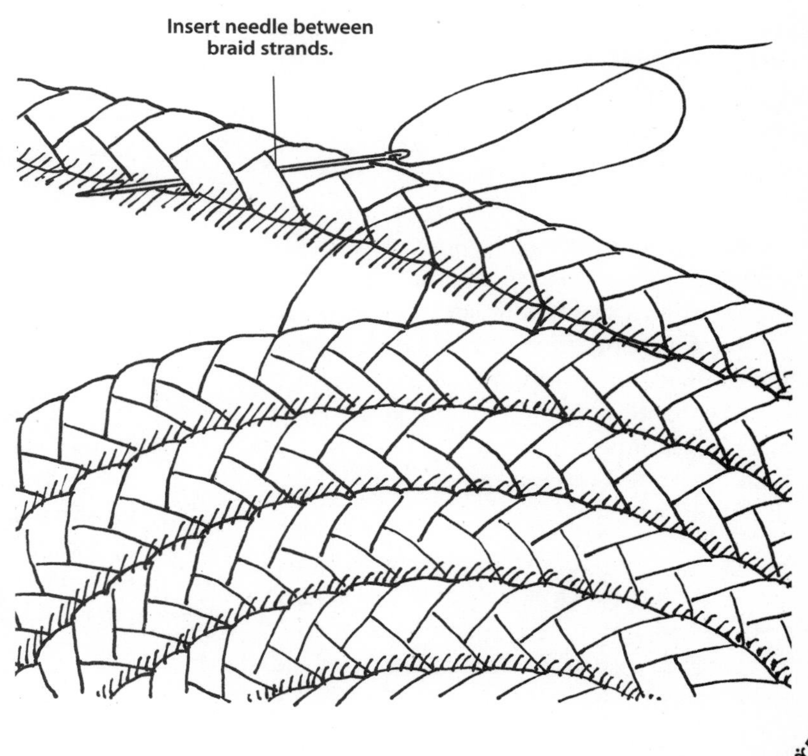

Old-Fashioned Projects for Modern-Day Homes

Busy as we are today, we have heaps more time for home decorating projects than our 18th- and 19th-century counterparts. Still, the homey touches that enhanced a pioneer woman's log cabin or Victorian lady's parlor are just as charming in our modern houses.

Bark for a Wastepaper Basket

▪ Bring the beautiful simplicity of Native American art into your home, at a price that ensures you can afford more than just one piece. Native artisans today make extraordinary crafts, most of them the legacy of hundreds of years of tribal crafting, from baskets to drums and carvings. These items bring a premium price that's worth every penny—but most of us could never afford all the native-look accessories we'd like. While you can't match the quality of these talented artisans, you can augment your collection with reasonable facsimiles, as long as you stick to simple projects and materials. One good starter project is a birch bark basket, for use as a magazine holder, a laundry receptacle, a toy basket, a wastebasket, or other storage. *The Good Housekeeping Manual of Home Handicraft* (1908) offers detailed directions.

"For this basket you need a strip [of bark] from fifteen to eighteen inches wide, and from thirty to thirty-six inches long, varying of course according to the size you wish the basket to be when finished." With a metal hole punch or a sharp nail, punch a row of holes along both short edges, every inch or so. Then "bring the two ends together and lace them with strips of wood fiber. Before reaching the bottom, slip in place a piece of wood cut round to fit the basket. In drying, the bark will probably shrink enough to hold the bottom in place, but it is just as well to drive in three or four small nails or tacks to make it very secure and guard against the bottom falling out at the most inopportune moment."

You can order birch bark for $5 to $8 per sheet from Internet suppliers (see Resources on page 349), or buy it at some craft stores, says Tom Russell, a graphic artist who designs craft and quilt projects for HGTV.

Historic Hints for Store-Bought Baskets

From the 1400s right up to the present, Native Americans have decorated baskets with colorful yarn and natural dyes made from huckleberries, sumac, and other plants. To decorate store-bought baskets in a similar manner, thread a darning needle with yarn and use it to stitch a geometric pattern around the side of a shallow basket. Or wind yarn or strips of colored ribbon around the top edge or handles of any basket. To be the most authentic, remember that yellow was the easiest color to make from natural dyes. Red, green, blue, black, and white were also within the realm of possibility.

Lively Lampshades, Victorian Style

A BEADED or fringed lampshade is a beautiful accent for many styles of furnishings, not just Victorian. It's easy and fun to adapt a modern lamp and shade to Victorian style. The best choice of lamp for this project is one with an off-white base and a long, sloped, light or off-white shade that has a finial and at least three top-to-bottom seams.

You will need:

- Cloth measuring tape
- Lamp with shade
- Scissors
- Off-white braid or beaded braid, about ¾ inch wide
- Hot glue gun
- Braid or beaded braid, about ⅓ inch wide
- Off-white beaded fringe, 2 to 5 inches long, depending on your taste
- Gold tassel

Step 1. Measure the height, top diameter, and bottom diameter of the lampshade and jot down the measurements.

Step 2. Measure and cut the ¾-inch braid or beaded braid to fit each seam of the lampshade. Hot-glue the braid to the seams and let the glue dry completely.

Step 3. Measure and cut the ⅓-inch braid or beaded braid to fit the top rim of the lampshade. Hot-glue it to the top edge, facing out and covering the top edges of the braid you applied in Step 2. Let glue dry completely.

Step 4. Measure and cut the beaded fringe to fit the bottom rim of the lampshade.

Step 5. Hot-glue the fringe to the bottom edge of the lampshade, facing out and covering the ends of the braid. Let the glue dry completely.

Step 6. Tie the tassel around the lamp finial and let it drape over the outside of the lampshade.

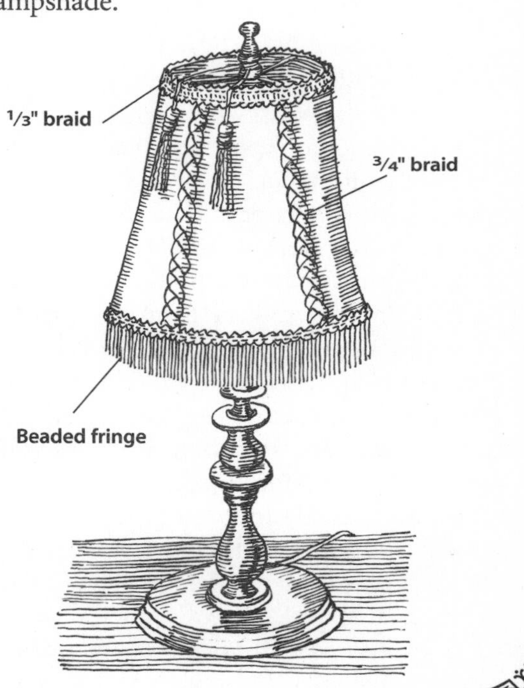

Catch the Sun with Colored Tissue

■ If you'd like one of those stained-glass sun catchers to cast colored rainbows from a sunny window, experiment first with a practically free tissue-paper version, following Elizabeth Sage and Anna Cooley's directions from *Occupations for Little Fingers* (1905). You can make these in virtually any color or design, limited only by your imagination and your ability to wield a craft knife. Hang several to get an idea of where the best rays in your home are, before you invest in a pricey store-made model.

To make this type of sun catcher, draw a simple pattern (such as a star and crescent moon) on a 4-by-6-inch card or heavy paper stock. Then cut along the lines with a craft knife and remove the patterned pieces. Paste colored tissue paper—yellow paper will provide a sunny look—over the openings in the card, and punch two holes at the top for a cord so you can hang your sun catcher in a window.

Toss Wastepaper into a Nostalgic Parasol

For a quirky, fun, yet practical accessory, transform a paper parasol into a fanciful wastepaper basket. The result will have a Victorian flavor, but without the heavy, dark tones that were common in Victorian furnishings. You can buy paper parasols at import or party stores, or order them from an Internet-based supplier (see Resources on page 349). You'll also need a cordless electric drill, a 2-inch-long wire pin or thin dowel, a wooden disk about 8 inches in diameter, and a 2-inch wood screw and washer.

Hold the parasol with the point facing up, open to the extent you desire for your wastebasket. Make a pencil mark on its shaft just above the inner push ring. Turn the parasol upside down, open it completely, and use the cordless electric drill to drill a hole through the shaft at the pencil mark. Be sure that the hole is large enough for the wire pin or dowel to fit through—that's what will keep the umbrella from popping open. (You may need a friend to hold the umbrella while you drill.) Partially close the umbrella and insert the wire pin or dowel through the hole.

If you'd like, use spray paint or acrylic paint to paint the wooden disk the color of your choice. Mark a point at the center of the disk and predrill a 1⁄16-inch-diameter hole all the way through at that point. Next, drill a 1⁄16-inch hole at least ½ inch into the tip of the umbrella to receive the screw. Place the washer on the bottom of the disk and thread the screw up through the hole and into the tip of the umbrella.

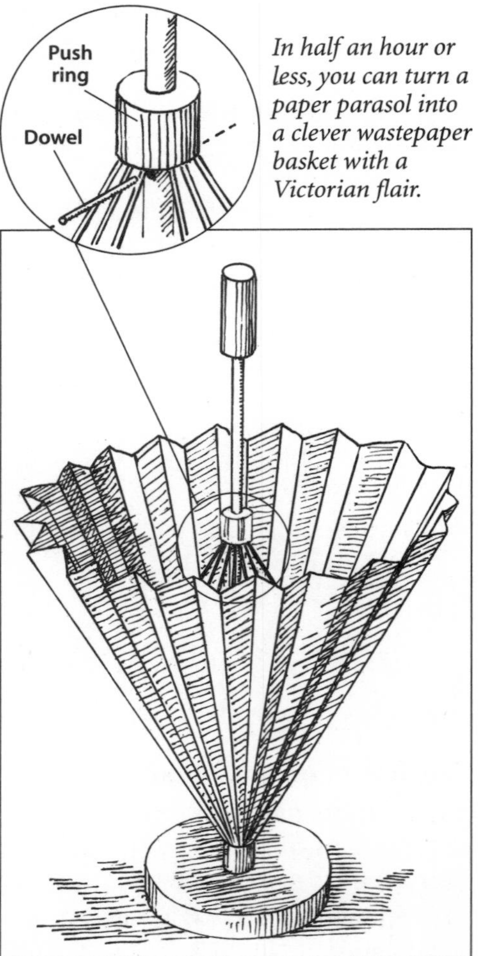

In half an hour or less, you can turn a paper parasol into a clever wastepaper basket with a Victorian flair.

A Houseful of Flowers

Decorate, create, enjoy! Use cut flowers to their fullest advantage with tips from Victorian and Colonial decorators and hostesses. When you've exhausted the bounty from your garden, see what Mother Nature has to offer—and what floral designers from another era can tell you about how to arrange these wonderful, unusual materials.

Match Centerpiece and Table Shape

■ If you're hosting a dinner at a big table, improve your odds of creating an eye-pleasing centerpiece with one simple choice. Regardless of the flowers in the display, it will look more harmonious if you pick a container that "conforms to the shape of the table; if round or oblong, the receptacle should be of similar shape," according to Edward White in *Principles of Flower Arrangement* (1925).

Stem the Thirst of Wild and Woody Cuttings

■ Expand your choice of floral materials beyond the carnations from grocery-store flower stands, and you can keep arrangements in your house much more often—and enjoy more creative fulfillment from your artistry. One oft-overlooked choice is cuttings from blooming shrubs such as lilacs or azaleas, or even bamboo or reeds. However, you can't just plunk them in water the way you would a bunch of cut flowers. "Bamboos and reeds, or anything that has a hollow, jointed stem, should have a notch cut in the upper part of each joint that will be under water, so that the stem becomes filled," Gertrude Jekyll points out in *Flower Decoration in the House* (1907). "The flowers of shrubs in general should have the stems slit up or the bark peeled up, leaving it on in ribbons . . . to expose as large a surface as possible of woody fiber and inner and outer bark to the action of the water."

This advice is just as valid as it was a century ago, says Lynn Byczynski, a cut flower producer based in Lawrence, Kansas, and author of *The Flower Farmer.* "This tactic—or just cutting the woody stem at a sharp angle—would work well with flowering shrubs such as butterfly bush, pussy willow, forsythia, lilac, and viburnum. But don't go to a lot of trouble until you're sure the branch isn't taking up water when you make an ordinary cut."

One old-fashioned tactic to disregard: smashing woody stems to provide more surface to draw up water. "The pieces of fiber will get in the water and start bacterial growth," warns Lynn.

Milk Warm Water into Milky Stems

■ Don't let milky sap keep you from expanding your floral repertoire with such blooms as hollyhock, poppy, or poinsettia. According to Gertrude Jekyll in *Flower Decoration in the House* (1907), it's a myth that these cuttings can't live in water, "though it is easy to see why it is so generally believed. Poppies and some other flowers, have a milky juice which has the property of drying quickly. If they are cut and not put in water immediately, this juice dries and seals up the cut end of the stalk so that it cannot draw up water."

To better your odds of success, make sure the water is deep and warm, which will force it up the stems, says Lynn Byczynski, a cut flower producer based in Lawrence, Kansas. "Don't rub your eyes when you're working with milky blooms, and make sure to wash your hands the second you're done. The milky sap can be caustic on skin."

Classic Containers for Displaying Flowers

■ When you arrange flowers, it's critical to place them in containers that will showcase the blooms—not detract from their beauty. Back at the turn of the 20th century, Gertrude Jekyll was a respected authority on home decor, and her expertise on vases still holds true today. If you don't own any (or enough) formal vases, follow these guidelines for choosing alternatives that won't sacrifice appearances, recommended by Miss Jekyll in *Flower Decoration in the House* (1907).

No pattern preferred. "As a rule it is well to avoid things that have much pattern, the chief exception to this being jars of oriental blue and white porcelain, which are singularly becoming to many kinds of flowers."

Set them in silver. Silver bowls, cups, and beakers are always excellent choices for displaying cut flowers, especially on dining tables. "They look best on well-polished dark mahogany, as in the days of our forefathers."

Serve them like soup. Search for cast-off serving dishes, particularly salad bowls and soup tureens, at flea markets and in the attic, "They will generally be admirable for flowers, both cut and in pots."

Don't shrink from finger bowls. Another kitchen castoff you can pick up: heavy glass finger bowls, which are excellent for violets.

A pint for peonies. If you have a pewter mug or commemorative beer stein hanging around in a cupboard, adopt it for displaying heavy-headed flowers, such as peonies or irises. "Such flowers might easily overbalance anything whose centre of gravity was not as well assured."

Don't toot the trumpet. Although trumpet-shaped vases are popular, they're often not the best choice, because they're prone to tipping and don't provide much volume for water at the base, where it's most needed.

Speak in the Language of Flowers

You can be thoughtful, mysterious, and creative all at once when you share a nosegay that you've arranged according to the Victorian-era "language of flowers." Suitors in that era would pick certain flowers according to their "flower dictionary" definitions, and the recipients might spend days decoding the floral message. Today, you could give a theme bouquet as a special treat for a friend, family member, or romantic interest, along with leads for deciphering your meaning. For example, a friend facing a job interview could be the recipient of a posy made of chamomile (energy in adversity), hollyhock (ambition), and basil (good wishes). Or you could present tickets for a date to spice up a longtime relationship, and present a small bouquet of fern (fascination), hyacinth (sport, game, or play), and chickweed (rendezvous) alongside.

Best of all, many of the most meaningful flowers are blooms you can cultivate yourself or find in a vacant lot, so you can indulge often—and the arrangements are far more original than most anything you'd find at the florist. Here are 20 flower messages from *Kate Greenaway's Language of Flowers* (1885).

FLOWER	MEANING
Alyssum, sweet	Worth beyond beauty
Amaryllis	Pride, timidity, splendid beauty
Azalea	Temperance
Basil, sweet	Good wishes
Carnation	Woman's love
Chamomile	Energy in adversity
Chickweed	Rendezvous
Chrysanthemum (white)	Truth
Columbine (red)	Anxious and trembling
Coreopsis	Always cheerful
Daffodil	Regard
Elm	Dignity
Fern	Fascination
Hibiscus	Delicate beauty
Holly	Foresight
Hollyhock	Ambition, fecundity
Honeysuckle	Generous and devoted affection

FLOWER	MEANING
Hyacinth	Sport, game, play
Ivy	Fidelity, marriage
Lilac (purple)	First emotions of love
Lily of the valley	Return of happiness
Moss	Maternal love
Nasturtium	Patriotism
Periwinkle (blue)	Early friendship
Primrose	Early youth
Rhubarb	Advice
Sage, garden	Esteem
Shamrock	Lightheartedness
Sweet pea	Departure
Tulip (red)	Declaration of love
Tulip (variegated)	Beautiful eyes
Tulip (yellow)	Hopeless love
Violet (blue)	Faithfulness
Zinnia	Thoughts of absent friends

Three Ways to Fill Out Flower Arrangements

■ You can make blooms from a store-bought bouquet the focus of three or four arrangements throughout your home if you augment them with finds from your garden or local fields (be sure to ask the owner's permission first). Also, be sure you can identify the species you're collecting, and never collect flowers from species that are rare or endangered. Whenever you experiment with wildflowers, cut and use just one stem at first, to test whether that variety will last well in a container of water. Some wild plants have great staying power in arrangements, but others wilt or drop their flower petals overnight, ruining the appearance of an arrangement.

Here are three ideas for unusual fillers you may never have thought of including

Can't-Miss Mini Bouquet—The Tussie-Mussie

RECEIVING FRESH FLOWERS is a wonderful gift. To spread the wealth, get in the mid-1800s Victorian habit of making tussie-mussies—round nosegays that include several varieties of flowers. Keep a stock of ribbon and tend a plot of annuals especially for cutting so you can whip up an unexpected gift for friends, family, a teacher, or a co-worker on the spur of the moment. Or save the idea for party favors or a centerpiece. Most any cut flower you have on hand will work for tussies. They're easy to make and they add joy to everyday life.

You will need:

- 1 large flower, such as a rose or chrysanthemum, or a cluster of small blossoms
- 1 or 2 varieties of filler flowers, such as baby's breath or pansies
- Large, leafy stems, such as violet leaves or lamb's-ears
- Florist's wire
- Florist's tape or colorful ribbon
- Paper doily (optional)

Step 1. Trim the flower stems to about 7 inches long and arrange them in a tight, round bouquet, with the largest bloom or cluster in the center. Gather the stems in a bunch just below the blooms.

Step 2. Add the leafy stems around the bunch of flower stems. Remove individual leaves from the bottoms of the stems to provide a few inches of bare stems.

Step 3. Wrap florist's wire around the stems, starting just below the leaves. Trim any uneven stems level.

Step 4. Wrap florist's tape around the stems to hide the wire, or tie a length of ribbon at the top of the bare-stem portion and wrap the two equal tails of ribbon around the stems to the bottom. Tie the tails together and trim.

Step 5. If you'd like, wrap a paper doily around the entire arrangement and tie it in place with a ribbon.

in arrangements, recommended by Gertrude Jekyll in *Flower Decoration in the House* (1907).

1. In early fall, fennel, "with its pretty yellow umbels and fine hair-like foliage . . . is effective cut long, with yellowish foliage of oak or ash or chestnut."

2. Before you dig your carrot crop in the fall, cut some of the tops. The fine-textured foliage will be an attractive mix of green, red, and copper to accent fall flowers.

3. If you live in an area (from New Jersey to Florida) where parasitic mistletoe grows on trees, seek some out after Christmas has come and gone. "March is the real time for the beauty of Mistletoe. When it is gathered for Christmas the berries are not yet mature; in fact, they are not fully ripe till April. But a nice branch or two, put in water with some dark-berried Ivy, will show its curious and quite special beauty to much advantage."

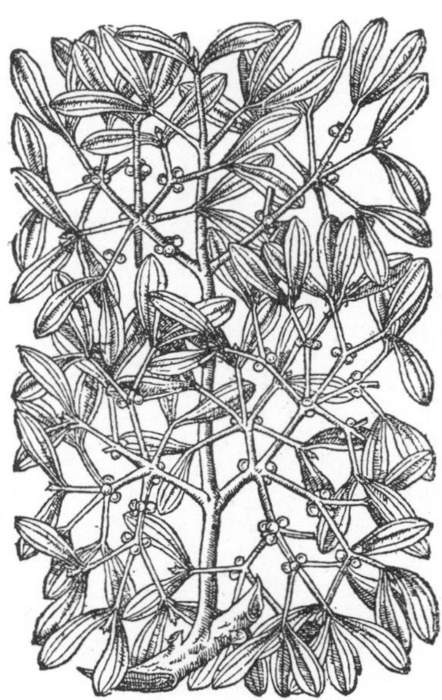

Toys and Games

OLD-FASHIONED TOYS and games are a breath of fresh air in our high-tech, low-touch society. In times gone by, a walnut and a scrap of cloth could be turned into a treasured doll, and a lively group of friends might gather in the parlor for the sole purpose of decoding each other's pantomimes. Inject some of that innocence and fun into your own life with these games and toys. If you don't have a young one to share them with, relive your own childhood—or use the homemade toys for folk art decoration.

Can You Make a Toy Canoe?

■ All you need is some strips of birch bark, and you can fashion a tiny canoe toy to rival any you see in a wilderness tourist store. Display the boat in a centerpiece or on the mantel—or give it to a youngster as a vehicle for those pricey Lego or Playmobil figurines. Elizabeth Sage and Anna Cooley offer directions in *Occupations for Little Fingers* (1905): "Take a piece of [birch] bark seven inches long and five inches wide. Find the centre of the two short sides, measure in from there toward the center one inch, and draw a curved line from that point to the outside edge at the corners." Use sharp scissors or a craft knife to cut along the lines you drew. Crease the bark down

☞ OLD-TIME ODDITIES ☜

Whirligigs

CARVED WHIRLIGIGS were once thought to be some sort of small weather vane. More recently, historians have decided that the gizmos were more likely children's "Sunday toys," whittled by indulgent 1700s papas. A child could hold a whirligig up while running and stir up enough air to make the flat arms of the contraption whirl—but quietly, as would befit the day of rest in the Colonial era. A few original whirligigs are on display in folk art museums, and crafters still carve reproductions by hand.

the center lengthwise. Then, with a small punch, make a row of holes through both layers of bark ¼ inch from the edge on the two short sides. "Lace through the holes twice with a piece of raffia, making the stitches cross. A decoration of some sort may be painted on the canoe or worked with raffia." You may have a birch tree in your yard from which you can peel a small piece of bark for a canoe, but if you don't, see Resources on page 349 for suppliers.

It's the (Peach) Pits to Lose at Basket Gamble

■ Dice games of many sorts were popular among tribal peoples in many cultures, and basket gamble probably dates back at least to the 1500s. No need to gamble your life's savings over the outcome, though. Instead, use the game as a fun way to choose who goes first in another game—or who does the dishes!

To make your own set of playing pieces for this game, wash and dry six peach (or plum) pits; then mark a large round dot on one side of each pit with ink, paint, or permanent marker. Break out a pack of colored toothpicks to use as counters to keep score if you plan to play more than one round.

To play the game, sit on the floor facing your opponent with a flat basket full of the marked pits between you. Take turns "making the throw"—holding the basket in both hands, giving it a shake upward so that the pits leap into the air, and then sharply slapping it down on the ground so the pits fall back inside. Your opponent should be able to clearly hear the slap. The pits that land with the marked side up count one point each for you. Players take turns.

A variation from the Zuni tribe involves five ¼-inch-thick blocks about 1 by 1½ inches, with one side painted in the design of your choosing. Scoring for Zuni basket gamble goes as follows after the throw: 10 points if all five show the painted side, 5 points if all five are plain, 4 points for four plain, 3 points for three plain, 2 points for two plain, and 1 point for one plain. The object of the game is to get 10 points. If you want to play without making the blocks from scratch, just use dominoes or mah-jongg tiles.

Ivory Soap Bubbles

■ Kids and grown-ups alike love blowing bubbles. Of course, you can buy ready-made bubble solution, but here's how to make your own, as described in *Unusual Uses of Ivory Soap* (1927). Try an 8-to-1 mixture of water and Ivory Liquid. (Any dish-washing liquid will work.) Add

Catch the Wind, Hold On to Memories

USED TO BE any kid with a piece of paper and a few spare minutes could fold up a pinwheel and race off for an hour or two of simple pleasure. To have a bit of nostalgic fun, brush up on these instructions for pinwheels from Elizabeth Sage and Anna Cooley in *Occupations for Little Fingers* (1905). To make a pinwheel that's a real work of art, try using fancy origami paper (available at craft stores). Pinwheels also serve as bright ornaments for potted plants on the porch.

You will need:

- 5-inch square of paper
- 8-inch-long, 1/4-inch-diameter dowel or plastic drinking straw
- Pushpin or straight pin
- Adhesive tape (optional)

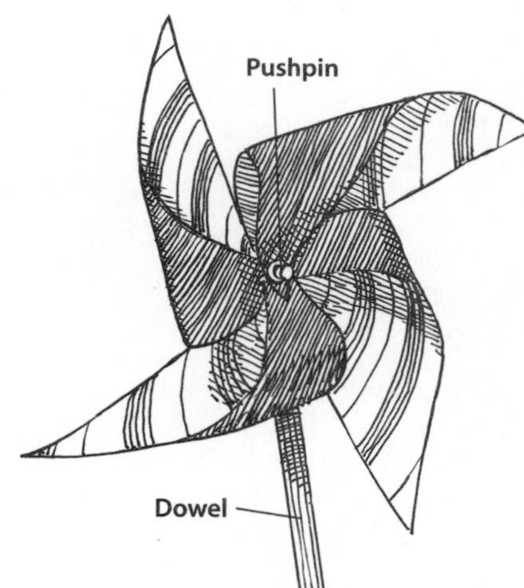

Step 1. Place a dot in the center of the paper.

Step 2. Fold the paper corner to corner, both ways, to crease the diagonals. Cut on these lines from each corner of the square to within half an inch of the center. After cutting, there will be eight points, two at each corner of the square.

Step 3. Lap over every other point to the center. You may choose to cover the overlapping points with a smaller square of contrasting paper.

Step 4. If you're attaching the pinwheel to a dowel, insert a pushpin through the center of the pinwheel and press it into the end of the dowel. If you're using a drinking straw, insert a straight pin through the center of the pinwheel and then through the straw, bending the end of the pin down and taping it to the straw.

To make a prettier pinwheel, stack two pieces of paper in contrasting colors. Proceed as you would with one sheet, folding and cutting the two sheets together, and when you cut the points, the sheet on the bottom forms a colored lining.

1 tablespoon glycerin (available at drugstores) for every pint of the mixture. *Unusual Uses* also recommends gum arabic, which is available in small quantities at art supply stores, to "make the bubbles more elastic," and suggests adding a little strawberry juice to "make them red." A few drops of red food coloring will do the same trick.

Do You Hear What I Hear?

Here's a Victorian-era party game that's similar to blindman's bluff. Choose one person to be "it" and blindfold her. Give her the blindman's wand—a stick about 2 feet long. The other players then take turns grasping the other end. Each time a new player takes hold, the "blindman" is allowed to ask that player three questions, with the aim of recognizing the voice of the player who replies. Players try to disguise their voices as much as possible. If the player's identity is guessed, he assumes the blindfold and wand.

A Fun Waiting Game

■ Stuck in the car during a traffic jam, or waiting in line with friends at the movies? Try playing "Cupid's coming" to pass the time. Designate one person to go first. That person chooses a letter of the alphabet, for example, the letter *T*. The first player then announces to the player on his right, "Cupid's coming." The second asks, "How is he coming?" The first player responds with a word that begins with *T* and ends with *-ing*, such as *tumbling*. The game continues from player to player, through all the players, as long as each person can come up with real words beginning with the chosen letter and ending with *-ing*. The next round starts with a new letter.

Don't Say It!

■ Taboo is another simple word game. Choose a letter of the alphabet; the object of the game is to avoid using the chosen letter. Designate one player as "it." The other players then take turns asking "it" questions, which she has to answer without using the forbidden letter. For example, if the letter is *D*, a player might ask, "What type of animal barks?" If "it" answered "Dog," her turn would be over. But if "it" answered "Puppy," her turn would continue. A time limit for answers is appropriate—5 seconds, perhaps. In a more difficult version of the game, players who are "it" must answer the questions in complete sentences, which must not include the forbidden letter.

Team Up for Dumb Crambo

■ If you have a group of six or more, you can enjoy dumb crambo, a Victorian parlor game that is similar to charades. Divide into two teams. Team 2 leaves the room while Team 1 chooses a secret word, such as *sky*, and a clue word that rhymes with the chosen word, such as *tie*. When Team 2 reenters the room, it is instructed that the secret word rhymes with *tie*. Team 2 then begins to act out words it believes might be the secret

☞ OLD-TIME ODDITIES ☜

The Jump Scooter

LONG BEFORE Flexible Flyers or snowboards were available for wintertime fun, creative parents crafted toys for their kids out of the wooden barrels in which many household goods arrived from the store. "Jump scooters" helped entertain children through the long winters in Colonial New England. The scooter was a simple seat mounted on a wide barrel stave, with a short rope knotted to the front, with which a child could hang on for dear life. *The American Agriculturist* (1880) describes a slightly more stable version called the *slew:* two barrel staves laid on the snow parallel to each other, like skis, and fastened together with crosspieces, with a plank on top as a seat. "This is not an easy thing to ride, as there is nothing to hold on to," *The American Agriculturist* warns. "To a new hand, if the hill is steep, it is a jumper which will sometimes leave [the rider] behind."

word. As Team 2 portrays incorrect words, Team 1 hisses loudly to let them know they are off base. Team 2 keeps acting out different words until they silently "guess" the correct word. Depending on your energy level, everyone on the team can act out at once or take turns. Then the teams switch places, and the roles are reversed. All the charades-type rules apply—no talking for the actors, no touching real objects, and so forth.

Mix Up Your Party Guests

Party games can bring a staid party to life just as well now as they did back in the 1930s. Here are two classic mixer games to try at your next get-together.

Solve the puzzle. Before your guests arrive, cut shapes out of construction paper, such as various-sized circles, triangles, or squares, and then cut each shape into two interlocking puzzle pieces. Make just enough so there will be one piece for each guest. Mix all the pieces together in a basket. As each guest arrives, ask him or her to select one puzzle piece. When all the pieces have been drawn, instruct your guests to find their partner by comparing puzzle pieces until they find their match. The random mixing will help people introduce themselves to one another. To add an extra twist to this game, write a "fortune" on each shape before you cut it in two. Then your guests can enjoy discovering their joint fortune when they match up the puzzle pieces.

Famous couples. Another way to play this mixer is to write out famous quotations, such as "A penny saved is a penny earned," on pieces of paper and cut the quotations in half. Have guests work the room to match up their quote and then see which pair finishes first and also knows the name of the famous person who authored their quote. You can

OLD-FASHIONED FAVORITES

Ask Away . . . 20 Questions

THOUGH IT'S BECOME more of an expression when someone's being nosy—"What is this, 20 questions?"—the game that was so popular beginning in the mid-1800s is still worth playing, particularly on long car rides or any other time a group of people are trapped waiting. If you've forgotten the basic rules, here's how the Victorians played the game: One person thinks of a person, place, or thing, and the other players try to guess who or what it is by asking only questions that can be answered "yes" or "no." The game progresses, with the players posing questions in turn, until one player correctly guesses the object (or place or person) or until 20 questions have been asked. The proverbial "Is it bigger than a bread box" question might have to be updated to "Is it bigger than a laptop (or a shoe box)?" If you're rusty on the tactics, remember that you want to eliminate as many possibilities with one question as you can. Therefore, ask questions like "Does anyone in our family see it on a daily basis?" or "Is it a tropical color?" instead of "Does Dad like it?" or "Is it orange?"

also mix the group by having them match two names of a famous twosome such as Romeo and Juliet, Antony and Cleopatra, Tom and Jerry, or Popeye and Olive Oyl.

No matter what your method of mixing, your guests will have more fun if they mingle and interact with new people. Your party will be a great success, and who knows where the new friendships may lead.

Spice Up Your Summer with Picnic Games

■ Add energy to a picnic gathering on a warm summer evening with popular party games from the early 1900s. For example, use ribbon to tie clever riddles written on white cards to branches throughout your yard. On yellow cards, write the answers and tie them around the property as well. Have your guests take a riddle and search through your garden to match it with the correct answer. Another way to play this game is to use pictures of famous people and match them to clues about their identity.

Silly races can also be lots of fun. Try dumping a bunch of walnuts on the driveway and have your guests push them to a finish line using dowel rods. Or have your guests race with a ripe cherry balanced on the blade of a dull butter knife. If the cherry falls during the race, the contestant must pick it up using only the butter knife. No fingers, please!

CHAPTER 6

Holiday Celebrations
Yes, There Is a Santa Claus

Preparing for holidays can be as much fun as celebrating them. Get started early with the bevy of fun holiday tips in this chapter. From carving two jack-o'-lanterns from one pumpkin to crafting handmade Christmas tree ornaments, and from making an Easter bonnet to growing real Irish shamrocks for St. Patrick's Day, you'll love these old-time holiday traditions. Old-timers knew how to make the most of seasonal and household items. They also understood that some of the best times in life are simple occasions spent with family and friends celebrating an ordinary day with a homemade glass of lemonade. (Add fresh mint leaves for zip!) Enjoy every day as if it were a holiday.

Delightful Decorations

Hang the wreath! Wrap the gifts! Color the eggs! Make the centerpiece! Bring out that special tablecloth! Every holiday involves creating a beautiful atmosphere for celebrating. No matter how grand or how simple you like your celebrations to be, old-time holiday decorating tips can add warmth and charm to your holiday presentation, without costing a small fortune for fancy materials and big-name brands.

Old-Time Tips for Colorful Easter Eggs

■ Here are some helpful tips from a 1911 *New York Times* article that will help you dye and decorate more-beautiful colored

Easter eggs today. Keep in mind that you should never eat eggs after decorating the shells unless you're certain that all of the materials used while dying the eggs are nontoxic, including paints and any dyes from fabrics.

Check for cracks. Before you boil your eggs, look them over carefully and remove any that are cracked. Wash each egg with warm water to remove any soil.

Watercolor works best. Choose a few eggs with the smoothest shells to use for painting. Watercolors work best on eggs because they dry quickly.

Dye them with ribbon. Boil inexpensive cloth ribbon in a small pot of water. Submerge your egg into the pot, and it will absorb the color.

Color with calico. Wrap your egg in a colorful piece of cheap, figured cotton fabric and submerge it in boiling water. In some cases, the pattern of the fabric will appear on the egg.

Throw onions in the pot. Boil your eggs with the red skins of an onion to obtain a lovely red hue.

Try some blown eggs. For a delicate effect, carefully prick both ends of an egg with a coarse needle. The hole should be just large enough to allow the contents of the egg to come out. Blow gently to start and then blow hard and steady until the egg is empty. Rinse the egg with warm water and allow to dry. Blown eggs can be painted or dyed and hung on egg trees.

Add a candy surprise. After decorating a blown egg, you can gently make a hole big enough to fill it with small candies. (Make sure your egg is thoroughly washed clean and dry inside.) After filling, glue a small piece of paper over the hole to keep the candy inside.

Make funny egg animals. Paint, markers, glue, and miscellaneous items such as feathers, buttons, yarn, beads, and fabric can turn plain eggs into fun creatures that can serve as place cards, favors, or decorations. Use your imagination to create rabbits, owls, pigs, chickens, clowns, old ladies, or pretty lassies.

BIZARRE BUT TRUE

An 88-Year-Old Easter Egg Masterpiece!

YOU MAY HESITATE to spend a lot of time and effort decorating Easter eggs because you figure you will just be making them into egg salad or, even worse, throwing them away after a few days. But the truth is that if you like the way you decorate an Easter egg (and it isn't cracked), you can keep it! Recycling your "egg-ceptional" decorations will save you time and money. And won't it be fun to display your favorite creations year after year?

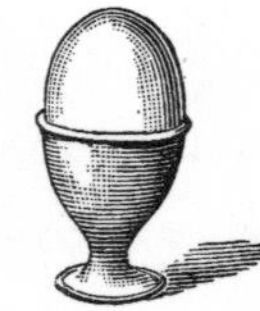

A 1939 *New York Times* article reported that Mrs. Ersil Stewart, of Linton, Indiana, showed visitors an Easter egg that had been dyed in 1851 by her grandmother, Clarissa Barb. The egg had been boiled in onion peel to dye it, and designs had been gently scratched on the shell with a pocketknife. Mrs. Barb was so pleased with her egg that she asked her family to pass it from generation to generation for 100 years. Mrs. Stewart kept the then 88-year-old egg wrapped in muslin in a tin can and carefully put it on display each Easter.

It would be interesting to know where that egg is today. Just think where your Easter eggs might be in 100 years!

Cozy Up Your Easter Eggs

CHILDREN will love helping you make a classic parade of Easter hens for the breakfast table. And you can tell them that their great-grandparents might have done the same thing, because this little project dates back to 1908! It's easy to whip up little hen cozies (like mini tea cozies) following directions from a *New York Times* article. You'll place the finished cozies on top of your soft-boiled eggs. This is a sure way to make your family smile on Easter morning, and to keep the eggs warm while you finish the last-minute breakfast preparations.

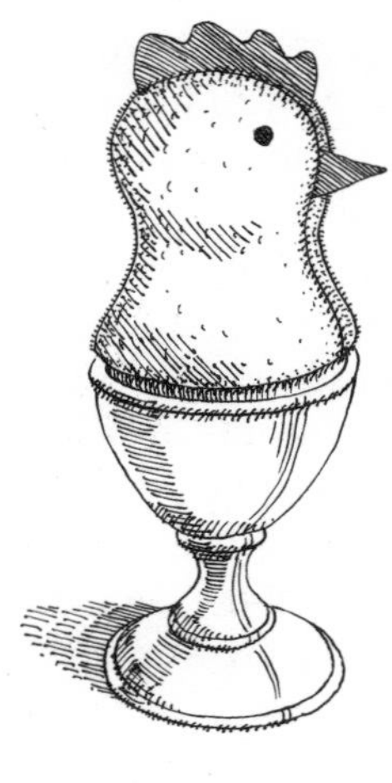

You will need:

Scissors
Two pieces of thin white flannel per hen (recycled from an old sheet or nightgown)
Needle
White and red thread
Red felt
Black permanent marker

Step 1. For each cozy, cut two pieces of flannel into the size and shape of the head and neck of a hen. (Make each piece about 2 inches wide × 3 inches high.)

Step 2. Whipstitch the two pieces of flannel around the edges, leaving the bottom edge open. Use white thread for this.

Step 3. Cut a little red comb and beak for each cozy.

Step 4. Use red thread to tack one comb and beak onto each hen.

Step 5. Draw two eyes on each hen.

Put the Decoration Back in Decoration Day

Re-create the original spirit of the holiday we call Memorial Day by making simple patriotic decorations. Memorial Day was originally called Decoration Day, and the holiday traces back to the early 1860s, when two daughters of a Michigan army chaplain "decorated" a Civil War soldier's grave with spring flowers. Over the years, Memorial Day evolved into a day to honor all fallen veterans. Some families also made it a day to visit the graves of deceased loved ones. It's easy to make traditional floral decorations like those from the Civil War era. All you need are some spring flowers (real or silk), small American flags, and several pieces of red, white, and blue ribbon. First, arrange the flowers into bouquets, each one including an American flag. Gather the flower stems together with a rubber band, if you like. Then tie each bouquet with a bow of colored ribbons. Hang one Decoration Day bouquet on your front door and take the rest to the graves of veterans, or give them to a local veterans' organization to be used to honor the men and women who defended our country.

Half a Pumpkin Is as Good as a Whole

For double decorative value from your Halloween pumpkins, try a trick from *The Butterick Book of Recipes and Household Hints* (1927) and carve *two* faces in one pumpkin. Just cut the pumpkin in half through the center cleanly, scoop out the pulp and seeds, and carve a face in each half. When your jack-o'-lanterns are finished, use pushpins or thumbtacks to attach a piece of cardboard for the back and insert a small flashlight or glow stick in each. Perch them at an angle on stairs or on a table in the corner of a room, and no one will be the wiser.

OLD-TIME HUMOR

Running Wild!

AT THE ANNUAL Halloween harvest dance held at the Field Club in Greenwich, Connecticut, on October 28, 1928, costumed society guests were entertained on the dance floor by the intentional release of crates of live pigs. Live turkeys also fluttered among dancers, much to the merriment of the guests. (But how did the Field Club smell after that party?)

Halloween "Special Effects" for Pennies

From the era before big-budget special effects, try this grab bag of simple, inexpensive tricks for creating a spooky ambience for a Halloween party.

Dim the lights. Hollow out several small pumpkins and decorative squashes and set a candle stub inside each one (leave these little lanterns uncovered). Then turn off most of your house lights. You can carve faces if you have time, but even uncarved jack-o'-lanterns offer an eerie glow.

Jack jump over the applestick. For candleholders that suit the season, use an apple corer to remove just half the core from several apples. Wedge a candle tightly into each apple and set your unique candlesticks around the house in locations where they won't be knocked over by an errant elbow or a running child. Put a coaster or plastic dish under each apple to trap any wax that may drip down.

Hang "spiderwebs." Tie small feathers (available by the bag at craft stores) onto lengths of thread or thin string, and use tape to suspend the threads from the ceiling, with the feathers at head height. As your guests circulate, the feathers will brush up against their faces and necks like spiders' webs tickling them. Eek!

Startle them with sound. At old-time Halloween parties, sound effects had to be improvised—footsteps on creaking stairs, doors opening and closing, and an occasional blood-curdling scream. You now have the convenience of buying a tape or CD of Halloween sounds to turn on at just the right moment to make your guests jump.

From Centerpiece to Soup

■ For a classic seasonal Thanksgiving centerpiece that you can turn into a hearty meal a day or two later, try this design featured in a 1932 issue of the *Ladies' Home Journal*. The *Journal* recommends using "golden fruits and vegetables," including a small pumpkin, "red and yellow corn in their husks and a few handsome green peppers," apples, oranges, even a rainbow of autumn leaves, to make a bountiful table display. Have fun and be creative by including "well-shaped, scrubbed carrots." Place the pumpkin in the center of your table and arrange the other fruits and vegetables around it. Set them up so that contrasting colors, shapes, and textures stand out. When you're ready to dismantle the centerpiece, use it to whip up a vegetable soup or a fruit cobbler!

One Centerpiece Makes All Places Holly Jolly

■ Next time it's your turn to host the crowd for a Christmas meal, put everyone in the holiday spirit and start a new holiday tradition based on a holly centerpiece—with a twist. Load a bowl or vase with holly branches (no taller than 15 inches so people can still see each other to talk across the table). Anchor red ribbons beneath the centerpiece and run one to each place card, where you pin a "small sprig of green for each person to wear" alongside the name, suggests Olive Hyde Foster in *Housekeeping, Cookery and Sewing for Little Girls* (1925). The radiating centerpiece unites the look of the table, and guests can have fun deciding where to attach their bit of holly—lapel, hair, shoe, snowman?

PEARLS OF WISDOM

"It is not the woman who has the most money, but the one who can make her guests 'take notice,' who is the most attractive hostess."

The New York Times (OCTOBER 21, 1900)

Victorian Elegance on a Modern-Day Schedule

■ More tree than ornaments? Don't sacrifice elegance to fill those gaps when with a few minutes of effort, you can give the tree an authentic Victorian touch—and maybe use up some wallpaper scraps while you're at it. Simply fold 4-inch squares of wallpaper into accordion pleats and staple them about ½ inch from one end to form small fans. Tie the bottoms with colorful ribbon and hang the fans from the tree. If you want to get fancy, hot-glue ribbon or lace on one of the paper edges before folding, or tie the fans with gold string. Prince Albert could ask for no better.

Pretty Peanutty Tree Decorations

HERE'S A QUICK, easy Christmas tree decoration from the turn of the last century. In 1901, *The Delineator* magazine showed readers how to turn peanuts and tissue paper into decorations that look good enough to eat. In fact, you may find that they disappear from the tree before Christmas Day arrives!

You will need:

Scissors
Tissue paper in various colors
Spool of colored string or yarn
1-pound bag of freshly roasted peanuts in their shells

Step 1. Cut the tissue paper into rectangles that measure about 2 inches × 5 inches.

Step 2. Cut the narrow ends of the paper rectangles into fringe as shown at right.

Step 3. Cut several lengths of string or yarn 18 to 24 inches long.

Step 4. Roll a peanut up in a paper rectangle and tie one end of a piece of string or yarn around the center of the peanut. Twist the fringed ends of the paper together tightly.

Step 5. Wrap another peanut and secure it to the same piece of string, about 3 inches away from the first peanut.

Step 6. Repeat Step 5 until you complete a string. (You can use between three and six peanuts per string.) Be sure there's enough string left at the end to make a loop, so that you can hang the decoration from a limb of the tree.

Step 7. Repeat the steps above until you've used up all your peanuts (snacking while you work is definitely allowed!)

Step 8. Hang the decorations at varying heights around your tree.

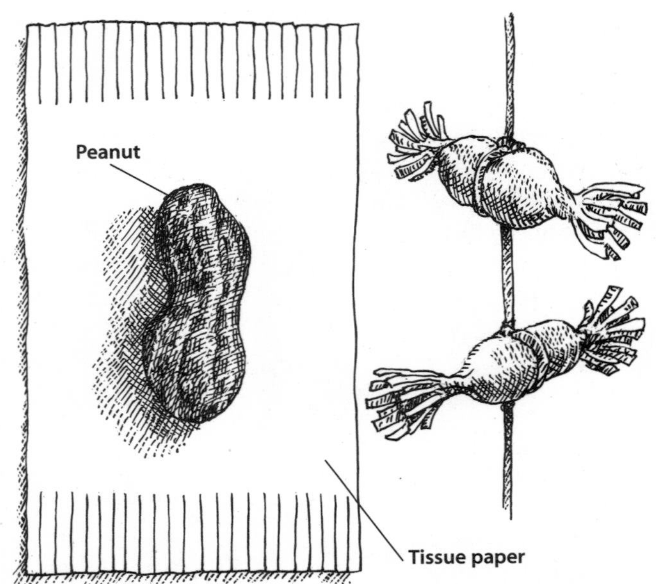

■ It's fun to invite any friends or neighbors who stop by during the holiday season to take a decoration with them as a souvenir (or healthy snack for their drive home). And if some of your peanut decorations still remain by the time you take down your Christmas tree, poke a few holes in the tissue paper and hang the strings on a tree outside. The squirrels and birds will love them!

From Ornaments to Applesauce

■ Ever considered disposable Christmas ornaments to avoid the hassles of packing and unpacking each year? If so, borrow a page from the junior homemakers of the 1920s. "Rosy apples will look pretty swung from the branches with [narrow] ribbon," writes Olive Hyde Foster in *Housekeeping, Cookery and Sewing for Little Girls* (1925). To execute this idea, choose shiny, smallish red apples and make sure they have stems. For each, center an 18-inch piece of narrow cloth ribbon or raffia at the base of the stem and tie a double knot. Then use the two ribbon tails (which should be about 8 inches long) to tie the apple about 3 inches from the end of a branch with a double knot and a bow. It should dangle down some 2 or 3 inches like any other ornament. That's all you do—the apples need no further adornment. When the tree comes down, as long as the apples haven't turned mushy, you can eat them or turn them into applesauce or Waldorf salad. As for the ribbon or raffia, it can go back in the craft supplies box or out with the recycling.

My Tree Is Like a Red, Red Rosebush

To simplify your Christmas decorating, try the specialty of the Victorian era—a tabletop Christmas tree—instead of that floor-to-ceiling extravaganza. Or use a tabletop tree in addition to your full-size tree to display your excess ornaments, in the den or on a buffet table.

To keep the Victorian theme going and end up with some fine dried flowers for future use, decorate the branches with live roses. "The Victorians favored dark red roses, putting them on the tree fresh and letting them dry out as the season wore on," says Linda Scimonelli, a floral and interior designer from Powell, Tennessee. You can do the same with cash-and-carry red roses from the florist or grocer. "Strip the leaves from the stems and cut the stems to about 4 or 5 inches," advises Linda. "Then clip each stem to a tree branch, using a bobby pin or paper clip. The blooms should sit on the branches and look like they're growing from the evergreen tree. They still look great after they dry, too."

☞ OLD-TIME ODDITIES ☜

Bubble Lights

HAVE YOU EVER put old-fashioned bubble lights on your Christmas tree? Benjamin Franklin actually discovered the theory behind the fascinating bubble lights when he demonstrated sealed glass tubes with bubbling liquid inside. The first patent for bubble lights was in 1936, and the first commercial sale of bubble lights for Christmas trees was in 1946. Multicolored bubbling lights make your Christmas tree look alive with motion and color. Comb shops and catalogs for reproduction sets.

"Wrap" Your Tree with Foil Ornaments

OUR GREAT-GRANDPARENTS had plenty of creative notions for making something pretty and fun out of whatever they had on hand. Here's an example: Christmas tree ornaments consisting of nothing but string and decorative foil.

You will need:

Scissors
Decorative foil or florist's foil
Strong, coarse string

Step 1. Cut three pieces of decorative foil of about the same length (6 to 12 inches long works well).

Step 2. Stack the pieces of foil and make crosswise cuts about ½ inch apart, leaving a 1-or 2-inch margin along the far edge of the stack, as shown in the illustration.

Step 3. Cut a piece of string a few inches longer than the foil and twist the foil fringe repeatedly around the string. Fluff the fringes as you work.

Step 4. Repeat Steps 1–3 until you have a bunch of these foil beauties. Your tree will sparkle without electricity!

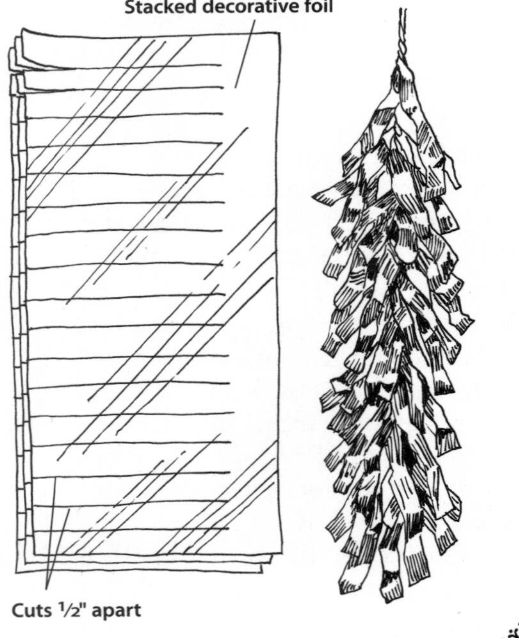

New Life for Old Christmas Cards

Many Christmas cards are works of art, but sadly, most end up in the trash by mid-January. Here are three ways that you can continue to enjoy your favorite Christmas cards after the holidays.

Frame them. The Victorians often turned Christmas cards into lovely gifts by framing them before sending them, explained *Harper's Bazar* in 1881. By doing the same, you can preserve your greeting for many years. Buy inexpensive picture frames at discount stores and yard sales throughout the year, and save them for Christmas.

Make tree ornaments. Collect pretty fringes and trims, and use white glue to fasten beautiful borders around the edges of your cards. (Save ribbons and trim from gifts you receive, and watch for clearance sales at local craft and fabric stores.) Punch a hole through the top of each card, and thread ribbon through it for hanging, or simply glue the ribbon in place. Voilà—you've created a decorative treasure. Present your Christmas cards to your recipients as gifts they can hang on a wall or on the Christmas tree. Your homemade gift will become part of their Christmas tradition.

Make do-it-yourself gift tags. Another use for old Christmas cards is to recycle them into pretty Christmas gift tags. Cut the cards into any shape you like. Trim around a bell or wreath, or just cut star or Christmas tree shapes out of patterned or colored backgrounds. Cut freehand, or trace Christmas cookie cutters as a guide. You can make your tags with or without a fold. Write your gift recipient's name with a calligraphy pen, and use a hole punch to attach a colorful ribbon for tying the tag to your package.

Poinsettias Lend Harmless Holiday Beauty

▪ Poinsettias are a holiday plant with a century-long history. "Nothing will be prettier for a holiday table decoration than the poinsettia," wrote a *New York Times* columnist in 1908. And turn-of-the-century Christmas-season brides chose poinsettias as wedding decorations. If you love these red, white, or pink beauties but hesitate to bring one home because you've heard that poinsettias are poisonous to pets, worry no longer. Join this long-standing holiday tradition, because poinsettias pose *no* danger to pets, say experts at the University of Pennsylvania School of Veterinary Medicine, in Philadelphia.

Holiday Treats

What's a holiday without some traditional yummy old-time food? Many of the best holiday memories come from the kitchen. Is there anything better than the smell of a Thanksgiving turkey roasting or the taste of a Christmas cookie fresh from the oven? Here are some old-fashioned recipes, ideas, and cooking techniques that you can use to create happy holiday memories for your family and friends.

A Hint of Mint for Holiday Dinners

▪ To add a special touch to your next Passover or Easter dinner, serve authentic homemade mint jelly with your roast lamb rather than a store-bought jelly. Mint complements the lamb nicely and fills the house with a fresh scent of spring.

Try this recipe for mint jelly, adapted from *The New American Cook Book,* by Lily Haxworth Wallace (1949).

1 cup finely chopped fresh mint
¼ cup plus ⅔ cup sugar
1 cup apple juice
Green food coloring (vegetable coloring, if possible)

Combine the mint with the ¼ cup sugar and ¼ cup water and let stand for several hours or overnight. Bring to a boil; then strain and set aside. Combine the remaining ⅔ cup sugar and the apple juice. Cook and test for jelly. When the jellying point is reached, add the food coloring and the prepared mint juice (1 or 2 tablespoons for each quart apple juice).

Homemade Halloween Doughnuts

DOUGHNUTS AND APPLE CIDER are a great Halloween tradition. These days, you can pick up doughnuts at any of several chain stores, but have you ever made your own doughnuts at home? It's a fun project for an October day, and there's nothing like the smell of fresh doughnuts in your kitchen. Try this recipe, adapted from *The Art of Cooking and Serving*, by Sarah Field Splint (1930). Yum!

- 1/3 cup sugar
- 1 1/2 tablespoons shortening
- 1 egg, well beaten
- 1/3 cup milk
- 2 cups flour
- 2 teaspoons baking powder
- 1/8 teaspoon ground cinnamon
- 1/8 teaspoon ground cloves
- 1/16 teaspoon ground mace
- 1/2 teaspoon salt
- Oil or shortening for frying
- Confectioners' sugar
- Ground cinnamon

Cream the sugar and 1½ tablespoons shortening together. Add the egg and milk, and mix well. In a separate bowl, mix and sift the flour, baking powder, cinnamon, cloves, mace, and salt. Add to the first mixture and mix thoroughly. Turn out onto a slightly floured board and roll to a ½-inch thickness. Cut with a doughnut cutter or knife, and fry in deep, hot oil or shortening until a delicate brown. Drain on paper towels. Sprinkle with confectioners' sugar and/or cinnamon before serving. Makes 24 doughnuts.

For extra flavor in your doughnuts, try this tip from *2,000 Useful Facts about Food* (1941): Place a few whole cloves or a stick of cinnamon in the fat while frying the doughnuts.

Basting Sauce Saves Time

■ If you'd rather not fuss with making mint jelly, you can still enjoy the hint of mint with your roast lamb dinner. Just baste your roast lamb with homemade mint sauce. Combine ¾ cup water, ¼ cup vinegar, 2 tablespoons sugar, ¼ cup chopped fresh mint, and a few drops of lemon juice. Cook on low heat for about 2 hours before using for basting.

Remember this basting tip, too: Stab the roast in several spots with an ice pick or thin, sharp knife before cooking. This will allow the basting liquid—and its flavor—to penetrate the meat even more.

Simple Stuffing Substitute

■ In the holiday grocery-store rush, if you neglected to buy that handy stuffing mix or those preseasoned dry bread cubes, try this cracker crumb stuffing recommended by the home economists writing for *The Woman's Institute Library of Cookery* (1928).

Moisten 3 cups of cracker crumbs with hot milk or water until they are quite soft. Brown 1 small onion, chopped, in ⅓ cup butter, and pour over the crackers. Season with ½ teaspoon salt, ¼ teaspoon powdered sage, and ¼ teaspoon pepper. Mix thoroughly.

These days, fear of foodborne illnesses keeps us from cooking stuffing in the bird, but this mixture can be used to stuff mushrooms, shrimp, or pork tenderloin. Or cook the stuffing alongside the turkey or chicken in a lightly greased baking dish during the last 45 minutes of baking. If you want that baked-in-the-bird flavor, be sure to baste it a couple of times during cooking with a tablespoon of turkey or chicken juices.

Thank Goodness for Thanksgiving Tomatoes

According to *The Butterick Book of Recipes and Household Helps* (1927), if you have unblemished green tomatoes in your garden in late September or early October, you should save them for a special Thanksgiving treat. Wrap each green tomato by itself in tissue paper and arrange them on a dry board in a cool place. The tomatoes will ripen so gradually that they will be ready for slicing just in time for your Thanksgiving dinner!

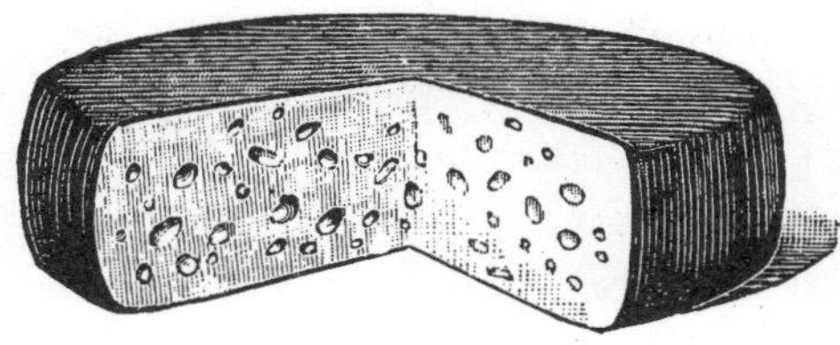

Cheesy Piecrust Party Treat

When you're making homemade pies for the holidays, make a little extra crust for a tasty appetizer that dates back 100 years. *The Inglenook Cook Book* (1906), a compilation of recipes contributed by sisters of the Church of the Brethren, offers these directions for making cheese straws, a "dainty dish and a good way to use left-over pie crust."

"Roll out the pastry to ¼ inch in thickness, sprinkle thickly ½ of it with grated cheese and a dash of salt, fold over the other half, press the edges together, roll out, and sprinkle with cheese as before. Fold again, and roll ¼ inch thick. Cut into strips as straw-like as possible" and about 3 inches long. Form several of the straws into circles. Leave the other straws straight and bake all about 8 minutes in a 400°F oven. To serve, thread several cheese straws through each ring and arrange on a plate.

Today's cooks have lots of cheeses to choose from, says Rob Stanford, a chef at the Tampa Yacht Club, in Florida. "Make sure you use something very flavorful, like extra-sharp Cheddar, Parmesan, Romano, or even hot pepper cheese," he says. "And if you're like me and the only time you make pastry anymore is when you're having a big family dinner, these are a great idea to pass around as appetizers. You might even want to make extra dough just for the cheese straws."

A Pineapple "Sugarplum" Tree

A pineapple can supply both the centerpiece and the hors d'oeuvres for an informal Christmastime event with this clever idea from *500 Snacks, Bright Ideas for Entertaining* (1940). All you need are a large jar of maraschino cherries, one large pineapple, and some bacon. First, rinse and drain the cherries so they won't be too sticky. Cut the top off the pineapple about 1 inch below the base of the leaves. Wash the leafy top thoroughly and wipe it dry. Set the pineapple top in the center of a large serving plate. Press the leaves outward, curving them to represent branches of a tree, and stick the cherries on the ends of the leaves. (If you prefer, use multicolored gumdrops instead of cherries.)

Now, make some pineapple hors d'oeuvres. Cut the fresh pineapple into 1-inch chunks. Wrap each chunk in bacon, secure with a toothpick, and broil until the bacon is cooked. Or just make sweet fruit skewers with chunks of pineapple and maraschino cherries.

Plum Pudding—Some Things Are Just Worth the Trouble!

VICTORIAN COOKS went to a lot of trouble to make their famous Christmas plum pudding. Remember Mrs. Cratchit fussing over her pudding in Dickens's *A Christmas Carol*? "In half a minute Mrs. Cratchit entered—flushed, but smiling proudly—with the pudding, like a speckled cannon-ball, so hard and firm, blazing in half of half-a-quartern of ignited brandy, and bedight with Christmas holly into the top."

A plum pudding recipe from *Godey's Lady's Book* (1860) illustrates the enormous amount of work that Mrs. Cratchit must have gone through to serve her pudding. The *Godey's* pudding contained 1 pound raisins (ground with a stone), 1 pound currants (washed and picked), 1 pound fresh beef suet (chopped very small), 2 ounces sweet almonds (blanched and chopped small or pounded), 1 ounce bitter almonds (blanched and chopped small or pounded), 1 pound flour (sifted), 1 pound bread crumbs (soaked in milk, then squeezed dry and stirred with a spoon until reduced to a mash, before it is mixed with the flour), 2 ounces preserved citron (cut into small pieces), 2 ounces preserved orange (cut into small pieces), 2 ounces preserved lemon peel (cut into small pieces), 1 ounce mixed spice, ¼ pound moist sugar, 2 wineglassfuls of brandy, milk as needed to moisten the bread crumbs and to adjust the pudding's consistency, and confectioners' sugar. (Just getting all of the ingredients together would tire most modern-day cooks!)

The recipe involves pouring the brandy over the fruit and allowing it to stand for 3 or 4 hours before the pudding is made, stirring it occasionally. Then, after a lot of mixing and stirring and beating of the rest of the ingredients in three different bowls, everything is combined. Then the pudding must be tied in a cloth and boiled constantly for 5 hours. When done, the pudding is turned out onto a dish, confectioners' sugar is sifted over the top, and it is served with wine sauce in a boat, and some poured round the pudding. Whew! After making this, Mrs. Cratchit must have needed a long winter's nap!

Double Duty for Jellied Cranberries

Cranberry jelly is a holiday classic, and this simple recipe from *The Butterick Book of Recipes and Household Helps* (1927) is relaxing to prepare and makes your home smell wonderfully good. Serve it at Christmas dinner and make extra to give as Christmas gifts for neighbors, teachers, and friends.

Pick over and wash 1 quart fresh cranberries and set them aside. Combine 2 cups sugar and 1 cup water in a saucepan and heat it until it boils slowly. Carefully drop the cranberries into the boiling syrup and cook until tender. When finished, the cranberries will have a transparent look. Using a washed and sterilized ladle, dip out the portion you want for serving with your holiday dinner and set it aside to cool.

As for the rest, pour the jellied cranberries and syrup into hot, sterilized half-pint canning jars. (Allow 2 inches headspace at the top.) Prepare the jar lids according to the manufacturer's directions. *Caution:* Be sure to consult an up-to-date reference guide and follow all safety precautions whenever you are doing home canning or jelly making.

Put your fresh-eating portion into the refrigerator after it has cooled. And once your jelly jars cool down, wrap the top of each one with a circle of pretty cloth or fancy paper. Tie it in place with a ribbon and add a miniature pinecone, a sprig of holly, or a cinnamon stick to make elegant, tasty gifts.

One-Egg Birthday Cake Saves the Day

At the last minute, you remember that it's your neighbor's (or your husband's) birthday. You want to whip up a homemade cake on the spot, but you have only one egg in the refrigerator. No problem! This cake recipe, adapted from the Depression-era pamphlet *Budgets to Make the Best Use of Your Food Dollar* (1937), requires only one egg.

- 1/4 cup shortening
- 1/2 cup sugar
- 1 egg
- 1 2/3 cups flour
- 2 1/2 teaspoons baking powder
- 1/4 teaspoon salt
- 1/2 cup milk
- 1/2 teaspoon vanilla extract

Preheat the oven to 350°F. Grease and flour a 9-inch round baking pan or an 8-inch square baking pan. In a medium-size mixing bowl, cream the shortening and mix in ¼ cup of the sugar. In a separate bowl, beat the egg, and then mix in the remaining ¼ cup sugar. Add the egg mixture to the shortening mixture and combine. In a small bowl, sift the flour, baking powder, and salt, and add alternately with the milk to the first mixture. Add the vanilla. Pour the batter into the pan and bake at 350°F for 25 to 30 minutes, or until a toothpick inserted into the center comes out clean. Decorate with your favorite homemade or canned frosting. (If you have two eggs, you can double the recipe and make two layers!)

When Eggs Are Easily Available . . .

Amaze your family and friends with a delectable egg-rich cake the next time you're hosting a birthday party or other family celebration. Lorraine Kiefer of Triple Oaks Nursery, in Franklinville, New Jersey, recalls that her mother made this delicious 11-yolk cake for all family birthdays. "This cake has been a family favorite for more than 70 years," Lorraine says. "It was made for family weddings, first communions, confirmations, and homecomings. We used the extra egg whites to make an angel food cake or to top cream pies. To this day, this cake is made for special days and birthdays. My aunt, who is eighty-seven, has promised my son, Joe, that when he marries she will make a small wedding cake for him from this recipe."

Here's the recipe for the Keifer family's time-honored celebration cake with Italian cream frosting.

1 tablespoon flour
1 cup cold milk
2¼ cups cake flour
2 teaspoons fresh baking powder
11 egg yolks
2 cups sugar
1 cup scalded milk, cooled
1 teaspoon vanilla extract
Two ¼ pound sticks of butter (no substitutes)
½ cup shortening
1 cup sugar
1 teaspoon vanilla extract

Start preparation of the frosting in advance by mixing the flour into the cold milk with a wire whisk. Cook the mixture in a microwave or double boiler, stirring often, until thickened. Refrigerate overnight or for at least 6 hours.

When you are ready to prepare the cake batter, preheat the oven to 350°F. Grease and flour two 10-by-10-inch baking pans (or, if you prefer, a sheet pan or two deep 9-inch pans). Sift together the cake flour and baking powder, and set it aside. Cream the egg yolks and 2 cups sugar until light and fluffy. Add the scalded milk and 1 teaspoon vanilla. Stir

Clever Cuts Keep Cake Fresh

BEFORE YOU CUT the birthday cake, ask yourself this: Will you have a lot of cake left over? If so, borrow a page from *Any One Can Bake* (1927), and cut *flat* slices rather than wedges from a round layer cake, removing the desired number of slices from the center of the cake. What you'll have left is two equal half-ovals of cake. "Push the two remaining pieces close together like a whole cake, and this will keep it moist and soft for several days." The same principle works for a rectangular sheet cake. Cut pieces from the center portion of the cake. Push the remaining outside portions together to form one smaller rectangle.

in the flour mixture and 1 stick of butter and blend with a spatula or wooden spoon. Do not overbeat. Pour the batter into the pans and bake at 350°F for 25 minutes, or until a toothpick inserted into the center comes out clean. While the cake cools, finish preparing the frosting. Beat 1 stick of butter, the shortening, and 1 cup sugar until very light and fluffy. Let sit for 30 minutes or so, add 1 teaspoon vanilla and the chilled milk-flour mixture (which will be very thick when you remove it from the refrigerator), and continue to beat well. When the cake is fully cooled, apply the frosting.

Garbage Pail Punch

■ At Fourth of July picnics in the early 1900s, a popular beverage was garbage pail punch. The picnic hosts pulled out a (well-cleaned) garbage pail, and everyone brought along their favorite drink and poured it into the pail. The result was a punch that was never the same twice! If you'd like to revive this tradition, but don't want to spend time arduously scrubbing out a garbage can, line the can with a jumbo-size plastic liner instead (double it up to safeguard against leaks).

Happy Holiday Traditions

Holiday traditions bind family and friends together through the comfort of rituals shared year after year—whether it's a special picnic potato salad recipe, the smell of glazed ham roasting, or the old family star that sits on top of the Christmas tree. Here are some practical and fun holiday traditions that you can share and enjoy with the ones you love.

OLD-FASHIONED FAVORITES

Refreshing Lemonade for Picnics and Parties

There's nothing like real lemonade on a hot summer day. This recipe from Irma S. Rombauer's *Streamlined Cooking* (1939) will help make your Fourth of July celebration a day to remember. Begin by boiling 1 cup water with 1 to 2 tablespoons sugar and a few grains of salt. Boil for 2 minutes, and then chill the syrup. Stir in 1½ tablespoons freshly squeezed lemon juice. Add ice and dilute with water to taste.

You can combine orange, pineapple, white grape, raspberry, loganberry, or other fruit juices with the lemonade, or mix it with chilled tea. The combinations are endless. And for added zip, put in a few fresh mint leaves.

Start the New Year with an Old Friend

■ Here's a New Year's resolution you'll be sure to keep, because you'll do it right on New Year's Day. Try the old-time "Knickerbocker custom" of renewing friendships at the turn of the year. *Peterson's Magazine* (1873) describes the Knickerbocker custom of making visits from house to house on New Year's Day for "the renewal of forgotten friendships, the forgiveness of injuries, the burial of old feuds." To prepare for your own Knickerbocker ritual, on the day after Thanksgiving, jot down a list of the friends and relatives whom you haven't been in touch with for a while. Then make a plan to reconnect with some of these special people on New Year's Day. Schedule a visit with old friends or relatives, or just look up the telephone numbers and take time for some ear-to-ear visits. Or set aside an hour or two for some chatty, affectionate e-mail exchanges. It's a sure way to start your year with a smile.

Spark Passion with Poetry on Valentine's Day

Do you want to wow your valentine this year? Forget store-bought valentines, and make your own special poetic Valentine's Day card. It will be sure to outshine the off-the-rack messages.

The Victorians understood that poetry is truly the language of love. Old-time magazines and newspapers were filled with poetry throughout the year to delight their readers. The following stanza is part of the passionate Valentine's Day poem "A Valentine," by Sir John Suckling, which appeared in *Godey's Magazine and Lady's Book* in February 1895.

Why should two hearts in
one breast lie,
And yet not lodge together?
Oh Love! Where is thy sympathy
If thus our hearts thou sever.

Follow Sir John's lead and write your own original poem, or call upon famous poets from long ago to help you express your sentiments.

Try a verse from Elizabeth Barrett Browning's *Sonnets from the Portuguese,* the sonnets of William Shakespeare, or John Keats's "Ode on a Grecian Urn."

After you write or find the perfect poetic message to tell your valentine how you feel, take some time to present it beautifully. Make an old-fashioned Valentine's Day card using sturdy red and white construction paper, white glue, and pieces of lace. Use a calligraphy pen to neatly write your poem. Or, if you'd rather put a modern spin on this old-fashioned approach to valentines, read your poem into a tape recorder and present your valentine with the tape tied up with a red bow.

Another Way to Send Your Love

If artwork isn't your strong suit, making a homemade Valentine's Day card may seem more like a chore than a happy expression of your love. Don't worry, there's an alternate route for sending Valentine's Day sentiments, as suggested in *Godey's Lady's Book* (February 1850): "Those who [do] not choose to write their own missives on the important fourteenth, would show their good taste by sending a beautiful book (with the sentiment or stanza they wished to make significant, underscored), rather than a fantastically flowered and printed sheet of paper, purporting to be a Valentine." Sounds like a great idea! Most bookstores feature books of love poetry or sentimental stories in honor of Valentine's Day. Enjoy browsing and picking out just the right book for your loved one. If you'd prefer not to mar the book by underlining the significant passages, make the fabric shop the second stop on your Valentine's Day shopping trip. Buy a yard of lace trim or red satin ribbon. Cut pieces 1 inch wide and the right length to fit the book. Slip these bookmarks between the pages you particularly wish your love to read.

Grow Shamrocks for St. Patrick

FOR AN OLD-FASHIONED St. Patrick's Day decoration, try growing shamrocks. It's an easy, fun project, but takes a little advance planning. Follow this advice from garden writer Lorraine Kiefer, who owns Triple Oaks Nursery, in Franklinville, New Jersey. Lorraine notes, "The shamrock most often seen at St. Patrick's Day is usually a sensitive houseplant called oxalis. In most cases, they only do well indoors." Shamrocks are native to the British Isles, and the plants have long been associated with St. Patrick's Day. It is said that St. Patrick, who died on March 17 more than 1,500 years ago, used the three leaves and the stem of a shamrock to explain the Christian doctrine of the Holy Trinity to the Celts.

Shamrocks grow from tubers. Lorraine advises ordering them from a mail-order catalog or local nursery in late October or November.

You will need:

- 4-inch flowerpot with a drainage hole
- Good-quality potting soil, such as ProMix
- About 10 oxalis tubers
- An organic plant food, such as fish emulsion or a liquid compost product

Step 1. Fill the pot with the potting soil, and plant the tubers in the pot. Add water until you see it running out the bottom. (You can add organic fertilizer for this initial feeding, following the label instructions.)

Step 2. Place your pot in a sunny spot that is fairly cool. "Usually near a window is a good choice," Lorraine notes. "Shamrocks don't like to be near a woodstove or fireplace, or a constantly blowing heater vent. Their favorite temperature is about sixty-five degrees. They aren't fussy about humidity."

Step 3. Water your shamrocks twice a week when conditions are dry, but don't overwater. "Too much water will cause the stems to become lanky," Lorraine says.

Step 4. Feed the plant once a week from February to August.

■ If your shamrock is happy, it will flower with either pink or, more commonly, white blooms. Although some shamrocks can grow in direct sunlight if watered very well, most don't like extreme conditions, such as excessive heat, dryness, or cold, and will probably go dormant. A dormant shamrock will dry up and look like it's dead. But never fear, shamrocks will usually come back to life when conditions become more favorable. According to Lorraine, "Once we put our shamrocks out on the deck, where it was very hot and sunny, and they just dried up. We thought they were dead, so we dumped them onto our shady compost pile. The next thing we knew, we had shamrocks sprouting in the compost pile."

Have a Pink Holiday Tea Party

Think pink! What a great way to celebrate Mother's Day, Easter, Valentine's Day, or a baby or bridal shower. Send each guest an invitation written on pink paper. Ask them all to wear something pink to the party.

Then adorn your home with pink crepe paper, balloons, ribbons, and vases and pots of pink tulips (or roses or carnations). Use pink dishes and tablecloths, if you have them. This is definitely an idea for a ladies-only get-together!

Take a tip from *Godey's Magazine and Lady's Book* (1896), and as each guest arrives, present her with a scarf of pink chiffon to "fling about her neck." (Buy a partial bolt of pink fabric and cut out pieces approximately 15 inches by 36 inches. Hem the edges on a sewing machine, or just cut them with pinking shears.)

Serve a traditional tea menu of tea sandwiches, scones, fruit, and sweets. Include as many pink foods as possible, such as raspberry cream cheese tea sandwiches, smoked salmon tea sandwiches, strawberry shortcake, heart-shaped cookies with pink icing, pink lemonade or champagne, cherry tarts, and strawberries.

Make sure that you also serve your guests a proper cup of hot tea by following these rules from *2,000 Useful Facts about Food* (1941):

- Have all equipment perfectly clean.
- Use freshly drawn water.
- Measure the water and tea with standard measuring equipment.
- Have the water boiling vigorously before pouring it into the teapot.
- Scald the teapot (pour a small amount of boiling water into it, swish it around, and then dump the water out).
- Place the tea leaves in the teapot (if the tea is not already in bags, use an infuser), fill the pot with boiling water, and steep for the desired length of time. Remove the tea leaves from the water and serve immediately.
- Provide a second pot of freshly boiled water to weaken tea for those who do not like it strong.
- Do not use tea leaves more than once.

TRASH OR TREASURE

Eggshell Bulb Pots

Reusing eggshells from Easter baking is a practice that dates back generations in the family of Lorraine Kiefer of Triple Oaks Nursery, in Franklinville, New Jersey. When Lorraine's family prepared Easter treats, they would gently tap the end of the eggshell to crack the egg and release its contents, leaving three-quarters of the shell intact. They'd wash out the eggshells and then tuck a small amount of soil and one crocus bulb into each one. (You can either dig the crocuses from your garden or start them in a pot a few weeks ahead of time, so they'll be just starting to bloom.) You can use a napkin ring, a small band of cardboard, or a tiny flowerpot to support these beautiful natural decorations for your Easter table place settings.

Make a Flowery Easter Bonnet

WEARING an Easter bonnet lends any woman extra feminine charm, and it has practical benefits for your hair and skin, too. Revive this tradition that originated in Victorian times and was celebrated in the 1948 movie *Easter Parade,* when Judy Garland wore an Easter bonnet while strolling down Fifth Avenue on Fred Astaire's arm.

Don't put your bonnet away after Easter—wearing it is helpful all summer long to protect your hair and skin from the harmful ultraviolet rays of the sun. To ensure that your bonnet has the look that's just right for you, make it yourself. Technically, a "bonnet" ties under the chin, but the tie isn't necessary. Instead, try fashioning your bonnet from a simple straw hat and some silk flowers. And if you want to lend a touch of Victorian authenticity to your bonnet, note this advice from *Godey's Magazine and Lady's Book* (1895): When it comes to Easter bonnets, "no flower is so much in favor as the rose."

You will need:

Plain straw hat
Ribbon (at least 1 inch wide)
Sturdy needle and thread (choose thread the same color as the ribbon)
Silk flowers
Hot glue gun (optional)

Step 1. If the hat you're using is a vintage hat recovered from your attic or found at a thrift shop, remove any decorations from it.

Step 2. Sew the ribbon in a band around the hat. Tack the ribbon in four or five spots around the crown of the hat to keep it secure. Make knots in the thread on the inside of the hat so they don't show.

Step 3. Play with the arrangement of flowers on the hat. (This is the fun part!) Before you sew or glue, take your time and try out various configurations. If necessary, use straight pins or a bit of tape to hold the flowers in place while you experiment. Try designs with lots of flowers and some with just a few, until you have a look that feels right.

Step 4. When you are happy with your arrangement of flowers, either sew or hot-glue them in place.

■ If flowers don't suit your style, try a different approach. At a fabric store, buy a yard of netting in one of your favorite colors. Scrunch it into a soft, dimensional hatband (as opposed to neatly folding the fabric into a flat hatband), wrap it around the hat (where the crown meets the brim), and tie the ends in a fluffy bow. Tuck under any edges so it lies smoothly along the line where the hat brim meets the crown.

Keep Easter Lilies off Your Cat's Menu

■ Easter flowers, especially Easter lilies, are a beautiful, old-fashioned Easter tradition. Easter lilies express the sentiment of the holiday because they are "flowers which are typical of burial, resurrection, and glorious fulfillment," said *Godey's Magazine and Lady's Book* in 1895. However, if you own a cat, Easter lilies can be a dangerous choice.

"One or two bites of an Easter lily can be fatal for a cat," says Robert H. Poppenga, D.V.M., Ph.D., diplomate, American Board of Veterinary Toxicology, and professor of toxicology at the University of Pennsylvania School of Veterinary Medicine, in Philadelphia. "Unless you can be absolutely sure that you can keep your Easter lily away from your cat, I wouldn't even bring one into your house." Dog owners: no worries. There are no reports of Easter lilies being toxic to other types of domestic animals.

BIZARRE BUT TRUE

"Lifting" Girls on Easter Monday

One of the strangest Easter customs was the Victorian practice known as *lifting*. On Easter Monday, any man meeting a woman on the street was entitled to lift her from the ground and give her a kiss. On Easter Tuesday, the women (if they could) lifted the men. This custom died out as respectable people began to strongly object to being "lifted."

Celebrate May Flowers

■ Celebrating with flowers on May Day (May 1) is an old and heartwarming tradition. One practice that remained popular until the middle of the 20th century was to hang a basket of spring flowers and small sweets on a neighbor's doorknob. Don't get caught, though, or you must accept a kiss! Another custom, as author Emma J. Gray describes in *Fun for the Household: A Book of Games* (1897), involved the trip home after a May Day party. "The girls might all carry wooden hoops, and having wound flowers around them, take them to some poor child or sick mother or sister on their return home, and so have the pleasantest sort of an ending to the . . . party." You can carry on this tradition today by taking a spring basket of sweet treats and blossoms to a nearby nursing home, or perhaps to older friends and relatives. These folks will enjoy the gift and understand the tradition, since they likely followed it as children themselves.

Revive the Fortune-Telling Fad

■ Do you wonder what the future holds for you? Do you daydream about where life will take you? Well, you're not alone. Accounts of old-time holiday celebrations often tell of parties featuring horoscope and palm readings and visits from the local fortune-teller. In 1932, the *Ladies' Home Journal* told readers, "If you have someone clever at reading palms the party is assured success from then on." Try reviving this custom on Halloween—a popular night for supernatural entertainment—or at a New Year's Eve party or any summer evening picnic.

Follow the lead of *Godey's Magazine and Lady's Book* (1896): After dinner, set your kettle for tea on the stove or a campfire (or barbecue) under the stars. Serve tea and dessert while having a "gypsy fortune-teller" tell fortunes. If you don't know a "gypsy fortune-teller" (shame on you), you can improvise with a deck of tarot cards, a Magic 8-ball, or even the horoscope section of the newspaper.

Give the Dreidel a Whirl

■ If the special children in your life become impatient and restless during the days before Christmas, entertain them with an age-old Hanukkah tradition—the dreidel game. The game is convenient and simple, and doesn't involve any fancy gadgets or preparation. All you need is a dreidel and some type of markers or prize pieces, such as pennies, M&Ms, candy kisses, cookies, nuts, stickers, trading cards, small toys—whatever you fancy. A dreidel is a spinning top with four sides marked with Hebrew letters standing for the Hebrew phrase, *Nes gadol haya sham*, or "A great miracle happened there." The great miracle referred to on the dreidel was the defeat of the Syrians by the Maccabees, a small band of Jews, about 2,000 years ago, and the amazing persistence of a tiny jar of oil, which burned in the temple for 8 days and nights.

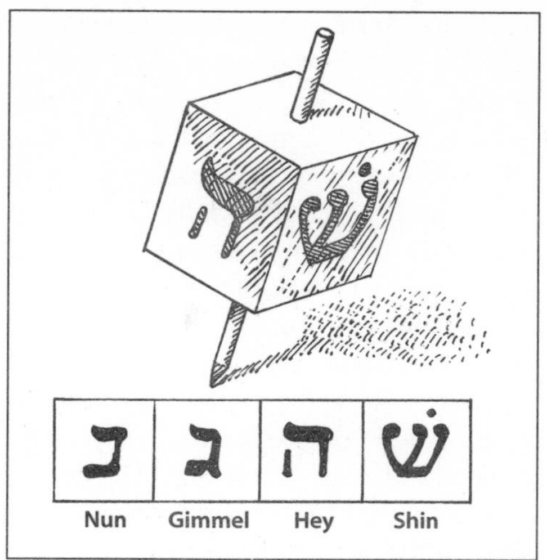

Although it's centuries old, the dreidel game is still a favorite holiday pastime.

To begin the game, each player gets an equal number of treats, and the rest are put in the center of the playing area. Then the players simply take turns spinning the dreidel. Depending on which side of the dreidel comes up, the player takes all (gimmel), half (hey), or nothing (nun), or adds to the kitty of treats (shin).

To buy a dreidel, contact a local Jewish community center or synagogue, or see Resources on page 349.

Progressive Caroling

■ The concept of an old-fashioned Christmas caroling party leaves many of us cold—literally—but here's a festive, new-fashioned caroling party idea that will warm both spirit and body. Plan a caroling party as you would a progressive dinner, where neighbors walk from home to home on the same block and enjoy a different dinner course at each residence. For your progressive caroling party, at each house on the route, head indoors for a few rousing rounds of Christmas carols along with warm drinks and snacks. If you're in charge of the evening, select about three songs to sing at each house. A simple way to do the research is to buy a compact disc of traditional Christmas songs. To find the words to each song, check out a songbook from your public library, or research them on the Internet by plugging the names of the carols into your favorite search engine. Make a copy of each song for each caroler to carry on the big night. Have one member of the traveling group carry a small CD player so you can broadcast the music of the disc to support your singing.

The Perfect Gift for Him

■ Do you have trouble finding the right Christmas gift for the man in your life? More than a century ago, women had the same problem, which an 1896 issue of *Harper's Bazaar* magazine addressed with this list of items that a Victorian lady might choose for her man at Christmas. Perhaps it will inspire an idea that will delight your man today.

Then. Silver: The lady could choose from "silver seals, silver pen-racks, silver pen holders or small silver stamp-boxes."

Now. Today's man might like a silver card case, pen, or money clip.

Then. Inkstand: There were many elaborate inkstands "in crystal and cut glass, with silver stoppers, plain and highly polished and silver trays to be placed underneath them."

Now. Maybe your man would like to try writing with a fountain pen, perhaps a classic one by Mont Blanc, Waterman, or Cross.

Then. Paperweights: A shopper could select from a vast variety of paperweights, including those made of bronze in the shape of animals.

Now. Paperweights are timeless and useful, a perfect gift for today. For something extra-special, Neiman Marcus offers paperweights made of glamorous materials including ivory, silver, and ruby-red French-made crystal.

Then. Decanters: "A heavy crystal decanter," perhaps of "the Queen Anne pattern," made a handsome gift.

Now. Decanters are still an elegant gift. Tiffany and Co. sells a beautiful line of crystal decanters in a range of patterns. For a less-expensive alternative, try home stores such as Crate and Barrel.

Then. Leather: Leather jewel cases, cigarette cases, and card cases were popular and useful.

Now. Leather is a fashionable, masculine gift for today. What about a leather belt, briefcase, wallet, or boots?

Then. Hymnal: "A very useful Christmas present is a hymnal and prayer book" bound in leather.

Now. A leather-bound Bible or other book of poetry or inspiration can make a memorable gift for a special man.

PART TWO

A Personal and Pet Care Compendium

"*Early to bed and early to rise* makes a man healthy, wealthy, and wise," wrote Ben Franklin in 1757. If only it were so! In our modern world, taking care of ourselves, our families, and our pets is more complicated than just getting a good night's sleep. There's a lot we can learn from old-timers about preventing and treating everyday health problems like coughs, colds, and aches, and about keeping our animal companions healthy, too. Some old-time remedies still work today, and many others have led to new health treatments that are more effective than the old-fashioned cures. We took a look at beauty secrets throughout the ages and distilled the best ideas, techniques, and formulas for beautiful hair, skin, eyes, nails, and more. Plus, we pored over fashion and etiquette guides from the Victorian era and found advice on matching colors, choosing accessories, and writing thank-you notes that still rings true for the 21st century.

◆ CHAPTER 7 ◆

Staying Healthy
An Apple a Day

Aches and pains, runny noses, annoying coughs, upset tummies—these common discomforts strike all of us from time to time. Fortunately, these sorts of ailments generally go away after a brief period and rarely require a physician's attention. Just as our ancestors did, the best we can do is wait out minor health problems and do what we can to relieve the symptoms. The following feel-better recipes, handed down from generation to generation, make the wait easier to handle—so you can concentrate on next week, when you'll be raring to go!

Simple Solutions for Sore Throats

Nothing's worse than the swollen, oh-so-sore throat that can accompany a cold, the flu, or allergies. That awful ache may even result from a rowdy afternoon spent cheering on your favorite team! Regardless of the origin, sore throats make us miserable. Fortunately, with a few vintage formulas for soothing mouthwashes, teas, and frozen concoctions, you can find relief.

Sage Advice

■ Gargling with cool sage tea is an old-fashioned sore throat remedy that has gone in and out of fashion. *Godey's Lady's*

Book (September 1876) notes, "As a medicinal herb, sage has lost much of its reputation in our own time, and that unjustly, for it possesses considerable aromatic and astringent properties; and sage tea is undoubtedly useful for debility of the stomach, and in nervous cases. For sore throats it makes a grateful and cooling gargle." To brew the real deal, boil 2 cups water and add 2 teaspoons fresh sage leaves; let sit for about 10 minutes and strain the liquid into a cup. Either sip at a comfortably hot temperature or chill the brew to gargle with later.

Be Sweet to Your Sore Throat

■ For the child in all of us, here's a sore throat remedy that's both tasty and soothing, based on a recipe from *The Household Guide or Domestic Cyclopedia* (1892), by Benjamin Jefferis, M.D., Ph.D., and James Nichols. Make 1 cup of flaxseed tea by mixing 1 to 2 teaspoons flaxseed in a saucepan with 1 cup cold water. (Flaxseed is available in some grocery stores and all health food stores.) Boil gently for 5 minutes; longer boiling makes a stronger tea. Remove the pan from the stove and let cool for 3 to 5 minutes. Pour the liquid through a sieve and discard the boiled flaxseed. Add fresh lemon juice to taste and float a few pieces of rock candy in the tea to sweeten.

Soothe That Ache with Slippery Elm

■ When searching for a lozenge to soothe a sore throat, look for one with slippery elm as its primary ingredient. In addition to being a wonderful sore throat remedy, slippery elm also helps you sing better, says Susan Clarke, president of Thayers Natural Pharmaceuticals, in Westport, Connecticut. The story behind this promise dates back to the 1840s, when company founder Henry Thayer, M.D., heard about a small choir in Cambridge, Massachusetts, that used slippery elm to soothe their tired, sore throats after long church services. Those who used the herb swore it healed the throat and returned a voice to its original strength within a day! Word of this natural remedy spread to church choirs throughout New England. One of Dr. Thayer's first products was slippery elm throat lozenges, and slippery elm lozenges such as Thayers are still recognized today as a safe nonprescription treatment that soothes inflamed mucous membranes in the mouth and throat.

BIZARRE BUT TRUE

Garlic Lure for Hoarseness

Be glad that no one will ever make you try this old folk remedy for hoarseness: applying crushed garlic to the feet. The garlic was said to draw the hoarseness to the feet, at which point the hoarseness was let out as the feet sweat. Of course, if this remedy worked, you'd have your voice back, but you'd have no one to talk to because of your stinky feet!

A Hot Trend in Treatment

■ For an "inflammatory sore throat," the author of *The Household Cyclopedia of General Information* (1881), Henry Hartshorne, M.D., encouraged a hot drink made with niter (a form of salt), honey, and rose water. Since you probably don't have niter in your kitchen or medicine cabinet, try this simple sore throat soother instead. Brew a cup of mild caffeine-free tea, such as chamomile, and add 2 teaspoons honey along with 1 teaspoon fresh lemon juice. If you don't have any caffeine-free tea in the cupboard, skip it! Mix honey and lemon to taste in hot water. Or go with plain hot water and lemon juice. However you choose to combine these basic ingredients, your throat should soon feel better.

Chill Out Your Sore Throat

■ A sore throat is "speedily arrested and cured by swallowing lumps of ice, continuously, until relief is afforded," stated William Whitty Hall, M.D., in the 19th-century publication *Hall's Journal of Health*. Dr. Hall was right: Ice is a great throat soother. But it's definitely lacking in flavor. A Popsicle is a tasty alternative, but not something we always have handy. Why not make your own throat-cooling treats instead?

Frozen paper-cup pops. Mix together one part juice and one part water. (You can use straight juice, but if your stomach's also upset, this may be too much sugar.) Fill 3-ounce paper cups halfway and place them in your freezer. When the liquid is partially frozen, slide a plastic spoon, fork, or knife in each cup. Once the juice has frozen solid, peel off the paper cup. Enjoy licking your ice pop, and you'll lick that sore throat while you do!

Homemade smoothies. Pour your juice-and-water mix into ice cube trays. Once it's frozen, put four or five cubes in a blender and blend the cubes until crushed to make a soothing smoothie.

Best Remedies for Colds and Flu

"We send humans to the moon, but we can't cure the common cold." This once-familiar saying isn't outdated—yet. Until that magical cold-curing pill is discovered, we can at least soothe our cold and flu symptoms with these favorite remedies, from chicken soup to a modern mustard plaster.

Combat Colds with Garlic

■ Our respect for the healing power of garlic goes way, way back. In 1100, Robert of Normandy stated, "Since garlic hath powers to save from death, bear with it though it makes unsavory breath."

No one believes any longer that garlic prevents death, but it does seem to have enough beneficial effects to be worth trying, even if garlic isn't your favorite scent. Research indicates that it may possess antibacterial and antiviral qualities. Herbalists suggest eating garlic to help prevent infection as well as speed recovery if you already have a cold or the flu. In addition, fans of this natural remedy claim that consuming garlic helps clear out phlegm.

No one knows for sure how much garlic a person needs to consume before its benefits kick in. (And people with diabetes need to monitor their insulin levels carefully if they eat a lot of it.) There's also debate about whether garlic tablets are better than fresh garlic. A few things are certain, though: Garlic probably won't hurt you; it may help you; and if you're sick, you won't be kissing anyone anyway!

To try a garlic cure when you're ailing, press or finely chop a few cloves of garlic and add them to a bowl of soup, mashed potatoes, or lightly buttered pasta—all yummy comfort foods when you're not feeling well. Or make garlic butter for toast, English muffins, or bagels by crushing 6 large garlic cloves and mixing them with 1 stick of softened salted butter. Toss in a tablespoon of chopped chives and a teaspoon of parsley, if desired.

Phoebe Reeve, an herbalist in Winchester, Virginia, praises garlic's health value. "I smash up one clove and just eat it—every day, if I remember. A lot of people find the flavor hard to tolerate, though. Maybe eating raw cloves is an acquired taste." Phoebe suggests toning down the potent flavor by placing ¼ teaspoon finely chopped raw garlic on a spoon with a blob of honey. Then, down the hatch!

The Chicken Soup Cure

Here's to chicken soup! Just a whiff of the stuff makes a throat feel better, clears the nose, and settles a queasy stomach. History books tell us that the origin of the chicken soup cure dates back to Moses ben Maimon, a 12th-century Jewish physician and philosopher who prescribed plain chicken soup—often called *stock, broth,* or *Jewish penicillin*—as a remedy for colds and asthma. In the 21st century, modern research indicates that chicken soup has genuine medicinal value. Coughs and congestion can result from an abundance of inflamed white blood cells (cells that help heal infection) accumulating in your bronchial tubes. A study conducted at the University of Nebraska Medical Center in Omaha found that chicken soup acts as an anti-inflammatory agent, preventing the

OLD-TIME ODDITIES

A "Magical" Cough Cure

TO CURE A COUGH, *Godey's Lady's Book* (August 1856) recommends: "Take one pint of strong vinegar; put in a quart bottle; add two new laid eggs, shells and all; let it stand in a warm place, shaking it well occasionally, till the vinegar dissolves the shells, which will be in two days if the vinegar is strong enough; then add one pound of strained honey; shake it well, and let it stand a day, when it is ready for use; take a tablespoon three times a day." While no modern doctor would recommend this remedy for curing a cough, if you stop right before the honey step, you have an at-home science experiment sure to delight every child. Yes, the egg's outer shell does disappear, leaving something sort of like a peeled hard-boiled egg. Magic!

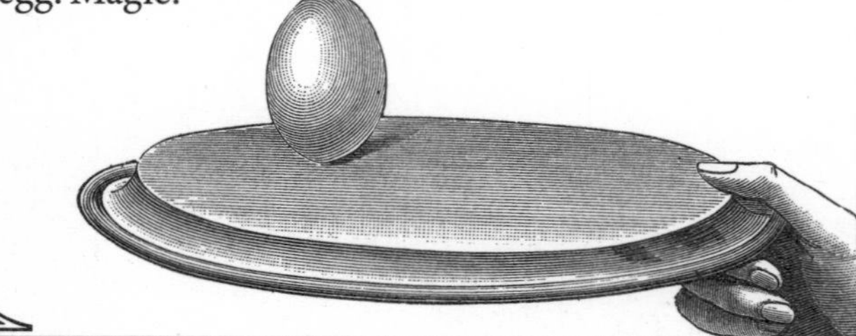

buildup of white blood cells without diluting their ability to heal. Here's the recipe used in this scientific study:

- 1 large stewing hen or baking chicken (5 to 6 pounds)
- 1 package chicken wings (10 to 12 pieces)
- 11 to 12 large carrots, peeled and sliced
- 3 large onions, peeled and quartered
- 3 parsnips, peeled and cubed
- 1 large sweet potato, peeled and cubed
- 2 turnips, peeled and cubed
- 5 to 6 stalks celery, sliced
- 1 bunch parsley, chopped
- Salt and pepper

Wash the hen or chicken and place it in an 8-quart soup pot. Fill the pot three-quarters of the way with cold water and bring to a boil. Add the chicken wings, carrots, onions, parsnips, sweet potato, and turnips. Cook at a low boil for 1½ hours, skimming off fat as it rises to the top. Discard the fat. Add the celery and parsley and continue cooking on a low boil for another 45 minutes. Remove the chicken, bones, and the vegetables from the pot. Discard the bones and place the chicken in one bowl and vegetables in another bowl. Place the vegetables in a blender and puree. (Put a cup of broth in the blender with the vegetables to speed up the pureeing process.) Mix the puree back into the broth to thicken it. Add salt and pepper to taste.

You can put the chicken back in the soup (if your stomach can handle it) or refrigerate it in an appropriate container until you feel better. It will make terrific chicken salad.

For a virtually fat-free chicken soup, refrigerate the bowls of vegetables and chicken once you've separated them from the broth. Let the broth cool, and then place the broth in the refrigerator, as well, for about 12 hours. A thin, solidified layer of fat will rise to the top. Remove this layer with a slotted spoon and discard. Then puree the soup as described above.

Also, if you don't feel like a thick soup, puree the veggies in four groups, each time adding the puree to the soup and then stirring. Stop when you feel the thickness is to your liking. Toss unused vegetables—their vitamins are already transferred to the broth, so there's no real nutritional value left in them.

A Little Spicy Zip Zaps Your Cold

■ To intensify the healing power of history's most respected chicken broth recipes, add spices. Garlic may help kill viruses and bacteria. Pepper—black, chile, or cayenne—acts as an expecto-

rant, thinning all the drips associated with colds, allergies, or asthma. This seems to help us more easily cough up or blow out various bodily fluids. (You might do well to skip spices in your chicken soup if your ailment includes stomach problems or nausea.)

Chicken Soup Cubes for Comfort

■ While our great-grandmothers probably stirred up homemade chicken soup for their families, they didn't have convenient electric freezers to store the extra, as we do. When packaged in a tightly sealed container, chicken soup freezes remarkably well, ready for defrosting as soon as you experience that first sniffle or cough. Try pouring chicken soup into ice cube trays. Freeze the trays; then pop out the cubes and store them in a resealable plastic bag. You'll need about four cubes for a single cup of homemade chicken broth. Plop your cubes in a mug, heat them in the microwave, and drink up, and hopefully you'll feel better soon.

Soak Your Feet in Mustard, Too

SOME FOLKS SWEAR that a warm mustard footbath eases every possible cold symptom. Try this simple folk recipe. Mix 1 tablespoon dry mustard with 2 quarts comfortably hot water. Dunk your feet in the mustard bath for about 10 minutes, several times a day.

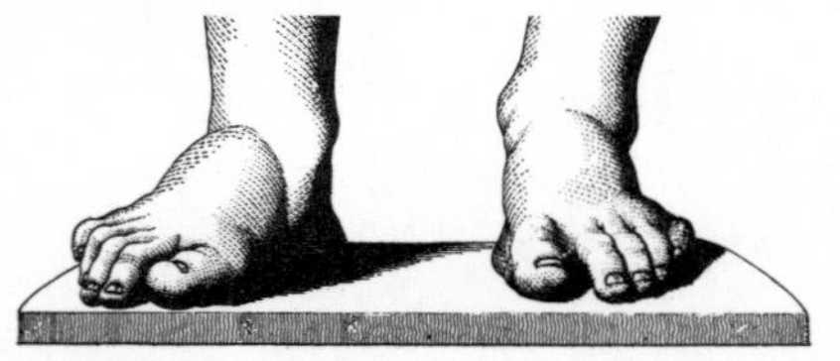

Plaster on the Mustard for Cold Relief

■ An old-fashioned mustard plaster may subdue cold symptoms, rev up circulation, and clear your nose. The mustard fumes may also cause your eyes to water, but that feels good if they're itchy. Home reference guides from the 19th century highly recommend the healing power of mustard plasters. In *The Household Guide or Domestic Cyclopedia* (1892), authors Benjamin Jefferis, M.D., Ph.D., and James Nichols advise, "If [a mustard plaster] does not afford relief, call the doctor, for the case is a serious one." Don't use the mustard plaster as a litmus test for when to call the doctor, but do give one a try the next time you have a cold. Here's a modernized recipe for a mustard plaster: Combine 1 tablespoon dry mustard and ¼ cup flour with enough water to create a paste. Spread the paste on a warm, damp washcloth and place the cloth on your chest. *Caution:* Dry mustard can irritate and even burn your skin if used too heartily. More is not better.

Hankies Are for the Healthy

■ Using a handkerchief is a civilized custom, but tissues are the thing to keep on hand when you have a cold. For a proper Victorian lady, carrying a handkerchief was an absolute necessity. Magazines such as *Godey's Lady's Book* (May 1885) even offered fashion advice regarding handkerchiefs: "If one has a dress trimmed with blue, a blue handkerchief is carried with it; if one trimmed with red, a red handkerchief, suggesting the thought that the wearer uses a piece of her dress-trimming as a handkerchief."

While blowing your nose with an accessory coordinated to your gown is a fetching concept, forgo cloth hankies when you have a cold and use that modern invention, the disposable tissue. One easy way to spread a cold or flu virus is by touching something infected with the germs, like when you absentmindedly pick up a used hankie. The best course of action is to immediately throw out anything that you've used to blow your nose when you're sick. Since one hankie can cost more than an entire box of tissues, it could be quite pricey to use those pretty cloth squares when you're ill. Save them for blotting your healthy brow while dining alfresco.

C for Yourself

■ Even our great-grandparents knew that eating foods rich in vitamin C was good for you, although they may not have known why. The first confirmation of the power of vitamin C came during the early 20th century, when it was discovered that the vitamin cured scurvy. (Another name for vitamin C is *ascorbic acid,* which is derived from *antiscurvy acid.*) What we've learned since then is that vitamin C may have a range of beneficial effects, from creating beautiful skin to curing common colds, although most of these claims are still being researched. We've learned for certain that our bodies can't store vitamin C, so we need to take it daily if we want to reap its benefits. Ask your physician what your daily recommended dosage is—this can change according to age or medications being taken, such as a blood thinner. Then, eat your citrus fruits, green and red peppers, strawberries, tomatoes, broccoli, turnip greens, sweet and 'Yukon Gold' potatoes, and cantaloupe! If you're doomed to catch that seasonal cold, bulking up on vitamin C may help the sniffles run their course more quickly.

Take Your Cold to Lunch

■ The old saying "feed a cold, starve a fever" seems to trace back to medical advice from the 1500s. Is it an old wives' tale or not? Recent research shows that the saying may have some basis in science. Dutch scientists found that eating a

OLD-FASHIONED FAVORITES

A Lemonade Tonic

One excellent source of vitamin C is lemons. In fact, back in 1879, *Godey's Lady's Book* advised readers, "Natural remedies are the best, and nature is our best doctor, if we will only listen to it. Decidedly, rub your hands, head, and gums with lemon, and drink lemonade in preference to all other liquids. This is an old doctor's advice. Follow it."

Here is a simple, tasty, and vitamin C–packed lemonade recipe, as offered by Lydia Maria Child in *The Family Nurse; Or Companion of the American Frugal Housewife* (1837): "Pour a pint of boiling water upon a tablespoonful of lemon juice, sweeten it to your taste, and place it where it will become cool. Some like to have a few pieces of the peel remain to season it . . . A very agreeable and cooling beverage in fevers."

meal boosts the immune response that destroys cold viruses, while fasting (no solids, but still plenty of water) stimulates a natural immune response that fights flulike *bacterial* infections. More research is necessary before we can elevate this maxim to medical truth, but in the meantime, it might be wise to eat hearty when you've got a cold and stick to clear liquids like water or broth when the flu strikes.

Relieving Aches and Pains

Generally speaking, a minor ache or pain is your body's way of saying, "Slow down! I need a rest." When you heed this advice and combine it with a few simple, timeless methods for relieving slight discomforts—including herbal soaks and hop-pillows—you have a prescription for get-up-and-go.

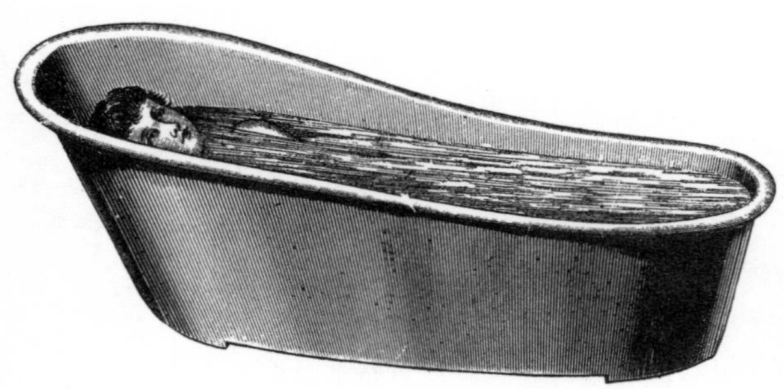

Go Soak That Ache!

■ To make an ache or pain more tolerable while on the mend, try an herbal bath like those recommended in 19th-century magazines. For example, *The Lady's Book* (December 1835) suggests the following bath for both its aromatic qualities and its ability to strengthen the limbs, remove pain, relieve a cold, and promote perspiration: "In sufficient quantity of river water, boil, for the space of two or three minutes, one or more of the following aromatic herbs: anise; clove; July-flowers; balm; basil, sweet; bastard marjoram; fennel; hyssop; laurel; lavender; rosemary; wild thyme; wild mint; or any other herbs that have an agreeable scent. Having strained off the liquor from the herbs, add to it a little brandy or camphorated spirits of wine."

These old-timers had the right idea, although collecting river water may be inconvenient for you! Modern research shows that some essential oils do appear to boost the body's natural ability to heal itself. And using regular tap water for an herbal warm-water soak works fine. Here are two recipes specifically recommended by Winchester, Virginia, herbalist Phoebe Reeve.

Stimulate sluggish circulation. This soothing herbal bath of ginger, cloves, orange, lemon, and cinnamon helps relax stiff joints and eases muscle pain. To prepare, put 1 pint of water in a pan on your stovetop. Add one sliced lemon with peel, the peel of one orange, one cinnamon stick, a 1-inch-long piece of fresh ginger cut into slices, and five whole cloves. Bring the mix to a boil, cover, simmer for 20 minutes, and then strain the liquid into a tub of warm water. Mix thoroughly before climbing in. As you melt away pain, slowly eat the orange that you peeled while preparing the herbal mix. There's an added benefit of this bath: "This recipe is filled with traditional Christmas scents. When you're feeling cold and miserable, nothing feels better than soaking in a warm bath and thinking about happy Christmas memories," Phoebe says.

Relieve inflammation. Add 6 to 10 drops total of lavender, peppermint, rosemary, and bergamot essential oils to your bathwater. Use more or less of each scent as desired, but no more than 3 drops of any one oil. A good soak in a warm bath infused with these anti-inflammatory essential oils should temporarily ease pain. You can boost your body's ability to absorb the oils by adding ¼ cup of Epsom salts to the bathwater.

The Proper Mattress Precludes Pain

■ Enjoy restful sleep and avoid morning backache by choosing the right mattress, advises Maria Parloa in *Home Economics, A Guide to Household Management, Including the Proper Treatment of the Materials Entering into the Construction and Furnishing of the House* (1898): "I am convinced that half the unrest, sleeplessness, and backache with which people are afflicted is due to the fact that most of the beds in use do not support the body in a perfectly horizontal position." A good mattress should support your body at all points, allowing your spine to be in the same shape as it is when you're standing with relaxed posture. Mattress firmness may be *too* high on many people's list when choosing a mattress, because a mattress that's too firm can cause uncomfortable pressure on your back. Unless specifically advised by a physician, an extra-firm mattress is probably not a good choice. However, mattress manufacturers have different definitions for "firm" and "extra firm," so don't buy a mattress based on the label alone. The

only reliable way to know what you're buying is to go to the mattress store and test the bed by lying down on it. And if you sleep with a partner, be sure to bring him or her along, too, so that you pick a mattress that will allow both of you to enjoy sweet dreams.

A Fishy Headache Remedy

■ Can too much thinking cause a headache? In Victorian times, that's what neurologists told their patients. Those old-time neurologists also pooh-poohed headaches as a form of hypochondria. Modern neurologists disagree, and recent studies indicate that fish oil may help reduce an inflammatory process in the brain that can cause headaches. More specifically, it's the oil's omega-3 fatty acids that are beneficial. While research on this subject continues, upping your omega-3 fatty acids may be worth a try if you're susceptible to throbbing stress headaches. By taking fish oil capsules or by including two 8-ounce servings of fish in your weekly diet, you can boost your omega-3 fatty acids. Omega-3 fatty acids are found in cold-water fatty fish, such as salmon, mackerel, trout, and herring. *Caution:* Because of concerns about the mercury content of fish, the FDA recommends that women who are pregnant or may become pregnant, nursing mothers, and young children avoid certain types of fish. Check with your health care provider before heading to the fish market.

There's also an old-fashioned fishy way to ease a tension headache: Hang a sign on your front door that reads, "Gone Fishing." Then do it! As you float in your boat, relax, think nice thoughts, and release all that tension. Whether you catch a fish or not, you'll likely go home without that headache.

Hot or Cold for Your Headache?

HISTORICALLY SPEAKING, keeping track of the advice about hot versus cold treatments for headaches is like watching a seesaw. But the current recommendation is that sinus headache sufferers should apply a warm compress around the eyes and nose. Conversely, the treatment for tension headaches is applying a cold compress.

An Improved Approach to Headache Treatment

According to Henry Hartshorne, M.D., author of *The Household Cyclopedia of General Information* (1881), a headache is brought on by wearing too-tight clothing and can be cured by applying leeches to the head, and then dressing the head in a cloth dipped in cold water. So the next time you have a headache, the first thing you need to do is loosen your corset. Oh, you aren't wearing a corset? Well, then, let's move on to the leeches. On second thought, let's skip the leeches. That leaves the cold cloth for your head, which is part of this safer (and more modern) approach to easing common headaches.

- Apply a cold compress or ice pack at the base of your neck and on your forehead.
- Eat smaller, more-frequent meals to maintain blood sugar levels.
- Massage your temples and scalp, with one drop of peppermint essential oil on your fingertips, if you'd like.
- If your spouse or a friend is available, ask him to massage your shoulders and neck.
- Natural herbs such as hops, skullcap, and catnip brewed in a cup of tea or taken in capsules may provide relief.
- Rest in a dark room. For an even more soothing effect, try a relaxation technique such as deep breathing while you're resting.

Hops Help a Headache

In *An Old-Fashioned Girl* (1870), author Louisa May Alcott refers to an old-fashioned headache remedy: "How we did laugh when he came up and explained that our neighbor, old Mrs.

Dodd, had sent in a hop-pillow for me, in case of headache, and a pie to begin house-keeping with." Miss Alcott's "hop-pillow" was an aromatherapy pillow—a cotton case stuffed with hops. The scent of hops is reputed to bring on restful sleep and relieve minor headaches.

To make your own hop-pillow in a matter of minutes, take a clean sock made of thin cotton and pour in two or three handfuls of dried hop flowers. (These and the following herbs are readily available at health food or herb stores.) If desired, bulk up your pillow with additional dried herbs, such as lime flowers, lemon verbena, chamomile, lavender, rose, crumbled sweet marjoram, or crumbled thyme. Tie the open end shut. As Miss Alcott might have done, take a nap with the pillow placed near your face. Sweet dreams.

BIZARRE BUT TRUE

Burn Away the Pain

WE ALL KNOW how painful even the mildest burn or scalding feels, so imagine granting your physician permission to burn various parts of your body. That's what people did in the early 1800s. Our ancestors believed that you could release a fever, ache, or pain by creating a blister and then letting the blister drain—which in turn released the ailment. Most physicians preferred blistering plasters made largely from mustard, although a few history books report hot irons also being used. Here's how William Buchan, M.D., explained the treatment's merit in *Domestic Medicine* (1785): "Blistering plasters may be applied at all times of the fever with great advantage. If the patient is delirious, he ought to be blistered on the neck or head, and it will be the safest course, while the insensibility continues, as soon as the discharge occasioned by one blistering-plaster abates, to apply another to some other part of the body, and by that means keep up a continual succession of them till he be out of danger."

Hot News about Mild Burns

From time to time, we all suffer superficial burns. This can happen if we brush against a hot pot on the stove or bump against a plugged-in iron. *Cassell's Household Guide* (circa 1880s) states that a burn can be assumed to be superficial—as in a first-degree burn, which affects only the outer layer of skin—when "the pain is severe for the moment, but rapidly subsides as soon as the surface burnt is protected." That's still a fair guideline. *Cassell's* recommends treating superficial burns by dredging flour over the burn, followed by a dry cotton wrap. Here, *Cassell's* is only half right. Today's medical professionals would urge us to skip the flour and proceed straight to the cotton wrapping. The goal is to keep first-degree burns clean and dry. Do not apply ointment, butter, salve, cream, oil, or ice. Instead, run cool water over the burn for about 5 minutes, or apply a clean, cool, wet towel to the area. (Using cold water or ice might cause shock.) Next, gently pat the burned area dry and cover it with a sterile bandage, making sure that the bandage adhesive stays clear of the burned area. The bandage should be loose enough to allow air in, but secure enough to protect the area from scrapes, which might open the burn and lead to infection. A minor burn should heal without any further treatment.

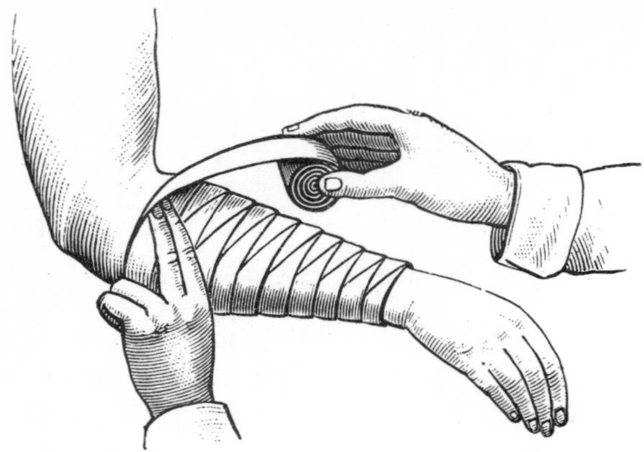

The Old-Time First Aid Kit

Keeping a first aid kit is as smart now as it was back in the early 1900s, when Clara Barton, American Red Cross founder, introduced the first official first aid kit. One 1915 kit, called the Household Accident Kit, contained two 3-inch bandages, three rolls of 3-inch compress bandages, three rolls of 3-inch gauze, two rolls of 2-inch gauze, and 1 yard of 4-inch gauze. When you assemble your home kit today, you'll want to include some of the same items that were in Miss Barton's kit, as well as several modern additions, says Diane Saint Germain, R.N., a nurse at Children's Memorial Hospital, in Chicago. Diane recommends using nonlatex products for first aid kits, because many people are allergic to latex.

- Ace bandage
- Adhesive tape (nonlatex)
- Antiseptic ointment
- Aspirin, acetaminophen, or ibuprofen tablets
- Bandages (nonlatex)
- Blanket (to warm up a shock victim)
- Disposable gloves (nonlatex)
- Finger splints
- Gauze pads and rolled gauze (assorted sizes, but at least 2-by-2-inch and 4-by-4-inch pads)
- Hand cleaner
- Instant freeze pack
- List of emergency phone numbers (including your physician's)
- List of your allergies
- Resealable plastic bags (to protect a severed digit for transport to the hospital with the patient)
- Scissors and tweezers
- Several doses of your physician-prescribed medications (each one in a clearly marked container)
- Small flashlight and extra batteries

You may be curious to know why the traditional syrup of ipecac is missing from the list. Diane explains, "Some poisons should not be vomited up. In all the panic, people grab that syrup of ipecac too fast, without knowing the facts. What you should do instead is call the Poison Control Center and get proper advice."

Sounds like a good number to write on that emergency phone list! The National Poison Hotline is (800) 222-1222. Diane also recommends keeping a first aid kit in your home, your car, and your backpack, as well, if you're planning an outdoor adventure. In addition, check your kits every 6 months, making sure that flashlight batteries work and no medications are expired.

The Newfangled House Call

In the old days, people knew they could request a house call from the doctor when someone in the family was suffering from an ache or minor injury. But most doctors don't make house calls today, and for a nonemergency medical problem, visiting the emergency room isn't a satisfactory substitute. Instead, we can sometimes make our own "house call" courtesy of informative Web sites, says Chicago mom Donna Shryer. When Donna's 8-year-old daughter cried about a stinging in her mouth, Mom suspected it was a canker sore. Turning to the Internet, Donna found a photograph that confirmed her thoughts, as well as a few home treatments—Popsicles to numb the pain and saltwater swishes to speed recovery. Donna also read that if the sore wasn't better within 3 days, she should call the pediatrician. Armed with a treatment and timeline, everyone calmed down, and the sore uneventfully ran its course in 2 days.

According to Rosalind Lett, an independent information consultant and a member of the Medical Library Association board of directors, the first thing you need to know about finding medical information on the Internet is that there are plenty of wacky, quackish sites out there. "When you read that something's a cure-all, be-all, end-all, it's a pretty safe bet that this site is not for real," Rosalind says. To locate reputable information, stick with sites sponsored by a hospital, academic medical center, government health agency, nonprofit association, or medical library. To find these sites, type your keywords into your favorite Internet search engine, such as Google. Scan the listing of search results for addresses with any of the following endings:

- Government agencies sponsor sites ending in *.gov.*
- Major educational institutions, including university-affiliated hospitals, have Web addresses ending in *.edu.*
- Professional organizations, nonprofit associations, or research societies usually have *.org* Web addresses.

Another good way to collect trustworthy Web sites is to ask your doctor for recommendations. And remember, don't try to use Web sites as a substitute for real medical care when a health problem is serious or persistent.

ROUGHING IT

Unusual Old-Time "Band-Aids"

THE NEXT TIME someone moans and groans about how much it hurts when you yank off that adhesive bandage, remind them about the alternative recommended in *The Housekeeper's Handy Book* (1915): "Bleeding of Severe Cuts may be stopped by the application of quantities of salt and flour, spread on thickly. This will answer in a moderate cut always. Cobwebs are used successfully also."

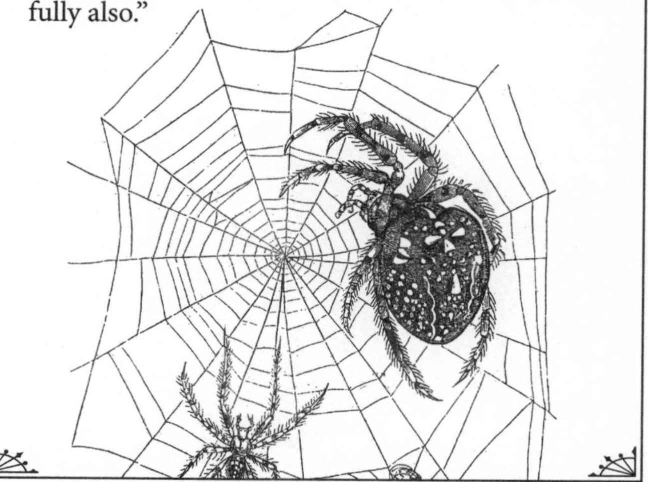

A Cut above the Rest

■ A popular over-the-counter treatment for fighting skin fungus has a long history as an antiseptic. Dr. Arthur Penfold, a curator and chemist in Sydney, Australia, is widely credited with verifying the antiseptic powers of tea tree oil—back in the 1920s. Dr. Penfold concluded that the essential oil of the tea tree, when used as an antiseptic, was up to 13 times stronger than carbolic acid, the standard antiseptic at the time. Pure essential tea tree oil remains an excellent and economical nonprescription antibacterial, antifungal, and anti-inflammatory treatment. You can use it to treat any minor cut, scratch, or abrasion. Clean the wound and then put two or three drops of pure essential tea tree oil on a cotton ball and gently dab the wound with the cotton ball. This essential oil temporarily relieves the itch associated with insect bites. It can also irritate your skin if applied too often and too heavily, so begin by applying only two or three drops to see how it affects you. If you know that you have sensitive skin, mix two drops of tea tree oil with one drop of carrier oil, such as sweet almond oil, olive oil, glycerin, or mineral oil, and then apply as needed.

Those Were the Days

According to guidelines set by the Medical Society of Washington County, New York, 1837, and the College of Physicians of Philadelphia, 1843, here are a few typical physician charges. The guidelines note that fees for house calls could be reduced if the doctor's horse was fed while the doctor was visiting the patient.

TYPE OF SERVICE	FEE IN RURAL NEW YORK	FEE IN URBAN PHILADELPHIA
Advice given in office	$0.50	$1.00–$10.00
House call (daytime)	$0.50	$1.00–$2.00
House call (nighttime)	$0.75	$5.00–$10.00
Labor and delivery	$4.00	$10.00–$30.00

Gotta Love Those Cloves

■ It's 8:00 P.M., and a pain shoots through your tooth. Your dentist's office doesn't open until 9:00 A.M. tomorrow. To survive the night, try this simple remedy: Put four drops of clove oil on a cotton ball and place the cotton over your painful tooth or gum. This is a less complicated yet perfectly effective version of an old-time toothache remedy described in *Henley's Twentieth Century Book of Formulas, Processes and Trade Secrets* (1912), which calls for mixing camphor, chloral hydrate, oil of cloves, oil of cajeput (a tree related to the tea tree), chloroform, and tincture of capsicum. That's a lot of blending—not to mention that several of the ingredients are no longer conveniently available or recommended. According to Evanston, Illinois,

dentist Michael Gordon, D.D.S., clove oil all by itself can temporarily numb toothache pain because it contains eugenol, a colorless aromatic liquid that has an anesthetic effect. Dr. Gordon adds, "Eugenol is an ingredient in many modern local anesthetics."

Exercises Overcome Eyestrain

■ "Whatever work you are doing, close the eyes every now and then for an instant. Let them wander to a distance, too, at intervals." So writes Baroness Staffe in her 1893 book, *The Lady's Dressing Room.* Modern vision experts would agree with the baroness and actually would recommend a more-specific set of eye exercises to help prevent eye aches and eyestrain. Keep your head still and move only your eyes up and down, 10 to 15 times. Close your eyes for about the time needed to inhale and exhale a deep, relaxing breath. Open your eyes and repeat the exercise, but move your eyes from side to side instead of up and down. Close your eyes and take a breath again. Open your eyes and repeat the exercise on the diagonal, moving first upper left to lower right, then the reverse. Close your eyes and take a breath. Finally, after opening your eyes, put your arm straight out in front of you, thumb up. Focus first on your thumb and then at a distance beyond your thumb. Repeat several times.

Oil Away Eye Irritation

■ To remove an annoying small particle of debris from your eye, use an oily technique similar to that recommended in *The Housekeeper's Handy Book: A Comprehensive Cyclopedia of Useful Information and Domestic Science in the Home* (1915): "A simple and effective cure may be found in 1 or 2 grains of flaxseed which can be placed in the eye without pain or injury. As they dissolve, a glutinous substance is formed, which envelopes any foreign body that may be under the lid and whole is easily washed out." Now, you probably don't have flaxseeds on hand, and putting the seeds in your eye could scratch your cornea. Instead, place a tiny dot of olive oil, vegetable oil, or sweet almond oil on your finger and gently tap the oil onto your eyeball. The oil will draw the bothersome particle into the corner of your eye, at which point you can use your pinkie finger to gently swipe it out. The oil will cause your vision to be blurry for about a minute, but don't worry; this procedure is safe, and your vision will clear up quickly. Just close your eyes for a few seconds, and all will be fine.

Taking Care of Digestion

The stomach is a ticklish subject, with a fine line between feeding it what it wants and upsetting it. If you find yourself suffering from indigestion, a few of our grandmothers' grandmothers' recipes may provide relief.

Ginger Ale Is an Old Tummy Tackler

■ When the flu leaves you feeling nauseated, good old-fashioned ginger ale may help. Knowledge of ginger's medicinal properties (ginger ale really does contain ginger) dates back to ancient times. Recent scientific studies prove that ginger is often more effective than some over-the-counter medicines for relieving nausea due to motion sickness, morning sickness, aftereffects of surgery, and the flu. The precise reason ginger works, however, eludes modern science. Who cares! The next time your stomach's feeling queasy, slowly sip ginger ale—as much as you can handle. You can also add about ⅓ teaspoon ground ginger to a cup of caffeine-free tea or nibble a few gingersnap cookies. If you have the energy, try this tasty old-time recipe from *The Household Cyclopedia of Practical Receipts and Daily Wants* (1873), by Alexander V. Hamilton: "A good remedy is a teaspoonful of carbonate of magnesia [available in health food stores], or carbonate of soda [baking soda] in a wineglass of peppermint or cinnamon water, with a little powdered ginger in it." To make the flavored water mentioned in this remedy, mix one or two drops of pure essential oil of cinnamon or peppermint with about 8 ounces of water.

Old-Time Belly Tamers

When it comes to upset tummies, some remedies prescribed by old-time medical practitioners are right on the mark. For example, Henry Hartshorne, M.D., author of *The Household Cyclopedia of General Information* (1881), recommends these simple and free treatments for an upset stomach: warm water, massage, and eating slowly. Chicago-area nurse Betty Guzman, R.N., offers a modern perspective on these old-time methods.

Heat brings relief. "Put the patient into the warm bath," instructs Dr. Hartshorne. Betty agrees, saying, "Warm water is a natural muscle relaxer. Also, when you slide into a warm bath, the body switches gears, concentrating more on the body's temperature change and less on sending messages about pain to the brain. It's a distraction, further helping the muscles relax." If you dislike baths, try putting a hot water bottle or heating pad gently on your stomach, Betty suggests.

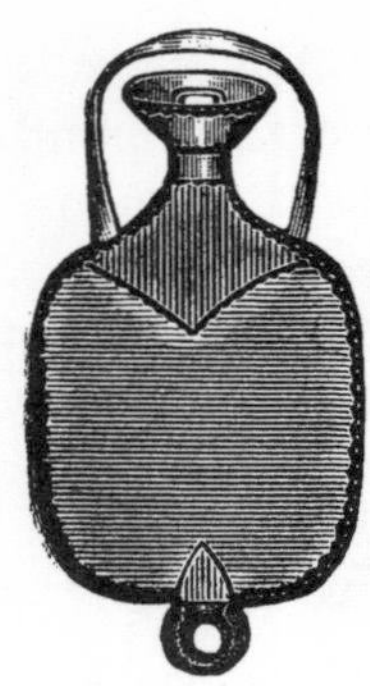

Try a soothing belly rub. "In rubbing the belly, the operation ought to be performed in a circular direction, as being most favorable to the course of the intestines, and their natural action," Dr. Hartshorne states in *The Household Cyclopedia.* This type of massage really helps, Betty notes. "The first thing we do when we get a stomachache is comfort ourselves by rubbing the painful area," she says. "You're instinctively relaxing the muscles—and increasing blood flow to the organ so it can begin healing itself." Go with the flow and give your belly a proper massage. Lie down in a comfortable position and move your fingertips over your belly in a circular motion. Apply as much pressure as you like.

Reduce your chewing speed. According to Dr. Hartshorne, stomachaches are often the result of hasty "overindulgence in the luxuries of the table." In other words, eating too much too fast. Properly chewing your food does take time, but it's time well spent, Betty says. "The stomach does not know how to break down chunks of meat. It will try to digest poorly chewed food, but then gastric juices start working too hard, acid builds up in the stomach, and pain follows." So how long should you chew your food to do it "properly"? Betty says, "Until it's mushy—like baby food." If you don't have enough time to properly chew and enjoy a full meal, then make your meals smaller but more frequent. Try six minimeals a day. For example, you might divide breakfast into two meals by eating a bowl of oatmeal at 8:00 A.M. and a banana and strawberries at 10:00 A.M.

Three Ways to Turn Down the Heat

"There is no such thing as heartburn. What is commonly heartburn, is nothing more nor less than acidity of the stomach, or a derangement of the digestive organs," proclaim Benjamin Jefferis, M.D., Ph.D., and James Nichols in *The Household Guide or Domestic Cyclopedia* (1892). Tell that to the 25 million Americans who suffer daily from some form of heartburn! Fortunately, we've learned a lot about heartburn since the late 1800s, and heartburn sufferers need not suffer. For minor heartburn that does not require a physician's attention or prescription medicine, try these tactics to curb flare-ups.

1. Keep a heartburn journal, noting when heartburn strikes and what you last ate. You may spot a pattern. If you do, eliminate these foods. If you don't, then this could be a clue that you should make a doctor's appointment to figure out what's causing the discomfort.

2. Elevate the head of your bed by 6 to 8 inches. Put blocks underneath the legs of your headboard, the front legs, or your bed frame. Or place a foam wedge under the top end of your mattress. This slows the flow of stomach acid into your esophagus as you sleep. Extra pillows won't do the job, because resting on pillows causes you to bend at the waist, squeezing stomach acid up further and intensifying heartburn.

3. Drink a cup of warm green tea. This is similar to, but more enjoyable than, the remedy offered by William Buchan, M.D., in *Domestic Medicine* (1785): "I have frequently known the heart-burn cured, particularly in pregnant women, by chewing green tea."

Hit the Sauce

That bottle of Worcestershire sauce in your kitchen not only adds flavor to food but may also help ease a tummy ache—because one of its primary ingredients is the spice tamarind, which is shown to soothe minor digestive problems. Here's how *London at Dinner, or Where to Dine* (1858), describes the sauce's benefits: "Those who require either a zest to enable them to relish their food, or

Cider on the Side

TO QUELL a tummy ache, try a home remedy that traces back to Hippocrates, the Greek physician born in 460 B.C., who is immortalized by the Hippocratic oath. Mix 2 tablespoons apple cider vinegar and 2 tablespoons honey into an 8-ounce glass of water (adjust the vinegar and honey to taste, but always use equal amounts). The theory behind this remedy is that indigestion sometimes occurs from a lack of stomach acid that's needed for optimal digestion.

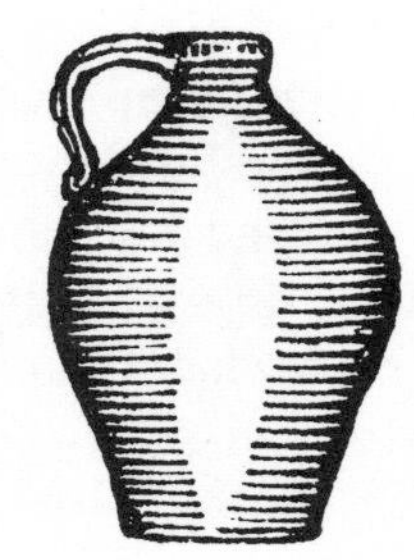

stimulant to assist the stomach in digesting it, should make trial of the Worcestershire sauce, which is world-renowned for the exquisite flavour it communicates alike to fish, flesh, or fowl, to soups, salads, or curries . . . Add a dessert spoon of this sauce to a bowl of dressed salad, and its aromatic properties will be found extremely agreeable, while effectually counteracting any tendency to indigestion." Yum! Add ½ teaspoon (or more) per serving to your basic oil-and-vinegar salad dressing. You can also mix this rich, flavorful liquid into gravy or meat loaf, or sprinkle it over vegetables. As a bonus, Worcestershire sauce is a healthful alternative to salt.

Overcoming Allergies with Ease

According to the Asthma and Allergy Foundation of America, more than 60 million Americans suffer some sort of asthma or allergy. While our ancestors would probably consider modern allergy medicines something akin to miracles, they weren't without their own remedies—many of which remain viable solutions for less-severe symptoms.

Poison Ivy Gets a Cold Reception

■ Nearly everyone knows that it's important to wash your skin as soon as possible after exposure to poison ivy in order to avoid the awful rash that's actually an allergic reaction to an oil produced by the plant. But should you wash with hot water or cold, with soap or without? Recommendations, often contradictory, abound. In *Dick's Encyclopedia of Practical Receipts and Processes* (1875), author

William Dick advises readers to "bathe the poisoned part thoroughly with hot water, without soap." No siree, Dick! say allergy specialists. If you're exposed to poison ivy, rinse the area as soon as possible with *cool* water and mild soap to remove the poison ivy oil from your skin. Using hot water tends to open the pores of your skin, allowing the oil faster entry, which could result in an allergic reaction that is even more intense. If a rash appears after you've washed the area with mild soap and cool water, you might also apply a compress of cool water and baking soda, or simply soak the area in cool water mixed with baking soda. An over-the-counter medication, such as hydrocortisone cream, calamine lotion, or an oral antihistamine, may also soothe the itch.

Gesundheit

■ If your allergies are rockin' and rollin', then a quick flushing of your nostrils may clean out the allergens lodged in the deep recesses of your sinuses. Baroness Staffe, author of *The Lady's Dressing Room* (1893), recommends pouring a little salt water into your palm and inhaling it, but perhaps you'll find the following procedure more convenient. Begin by purchasing a bulb syringe, which is available at drugstores. Next, mix a simple saltwater solution of 4 ounces warm water, ¼ teaspoon salt (table salt is fine), and ⅛ teaspoon baking soda. Fill the bulb, tilt your head sideways over a sink, and squeeze a comfortable amount of the solution into the nostril that is closer to the sink. Then blow the saline solution out of your nostril into the sink. If any solution trickles down into your throat, either spit it out or swallow—it won't harm you. Repeat the procedure in your other nostril.

Sheets Shut Out Pollen

People who suffer from allergies know that air-conditioning can help prevent symptoms, because it cuts down the amount of pollen infiltrating a room. But if you're an allergy sufferer who's also a fresh-air lover, try this trick from the July 13, 1929, issue of *Literary Digest*. Immediately after making your bed in the morning, drape it with a large sheet (foot to head, and well over the sides). Use a flat sheet one size bigger than your bed size: full size for twin beds, king size for queen beds. (If you have a king-size bed, buy two inexpensive full-size flat sheets and stitch the two long edges together.) Before climbing into bed at night, gently remove the sheet without shaking or excessive handling. The cover will significantly reduce the quantity of pollen scoundrels hiding in your pillows and blankets, resulting in a more restful sleep. As the magazine promises, "Many patients after sleeping in such a room find they can go through the day with much less inconvenience."

Hum Your Allergies Away

When allergy symptoms settle in your sinuses, try humming. Swedish scientists recently discovered that humming (producing a tune without opening your lips or forming words) effectively increases ventilation in your sinuses. Perhaps these scientists are just rediscovering a concept reported in a February 1861 article in *Godey's Lady's Book,* which sings the praises of singing—as well as reading aloud—in order to breathe more efficiently: "The effect is to induce the drawing of a long breath every once in a while . . . These deep inhalations never fail to develop the capacity of the lungs in direct proportion to their practice." Singing with a closed mouth, moreover, apparently increases nitric oxide levels, which is what you want for healthy sinuses.

Every Cloud Has a Silver Lining

If you have pollen allergies but also love long, lazy walks, then you're in luck! Simply schedule your outdoor strolls immediately after a good downpour. As reported in the *Literary Digest* (June 14, 1930), "The principal varieties of pollen have been tested in our biological laboratory and it has been found that the submersion of the pollens in a large amount of water removes their irritating properties." Translated into layman's English, after about 30 minutes of rain, the air is virtually pollen-free! "A heavy rain will effectively wash airborne pollen out of the air," says Peter Jensen, vice president of Surveillance Data, the company that sponsors www.pollen.com. "But you have to remember that pollen has spent millions of years learning to travel, so things like strong wind or heavy damp air can bring it right back or hold it in place." Peter adds that most pollination occurs in the morning, so if there's a late-afternoon rainfall in your area, and afterward the air is relatively calm, go and enjoy the evening. You certainly have time to enjoy at least a half-hour walk.

Excellent Energy Boosters

That sluggish feeling that occasionally weighs us down is the body's instinctive way of forcing us to ease the pace of life. Maybe you're doing too much or, as our ancestors called it, "overindulging in luxurious food and drink." Because listlessness is such a natural reaction to stress, natural energy boosters that our ancestors relied on—such as fruit, music, and sunshine—are often the safest way to counteract fatigue.

Add Zip to Your Water Supply

It's simple—but important—advice: Drink water for health. And in a dramatic yet accurate article in the *Ladies' Home Journal* (July 1921), Dr. Woods Hutchinson tells readers why: "Water is the most important element in the whole mixture [of the human body]; in it we live and move and have our being. It is vital that our contained water should be changed frequently;

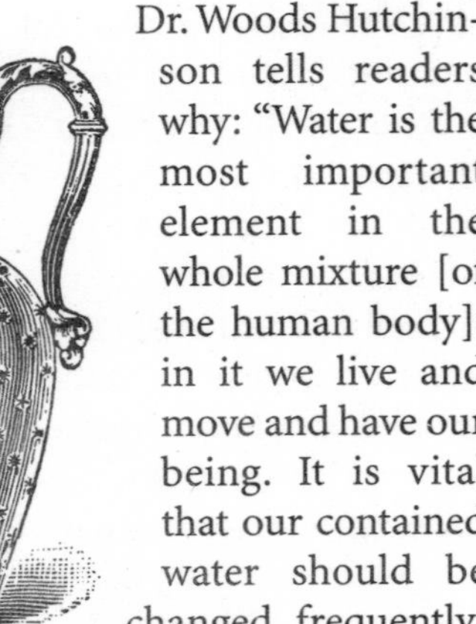

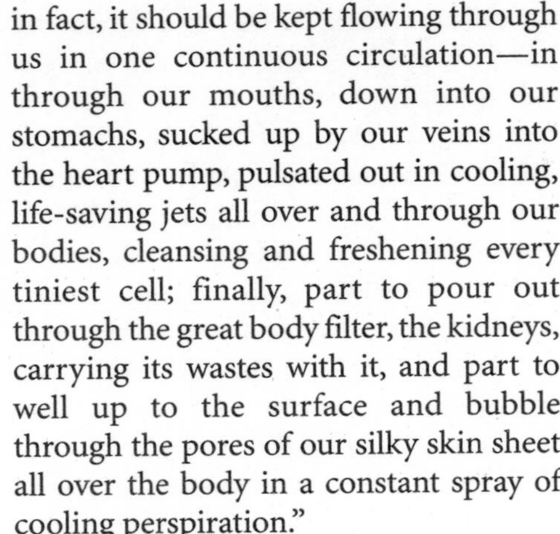

in fact, it should be kept flowing through us in one continuous circulation—in through our mouths, down into our stomachs, sucked up by our veins into the heart pump, pulsated out in cooling, life-saving jets all over and through our bodies, cleansing and freshening every tiniest cell; finally, part to pour out through the great body filter, the kidneys, carrying its wastes with it, and part to well up to the surface and bubble through the pores of our silky skin sheet all over the body in a constant spray of cooling perspiration."

Whew! That should be enough to inspire anyone to keep up their water intake. But the current recommendation of six to eight 8-ounce glasses of water per day can be daunting to many. It can help if you liven up this essential daily liquid with a dash of flavor or refreshing ice. Try these tricks.

Add a splash of fruit juice. Stick with 2 or 3 tablespoons, since most fruit juices are high in sugar, which adds unwanted calories.

Make juice cubes. Fill an ice cube tray with your favorite fruit beverage and freeze as usual. Float the cubes in your water.

Freeze fruit in cubes. Fill an ice cube tray with water, and then plop a strawberry into each cell before popping the tray in the freezer. Float the cubes in your water. It's fun to nibble on the tasty berries as they free themselves from the ice.

Squeeze in a little citrus. Add a squeeze of juice from a slice of fresh lemon, orange, or lime (or all three) to your water glass. Toss the squeezed citrus slice into your glass, too.

Drink half and half. Fill a water bottle halfway with water and put it in the freezer. Top it off with fresh water when ready to drink. The frozen half makes the entire portion ice-cold.

Fruit Fights Fatigue

■ Low-carb and no-carb diets are a hot modern trend, but one possible negative side effect of these diets is sluggishness. To combat this, follow some old-time advice and boost your energy by eating fruit. As an article in the August 21, 1851, edition of *Frederick Douglass's Paper* notes, "No one, we imagine, ever lived longer, or freer from the paroxysms of disease, by discarding the delicious fruits of the land in which he finds a home. On the contrary, they are necessary to the preservation of health, and are therefore caused to make their appearance at the very time when the condition of the body, operated upon by deteriorating causes not always understood, requires their grateful, renovating influences."

Here's the modern take on low-carb diets and fruit from endocrinologist David Schteingart, M.D., associate director of the General Clinical Research Center at the University of Michigan Health System. "People who are on very low carbohydrate diets tend to feel tired. Carbohydrates provide a quick source of energy, and you need energy for muscle metabolism. Your endurance may be decreased by low carbohydrate intake because the body has to use fat to provide energy for muscle contraction." Using fat to provide energy is not the body's first choice; thus the process of making fuel is less efficient. So when the scale says your diet is working, but you're too tired to enjoy your new lower-weight life, try a compromise by snacking on low-calorie, carbohydrate-rich apples, cherries, cranberries, grapefruit, melon, oranges, peaches, pears, plums, raspberries, or strawberries—and enjoy their invigorating influences!

Teatime, Please

To extend the effects of an energizing, healthy carbohydrate snack, try indulging in a modern version of a Victorian tea. This is a great idea for a midafternoon nibble, just as lunch's fuel begins wearing off but before you sit down to dinner. Victorian ladies honored "taking tea" as a daily ritual. While these ladies tended to dress in fine clothing and use their best serving pieces for this 3:00 to 5:00 P.M. event, you can make the practice just as beneficial by simply taking a few minutes to relax and enjoy a cup of mint tea along with protein-packed peanut butter spread on top of a rice cake, for example. Or mix some wheat germ or whole grain cereal into protein-rich yogurt, or tuck a slice of cheese inside whole grain pita bread, and heat it just enough to melt the cheese. Following the 19th-century ladies' lead, invite a friend or two over to share tea, a light snack, conversation, and, in true Victorian style, a little harmless gossip.

Build Momentum with Molasses

When you don't get enough iron in your diet, you may feel a little run-down. If you're certain the problem is not serious enough to warrant a physician's attention, then you could try treating your symptoms by taking blackstrap molasses, which is loaded with iron. This modern-day treatment is much like the advice offered back on October 5, 1882, in *The Christian Recorder:* "The blood is the foundation of life, it circulates through every part of the body, and unless it is pure and rich, good health is impossible. If disease has entered the system the *only* sure and quick way to drive it out is to purify and enrich the blood. These simple facts are well known, and the highest medical authorities agree that *nothing* but iron will restore the blood to its natural condition." Today, you can purchase over-the-counter iron boosters, but for less money and better taste, select instead muffin recipes with blackstrap molasses, or simply stir a teaspoon of blackstrap molasses into a cup of tea. For the record, there's also a megadose of iron in oysters, beans, and red meats.

Aphrodisiacs: Fact or Fiction?

NOT IN THE MOOD? Too tired? Don't have the energy? Perhaps an aphrodisiac can combat your low libido. For centuries, people have looked to certain foods and drinks to inspire passion. The French poet Paul Verlaine (1844–1896) is often credited with starting the 19th-century fad of drinking absinthe, an extract from the wormwood plant that was celebrated as an exotic and erotic tonic. (*Caution:* It's now known that this beverage has horrid side effects, including blindness and nerve injury, so don't try it!) Today, there is no scientific proof that any food can arouse or intensify desire, but researchers are testing certain theories. Regardless of the results, it's fun to see which foods make the list.

- Alcoholic beverages, particularly champagne
- Asparagus
- Bananas
- Cappuccino
- Caviar
- Chocolate
- Figs
- Garlic
- Ginseng
- Oysters
- Puffer fish
- Radishes
- Truffles

Three Ways to Bounce Back from the Blahs

Our ancestors so frowned on drunkenness that the subject was avoided at all cost, as were any cures for the resulting hangover. Oh, they had next-morning recipes, but these concoctions were often simply dumped into a bartender's guidebook, with the understanding that everyone knew when to drink them. For example, Jessup Whitehead offers a recipe for the Prairie Oyster in his book *The Steward's Handbook and Guide to Party Catering: In Five Acts* (1889). A common hangover cure long into the 1930s, this recipe requires a mix of "½ teaspoon vinegar, 1 new-laid egg, little salt, pepper and dash of Worcestershire sauce; to be drunk off raw." You do *not* want to drink a Prairie Oyster today, since we now know that raw eggs may contain salmonella. Instead, here are three safe ways to survive the inevitable next-morning blahs.

1. Sip a cup of caffeine-free ginger tea, available in convenient tea bags at most grocery stores.

2. Alcohol is dehydrating, so while enjoying your cocktails, drink one glass of water for every alcoholic beverage. In addition, drink one or two glasses of water before bed and several more immediately upon waking up.

3. Since you're already dehydrated from the alcohol, avoid all caffeine-containing beverages, including coffee, caffeinated soft drinks, and tea. Caffeine is a natural diuretic, and that's the last thing you need.

Build Energy with a Lively Melody

▪ It's common knowledge that music can soothe and calm, but by tweaking your selection, it can also wake you up and boost your energy. "Music has a very happy effect in relieving the mind when fatigued with study. It would be well if every studious person were so far acquainted with that science as to amuse himself after severe thought, by playing such airs as have a tendency to raise the spirits, and inspire cheerfulness and good-humour." So reported the 1785 edition of *Domestic Medicine,* by William Buchan, M.D. How right the doctor was. Today, many hospitals play music to elevate patients' moods, counteract depression, and promote movement for physical rehabilitation. When it comes to revving up the human engine, Barbara Reuer, Ph.D., director of MusicWorx, a San Diego–based music therapy provider, mentions the old-time marching bands once used to fire up our boys going off to war. While a rousing John Philip Sousa tune may be overkill for an afternoon pick-me-up, Dr. Reuer does suggest playing something stimulative, with lots of rhythm, to get the juices flowing. "Depending on your era, you might play Three Dog Night, Glenn Miller, Elvis Presley, or anything upbeat. Try playing along with your musical selection, using what I call musician-proof instruments, like a drum or marimbas—the sort of instruments that sound better with training but *never* sound bad!" Is listening to upbeat music a fair (and some might say healthier) replacement for a cup of coffee? Dr. Reuer says that she hears a frequent and resounding yes from many clients.

PEARLS OF WISDOM

"This is the only body you will ever have in this world. A large share of the pleasure and pain in life will come through the use you make of it."

BENJAMIN JEFFERIS, M.D., AND JAMES NICHOLS, *The Household Guide or Domestic Cyclopedia* (1892)

Let the Sun In

▪ You wake up, pull back the curtains, see a bright blue sky filled with sunshine, and exclaim, "What a beautiful day!" Truth is, this beautiful sight is pleasing not only to your eyes but also to your body. We humans need sunshine every day, winter and summer, to keep our mental health and energy level in tip-top shape. Why is sunshine so important? In

The Household Guide or Domestic Cyclopedia (1892), Benjamin Jefferis, M.D., Ph.D., and James Nichols explain the sun's value this way: "Seclusion from sunshine is one of the great misfortunes of our civilized life. The same cause which makes the potato vines white and sickly when grown in dark cellars, operates to produce the pale, sickly girls that are reared in our parlors. Expose either to the rays of the sun, and they begin to show color, health, and strength."

Although he's never drawn an analogy to the potato, Norman Rosenthal, M.D., of Rockville, Maryland, does agree in theory with this old-time information. Dr. Rosenthal is a psychiatrist and leading national authority in the study of seasonal affective disorder (SAD), a form of depression that's associated with short daylength in the winter months. In severe cases, SAD can be quite debilitating. Your health care provider may recommend newfangled treatments involving artificial full-spectrum light. But if you find yourself generally lacking energy or feeling a little less productive, you may have a mild and self-treatable form of SAD. As Dr. Rosenthal says, "Mild cases are very common, and they can be greatly helped by stepping outside. Fifteen to 30 minutes, especially in the morning, can make a big difference." So, weather permitting, put on the appropriate clothing, slather on that sunscreen (winter and summer!), take a walk outdoors, and let your body drink in the sun.

CHAPTER 8

Beauty and Body Care
A Thing of Beauty Is a Joy Forever

BEFORE DEPARTMENT STORES built sprawling cosmetics counters and pricey spas taught us that good health begets loveliness, women and men depended on homemade treatments and common sense to enhance their natural beauty. Concoctions consisted of one part ingenuity, one part heirloom recipe, and one part accessible ingredients found in most kitchens or gardens. From skin care to tooth polish, slim waists to gorgeous hair, these antique prescriptions always resurface—because they work! In this chapter, you'll see how our great-grandparents' wisdom influenced many of today's most technologically advanced personal care therapies.

Terrific Tips for Teeth and Breath

WHEN ARCHAEOLOGISTS dig up skulls of prehistoric humans, they often find grooves in the teeth—indicating that these very old-time folks used some sort of device to clean their pearly whites. Even cave dwellers wanted a beautiful smile! Fortunately, oral hygiene has evolved, but many modern products are little changed from the homemade formulas that gave our great-grandparents whiter teeth and pleasant breath.

Baking Soda for Super Smiles

■ As the race for whiter, brighter teeth heats up, with more and more bleaching products introduced every day, baking soda remains in the lead. *A Friend in Need,* published by Arm & Hammer in 1922, recommends baking soda for cleaning teeth because it's gritty enough to remove ugly yellow plaque but not abrasive enough to remove healthy tooth enamel—which can't be said for some modern toothpastes. Combine baking soda with hydrogen peroxide for an effervescent effect that lifts particles caught between teeth, while also helping to kill bacteria and providing a slight whitening effect. To make this terrific tooth-cleaning formula, mix about ¼ teaspoon hydrogen peroxide with about ½ teaspoon baking soda in any small cup (a 3-ounce paper cup is fine). Scoop the paste up with your toothbrush and proceed! The baking soda tastes a little salty, and the hydrogen peroxide may give your gums a refreshing tingle, but rest assured, this old-fashioned recipe is completely safe, even if you should swallow a bit. A quick swish of clear water after brushing eliminates the salty aftertaste. Mix a fresh batch each time you brush. Once you've done it a few times, you'll find it just as easy as squeezing that old tube of toothpaste.

BIZARRE BUT TRUE

An Ancient Toothpaste Recipe

Believe it or not, a toothpaste recipe that's more than 1,500 years old actually contains a natural ingredient that dentists are now researching as an aid in fighting gum disease: the iris flower. The recipe, written on a piece of papyrus currently on display in Austria's National Library, describes a "powder for white and perfect teeth." The ingredients, according to the translation from Greek to English, include 1 drachma of rock salt (a drachma equals one-hundredth of an ounce), 2 drachmas of mint, 1 drachma of dried iris flower, and 20 grains of pepper, all of them crushed and mixed together. Before you prepare a batch of this ancient mix, give dental experts time to complete their research and declare this ancient formula safe and effective.

Mint Makes a Tasty Difference

▪ Add a minty zip to your baking soda toothpaste, and you not only clean your teeth but also freshen your breath! Here's a recipe that's a takeoff on a recommendation for a homemade peppermint mouthwash from *Godey's Lady's Book* (October 1855): Mix together 6 teaspoons baking soda, ⅓ teaspoon salt, 4 teaspoons glycerin, and about 15 drops of peppermint or wintergreen extract. (All of these ingredients are available in most grocery or health food stores.) The mixture should have a traditional toothpaste consistency. This recipe makes enough for 15 to 20 applications, depending on how much you use at one time. Store the mixture in any appropriately sized container with a snug lid—such as one of those handy plastic containers you use when traveling.

Old-Time Toothpicks

▪ Next time you select a packet of flavored toothpicks from the shelf, count your blessings. One hundred years ago,

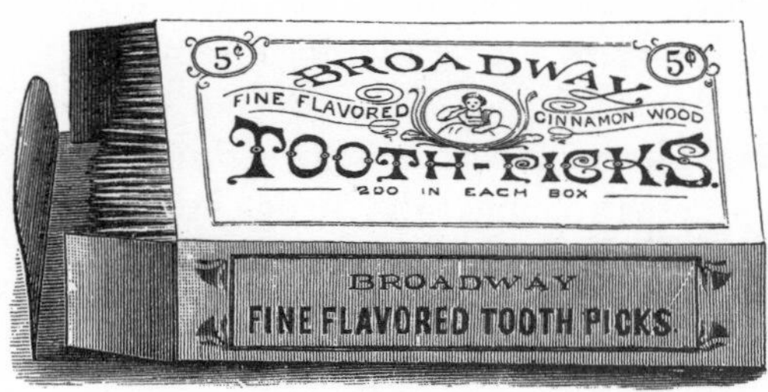

our ancestors weren't so lucky. *Mothers and Daughters* magazine (1890) gives some prickly advice: "If using a toothpick, use a quill or a bamboo splint, or a thorn from a hawthorn bush." Thorns for cleaning your gums? Ouch!

For Cinnamon Fans

Everyone wants fresh, clean, sweet-smelling breath. But we don't all agree on which sweet smell is best: mint or cinnamon. Cinnamon lovers will enjoy this report from Baroness Staffe in *The Lady's Dressing Room* (1893): "The people of Java eat the bark of cinnamon to perfume their mouths and make them sweet. The famous little dancers of Kampong, at the Paris Exhibition, had brought a large provision of it." Now, you probably don't want to walk around with a clump of cinnamon bark tucked in your cheek, but you can enjoy cinnamony-fresh breath with this simple homemade mouthwash: Boil 5 cinnamon sticks with 1 cup water in a covered pan. You can make as much as a 3-day supply (after that, it may taste stale) by adding more water and sticks; just keep the ratio the same. After boiling for 5 minutes, remove the pan from the heat, remove the lid, discard the cinnamon sticks, and let the liquid cool. Store in a clean bottle and rinse your mouth as desired. There's an extra benefit to this mouthwash, too: Your home smells delicious as the sticks boil.

A Berry Good Idea

Eating fresh strawberries is a tasty treat, and the acid they contain serves to whiten your teeth. The *London Pharmacopoeia* (1679) reports that the gritty outer skin of the berries helps loosen plaque and trapped food particles. While modern dentists wouldn't recommend brushing your teeth with mashed berries, biting into some fresh red strawberries works nicely during a picnic or other occasion when conventional toothbrushing isn't an option.

OLD-TIME ODDITIES

Hog Hair Toothbrush

THE FIRST TOOTHBRUSH, invented by a Chinese emperor in 1498, was made of bristly hairs from the neck of Siberian hogs. These hog bristles were plucked and then embedded into a handle made of bone or bamboo. In short order, the toothbrush became quite popular throughout Europe. The only problem back then was cost—collecting all those bristles was expensive! So in many cases, less-affluent families shared one brush.

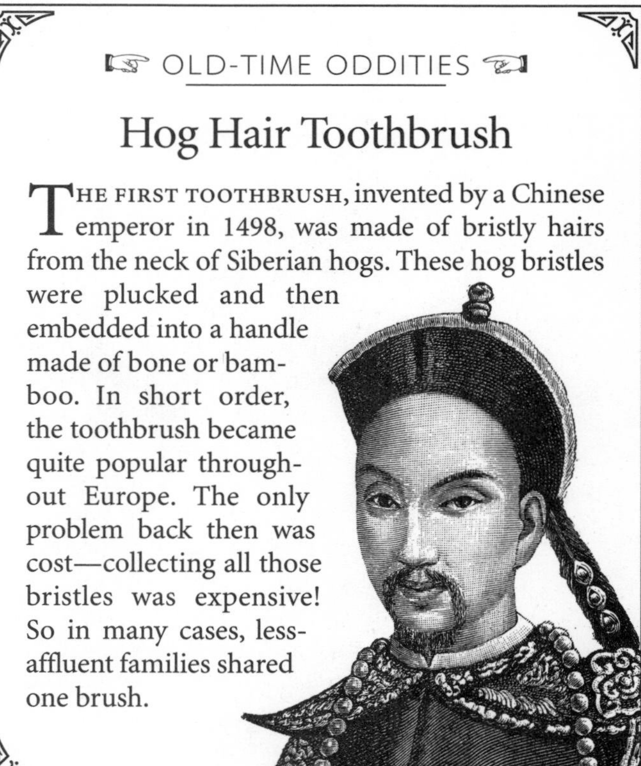

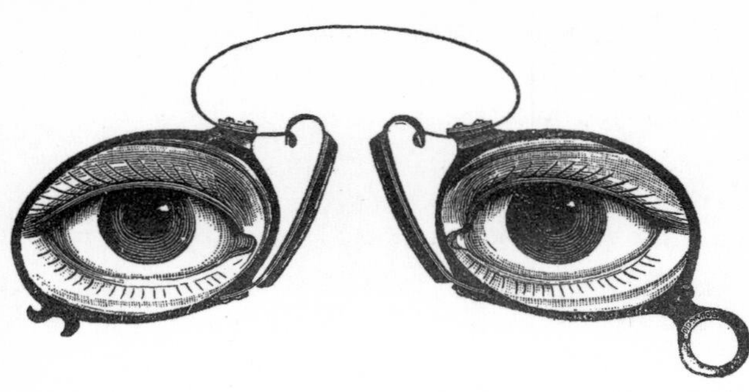

Excellent Eye Care Advice

Poets, songwriters, and fine artists have long paid tribute to the eyes' beauty, although how we embellish their loveliness flip-flops from era to era. At times, outlining the eyes with dramatic black make-up was the standard; during other periods, the height of beauty was to leave eyes completely unadorned. Here you will find the best ideas from each period—from eyewashes to make-up removers, crow's-foot creams to eyebrow grooming—sure to enhance your eyes' natural beauty.

Appreciate Your Wrinkles— And Then Moisturize

■ The best recipe for those dreaded crow's-feet is one part moisturizer and one part attitude adjustment. Let's begin with the latter, since it's gloriously free. In *The Lady's Dressing Room* (1893), Baroness Staffe explains that those who laugh a lot may be prone to little wrinkles around their eyes and mouth, "but these are rather pleasing. There need be no anxiety except about wrinkles that come from causes we ought to fight against: cheerfulness is a virtue to be encouraged." In other words, consider eye crinkles a valuable accomplishment! As for the formula's second part, you can minimize eye wrinkles by choosing a moisturizer that contains retinol, antioxidants, and/or glycolic acid—three ingredients shown to help the skin renew and repair damage due to age. Although the body continually renews its supply of elastin and collagen, production decreases with age. As the skin loses both collagen and elastin, it becomes thinner and less able to hold in moisture. Eye creams with retinol, antioxidants, and glycolic acid cannot reverse the aging process, but they can slow it down.

Castor Oil Chases Wrinkles

■ Following her grandmother's lead, Chicago health writer Donna Shryer dabs two drops of pure castor oil around her eyes before bed. "I have no idea where my grandmother got this idea," Donna explains, "maybe in Germany, where she was born in 1904. But I must say, her eyes remained wrinkle-free until the day she died . . . at the very old age of 98!" There is a scientific basis for Donna's grandmother's eye care regimen. Castor oil acts as a humectant, which means it attracts moisture to the skin and retains it, promoting healthier skin cell rejuvenation. This is also why some plastic surgeons apply castor oil to the area around an incision after surgery. You can find pure castor oil in many pharmacies, as well as health food stores.

Eyebright Takes the Red Out

■ In the 17th century, Nicholas Culpeper, renowned English herbalist and author of *The English Physician,* wrote that eyebright has a powerful ability to heal every possible eye problem, including loss of sight. Today, eyebright herb (*Euphrasia*) is not quite so highly regarded as a miracle cure, but it is still respected as an excellent eyewash ingredient, shown to revive red, irritated eyes. Steep 2 tablespoons eyebright herb in 2 cups hot water until cool, which will take about 3 minutes. Strain the mix for a clear liquid. Dip a cotton ball into the liquid and wipe your eyes with it. Eyebright is available in health food or herb stores and may help relieve eyestrain, eye inflammation, and those itchy eyes brought on by colds or allergies.

A Therapeutic Tea for the Eyes

Those late nights spent laughing with friends and sharing silly stories are not so funny the next morning—especially when you glance in the mirror and see drowsy eyes rimmed with unsightly dark circles. To restore your beautiful eyes, try a technique used by high-living flappers in the 1920s. They soaked cotton balls in chamomile tea and applied the cotton to their eyes to reverse dark circles. Today we have the convenience of commercial chamomile tea bags for this trick. Steep two cups of tea, so you'll have one bag for each eye. Remove the bags, squeeze out the excess liquid, and set them aside to cool. Meanwhile, sip and enjoy your tea. (Since you made two cups, put the second in the fridge—chamomile is excellent as an iced tea.) When your cup's drained, lie down and place one cooled tea bag over each closed eyelid. After resting for about 20 minutes, your eyes should be refreshed and the dark circles less noticeable.

PEARLS OF WISDOM

"The most beautiful eyes are those which express all the feelings sincerely and directly. I know some that are good, tender, and sweet, but they can flash like lightning in moments of indignation or enthusiasm. These eyes can hide nothing; you may have confidence in those who have them."

BARONESS STAFFE,
The Lady's Dressing Room (1893)

Take Off Make-Up with Old-Fashioned Oil

If you wear eye make-up, don't bother buying a special eye make-up remover. All you need to make your own remover is castor oil and two ingredients you probably have on hand in your kitchen. This perfectly safe and absolutely gentle eye make-up remover uses ingredients that our Victorian foremothers kept on their toilette table. Mix together 1 tablespoon canola oil, 1 tablespoon castor oil, and 1 tablespoon light olive oil. Store the mix in a clean container with a tight lid. To use, saturate a small, clean cotton ball. Dab the lash line and lid; then gently wipe off the make-up. Due to the

☞ BIZARRE BUT TRUE ☜

Lash Pearls

THOSE DECADENT FLAPPERS in the 1920s were not satisfied with mascara alone—no, they desired lashes of inhuman length. To accomplish this, they dipped a toothpick into melted wax and then applied a bead of the wax to the end of each lash. When the wax hardened, it gave the impression of a tiny row of pearls.

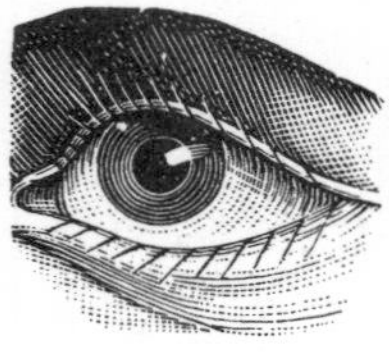

mixture's emollient nature, there's no need to rub—make-up should slide right off—and you do not need to wash off any oily residue, since the remover also acts as a nice moisturizer.

Deflating Under-Eye Bags

■ Trapped fluid is a common cause for those droopy bags under the eyes, which often look the worst when you first wake up. The bags may be due to allergies or sinus problems, and for mild situations an over-the-counter allergy treatment sometimes helps. Or you can place two cool cucumber slices (no need to peel the cukes first) over each closed eyelid, lie down, and relax for 15 to 20 minutes.

This treatment became quite popular in the late 1800s, when cucumber juice was a common beauty aide, as reported in 1870 in *Personal Beauty, How to Cultivate and Preserve It in Accordance with the Laws of Health*. "In France they attribute sovereign cosmetic virtue to the juice of the cucumber," wrote Daniel Brinton, M.D., and George Napheys, M.D. "All the shops keep a *lait de concombre,* or a *pomade de concombre.*" Those French shopkeepers probably didn't know why cucumber helps—cucumber has an astringent property that slightly and safely constricts blood vessels, which in turn helps to deflate under-eye bags.

Treat Your Brows with a Toothbrush

■ Heed some old-time beauty advice and choose your eyebrow pencil with care. In *Our Deportment* (1881), John Young advises, "The eyebrows may be brushed carefully in the direction in which they should lie. In general, it is in exceedingly bad taste to dye either lashes or brows, for it usually brings them into disharmony with the hair and features." To achieve the tonal harmony Mr. Young prescribes, stick with eyebrow pencils that match your current hair color, or if your hair is gray, pencils close to your original hair color. "Very dark eyebrows make us look older," says Chicago-based make-up artist Lori Neapolitan. "Big, soft eyebrow pencils work best because they give a softer, more natural line." And here's another modern hint for eyebrow care. Skip the pricey eyebrow groomer and buy a soft, cheap toothbrush instead. Use that toothbrush to sweep the brow hairs up after applying pencil, gently blending the color and removing any hint of a harsh line.

Simple Substitute for Mascara

■ When you're out of mascara, you're not out of luck as long as you have a tube of petroleum jelly at hand. For a quick and subtle darkening of your lashes, put a dot of petroleum jelly one-quarter the size of a pea on your finger, and stroke over the tips of your upper lashes. (Skip the bottom lashes, as the jelly could creep into your eye and temporarily blur your vision.) This is a neat trick from the early 1900s, and it inspired chemist T. L. Williams to create the first mascara by blending petroleum jelly with coal dust. Mr. Williams had watched his sister, Mabel, applying petroleum jelly to her lash tips, and that sparked his brainstorm, which is why he named his invention and the company he founded in 1915 *Maybelline*.

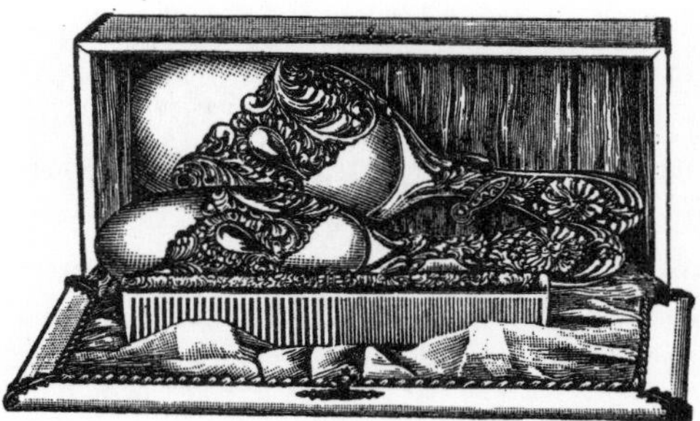

Helpful Hair Care Hints

By today's standards, truly beautiful hair is naturally healthy hair. It's a concept that comes and goes—for example, leaving hair natural was very much in vogue during the mid-1800s, but in the 1960s, we ripped and ratted our hair to achieve big bouffant fashions. Back now in style, these old-time hints have a remarkably modern twist.

Six Ingredients for Shampooing Success

■ Essential oils that old-timers relied on for hair care really do work. Rosemary was a favorite—*Godey's Lady's Book* from April 1860 recommends several hair washes that include rosemary. Whatever your hair type, there is an essential oil that comes highly recommended for contributing to its ultimate health.

Nourish and moisturize. Try cedarwood, chamomile, clary sage, lavender, rosemary, thyme, or ylang-ylang.

Add thickness and body. Use cedarwood or clary sage.

Reduce oiliness. Try bergamot, cedarwood, lavender, lemon, pine, rosemary, or ylang-ylang.

Add luster. Try sweet basil, Roman chamomile, or lavender.

Detangle hair. Use chamomile, grapefruit, marigold, passionflower, or sweet clover.

Relieve dandruff. Try cedarwood, clary sage, lemon, pine, rosemary, or tea tree.

You can buy a commercially formulated shampoo and conditioner containing the essential oils that produce the effect you're looking for, or buy your regular shampoo and blend in the essential oil of your choice each time you wash your hair. Just pour some shampoo or conditioner into your palm, add one drop of your preferred essential oil, mix them together, and spread the shampoo or conditioner on your hair.

Old-Fashioned Soap Is Shampoo, Too

■ The most popular type of soap in 19th-century households is still a great choice today. In the 1800s, Americans relied on castile soap for much of their personal toilette. They washed their face with it, shaved with it, and dissolved it in warm water for shampoo. This one-bar-does-it-all product is very economical to use, and because pure castile soaps are made of natural ingredients (water, olive oil, and sodium hydroxide), they are incredibly gentle cleansers. In fact, *Cassell's Household Guide* (circa 1880) advises that newborns be washed only in warm rainwater and castile soap. So try some for your own baby-soft skin. Castile soap is available in health food stores as well as many grocery stores and drugstores.

Take a Shine to Baking Soda

■ There's no need to buy a pricey shampoo to bring out the natural highlights in your hair. Instead, follow the lead of *The Delineator* magazine (October 1894), which suggests that women wash the dark ends of their hair with bicarbonate of soda (baking soda) in order to bring out lighter tones. This tip is effective because baking soda is a gentle but thorough cleanser that leaves hair squeaky-clean and removes any residues of hair spray or styling gel that might dull your hair. Even the slightest natural highlight can shine through. Mix about a teaspoon of baking soda in with your usual single application of shampoo, and apply the baking soda–shampoo mixture to all of your hair, not just the ends. Massage it into the hair, and rinse as usual.

OLD-FASHIONED FAVORITES

Olive Oil for Improved Shine

In the 1920s, shampoo makers such as Palmolive boasted that their products not only cleaned but also conditioned, due to their use of olive oil as a primary ingredient. Those shampoo manufacturers were onto something! You can give yourself silky and shiny hair—for pennies—by treating your hair with olive oil straight from the bottle. Simply distribute about ¼ cup of olive oil evenly into your hair. Massage it onto the scalp, as well. After about 15 minutes, use warm water to rinse out the oil, and then shampoo as usual.

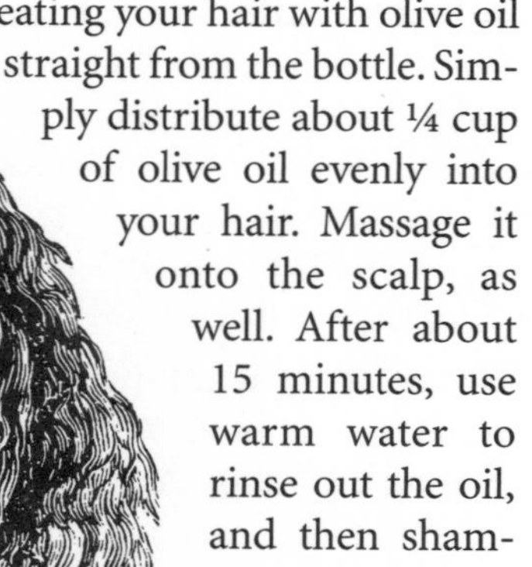

Turning Lemons into a Lemon Aid

■ For truly clean hair, rinse with lemon juice after you shampoo. "When you shampoo your hair a curd is formed by soap. It settles on the hair and stays, no matter how frequently you rinse with water alone. The hair is sticky and unclean, although you 'washed it good.' The lemon juice eliminates the curd completely. The hair is really clean," reports a booklet produced by a major citrus grower in the early 1920s. Squeeze one lemon into a quart of water and use the lemon solution as a final rinse after shampooing. You'll see and feel the lemony difference!

Valuable Vinegar Rinse

■ Victorian legend as well as American Colonial wisdom tells us that apple cider vinegar (one part vinegar to eight parts water) adds shine to dark hair. After shampooing, saturate your hair with the vinegar solution, let it rest for 5 minutes, and then rinse out.

Cap Trick for Terrific Hair

■ Here's a nifty trick that comes from our Colonial foremothers' practice of wearing mobcaps to protect their hair from dust and dirt. To prevent your hair from becoming tangled or dirty when you tackle gardening chores or heavy housework on a warm day, cover your hair with a cap before you start. You don't literally

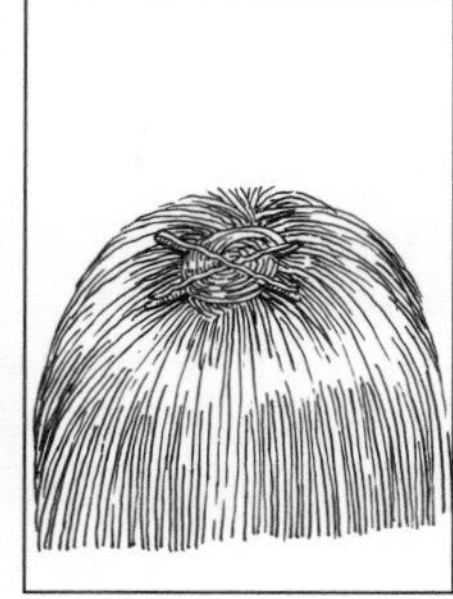

To make a pin curl, twist a section of hair around your finger and slide your finger out. Use two bobby pins to secure the curl.

have to use a mobcap, which is a plain cotton cap with a gathered ruffle around the edge. You can use your regular gardening hat, a straw hat, or any square cotton scarf. Fold the scarf into a triangle, place the fold along your forehead hairline, bring the corners behind your head, and tie. To gain an extra reward from this technique, loosely roll your hair into pin curls before donning your 21st-century "mobcap."

To make a pin curl, use one hand to hold a section of hair, and place a finger from your other hand against and under this section, about ½ inch from your head. Wrap the hair around your finger. Next, slide the finger out while holding the curl secure with your other hand. Twist the curl so it lies flat against your head and insert two bobby pins, crisscrossed, to fasten the curl.

For looser curls, use two or three fingers to form the loop. Don't be concerned if your curls appear a bit messy. You're not aiming to mold an exact shape but rather to boost volume, so random pin curls work fine. Your body heat sets the curls like a hair dryer would! When you're done weeding or vacuuming, swap your hat for a shower cap and take a quick shower. Then get dressed and remove your pin curls, and you'll be ready for a night out with beautiful, bouncy hair.

Vaseline to the Rescue

■ Vaseline has a long history in American homes. In October 1896, the *Ladies' Home Journal* reported that Vaseline, rubbed on the hair and then brushed into the hair, creates a wonderful shine. However, this technique also produces a greasy look. Instead, try these modern practical approaches to hair care using petroleum jelly.

Keep hair dye under control. If you color your hair at home, keep dye from creeping onto and discoloring your skin by applying a thin coat of Vaseline along the skin that follows your hairline.

Fight frizzies. For humid days, tame the frizzies by pulling your hair back into a ponytail. Next, rub a pea-size amount of Vaseline on your palms. With palms against your head, run your hands over your head, from hairline to ponytail.

Remove stuck gum. Apply a dollop of Vaseline to the problem area and massage it into the hair, and the gum should comb out. Any remaining Vaseline will wash out with the next shampoo.

Avoid tears at shampoo time. If you need to wash the hair of a tot or an elderly or disabled loved one, swipe Vaseline along the person's eyebrows. This repels soapy water, causing it to drip over to the sides of the face, rather than into the eyes. Afterward, wipe the Vaseline off with a washcloth and warm water.

Skip Soap When Cleaning Brushes

CLEAN YOUR COMBS and brushes often, instructs Baroness Staffe in *The Lady's Dressing Room* (1893): "The greatest neatness is necessary for all implements used for hair-dressing . . . There is nothing better than ammonia for cleaning hair-brushes; it does not soften the bristles as soap and soda do. Put a teaspoonful of ammonia in a quart of water; dip the brush into this, preserving the ivory or wooden backs as well as possible. An immersion of a few seconds will suffice to take out all the grease. The brush should then be dipped in clear water and dried in the open air, but not in the sun."

Diluted ammonia is indeed a viable brush cleaner for natural as well as synthetic bristles. Or you can add about 1 teaspoon of your shampoo to a quart of warm water and let your brush soak in the soapy solution for about 10 minutes. Then rinse it with clean warm water. Whether you use ammonia or shampoo, always remove loose hair caught in the brush before washing. To do this, comb the hair out with a wide-tooth comb or pick the hair out with the handle of a rat-tail comb.

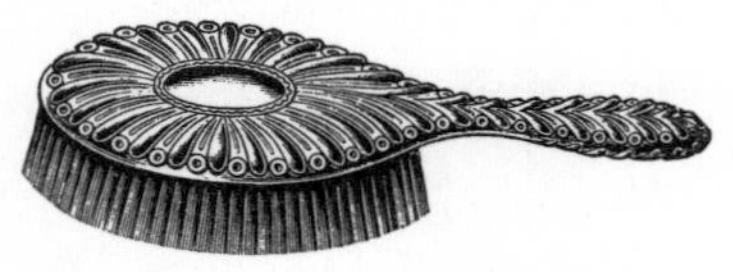

Best Ideas for Brushing

■ The old-time idea of a good daily brushing really does result in better-looking hair—if you do it right and use a quality brush. Old-time brushing regimens made a woman a slave to her hair, though. For example, *Decorum* magazine (1880) instructs, "The hair should be brushed for at least twenty minutes in the morning, for ten minutes when it is dressed in the middle of the day, and for a like period at night." Fortunately, that's overkill. Brushing does help distribute natural moisturizing oil along the hair shaft, which in turn promotes better shine and gloss, but 20 daily strokes is enough for healthy hair. More important than the number of strokes is the pressure used and the quality of your brush. Always be gentle; never rip snarls out. Place the palm of one hand underneath the snarl, hold your brush with the other hand, and brush the snarl with short, gentle strokes until gone. If it's a stubborn knot, dab a pea-size amount of conditioner onto the tangle and try again.

Our Victorian sisters used brushes made with natural boar bristles. This is still the best option, says Caroline Shamoun, proprietor of a hair salon in Skokie, Illinois. "You want a brush with natural boar bristles set in a ceramic base. They're more expensive, but natural bristles won't pop out or break in half like plastic, so these brushes should last for years . . . at least five, maybe ten." As for your hair's beauty, Caroline explains, "Natural bristles grip hair much better, which significantly cuts back on the ripping action of nylon bristles and also helps move natural oils from your scalp to the hair ends. Your hair really will look shinier." A ceramic base offers another benefit, Caroline points out: It holds heat from your blow dryer, so you end up with a heat source above the hair being dried (from the blow dryer) and below the hair (from the ceramic base). This significantly speeds up the drying process. It also helps distribute natural oil to all sides of the hair, which in turn raises the shine factor. And when it comes to detangling wet, snarled hair after a shampoo, Caroline says, "Don't use a brush at all. What you want is a wide-tooth comb, with the teeth about ¼ inch apart. It's less likely to break your hair."

Skin Care Secrets

Throughout history, ladies and gentlemen have dedicated untold time and care to their skin's beauty. Read on to learn their old-time secrets, including homemade shaving cream, luxurious milk baths, and simple moisturizers.

Enjoy an Old-Time Shaving Cream Blend

■ Daily shaving became the norm in the 1920s (thanks to magazine advertising campaigns that praised the clean-shaven man), before the days of canned shaving cream. A homemade shaving cream made from bar soap and a few additional ingredients is exactly what your grandfathers and great-grandfathers used for shaving—and it's still an economical, environmentally friendly, and efficient shaving solution. To prepare your own moisturizing shaving cream, try the following recipe.

Dissolve ½ cup grated hard white soap (a pure, gentle soap without fragrances works best) in ⅔ cup boiling water. Transfer your mix to a blender. Add 1 tablespoon borax, 2 tablespoons melted coconut oil, 3 tablespoons almond oil, and, if desired, approximately 20 drops of your favorite essential oil. (Coconut oil changes from solid to liquid form at 76°F. On warm days, it will be a liquid in the jar, and on cooler days, a white solid rather like Crisco. This natural transformation will not harm the product, and it need not be stored in the refrigerator.) Blend until fluffy and pour the results in a proper shaving mug or plain old coffee mug. Let harden. To use, cleanse your face (skip this step if you've just showered), dip a shaving brush in warm water, shake off any excess liquid, and promptly swirl the brush over your hardened shaving cream. Apply the lather on the brush to your beard and shave with a razor. Yes, preparing your own batch of shaving cream takes some time, but you'll enjoy it for weeks to come.

Vintage Aftershave

■ "No one shaving himself should neglect the use of Bay Rum . . . after shaving. It keeps the skin smooth and soft, and makes shaving an easy task," report Benjamin Jefferis, M.D., Ph.D., and James Nichols in *The Household Guide or Domestic Cyclopedia* (1892). Bay rum as an aftershave is just as soothing, gentle, and nicely fragrant for use today as it was at the turn of the 19th century. (Yes, women love it!) Don't look for bay rum in fancy department stores, though. Available from online suppliers and sometimes found in health food stores, pharmacies, and ethnic food markets, bay rum is not produced under any designer label.

If you're feeling adventurous, brew your own bay rum aftershave. This recipe is courtesy of Annie B. Bond, executive producer of the Care2.com Healthy Living section. "It's a very masculine aftershave. Truly, it smells divine. And you might want to make a double batch, since this recipe makes a great gift for men," Annie says. You'll need about 3 cups of dried bay leaves. Break each leaf in half and put the leaves in a quart jar with a screw-on lid. (You can recycle any old jar, as long as it's thoroughly cleaned first.) Add rum to the jar to cover the leaves, plus 2 inches. Screw on the lid and let this mix sit in a cool, dry place out of direct sunlight for 1 month. Finally, strain the mixture, reserving only the liquid. Splash it on after shaving. This recipe makes about 2½ cups of bay rum, which has an indefinite shelf life. As an alternative, you can replace the rum with witch hazel.

Milk Bath for Beauty

Tales of Cleopatra, queen of Egypt in the first century B.C., inevitably mention her famous beauty—in particular, the queen's radiant skin. Her secret, according to history books, lay in frequent baths of fresh milk. Modern research tells us that milk baths produce stunning skin because of milk's high levels of lactic acid, one of the alpha hydroxy acids (AHAs). AHAs naturally dissolve the "glue" that holds dead skin cells together. When you sit in milk, the skin receives a deep cleansing, with dead skin cells loosened and shed, or sloughed off.

It's easy to treat yourself to a luxurious milk bath at home. Pour 2 cups to 1 quart fresh milk or buttermilk into the tub as it fills. Soak for at least 20 minutes in the milk bath. Gently massage your skin with a washcloth or loofah to encourage sloughing. Try these variations, too.

- Instead of using fresh milk, mix 1 cup powdered milk into a warm bath.
- When you've had a hectic day, adding a few drops of lavender essential oil may increase the milk bath's relaxing effect.
- If you find yourself a bit pink after a long afternoon in the sun, add a cooling effect to your milk bath by slicing two or three medium cucumbers (no need to peel them) and floating them in your tub. In this scenario, skip even a gentle washcloth rubdown—your skin may be too sensitive.

Regardless of how your milk bath is prepared, when you're finished soaking, drain the tub and take a quick shower to thoroughly rinse all the milk off your body.

Lemon for Lovely Skin

A little lemon juice helps fade freckles, age spots, or mild brown splotches that naturally occur as our skin ages. It's an old-time treatment recommended by *The Manners That Win* (1880) for the whitest, palest skin possible. Given time, the acidity in lemon juice likely will fade dark spots. But straight lemon juice can also be very drying, so try diluting

A Sweet Way to Remove Body Hair

OUCH! Waxing to remove leg or armpit hair is no fun. Instead, try a method that dates back to ancient civilizations: body sugaring. Sugaring removes unwanted body hair by the root, in a process that's similar to body waxing. Unlike depilatory waxes, though, body sugar is made from all-natural ingredients. The sugar is not applied hot, so there's no worry about burning your skin. Fans swear that it's less painful than waxing. Annie B. Bond, executive producer of the Care2.com Healthy Living section, recommends the following body sugaring procedure.

You will need:

- Clean cotton fabric (choose fabric that is not coarsely woven)
- 2 cups sugar
- 1/4 cup lemon juice
- 1/4 cup water

Step 1. Cut the cotton fabric into 1-inch-wide strips 8 inches long or longer. The number of strips you will need depends on how large an area of skin you plan to sugar.

Step 2. Combine the sugar, lemon juice, and water in a heavy saucepan and heat on low. Heat the mixture to 250°F, using a candy thermometer to monitor the temperature. Watch the mixture carefully. Do not let it boil over.

Step 3. Remove the pan from the heat. Let the mixture cool so that it won't burn your skin. Test by applying a bit of the mixture to the palm of your hand, but bear in mind that this skin is tougher than the sensitive skin under your arms.

Step 4. When the mix is cool, use a dull knife or a Popsicle stick to spread the sugar mix on your skin. Once you've covered an area equal to three of your cotton strips, immediately cover this area with the strips. Keep repeating this process until you have covered the entire area from which you want to remove hair.

Step 5. Let set for a few minutes, pull the skin taut, and then rip strips off quickly in the direction of hair growth—as you would a Band-Aid.

1 tablespoon freshly squeezed lemon juice in ½ cup water. With a cotton ball, dab dark patches before applying your morning make-up and bedtime moisturizer. Instead of water, fans of this natural remedy sometimes mix ¼ teaspoon lemon juice with a single application of pure aloe vera gel (look for this in health food stores). You can also snap off a leaf from an aloe vera plant and rub your finger over the natural aloe vera juice from the leaf. Then dip this finger into freshly squeezed lemon juice. Now dab the mixture onto your skin where needed. Since aloe vera is reportedly another natural solution to fade dark skin spots, the two combined may work even better than lemon juice alone.

Honey Mask Helps Your Skin

■ Victorian women often relied on the following facial mask to promote a smooth complexion and wrinkle-free skin. To mix up a little magic for yourself, here's the recipe, as provided by *The Housekeeper's Handy Book, A Comprehensive Cyclopedia of Useful Information and Domestic Science in the Home* (1915). You will need 3 ounces finely ground barley or oatmeal, 1 ounce honey, and 1 beaten egg white. "Mix to a paste and spread thickly over the nose, cheeks and forehead before retiring. Cover the portions where the paste is applied with bits of old thin lawn, and let remain on all night. Wash off with warm water, first dampening and allowing to soften while dressing." Tweaking this recipe from a modern perspective, you can skip applying scraps of lawn fabric (very finely woven cotton with a silky feel), and overnight may be overkill, not to mention the downfall of a perfectly nice pillowcase. Instead, mix the ingredients and apply as explained above, then rinse off after 15 to 20 minutes. As you gently massage the mask onto your skin, the barley or oatmeal offers a mild exfoliant to help shed dry, dead skin. After the mask has been rinsed off, the honey leaves skin quite soft.

☞ BIZARRE BUT TRUE ☜

No Sting Intended

You know the expression "Mind your own beeswax," as in "Mind your own business"? Well, it waxes more interesting when you discover its unusual origins. In the 19th century, this cautionary saying made reference to the state of a woman's "make-up." Back then, make-up was considered vulgar, but because smallpox was rampant, many pockmarked women evened out their scarred complexions by applying beeswax. The expression alludes to sitting too closely to the fire, where one's beeswax could melt! Incidentally, fire screens like the one shown on page 73 became popular accessories partially to protect women wearing beeswax from too much direct heat.

Essential Oils for Bathing Excellence

Aromatherapy isn't a newfangled fad. Victorian women relied heavily on smelling salts laced with lavender to calm "the vapors"—fainting spells caused by tight corsets that severely restricted oxygen intake. While lavender did not solve the problem (only loosening the corset could do this), its relaxing effect when inhaled may have dispelled the dizziness these tightly bound women felt, and soothed the panic that precedes fainting. Aesthetician Valerie Fulbright of Evanston, Illinois, says that lavender remains a respected scent for inducing relaxation. Valerie explains that adding lavender, or any essential oil, for that matter, to your bathwater supplies a few more benefits beyond aromatherapy.

"All essential oils are hydrating, so a few drops in a warm bath helps moisturize your skin. Also, when you soak in water with an essential oil, the oil enters your skin and travels through your bloodstream, slightly intensifying the oil's healing power." Here are eight essential oils that Valerie suggests for your bath, along with their primary benefit.

Chamomile. Helps relax jangled nerves. It's also balancing, which means that it has a calming effect—taking the edge off extreme emotional states.

Eucalyptus. Used to refresh and energize, as well as clear congestion and soothe troublesome sinuses.

Lavender. A relaxing and soothing oil.

Lemon. All citrus oils (orange, grapefruit, lime, and the like) are balancing oils that lift the spirits.

Rose. An enchanting scent that simply pleases many women. This essential oil should not be used if you're pregnant.

Sandalwood. Selected to calm tension and induce relaxation, this oil is also recommended to soothe mild digestive problems.

Tea tree. Enjoy an energizing soak with tea tree oil. Because of its antibacterial and antifungal properties, it's also an excellent choice if you're suffering from a mild rash such as heat rash.

Ylang-ylang. A calming oil that is also good for regulating sluggish circulation.

Caution: Never use essential oils in place of a physician's treatment. If a health situation goes beyond mild, seek medical care before self-treating with an oil.

Almond for Kissable Lips

■ For lips that are soft, softer, softest, rely on almond oil. Victorian ladies understood well the value of this remarkable oil. *Godey's Lady's Book* (September 1876) suggests that mixing equal parts of almond oil and white wax would make a good lip salve. You can find pure white wax suitable for cosmetics in many health food stores; it may be called *beeswax* or *carnauba wax.* Slowly melt the wax in a double boiler, or fill a larger pan halfway with water, place a smaller pan into the larger one, put your wax into the smaller pan, and heat until melted. Once melted, add the almond oil (which is available at drugstores or health food stores), mix thoroughly, pour into a small container with a lid (plastic is fine),

and set aside to cool and harden. What we know now is that almond oil is just as effective straight from the bottle for sloughing off dry skin on your lips, so you don't have to fuss with making the salve. Just apply a few drops of sweet almond oil to your lips and then gently brush your lips with an unused, medium toothbrush. Rinse your lips with warm water and reapply a bit of oil to maintain the smoothness.

PEARLS OF WISDOM

"Discontented people, you may notice, always look ten years older than they are. The face gets wrinkled by frowning, pouting causes the mouth to protrude disagreeably, and they rapidly grow old and ugly. Compare with them a woman with a cheerful face . . . Her mouth curves delightfully, benevolence softens the expression of her eyes, and goodness beams from her smooth brow. She is perhaps older than the ill-tempered woman whom you see beside her, but she will always look like her younger sister."

BARONESS STAFFE,
The Lady's Dressing Room (1893)

Pearl Water

To make a moisturizing face soap using castile soap, try this recipe for Pearl Water from *The Household Guide or Domestic Cyclopedia* (1892): "Dissolve 1 pound castile soap in one gallon of water, then add alcohol, one quart; oil of rosemary and oil of lavender, each 2 drachms [2 teaspoons]. Mix well." What you will have is a homemade version of liquid soap. So when your store-bought liquid soap runs out, fill the empty (and thoroughly rinsed out) pump dispenser with Pearl Water.

Make-Up Magic for Mature Women

In *The Lady's Dressing Room* (1893), Baroness Staffe writes, "Let us accept our age. An octogenarian who continues to take care of her person can still be beautiful, charming, beloved by her children and her friends, young and old." Ah, wise words . . . although not our natural inclination when it comes to cosmetics. Chicago make-up artist Lori Neapolitan explains that part of recognizing our age means accepting that our skin has changed. "We tend to use the same products we loved 20 years ago. Or we resort to using nothing. Either way, we end up looking older." Instead, Lori offers these four bits of advice for 40-plus youngsters—guaranteed to enhance natural beauty.

Blend and smudge make-up colors. Harsh lines produce an aged effect. Eyeliner, applied to the top lid only, should be blurred to a whisper of definition; lip liner should be natural or in the same shade as your lipstick.

Try light-reflective products. These are available as moisturizers (worn alone or under foundation), as foundations, and as powders or creams to be gently applied over foundation. They diffuse light as it reflects off your face, which diminishes small lines and imparts a natural glow.

Avoid overdoing it. Minimal coverage should be your goal. Translucent and light-reflective foundations and blushes are a dynamic duo. Products labeled *full* or *maximum coverage* tend to cake on older skin, falling into and accentuating wrinkles.

Choose softer colors. Soft doesn't have to be boring. If you've always worn red lipstick, go pink; orange becomes peach; purple eye shadow becomes lavender.

Play It Cool

■ Here's a refreshing remedy for hot, dry summer skin based on a simple ingredient that's been around since 1846: witch hazel. Fill a spray bottle with one part witch hazel, one part lemon juice, and two parts water. Store it in your refrigerator. Before heading out into the hot summer sun (and after applying your sunscreen!), grab the bottle. When your skin becomes parched or sweaty, spritz your face. The witch hazel cools, and the lemon provides a terrific astringent as well as an invigorating scent.

Caution: This solution might sting if sprayed directly into the eyes. Be sure to close your eyes before you spray your own face, and be careful to avoid the eye area if you spray someone else.

A Shot of Sunscreen

■ The old-fashioned way to protect yourself from harmful ultraviolet rays is with a parasol, and it's the very reason Victorian ladies carried them! While toting a parasol remains a valid option for sun protection, applying sunscreen gives you more freedom of movement, especially when playing tennis, hiking, biking, picnicking, or simply enjoying the great outdoors. To figure out how much sunscreen to apply, turn to another old-time device—a shot glass. Using a shot glass to measure sunscreen never crossed the minds of old-time bartenders, but it works! As a general rule, one shot glass of sunscreen is enough to cover the exposed areas of your body.

Another effective way to protect your skin from the sun is to wear a wide-brimmed bonnet or hat. Turn to "Make a Flowery Easter Bonnet" on page 157 for simple directions for a do-it-yourself decorated sun hat.

Blend Your Own Vintage Scent

■ Victorian women understood well that when it came to eaux de toilette (toilet waters), colognes, and perfumes, it was crucial to use a very gentle hand. They preferred delicate floral scents, such as violet and rose, or citrus scents, such as lemon and orange. One of their favorites was lavender water, a wonderfully light scent that is especially appropriate for hot summer days when heavy perfume can literally take your breath away. Recipes for toilet waters were sometimes elaborate, like this one from *Beauty: Its*

Attainment and Preservation (1890): "Take spirits of wine [rectified ethyl alcohol], 1 pint; oil of lavender, 2 ounces; orris root, ½ ounce. Keep the mixture two or three weeks and then strain it through [a] thickness of blotting paper. It will then be ready for use." All of these ingredients are available in health food stores, and yes, you could follow the recipe to a tee, but there is a much simpler method. Visit your favorite store that offers pure essential oils (it's important that they be pure) and select several that please you. In a bottle with a tightly fitting cap, mix 4 or 5 drops of essential oil with 4 ounces distilled water. Shake gently. Now dot your fragrance gingerly on your wrists, behind your knees, and on each side of your neck. Begin by using one type of oil only; then try mixing several oils with the water for a custom blend. Be sure to keep the total amounts of oil and water in line with the basic proportions. For a light spritz when away from home, you can also pour your homemade toilet water into a small portable spray bottle—the kind you might use to carry hair spray in your handbag or when traveling.

Help for Nails, Hands, and Feet

The hands and feet are four of our most-used body parts, yet often the least pampered. We would do well to incorporate a few time-tested techniques for manicures and pedicures, with some modern suggestions added for good measure—giving these vital extremities the respect they deserve.

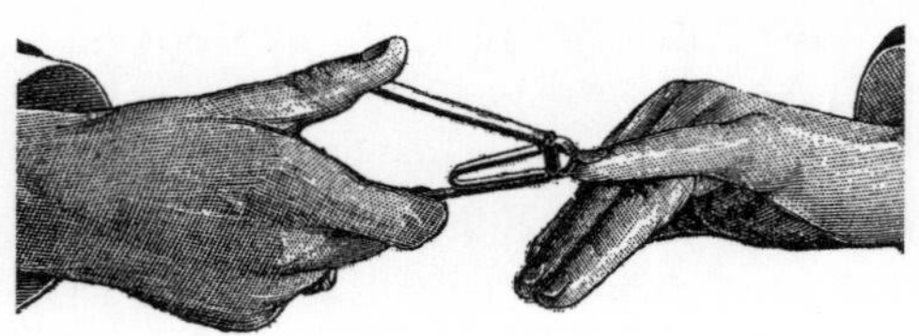

Choose Clips and Files, Not Knives and Scissors

"To properly protect the finger the nail should extend just a little beyond its tip, and its length and shape should result from the use of a nail-file, as cutting the nails with a knife or scissors has a tendency to make them coarse and thick." That's the recommendation of *Beauty: Its Attainment and Preservation* (1890). Manicurist June Park, of Skokie, Illinois, agrees that knives and scissors are a no-no for nails, but she recommends an option that wasn't available in the 19th century: a sharp nail clipper. June says that using a common scissors or a pocketknife for cutting nails causes problems not because these tools make your nails thick, but because they cut roughly, causing nails to split, peel, and break. Sharp clippers cut cleanly, so your nails will be easier to maintain and less likely to break.

After you clip, you can refine the shape of your nails by filing. But never file your nails with a back-and-forth method, June says. That will also leave your nails more likely to split, peel, or break. Instead, begin on the outer corner of a nail and file in one direction, toward the center. Repeat on the other side. Then, still filing in one direction only, gently shape the nail as an oval or a straight edge with softly rounded corners.

Lovely Nails for Ladies (or Gents)

If you love gardening, painting, or revving up that pottery wheel, then you know well the results—creative artwork and 10 grimy nails! To clean those dirty nails, heed this handy advice from a 1922 issue of the *Ladies' Home Journal*: "Spend only ten minutes on your nails regularly, once or twice a week, and you will keep them always in perfect condition." The *Journal* offers this 10-minute approach to keeping the nails looking great. We've updated the procedure a little, offering modern alternatives to some old-time products that are no longer available.

You will need:

Cuticle softener
Small dish
Orange stick
Cotton ball
Soap
Towel
Nailbrush or unused hard toothbrush
Nail polish
Olive oil, sweet almond oil, or hand cream
Chamois cloth or professional nail buffer
(available at beauty supply stores; optional)

Step 1. Apply the cuticle softener of your choice. Olive oil, sweet almond oil, your favorite hand cream, or any drugstore product marked *cuticle remover* will do nicely.

Step 2. Plunk all 10 nails, coated with cuticle softener, into a small dish of plain warm water. Let them soak for about 3 minutes to loosen dirt and soften the cuticles.

Step 3. Remove your fingers from the water. Wrap the end of the orange stick with a bit of cotton ball and use the padded end to gently push back each cuticle.

Step 4. Wash your hands with soap and water. Before drying your hands, push back the cuticles one more time. To do this, place the towel over one fingernail and then place the thumb of your other hand over the towel-covered nail. Gently push the cuticle back. Repeat with each fingernail.

Step 5. Wash your hands again, using the nailbrush or toothbrush to remove any last bits of dirt.

Step 6. Paint your nails with your favorite color of nail polish, or buff them to a natural shine. To create a subtle luster, dot a bit of the oil or hand cream onto each nail. Using the chamois cloth, the nail buffer, or the heel of your opposite hand, buff your nails.

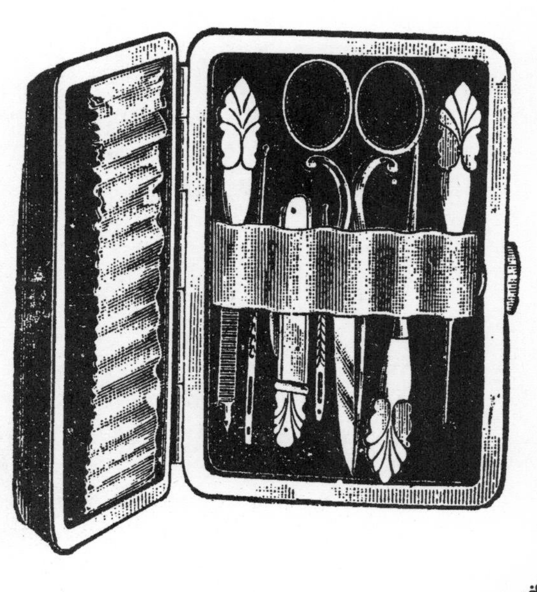

Tame Rough Cuticles in 2 Minutes

If time is of the essence, you can squeeze in a 2-minute manicure by simply performing Steps 1 and 3 from "Lovely Nails for Ladies (or Gents)," on page 205. (Skip soaking your nails in warm water.) Afterward, wash your hands and apply your favorite hand cream. *Never* try to save time by hacking away at thick cuticles. Cutting off unsightly cuticles was once the norm, as described in *Beauty: Its Attainment and Preservation* (1890), which claimed that "you will have to endure a little martyrdom in the cause of beauty." The old-time procedure included using acids and scissors to remove overgrown cuticles, but that's entirely too rough, says Jom S. Kim, proprietor of a nail salon in Skokie, Illinois. "If you're slicing off chunks of cuticle, it's easy to accidentally cut yourself, and this can lead to infection since you're probably not using sterile tools," Jom says.

Soap Blocks Grease

■ If you're a person who likes to do fix-it projects around the home or on your car, here's a simple way to prevent a fingernail-cleaning problem, offered by the March 1929 edition of *Better Homes and Gardens.* Before you paint or work with oil or grease, which always seem to leave intractable smears of grime under the fingernails, scratch your fingers sideways across a bar of soap so the space under your nails fills with soap. This will block grease and dirt from getting under the nails and make it much easier to clean up after the job is done.

Old-Time Nail Repair Tip

■ In the 1930s, before fiberglass and silk wraps were available for repairing nails, women fixed fingernail splits and breaks with a dab of glue and a tiny patch cut from a tea bag, cigarette paper, or perm paper. Manicurists used airplane glue, intended for miniature airplane, car, and ship model kits. Today, superglue works fine. Since you probably don't have cigarette or perm papers lying about the house, use a bit of tissue or coffee filter, or the proverbial tea bag. Put a dot of glue on the break, place your patch over the glue, tap gently with an orange stick, and let dry. Lightly file the patch so it's almost level with the nail. Apply polish, and the patch disappears.

Sweet Softness

■ To moisturize your hands and simultaneously slough off dead, dry skin, all you need is a bit of honey and sugar. It's a modern version of a recipe offered by William Dick in *Dick's Encyclopedia of Practical Receipts and Processes* (1875). Called Pâté d'Amande au Miel, the original recipe combined honey, egg yolks, a few essential oils, and coarsely ground almonds. You can skip the eggs, essential oils, and almond grinding, and simply mix 1 teaspoon honey and ¾ teaspoon sugar in the palm of your hand. Gently massage this mixture into your hands for 2 minutes. It will feel gritty, and you'll have to rub for about 10 seconds before the honey picks up your body heat and becomes pliable. Afterward, rinse with warm water (no soap necessary), then apply your favorite hand lotion. The results are remarkably smooth hands.

Don't Forget Your Gloves!

■ Sleep gloves, which are made of thin, pure cotton, have nothing to do with warmth. They're meant for donning after you slather on hand lotion just before going to bed. Leaving the gloves on overnight is said to intensify the lotion's moisturizing ability. It's an old-fashioned beauty trick described in the 1915 edition of *The Housekeeper's Handy Book*. Back then, the gloves were called "cosmetic gloves" and were made of "strong kid or dog-skin." The homemade hand lotion described in *The Housekeeper's Handy Book* involved a lot of blending and boiling of uncommon ingredients. How fortunate we are that ready-made hand lotions are plentiful today! The concept, however, remains a good one. And if you prefer naked hands as you slumber, here are a few ways to slip in lotion/glove therapy during your waking hours.

◆ Before you set out on your brisk daily walk, apply hand cream and pull on gloves.

◆ When washing dishes, apply lotion before donning those rubber gloves. The water's heat intensifies the softening results.

◆ When gardening, apply a thicker, jellylike cream before slipping on your work gloves. You can use plain petroleum jelly or products labeled *extra emollient* or *night cream*. This not only moisturizes your hands but also makes it easier to wash off the inevitable bits of flying mud that fall into your gloves.

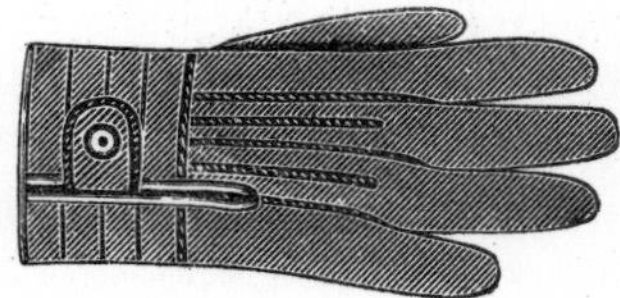

OLD-TIME ODDITIES

Hand Over the Eggs and Bacon

THIS RECIPE for soothing chapped hands will make you very glad you live in the 21st century rather than the 19th. *Godey's Lady's Book* (1854) advises readers: "Mix a quarter of a pound of unsalted hog's-lard, which should be washed first in water and then in rose-water, with the yolk of a new-laid egg and a large spoonful of honey. Add to this as much fine oatmeal or almond paste as will make the whole into a paste, and apply this after washing the hands."

Refreshing Footbath Favorites

■ If you could add up all the miles you walk in your lifetime, the sum might equal two to four trips around planet Earth. That's a lot of walking! Treat your feet with proper respect and give them a revitalizing soak. They'll thank you by looking rosy and feeling softer. (Remember, water is the best and original skin hydrator!) Everyone knows about the old-time method of soaking your feet in Epsom salts, but perhaps you didn't know that a plain footbath with 2 cups Epsom salts for every 1 gallon warm water helps draw fluid from your feet and reduce swelling. Beyond being uncomfortable, puffy ankles are a real beauty-buster.

Another excellent footbath ingredient that moisturizes and revives tired feet springs from *The Lady's Dressing Room* (1893), which recommends floating lime-tree flowers in your footbath. Of course, most of us don't have fresh lime blossoms on hand, but an easy alternative is to put 5 drops of pure essential lime oil in about 3 gallons of cool water. According to Chicago skin care expert Victoria Fulbright, you can really use any citrus essential oil, including grapefruit, lemon, or orange. They all share hydrating as well as energizing qualities.

OLD-FASHIONED FAVORITES

Rose Water Hand Cream

PLEASANT-SMELLING ROSE WATER has long been a favorite for scenting lotions and perfumes. The *Manual of Formulas: Recipes, Methods, and Secret Processes* (1932) offers this simple hand cream.

- 4 ounces glycerin
- 4 ounces rose water
- 8 ounces witch hazel

"Mix glycerin with rose water, then add the witch-hazel." What could be simpler? You can buy these ingredients at any drugstore. This cream is effective because glycerin softens, soothes, and moisturizes the skin; rose water smells wonderful and also soothes dry, sensitive skin; and witch hazel is a natural extract from the witch hazel plant that gently cleanses and conditions the skin.

Pedicure Procedure for Refined Feet

"Well pedicured feet are as much an evidence of refinement as well manicured hands; and it is not certain, but that they are more so, since human nature is prone to neglecting what is usually hidden." Wise words as printed in *Beauty: Its Attainment and Preservation* (1890). So without further ado, let's take our feet out of hiding and look at a quick, no-nonsense pedicure. Some of the steps are similar to the manicure procedure described in "Tame Rough Cuticles in 2 Minutes" on page 205, but there are some differences, too.

Dab cuticle remover around each toenail and soak your feet in warm water for 15 minutes. (A manicure does not always require commercial-strength cuticle remover. However, toe cuticles are tougher. It's often worth the money to buy cuticle remover for a proper pedicure.) Dry your feet with a towel and massage lotion into each foot. Gently push back each cuticle, using an orange stick with its tip wrapped in a bit of cotton ball. Clip your nails and use an emery board to smooth any rough edges. (Most people prefer the toenail to be even with the tip of the toe or slightly shorter, filed more square than oval.) Rinse your feet with warm soapy water, particularly rubbing each toenail. This removes any oily lotion residue. To finish, paint your toenails. Polish takes a full 20 minutes to thoroughly dry; put your feet up and enjoy a little break while you wait.

Exercise the Old-Time Way

A trim figure and firm physique have always been held in the highest regard. However, our emphasis on superthinness and extreme musculature is distinctly modern. For most of history, it was fashionable to carry a little natural padding. To keep their comely build, our ancestors enjoyed healthy exercise, sometimes involving little more than living life to its fullest and letting nature take shape.

Put "Old-Time" Effort into Your Chores

■ Take an exercise cue from women of generations past, and look to daily chores to stay trim. These women performed tough manual labor sunup to sundown, says Lauren Link, an aerobics instructor from Milwaukee. "Old-fashioned household chores burned more calories in one day than many Americans today burn in two days. All that physical activity kept their muscles toned," Lauren notes. "Doing the laundry back then was a terrific workout, since wringing clothes by hand used so many muscles and even got the heart going. Women got down on hands and knees to scrub floors, and that exercised their arms, glutes, and abs. Hanging laundry out on the line and repeatedly raising their arms above their heads worked their backs. They walked and climbed stairs—a lot—and both are terrific for toned thighs." No one's suggesting that you give up modern conveniences in order to lose inches, but you can

Burning Off the Pounds

For centuries, tending to the home was precisely how women remained in shape. Remember, until the recent past, there was no such thing as a fitness club or day spa! The amount of calories burned in any activity varies from person to person depending on individual height and weight, but generally a 150-pound person will burn 150 calories when performing the following tasks for the designated amount of time.

ACTIVITY	TIME REQUIRED
Cooking	48 minutes
Washing windows	45–60 minutes
Stocking shelves	40 minutes
Cleaning blinds, closets, and shelves	36 minutes
Mopping floors	36 minutes
Dusting	34 minutes
Vacuuming	34 minutes
Gardening	30–45 minutes
Raking leaves	30 minutes
Mowing the lawn (with a power push mower)	29 minutes
Shoveling snow	15 minutes

take modern-day activities and enhance their figure-slimming benefits.

Mowing the lawn. Move a little faster than usual and really use your upper body to push the mower.

Hoeing or raking the garden. Take longer strokes for full range of motion with your arms.

Washing windows. Use large, larger, largest circular motions to strengthen shoulder joints. Be sure to switch that cleaning rag from hand to hand.

Kitchen duty. Leave the sponge mop aside, and use a bucket and scrub brush to clean the floor on hands and knees. Use your garden kneeling mat to cushion your knees.

Head for a Heated Pool

■ For more than 100 years, doctors have recommended the benefits of heated water. In *Personal Beauty* (1870), for instance, Daniel Brinton, M.D., and George Napheys, M.D., report that "the effect of frequent and long-continued tepid bathing on the skin is so salutary, that recently Professor Hebra, of Vienna, one of the most celebrated physicians of skin diseases now living—probably we ought to say *the* most celebrated—has adopted the plan of placing some of his obstinate cases in water up to their neck, and leaving them there for several days!" We know now that spending several days underwater is overdoing it. However, swimming or working out in a warm-water pool is a highly respected mode of exercise. Ideal water temperature for water exercise is 83° to 86°F, because exercising in warm water is less stressful than swimming or exercising in cold water. Water adds buoyancy, which supports joints and muscles. Warm pool water further helps to keep muscles and joints relaxed and soothed. If you don't like to swim laps, try a water exercise class instead. Call your local YWCA, JCC, or fitness center to inquire about classes. In the meantime, here are three easy water exercises to start with, all done in water no higher than your shoulders.

Hip warm-up. Stand facing the side of the pool and holding the edge of the pool. Now lift one leg out to the side, as high as you can, then bring it back to your beginning position. Repeat 12 times, or whatever amount is comfortable for you. Repeat with the other leg.

Spine twist. Stand with your feet about shoulder-width apart and your hands on your hips. Now twist from the waist, first to one side and then to the other. Repeat as many times as feels comfortable.

Arm sweeps. Extend your left arm in front of you, underwater, palm facing down. Place your right arm by your side, palm facing forward. With straight (but not locked) arms, bring your left arm to your side, pushing down on the water, while you move your right arm up, pushing up on the water. After completing this movement, turn both palms over, and repeat the process. Be sure your palms are always pushing water as you lift or lower your arms. Repeat as many times as you can.

Let the Good Times Roll

■ Bicycles became all the rage in the late 19th century. For women in particular, bicycles afforded the first opportunity of getting around without the obligatory chaperone. Some historians even credit the bicycle for helping to emancipate women! Bicycling is a wonderful way to tone muscles and force that heart to pump harder, whether you bike alone or with a partner. Follow these words of wisdom from *The Household Guide or Domestic Cyclopedia* (1892) when you cycle: "To get the real benefit a bicycle can give, don't race, or attempt phenomenal distances. Walk up the severe hills, i.e., those . . . which cause the slightest inconvenience in breathing . . . Go if possible, into an interesting country, so as to have occasion for little detours afoot, off the road, and so vary the exercise. Go alone if you can not [find a cycling companion] who will stop and rest when you feel like it."

Safety First

WHILE PROMENADING and bicycling are great timeless activities for both relaxation and exercise, a few simple and effective contemporary protective measures make these activities safer. For instance, to avoid dehydration, always carry water with you. A water bottle holder with shoulder strap is convenient. Wear the strap diagonally across your chest. Clothing with reflective material stitched on makes evening excursions safer. And don't forget that bicycle helmet—a helmet reduces the risk of serious head injury by 85 percent.

Take a New-Fashioned Walk

■ Walking for exercise has always been in fashion. In July 1862, *The Christian Recorder* offered its readers this remarkably timeless advice: "Of all forms of exercise, walking is the most useful, as it brings into play the greatest number of muscles, without unnatural strain upon any." To help readers fit more walking into a day, the newspaper suggested, "Those who are engaged in business, where the dwelling and the place of business are at a distance from their place of residence, ought to walk at least part of the way, both in the morning and afternoon, if confined within doors during the day." From a modern perspective, you can "walk at least part of the way" by exiting your commuter bus or train one stop early and then traveling the last bit by foot. Here are several more ways to incorporate walking into your everyday life.

Join a club. Call a local fitness center and ask if it hosts an outdoor walking club. As part of the class, a qualified instructor will provide walking tips, and your fellow classmates will provide instant camaraderie, which boosts motivation.

Forget the exercise video. Instead of driving to your local video store to check out an exercise video, walk there—and then rent a movie instead. You've already got the exercise covered!

Try dual-purpose walking. Exercise your mind as well as your muscles by visiting a museum, art gallery, or historic

district. We tend to forget that 30 minutes spent viewing beautiful things is also 30 minutes spent walking. There's no need to plan a big trip. Many neighborhoods have local historical museums and mapped walking tours of historic residential areas. Call your town or city chamber of commerce or visitor's bureau to see if such options are conveniently located near you.

Take an idea walk. Select a nearby neighborhood that's currently undergoing a general face-lift, with trendy new stores moving in and homes being rehabbed. (If you need a clue to find these areas, look for giant Dumpsters along residential streets!) Park your car and take a stroll. In addition to exercise, you'll garner some great ideas for fixing up your own garden, since many rehabs include input from professional landscape designers.

Deliver the mail. Walk to a mailbox at least four blocks away instead of leaving stamped letters in your mailbox for the letter carrier to pick up.

Walk with a friend. Whether your partner has two legs or four, it's more fun to stroll with a companion.

CHAPTER 9

Fashion and Etiquette
If the Shoe Fits, Wear It

In times past, fashion rituals and social customs were a major occupation of daily life. Creating and maintaining a wardrobe, writing a thank-you card, or visiting a next-door neighbor were not laborious entries on a to-do list; they were labors of love. Although our 21st-century fashion and social scene is worlds different from that of 100 years ago, we can still apply old-time fashion and etiquette wisdom and experience to topics such as developing a personal fashion style, shaping and caring for a wardrobe, and handling social situations with ease and charm.

Fabulous Fashion Advice

In centuries past, getting dressed was as much an art as a science. Some fashions seemed to be mainly for fashion's sake (bustles and hoopskirts come to mind!), but most clothing was methodically adapted to suit people's physical needs and purchased not only to bring pleasure but also to meet a need. You can adopt this remarkably efficient and thrifty way of thinking to find a perfect little black dress, accommodate hemline trends, zero in on your best color palette, and select the right walking shoe.

When Hemlines Have You Up in Arms

■ Hemlines go up and down faster than gasoline prices, but there are clever ways to keep ahead of the fashion game.

Follow the lead of Lillian Eichler, author of *The Book of Etiquette* (1921): "They [men and women] do not realize that to be fashionable does not mean to follow conscientiously every new fad, but to adjust the prevailing style to conform with the lines of their individual faces and forms." Thus, when miniskirts come back in fashion (as they inevitably will), don't feel obliged to wear the short look if it's not comfortable for you. Try some simple alternatives or alterations that create the impression of a mini without straying out of your preferred fashion zone. Here are some examples.

Choose a hankie hem. A hankie hem, also known as the handkerchief or scarf hem, creates the illusion of shortness. It falls into several distinct, fluid points around the entire hem (this effect works best with soft, flowing fabrics such as rayon or silk).

Slit your skirt. Add side or back slits to a skirt, so that just enough (but never too much) leg peeks out.

Use tights to cover flaws. During chilly months, flex your fashion muscle by wearing a shorter straight skirt with thicker cotton/Lycra tights and a pair of stylish lace-up oxfords all in the same color.

Slip into a skort. For summer, you'll find options galore if you expand the definition of a miniskirt to include skorts, which have a front skirt panel that covers the shorts. The skirt panel sometimes carries around to the back of the garment as well.

BIZARRE BUT TRUE

Hemlines Make Economic Headlines

BACK IN THE 1920S, a Wharton School of Business economist named George Taylor introduced the hemline theory. He noticed that hemlines went up during favorable economic times, so women could show off the expensive silk stockings they could now afford. Conversely, during tight economic times, women lowered their skirts to hide the fact that they weren't wearing silk stockings. While silk stockings are no longer an issue, some fashion theorists claim that during strong economic times, American women tend to express their happiness by tolerating less-traditional clothing trends —such as miniskirts.

Finding the Best Little Black Dress

The trick to finding the perfect little black dress is to select a silhouette (dress shape) that enhances your figure and emphasizes your style. To do this, think like a clothing pattern designer, as author Harriet Pepin explains in *Modern Pattern Design* (1942). "Because the feminine figure is a mass of curves, both convex and concave," she writes, pattern designers must learn how to create simple patterns that will "fit the garment to conform to the curves" and add "design interest or drapery which will improve the silhouette" but "retain a beauty in line and form of the finished silhouette."

With these points in mind, here's how to find the perfect little black dress for *you*.

Be a show-off. Find a dress that enhances your best curve. In other words, show off your ample bosom, great shoulders, beautiful back, or stupendous Rockette legs. Your own best feature is your best accessory! Finding a little black dress that focuses on your finest physical attribute makes the dress your own. If you're lucky enough to have multiple best features, choose only one to emphasize.

Remember the ratio. When it comes to "additional design interest or drapery," use a three-to-one ratio: three parts classic to one part razzmatazz. In other words, choose a dress with *one* flashy feature, not two or three. The element of razzmatazz might be a halter neckline, a fitted waist, or the proverbial favorite: spaghetti straps.

Seek a strong foundation. Make sure you have the right underwear, since nothing spoils the "beauty in line and form" faster than an ill-fitting bra or a tummy bulge. Take the dress with you to your favorite lingerie department and try it on over the undergarments. You don't need to be rail thin, just smooth and chic.

Looking Good in Any Color

■ Fashion magazines dictate the "in" colors for clothing each season, but what can you do when the "hot" color is one you can't wear? Follow the advice from the Fashion Institute's *New-Way Course in Fashionable Clothes-Making* (1926), and you can look beautiful in absolutely any color! "Study your type and if you fall in the classification known as the warm type, that is, those of high coloring, brown eyes, red or dark hair, the most satisfactory colors will be those falling on the warm side of the color chart. If, however, you are of the cool type, that is, the typical blonde with golden hair and fair skin, the cool colors will suit you much better." The secret to following this advice well is to know that *every* color has both warm and cool versions.

PEARLS OF WISDOM

"Don't copy the best selling design in the biggest department store in your city. Almost anyone can own a Ford."

GRACE DIMELOW,
Paris Frocks at Home (1930)

First, determine your skin tone by examining your face without makeup and in natural lighting. A warm complexion has a yellow, peach, or reddish undertone and looks best against warm colors—red, yellow, and orange. Cool complexions lean more toward pink, violet, or blue undertones and look best against cool colors—green, purple, blue. If you can't quite make up your mind, consider the skin inside your wrist, under your arms, or on your stomach—spots that don't tend to get tanned. As a final clue, consider this: Those with a cool undertone tend to prefer silver, white gold, or platinum jewelry; those with a warm undertone generally prefer gold-colored jewelry.

Once you've determined your skin tone, refer to "Fashion Color Chart" on page 216 to find the color tones that will work for you.

Take a Paint Chip to Shop for Clothes

■ If you have trouble buying clothes that actually match what's already in your closet, then what you need are handy color cards to take along when you shop. This trick dates back to the early 20th century, as Mary Picken describes in *Harmony of Dress* (1922). An organization called the Textile Color Card Association created a standardized collection of colors, numbered each color, and then printed each color with its respective number on an individual card. Fabric and sewing notion manufacturers based their product colors on these color cards, and women used the cards to match materials and threads for their personal sewing needs.

This association and its color cards may no longer exist, but there's a terrific alternative that's available at any home store: paint chips! Perhaps you're looking for a scarf to match your robin's-egg-blue blouse, or maybe you have a handsome plaid sport coat and you need a tie that picks up the unusual eggplant color in the weave. Take the item of clothing with you to the paint department (you only have to do this once) and select a chip to match. Or collect several chips in the right range, compare the chips and garment at home, and toss all but the chip that matches. Tuck the chip in your purse or wallet, and it will be ready to refer to as you browse at the mall. Here's another alternative: If a garment needs fabric removed during alterations, ask your tailor beforehand to save all the material scraps for you. Cut a 2-by-4-inch snippet of fabric, glue the swatch to a 3-by-5-inch card, and you've created a custom-made color card.

Fashion Color Chart

THE TABLE BELOW lists seven popular colors and their warm and cool variations. Black is a universal color, although cool skin undertones sometimes look even more beautiful against charcoal, which is a cooler form of black. Letters in parentheses indicate whether the base color is warm (W) or cool (C).

COLOR	WARM TONES	COOL TONES
Red(W)	Tomato; strawberry	Raspberry; magenta
Orange (W)	Pumpkin; peach	Terra-cotta; coral
Yellow (W)	Butter; sunflower	Butterscotch, celery
Green (C)	Olive; lime	Mint; forest
Blue (C)	Turquoise; aqua	Royal; sky blue
Purple(C)	Mauve; wine	Lilac; eggplant
White (C)	Ivory	Bright white

Seasonal Color Strategies

■ Freshening up one's wardrobe with seasonal fashion colors seems like a modern-day concern, but it's not. Even our Pilgrim ancestors dealt with seasonal color trends. The stereotypical image of the Pilgrims clad only in somber black, white, and gray is not true! Pilgrims enjoyed colorful wardrobes, and records of Pilgrim wills list detailed inventories of goods passed on to relatives. For example, Mary Ring, who came to Plymouth around 1629 and died sometime in 1633, bequeathed to her children cloth and clothing in violet, red, blue, "mingled color," and green "to make a coat."

Few examples of actual Pilgrim clothing still exist, because unlike most of us, the Pilgrims literally wore their clothes to shreds. We can be glad that we have the option of adding new clothes to our wardrobes each season, but it can be a dilemma when you don't like the color that's the current hot trend. How can you blend this undesirable color into your wardrobe? The most important thing to remember is to keep your best colors next to your face and use the trendy color as an accent. Here are some clever strategies to try.

◆ Buy a skirt or a pair of pants in the trendy-but-odd color, splurge on matching shoes, and complete the look with your favorite black, white, or ivory blouse. Those shoes can also instantly update the simplest perennial outfit—like a plain pair of black pants with a white blouse, or a black dress.

◆ Choose an outfit in a neutral color—tan, black, or white—and buy a purse, belt, or long necklace in the fashionable color to wear with it.

◆ Try a camisole in the trendy color, and wear a shirt of your favorite color over it.

◆ Don't forget those toes! Put on a pair of great summer sandals and head over to your favorite nail salon. Ask them to decorate your toenails with polish in that hot seasonal color.

Fitting Advice about Alterations

■ How important is it to find a reputable tailor? Let's let *Beadle's Guide to Dress-Making and Millinery* (1860), supply the answer: "The handsomest dress looks ill if the corsage [bodice] does not fit nicely; the commonest calico, if this essential part is managed artistically, looks well." That is to say, a bargain is *no* bargain when the garment doesn't fit right. If you've found an outfit you just can't live without, even though it doesn't fit quite right, find an alterations expert to save the day. Perhaps you are handy at sewing, or you may know a reputable tailor or a talented seamstress in the area. Your favorite dry cleaner may even have someone on staff to do alterations. Whoever tackles the alterations, keep these fitting tips from modern-day image consultant Susan Fignar of Chicago in mind.

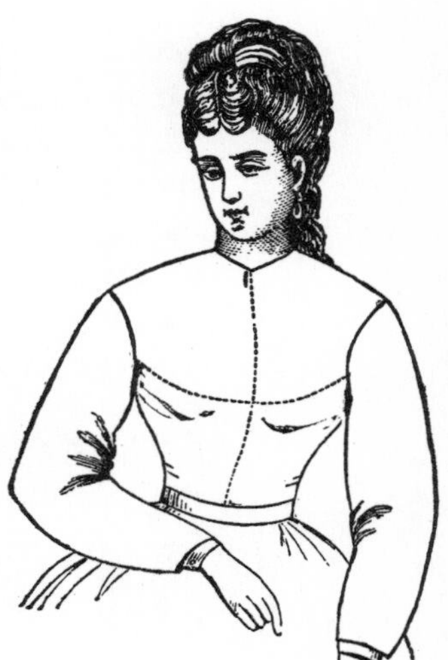

◆ Pleats in a skirt or trousers should lie flat and fully folded when you're standing. If the pleats pull apart when you are standing, fix the problem by letting out the side seams and waistband.

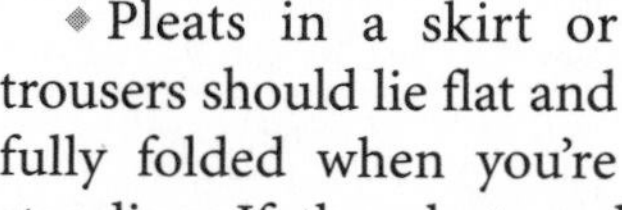

◆ A double-breasted jacket should comfortably button when standing. If it pulls when buttoned, won't button at all, or hangs loose like a sack, have it altered.

◆ Trouser legs should rest gently against your instep with a slight break. Different heel heights affect this break, so if you plan to wear specific shoes with a pair of trousers, put them on before pinning the new hem.

◆ The ends of jacket sleeves should hit the bony protrusion on the outside of your wrist.

Wrapped in Comfort

During the Civil War era, women relied on shawls for warmth. Those shawls were often nothing more than a square of wool folded in half diagonally to form a large triangle. We can enjoy shawls as a fashion accessory rather than a primary source of protection from the weather and wear them as creative accessories.

To make a low-cost shawl with a touch of whimsy, buy a 100 percent cotton tablecloth about 52 inches square. Wash the tablecloth to remove the stiff sizing and fold it diagonally, and you have a classic shawl! For the holiday season, select a plaid tablecloth in red, green, and gold; wear it with black velvet pants and a black shirt. To dress in style for viewing fireworks on the Fourth of July, choose a solid red tablecloth and wear it over a white T-shirt and blue jeans.

If your approach to your wardrobe is more traditional than improvisational, you may prefer a modern variation on a pashmina, which is a classic shawl made from the underhair of Himalayan goats. Real pashminas are expensive and too warm to wear except during cold winter months, so it's difficult to justify the wrap's high cost. However, pashmina lookalikes are now available in cashmere-and-silk blends, resulting in a lighter texture and year-round wearability. Drape one of these light shawls over your shoulders to create a sophisticated look for dining alfresco or beside a restaurant's roaring fireplace.

Boost Your Blazer with Beautiful Buttons

If your navy blazer or everyday cardigan has become a little too predictable, jazz it up with a new set of unusual buttons. This idea is inspired by unusual button treatments born from necessity, described by Parthenia Hague in her memoir of daily life on an Alabama plantation, *A Blockaded Family: Life in Southern Alabama during the Civil War* (1888). The author writes about making buttons out of wood, sometimes polished with sandpaper and varnish. Other buttons were made of cloth "cut round, stacked in as many plies as needed for firmness with the outside worked with a heavy button hole stitch." The ingenious plantation dwellers even fashioned buttons from persimmon seeds, common gourds, and homemade pasteboard (cardboard) cut to size and shape, and then covered with fabric.

You don't need to make your own buttons, and you can search out unusual buttons for the pure joy of it rather than necessity. Try dyed wood, faux emeralds, bamboo, or unusually shaped buttons. And yes, buttons made from seeds are still available! You'll find wonderful button selections at fabric stores, and when you go, be sure to bring an original button from the garment with you, so you choose the right size (for a blazer, you'll also need to bring one of the smaller buttons from the blazer cuff).

Five Ways to Find the Right Walking Shoe

■ Fashion advice from *The Book of Etiquette* (1921) still rings true today. Author Lillian Eichler advises, "Practicability should never be sacrificed to fashion, and however beautiful they may be to look at, an automobile coat that cannot stand dust, a bathing suit that cannot stand water, and a hiking outfit that cannot stand wear are merely ridiculous. There are three questions that the man or woman should first ask themselves before buying a sports outfit. First, Is it comfortable? Next, Is it practical? And last, Is it pleasing?"

Those first two questions, about comfort and practicality, are especially important when you're buying walking shoes, where choices of styles and features are legion. Follow these guidelines to select a pair of walking shoes that does its intended job: protecting the health of your feet!

1. Always try on both shoes, and wear the same socks you'll be wearing when walking.

2. After properly lacing both shoes, walk briskly around the shoe department for at least 1 minute. Your feet should land firmly on the floor, without any sensation that they are sliding to the left or right. This is your stability factor.

3. Look for a shoe that provides a snug fit in the heel but a little wiggle room for your toes—one-half to one full thumb's width between the toe of the shoe and the end of the longest toe on your larger foot.

4. Shop for walking shoes later in the afternoon. Your feet are slightly swollen at this time of day, thus ensuring a great fit no matter what time of day you decide to walk.

5. Try on three or four pairs of shoes. Two shoes of the same size made by different manufacturers will fit slightly differently. For example, some shoes fit a wide foot better, while others are cut for a slimmer foot.

☞ BIZARRE BUT TRUE ☜

Saved by Her Skirt

FASHION HISTORIANS dedicate pages of criticism to our foremothers' infatuation with hoopskirts, calling these huge undergarments cumbersome and rude. Innocent bystanders could be knocked over by a woman's hoopskirt. The ballooning garments also toppled end tables and took up entirely too much space in a carriage. But apparently hoopskirts did provide one very unexpected benefit, as reported in *Emerson's United States Magazine* (July 1857): "As the steamer *Commonwealth* came alongside the wharf at New London on Friday night, on the passage from Norwich to New York, a lady walked overboard, and would have been drowned but for the hoops in her dress, which rendered the same somewhat balloonish, and withal answered the purpose of a more complicated life preserver. The night was very dark, and it was nearly half an hour before she could be extricated from her perilous situation, during which time the hoops were sufficiently strong to buoy her up and prevent her from sinking."

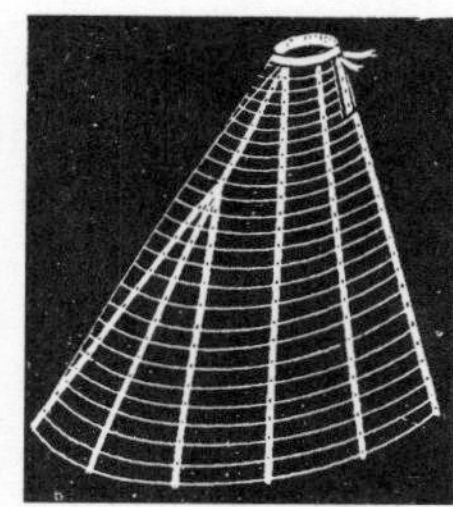

Clean Out Your Closet

"It is ridiculous to have too great a number of toilettes [outfits] at once. We know how short a time a fashion lasts, and it is unpleasant, and almost ridiculous, to be out of the fashion." This timeless advice from Baroness Staffe, author of *The Lady's Dressing Room* (1893), is even truer today, and a simple, three-pile process will make cleaning out your closet a breeze. Keeping your closet in order will ultimately help you dress faster—and protect you from absentmindedly pulling on outlandish leftovers from 1974.

Here's how this closet-organizing scheme works.

You will need:

Sewing kit
Extra clothes hangers
Storage boxes
Wardrobe bags
Garbage bags

Step 1. Remove everything from your closet. As you do, put items into one of three piles: (a) clothing worn within the past 3 months, (b) clothing worn more than 3 but less than 6 months ago, and (c) clothing you haven't worn at all during the past 6 months.

Step 2. Return the items in the 3-month pile to your closet. These are clothes you wear on a regular basis. But as you handle each item, check if anything needs repair or cleaning. Tend to these maintenance matters as soon as possible and then rehang the clothes in your closet.

Step 3. Turn your attention to the 3- to 6-month pile. Most of these items are probably off-season clothing. Pack these items away in storage boxes or a spare closet until the right weather returns for wearing them. Be careful never to pack soiled clothing, though. That's like sending out engraved invitations for a moth party!

Step 4. Sort the over-6-month pile into two more piles: clothing that you wear infrequently but that has real value (such as classic formal attire), and clothing that doesn't. Prepare the first pile carefully for storage in wardrobe bags or other protective coverings as needed. Put the items in the second pile into a garbage bag, so you can carry it to your favorite local clothing thrift shop and donate these items. (If you haven't worn a piece of clothing in more than 6 months, you really don't need it anymore!)

Follow the 48-Hour Rule

■ Closets filled to bursting are not a new problem, as this excerpt from Lillian Eichler's *Book of Etiquette* (1921) reveals: "Fashion is a temptress . . . The extravagant woman fills her wardrobe with numerous dresses, blouses and hats for which she has no real use. But how much more sensible it is to have just enough for one's needs, a few stylish, well-made garments—each one an expression of the wearer's own personality." To keep your wardrobe limited to "a few stylish, well-made garments," follow the 48-hour rule: If you're still thinking about an item of clothing 48 hours after first spotting it in the store, and no other pretty thing has taken its place in your thoughts, then it's probably a wise investment—or at least a luxury that you will use and enjoy. Go buy it and enjoy wearing it.

Keeping Your Wardrobe in Trim

Often with astounding ingenuity, our ancestors speedily repaired their clothing to last through the reign of the current fashion trend, and they also restyled garments to match the next trend. Today, most of us lack the know-how to take apart a dress and reassemble it for a completely new look, but we can use bits of old-time ingenuity to freshen up or preserve our wardrobes.

Scribble Away Shoe Scratches

■ Disguising scratches on leather shoes is easy if you take your inspiration from this suggestion from Baroness Staffe in *The Lady's Dressing Room* (1893): "A mixture of cream and ink is excellent for keeping kid boots in good order." Rather than fussing with cream and a bottle of liquid ink, though, gently tap the scratch with the tip of a permanent marker of the appropriate color. Keep tapping until the exposed leather is completely colored. Let dry for about 15 minutes and then dab the scratch with a paper towel to remove any ink that did not seep in. A crayon also works for this task, and while it's not as permanent as marker, it may be your best choice for scratches on leather shoes that are dyed an unconventional color. Because a marker or crayon covers but does not remove a scratch, this trick works best in inconspicuous spots, such as the heel of a shoe.

Oil Improves Leather Shoes

■ To freshen up leather shoes, *A Thousand and One Formulas* (1920) offers this practical recipe. "Shabby leather can be much improved by either *Linseed Oil* or the well-beaten *Whites of Eggs* mixed with suitable coloring matter," writes author Sidney Gernsback. "The surface can be brought to a gloss by the use of a soft duster." Using egg whites is way too gooey to be worth the trouble, but coating shoes with boiled linseed oil remains an excellent idea for sturdy footwear made from thicker leather, such as work boots, hiking shoes, or shop-'til-you-drop leather walking shoes. In addition to reviving shabby leather, the oil also renders leather water-resistant and silences squeaky soles on new shoes or boots. Use a clean rag to apply the oil in a thin coat. Let the shoes dry for 10 to 12 hours; then reapply. Optimally, apply three coats. Aim to apply a very thin coat each time, because applying too much oil too fast will produce a gummy texture that won't dry properly. *Caution:* Be sure to dispose of oil-soaked rags properly, following the instructions on the oil container.

☞ TRASH OR TREASURE ☜

Old Newspaper Restores Shoes to Shape

WET SHOES OFTEN DRY misshapen, and then all you can do is give them their walking papers. To prolong the life of your shoes should you step in a puddle, grab some old newspaper from the recycling bin, and try this technique suggested by Baroness Staffe in *The Lady's Dressing Room* (1893): "When you come in with your leather boots wet, take them off at once, and have them filled with very dry hay. This absorbs the damp rapidly, stretches and fills out the boots, and so prevents them from stiffening and losing their shape. Above all, avoid putting them near the fire. The next day the hay is taken out, and may be dried for another occasion or thrown away. By stuffing the boots with paper you will obtain exactly the same result." Keep stuffing newspaper inside those damp shoes until each takes on the correct and original shape. Then wrap the shoes in more newspaper. Leave the shoes in a warm, dry spot for about a day, giving the paper time to absorb all the moisture—and as suggested, do *not* place your shoes by the fireplace. Old newspaper also works for fashioning supports that prevent tall fashion boots from sagging or creasing between wearings. Roll enough newspaper to make two sturdy tubes, and stick a tube straight into the leg section of each boot. Now your boots will stand at attention in your closet until you wear them again.

Quick-Fix Shoe Polish

■ Late for a meeting but out of shoe polish? Rub a half-section of lemon over the shoes and buff them with a soft cloth, suggests *1001 Entirely New Household Hints* (1937). Another nontoxic approach to cleaning leather shoes is to mix a few drops of lemon juice in a few tablespoons of olive oil and use this mixture to polish your shoes.

This Shine Commands Attention!

■ Every old soldier knows how to make dull, scuffed shoes look like new. William E. Meehan Jr., of Haddonfield, New Jersey, recalls that his father, Lieutenant Colonel William Meehan, a retired U.S. Army artillery officer, really knew how to make his shoes shine. "Dad advised to invest in two shoeshine brushes—they look like scrub brushes, but they have long, soft, furry bristles. Use one brush for shining black shoes only; the other for lighter colors."

To begin, gently dust off the shoes using one of your brushes. Next, using a cotton rag (old cotton briefs work best), apply a thin coating of shoe polish in the appropriate color. Then shine the shoes by gently but briskly buffing them with the brush. To finish, use an old cotton T-shirt to remove any excess polish and increase the shine.

Not shiny enough? Apply a "spit shine"! No, you don't use saliva. Just dampen your cotton rag with a drop of water before putting the polish on the rag, and apply as before. The mixture of water and polish will give your shoes a mirror finish rivaling patent leather.

Don't Let Bugs Bug Your Clothes

■ Come spring, there's nothing more liberating than packing away heavy sweaters. But do this with care, or else you'll pull these warm woolens back out next winter with unappealing moth holes! Lydia Maria Child, author of *The American Frugal Housewife* (1833), explains: "About the last of May, or the first of June, the little millers [clothes moths], which lay moth-eggs begin to appear. Therefore brush all your woolens, and pack them away in a dark place covered with linen. Pepper, red-cedar chips, tobacco,—indeed, almost any strong spicy smell,—is good to keep moths out of your chests and drawers." Using pepper and cedar chips to repel moths is a good idea, but don't try tobacco. Here are a few more ways to debug your clothing.

Store it clean. Always dry-clean or hand-wash wool clothing before packing it away; this eliminates skin flakes, hair, and other substances that moth larvae like to dine on.

Seal it up tight. Invest in plastic containers with snap-shut lids (available at any discount store and often available at sale prices in April or May). Cardboard boxes or paper bags are poor choices for storing woolens, because you can't seal them shut and they won't protect woolens from water damage if your normally dry storage area should suddenly spring a leak.

Toss in some cloves. Sprinkle loose whole cloves, which are an inexpensive, effective moth repellent, over clothing placed in storage boxes. Next season, just shake out your clothing, and the cloves will roll right off.

Use sachets. Buy lavender or rosemary sachets (available wherever closet-organizing equipment is sold), and tuck them into your storage boxes. Or make your own moth-repelling sachet. Mix 8 ounces whole cloves with 1 ounce dried thyme, 2 ounces dried mint, 2 ounces dried rosemary, and 1 ounce dried ginseng. Take a pair of clean, cast-off panty hose (a pair with a run is perfect), and cut off the end section of one leg of the hose. Pour the mixture into the "toe" of the hose, knot the hose closed, and put your sachet in with stored clothes. Not to worry—although this mixture repels moths, humans find the scent pleasant.

Don't Wrinkle Your Nose at Velvet

■ A tip from the 1930s saves the day when you discover that your rarely worn but much-loved black velvet skirt is a wrinkled mess from being smashed in the back of your closet. *Home Laundering and Dry Cleaning* (1931) explains how to use a press cloth to remove the wrinkles without damaging the nap of the velvet:

"Dampen the press cloth, but do not have it too wet. Place over the material and press lightly, moving the iron always in the same direction; that is, with the nap of the material. If the material is not pressed in this way, it will have a rough surface. If the material is hung in the open air after pressing, the nap will be raised, thus giving it a softer finish." For the record, a press cloth is a second piece of fabric, like a tea towel. To dampen it, use a spray bottle filled with plain water. Set your iron on the cotton setting. Use light to normal pressure and always keep the iron moving with the nap of the fabric, as the old-time tip suggests. This procedure works equally well on any fabric with a nap, such as corduroy or Ultrasuede.

A Sewing Basket to Brag About

■ A well-equipped sewing basket, according to Helen Hall's *Home Sewing Course* (1936), should include a sharp pair of shears, a thimble that fits, plenty of pins, and needle and thread, and that's just as true for today's home sewer. The author notes, however, that the most important attribute of any sewing basket is that it is easy to lift and carry. "A modern sewing room, well-equipped with all conveniences, is every home sewer's dream; but this luxury is seldom enjoyed by the average home sewer of moderate means. Her sewing room may be her bedroom or her kitchen with only a few tools with which to work, but her sewing may be a work of art." In addition to the items listed in the *Home Sewing Course,* consider tossing in spare needles for your sewing machine (if you have one), a tape measure, a seam ripper, and a pencil or washable marking pen (to mark button placement). None of these handy items will add much weight to your basket. And speaking of buttons, find a lightweight container to hold stray buttons, such as a 4-ounce plastic container or a resealable plastic bag. Or start a button box (see "Hit the Fashion Button with . . . Buttons!" on page 225).

Exceptional Accessory Ideas

With the flutter of a chiffon scarf or a pair of elegant shoes, you can transform a single outfit from flirty to formal and back again. It's all about the ancient art of accessorizing. These wardrobe embellishments are often impervious to seasonal trends, so with proper care, they'll be part of your wardrobe for decades—maybe centuries, if you add in heirloom-quality jewelry. A peek into the past shows us how to select and maintain accessories, from embellishing a hat to cleaning classic pearls.

Dressing Up a Classic Suit

■ Every season, women's fashion magazines remind us that everyone should own one classic black suit (jacket and trousers or skirt) made from a four-season lightweight worsted wool, along with plenty of seasonal or trendy accessories that complement the suit. It's the same notion our Victorian foremothers followed, although back then the wardrobe staple was not a suit but a handsome black silk dress. In April 1872,

Godey's Lady's Book suggested that women wear this versatile dress with different "polonaises" (an overdress rather like a knee-length jacket) in order "to make a variety of house and street dresses."

You may already have a few favorite accessories to pair with your black suit, but here are some new tricks and styles to try.

By day. For a casual outdoor summer brunch, pair your black suit with a white camisole or silk tank top, and then think pink mules (backless, slide-on shoes with closed toe), a pink oblong scarf tied in a soft bow at your waist (instead of a belt), and pink sunglasses. Feel free to replace pink with the color of your choice. The point is to wear accessories of a similar color, so you make a grand statement.

By night. Go glam by replacing your single strand of pearls with a multistrand pearl bracelet or snug-fitting multistrand choker. Rather like a formal turtleneck, a choker accents a graceful neck but hides wrinkles. Or wear a very long pearl necklace, pinch the necklace together just below your bosom, bring the pinched part up to either shoulder of the suit jacket, and secure the pinched part with a big, bold complementary brooch. Let the necklace dangle vertically off-center. (Faux pearl accessories are plentiful at any department store costume jewelry counter, so you need not break the bank with the real deal.)

Any time. The "basic black suit, basic black shoe" rule is a thing of the past. Try a bold red high-heeled sandal; leopard-, Dalmatian-, or cheetah-print pumps; or a dressy mule of leather embossed to imitate crocodile, snake, or alligator hide.

☞ TRASH OR TREASURE ☜

Hit the Fashion Button with . . . Buttons!

BEFORE YOU TOSS a stained or outmoded garment, be sure to remove the buttons—you never know when they'll come in handy. Back in the 1940s, as World War II raged, many Americans saved buttons of necessity. Mary Cieslik, of Milwaukee, recalls the process: "If something was too worn to wear, I took off the buttons, cut apart the material, remade the fabric into something for the kids—like pajamas, a dress, or a coat—and then reused the buttons. If I didn't need the buttons, I saved them. I was always gathering buttons." And even though Mary now lives a comfortable life in a beautiful home where she often welcomes her four grown children and three grandkids, she still has a button box. Start your button collection today, and put your extra buttons to good use with these quick ideas.

A button "necklace." Sew an assortment of mismatched buttons around the neckline of a plain T-shirt to simulate a necklace. Use as few or as many buttons as you'd like.

Pants with a button accent. Give a pair of capri pants a leg up on fashion by sewing colorful buttons (matched or unmatched) around the bottom of each leg, about 1 inch up from the hemline.

A button-bedecked hatband. Whip up an eye-catching hatband for your summer hat. Sew the decorative buttons of your choice onto a piece of grosgrain ribbon at least ½ inch wide. See "Make a Flowery Easter Bonnet" on page 157 for instructions on attaching the hatband to your hat.

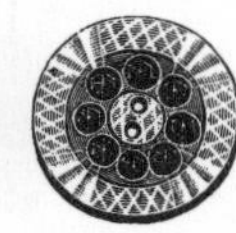

Hats You Can't Do Without

▪ It wasn't too long ago that a proper lady never left her house without a hat. Fortunately, this rule has been overruled, but it's still useful to keep hats on hand for certain occasions. Here are three hats that everyone will find useful now and again.

Bad-hair-day hat. If you're getting ready to meet a friend for a casual lunch and your hair simply won't behave, tuck it under a hat—just as Jane Austen explained in 1798, in a letter to her sister

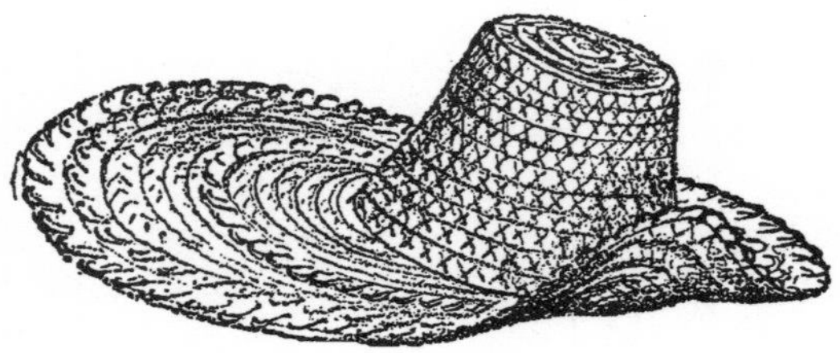

Cassandra: "I have made myself two or three caps to wear of evenings since I came home, and they save me a world of torment as to hair-dressing." Select a decidedly feminine baseball cap or a smart straw hat, or slick your hair back (with gel or in a ponytail) and toss on a jaunty beret. Just make sure your bad-hair-day hat is comfortable, since you'll be wearing it for several consecutive hours.

Fun-in-the-sun hat. In *Personal Beauty, How to Cultivate and Preserve It in Accordance with the Laws of Health* (1860), authors Daniel Brinton, M.D., and George Napheys, M.D., advise Victorian ladies, "Now-a-days, we are content to parry [the sun's] attacks with parasols, veils, and 'sundowns.' These are sufficient in our more active lives."

Veils and parasols aren't practical; however, sundowns are very much in vogue. A sundown is a hat with a brim that can be worn either curled up or turned down. This type of hat can help prevent the dreaded sunburned head, as well as a scalded forehead and nose. Modern sundowns are available in styles to suit both women and men. Choose a lightweight sundown made of a technologically advanced fabric that's described as blocking up to 98 percent of the sun's harmful ultraviolet rays.

Let-it-snow hat. People lose a lot of body heat through the top of the head, and ears nipped by winter cold can be very painful. Without a doubt, everyone who lives in or visits a cold winter climate needs a warm hat. In her *Book of Etiquette* (1921), Lillian Eichler notes that even the strict rules concerning a gentleman's hat and good manners should be bent during the cold months. "Many gentlemen, while speaking to ladies in the street, stand with their heads uncovered. While it is a polite custom, it is dangerous to the health and therefore should not be indulged in except in warm weather."

Today, cold-weather hats run the gamut. Faux fur keeps you just as toasty as the real deal. Advanced synthetic fabrics such as Thinsulate, Primaloft, and Liteloft are billed as synthetic replacements for down; they tend to resist wetness and maintain their warmth even when drenched. Despite their heat-preserving qualities, these fabrics are remarkably thin and comfortable. They're ideal for long outdoor adventures or standing outside to watch Thanksgiving or Christmas parades.

Hatboxes Come in Handy

With the pleasure of wearing hats comes the responsibility of caring for them. The best way to store your better hats and those that can't withstand crushing (such as most straw hats) is in hatboxes. Follow in the footsteps of an imaginative young woman, Hannah Davis, who lived in Jaffrey, New Hampshire, in the early 1900s, and decorate your hatboxes. Hannah was a single woman in need of an income, so she decided to design, construct, and sell wooden bandboxes—small oval boxes used to store and carry hats, bonnets, clothing, and other accessories. Hannah began what would soon become a booming business, eventually offering special decorated boxes (she used wallpaper to cover them). Today, Hannah's hatboxes are considered collectibles.

You can still find plain wooden bandboxes in contemporary craft stores, as well as economically priced, sturdy cardboard versions. Pick up a few for your hats and decorate them with the same wallpaper that hangs in your bedroom (following Hannah's lead), purchase some pretty peel-and-stick paper, or simply paint them. Of course, you can also find slightly more expensive colored plastic hatboxes in many home stores.

However you collect your hatboxes, here's the best way to use them. Form an open ring of tissue paper in the bottom of the box. Place the crown of the hat inside this ring, so the hat is upside down. Now gently tuck (do not jam) tissue paper into the crown to help hold the hat's shape. Stack your hatboxes in that unused empty corner beside your dresser.

TRASH OR TREASURE

New Tricks for Old Accessories

COMMON ACCESSORIES from past eras take on new life when you use them as jewelry. *American Etiquette and Rules of Politeness* (1882) suggests: "No well-bred gentleman will load himself with jewelry. He may wear one ring, a watch chain, studs and cuff buttons." Since these pieces once were worn in abundance, you can easily find them in antique shops.

Look for an old-fashioned pocket watch (with or without its chain) and use it as a necklace. Slip the round watch onto a long black silk cord (found in any good fabric store), tie the ends securely, and put it around your neck.

Another old-time accessory that you can adapt as jewelry is the hatpin. Stick the hatpin through a jacket lapel; do your hair in a French twist, and slide the hatpin into the twist; or use it to secure a scarf. For the scarf trick, which works best with heavy fabrics, place a scarf around your neck with the ends hanging in front. Crisscross the scarf, and then insert your hatpin down through both layers of the scarf and back up to the outer layer. For a different look, crisscross the scarf and position the intersection off-center on the shoulder of your sweater or jacket. Then stick the hatpin through the scarf and the sweater fabric, back out through the fabric, and back through the scarf. If your scarf fabric is lighter weight and you're pairing it with a blouse, try the same technique using an antique stickpin, which is smaller than a hatpin.

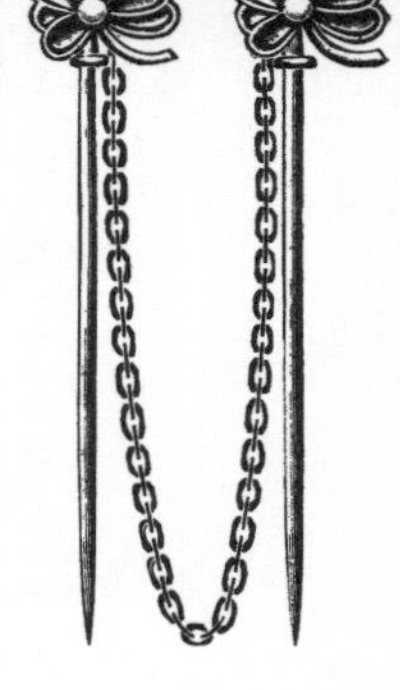

From Orphan Earring to Independent Accessory

■ Most women seem to end up with a few earrings that have lost their mates. It's not a tragedy, except when an earring is very valuable or is a sentimental family heirloom. Don't despair! If you've been mourning that precious solo earring in your jewelry box, and hoping against hope to find its other half, it's time to turn a negative into a positive. Take a tip from our Victorian sisters, who were quite fond of redesigning jewelry, and restyle that earring into a smart pin or pendant.

PEARLS OF WISDOM

"Elegant dressing is
not found in expense;
money without judgment may
load, but never can adorn.
A lady may be covered with
jewels, and yet not show
the slightest good taste."

American Etiquette and Rules of Politeness (1882)

When you have the earring reset, keep in mind this advice from *Godey's Lady's Book* (September 1879): "Should any of our readers require family diamonds reset, they will do well to remember that the chief thing to aim at is lightness, actually and in appearance." This fashion rule applies whether your earring is a diamond or any other type of precious stone or metal, and should also help hold down the costs of restyling.

Compliments for Complementary Colors

■ In the time it takes to say, "What should I wear?" you can transform a so-so outfit into va-va-va-voom. A fast, simple, and inexpensive place to begin is with this sage advice from *Godey's Lady's Book* (March 1869): "A French fancy popular at present is to wear jewelry in contrast with the dress. Turquoise is worn with rose-color, coral with blue, and malachite with crimson." This trendy whim was nothing more complex than pairing complementary colors as found on a classic color wheel. It's still a great way to make a fashionable color statement. What are complementary colors? Green complements red, which explains *Godey's* recommendations of malachite with crimson and turquoise with rose. Orange complements blue, which relates to coral with blue. The third basic complementary combination is purple and yellow.

To quickly add pizzazz to a monotone outfit, throw on an accessory in the complementary color. Try one large statement piece, such as a necklace with a large painted wooden pendant, a string of chunky plastic beads, a scarf, or even a shawl. Remember, your accessory doesn't need to be expensive, just complementary.

You Can't Beat Pearls

■ Twentieth-century fashion icon Coco Chanel once said, "A woman needs ropes and ropes of pearls." Note that Miss Chanel didn't specify pearls mixed with extravagant gems or pearls within elaborate settings, but rather a rope—simply a long strand of pearls. Today the long pearl rope, as well as its sister, the shorter strand of pearls, remains a timeless classic. Here are a few hints to help you find your own string of classic beauties.

Know which type you want. There are three types of pearls: natural, cultured, and imitation. The most inexpensive are imitation pearls, although modern technology makes them often difficult to spot. The majority of pearls sold today are cultured, which simply means that a human hand helped the oyster along.

Look closely before you buy. Inspect a cultured pearl directly under a light on a flat, white surface. A 10× magnifier, or jeweler's loupe, is helpful.

Select for shine. Choose pearls that are shiny, with crisp reflections and contrast between light and dark areas. Reject pearls that look like dull, cloudy white beads.

Follow the rainbow. Look for the subtle, iridescent rainbow colors characteristic of better pearls. A pearl with a very slight pinkish cast is preferred over one with a green or blue tint.

Avoid most imperfections. Check for minimal surface blemishes (such as nicks, cracks, divots, or discoloration). Keep in mind that you do not want pearls with absolute color uniformity and perfect shape, because these characteristics create a lusterless pearl and indicate the pearls are fakes.

Try the tooth test. Run the pearl lightly along the biting edge of your top front teeth. Real pearls (natural and cultured) feel slightly gritty or sandy; fakes feel smooth. This is a standard jeweler's test for authenticity, and most retailers actually allow it—as long as you ask first.

Dust Off Your Pearls

■ Caring for your pearls need not be a laborious task, but it does need to be done. And modern methods are far more practical than our ancestors' techniques. For example, in 1893, Baroness Staffe instructed readers of *The Lady's Dressing Room,* "If pearls are shut up with a piece of ash-tree root, it prevents them losing their colour. Should wiseacres laugh at this recipe, let them laugh, and believe the experience transmitted in old families from generation to generation." Instead, Helena G. Krodel, media liaison for the Jewelry Information Center, in New York (a nonprofit trade organization representing the fine jewelry industry), recommends gently wiping your pearls with a soft, dry, lint-free cloth after each wearing. "Most important," Helena adds, "is that you always want to put your pearl necklace on last, right before you step out the door." The reason, she explains, is that pearls are porous and can absorb hair spray, perfume, or any liquid you spray or splash near your head and neck while getting dressed. This can dull your pearls' luster. As for long-range maintenance, better pearl necklaces are usually strung on a silk or natural-fiber strand, and it's a good idea to have the necklace restrung by a professional jeweler every year if worn often; every other year if worn infrequently. There should be a knot in the strand between each pearl (this is standard if done by a professional jeweler). "The knots keep the pearls from rubbing against each other. Also, if for some reason the strand breaks and the necklace falls off your neck, the knots prevent your beautiful pearls from skittering across the floor," Helena says.

Diamonds Aren't for Gaslight Anymore

"A rich silk dress, with lace at the neck and wrists, with plain jewelry by daylight, but diamonds by gaslight, must be worn by a young hostess," proclaims *American Etiquette and Rules of Politeness* (1882). Be glad that women don't have to follow such rigid guidelines about jewelry anymore! Let your jewelry rule be, I'll wear what I want when I want. "Today's independent women work, they earn good salaries, and they know they deserve the best. They wear their better jewelry on a daily basis—to the office, on the weekends, even with blue jeans and a T-shirt," says Helena G. Krodel, media liaison for the Jewelry Information Center, in New York (a nonprofit trade organization that represents the fine jewelry industry). One new jewelry style you may want to try is the right-hand ring, which is quickly becoming a popular trend. As the name implies, such rings are worn on the right-hand ring finger. They often incorporate diamonds, but as Helena explains, these rings are different from an engagement ring in that they tend to be more artistic—for example, the setting is often vertical and open.

Keep Your Diamonds Sparkling

If diamonds are our best friends, then it only makes sense to keep them sparkling clean. Of course, gemstone maintenance was not what Anita Loos, a popular writer during the flapper era, had in mind when she wrote these words (which inspired the song "Diamonds Are a Girl's Best Friend"): "I really think that American gentlemen are the best after all, because kissing your hand may make you feel very, very good, but a diamond and sapphire bracelet lasts forever."

Whether your American fellow gave you diamond jewelry or you bought it for yourself, there are two ways to keep these precious stones clean.

The preferred method is to take diamond jewelry to a better jewelry store for professional cleaning. Have diamonds that you wear often cleaned every 6 months. This service should be free, especially from the shop where you bought the jewelry. Also, ask the jeweler to double-check all prongs holding the diamonds—another free service, although you may be charged a minimal fee to repair a loose setting.

The do-it-yourself method for cleaning your diamond jewelry is to swirl together a few drops of very mild dish detergent in about a quart of warm water and then dip your diamond into the sudsy water. With a soft toothbrush, gently brush the submerged diamond and its setting. (A soft touch is not so much to protect the diamond, but rather to prevent scratching its metal setting!) Give the back of the jewelry special attention, as this side is where dirt and oils collect. Run warm water over the diamond to rinse, and then pat dry with a soft, lint-free cloth.

Proper Suggestions for Good Manners

The strict etiquette rules of past generations simplified social interaction: There were rules for everything from greeting a casual acquaintance to proposing marriage. On the other hand, there was little room for individuality. Contemporary Americans have compromised. Good manners are back in fashion, but they're more an expression from the heart than unwritten law. Borrowing the best of our ancestors' wisdom (with a modern outlook), let's look at the fine art of shaking hands, selecting a hostess gift, writing a proper thank-you letter, and more.

Shake Hands in Style

We Americans have been shaking hands as a greeting for a long time. As long ago as June 3, 1852, this action (which originated as physical proof that a man had put down his sword) had already gained historical status, as an article in *Frederick Douglass's Paper* explained: "Shaking hands itself was but a token of truce, in which the parties took hold each of the other's weapon-hand, to make sure against treachery."

Since shaking hands has such a rich history, it pays to do it right, but many people don't know how to properly shake hands.

A handshake is between right hands only (unless your right hand is disabled), with the skin between your thumb and index finger touching the same area on the other person's hand, explains Susan Fignar, a Chicago image consultant. You want a firm grip—please, nothing that threatens blood circulation—just long enough for two to five substantial pumps. "The only time you might want to loosen your grip and soften your pump," Susan stresses, "is when shaking hands with an elderly person. Many older people have arthritis, and it may be painful to have someone strongly shake their hand."

There is one change in this old-time tradition, of course: It's not just for men anymore. It's perfectly permissible for women to initiate a handshake—with men as well as women—and the same grip described above applies.

A Tip of the Hat

WITH A NOD TO strict policies of politeness, here are a few rules concerning a gentleman and his hat from Lillian Eichler's *Book of Etiquette* (1921)—with a few modifications to suit today's society.

- When acknowledging a woman in his conversation circle, whether he is acquainted with her or not, a gentleman raises his hat.
- When introduced to an elderly gentleman, superiors in office, clergymen, and men of distinction, the hat should be lifted.
- When greeting or being introduced to anyone, if you doubt whether or not a tip of the hat is called for, go ahead and do it. As the *Book of Etiquette* explains, "Surely it is better to be too polite (if such a thing were possible) than to be rudely discourteous to someone."
- And finally, here's a note about the gesture itself: "While lifting the hat one should incline the head slightly and smile. But it must be remembered that the unmannerly habit of touching the hat, instead of lifting it is an indication of sheer laziness and a lack of gallantry."

Greet New Neighbors the New-Fashioned Way

In *Polite Society, at Home and Abroad* (1901), Annie White offers this neighborly guidance: "When a stranger comes into town, the residents should call on her. In a city, the immediate neighbors should pay her the compliment of calling [to visit]." Yes, knocking on your neighbor's door is a simple act of kindness, and it can mean a great deal! Here are a few excuses to start a conversation with a new resident on your block or in your building.

Share a store list. Bring over a list (with directions!) of nearby home stores, like Lowe's or Home Depot. Every new homeowner needs lightbulbs, nails to hang pictures, and other household items right after moving in.

Recommend resources for kids. If you notice that your new neighbors have children, share a list of reliable teenage babysitters, as well as nearby parks or swimming pools.

Help them find takeout. Write down the names, addresses, and phone numbers of your favorite local take-out restaurants. Until the boxes of pots and pans are located, your neighbors will need this list.

Caution: You may want to avoid the old-time practice of welcoming new neighbors with fresh baked goods. They may have food allergies. Also, we live in a far less trusting world than a few generations ago, and folks may be reluctant to accept food from people they don't know. Until your neighbors get to know and trust you, stick with lists as welcome gifts.

☞ OLD-TIME ODDITIES ☜

The Secret Language of Fans

IN THE 19TH CENTURY, a lady used her handheld fan as much more than just a cooling mechanism and a fashion accessory. This seemingly innocent item that dangled from every proper lady's wrist was vital for communication between young men and women. All the emotional expressions deemed inappropriate for polite society were "spoken" with the fan. Michele Cox teaches the long-lost art of silent fan language at Southern Oaks, a restored turn-of-the-century house in Fayetteville, Georgia, that offers hands-on historical programs. Here's how Michele translates a few simple fan gestures.

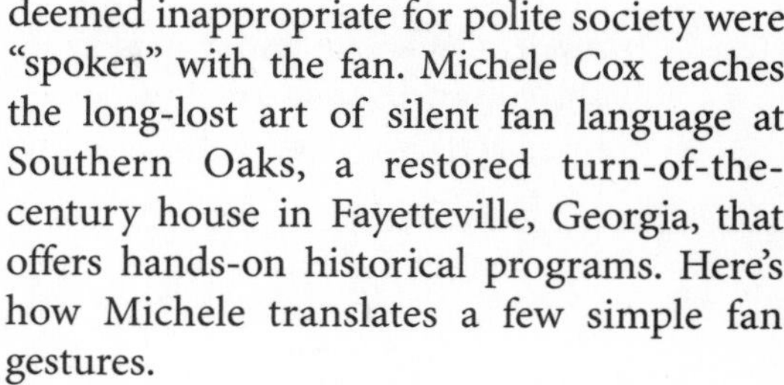

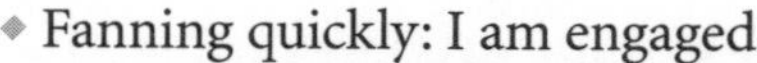

- Fanning quickly: I am engaged.
- Fanning slowly: I am married.
- Pulling a fan down either cheek: I love you.
- Holding an open fan in front of your face with your right hand: Follow me.
- Drawing a closed fan across your forehead: We are being watched.
- Drawing a closed fan across your eyes: I am sorry.
- Twirling a closed fan in your right hand: I love another.
- Twirling a closed fan in your left hand: I wish to be rid of you.
- Holding a closed fan against your lips: Kiss me!

Old-Time "Calling Cards" with a Twist

■ When swapping phone numbers with a new friend, we usually dig around inside our purse or pockets, grab an old grocery store receipt, jot down the numbers, and stuff the paper back into our purse or pocket. Finding that paper scrap again, days later, can be a major project. To avoid this frustration, adopt a useful custom that dates back to the 18th century: the calling card, also known as the *visiting card.* This slip of paper, about the size of a modern business card, was a vital and ceremonial part of the equally ceremonial house call of earlier eras. A woman or man would call on an acquaintance, engage in small talk for about 15 minutes, and then depart, leaving a card imprinted with her or his name on a designated tray. In *Our Deportment* (1881), author John Young described the calling card's importance: "To the unrefined or underbred, the visiting card is but a trifling and insignificant bit of paper; but to the cultured disciple of social law, it conveys a subtle and unmistakable intelligence. Its texture, style of engraving, and even the hour of leaving it combine to place the stranger, whose name it bears, in a pleasant or disagreeable attitude."

Nowadays, a calling card need not be so formal (or pricey), but it's a great alternative to a standard business card when sharing phone numbers in a social situation. If you have a home computer and a printer, an inexpensive option is to buy a package of clean-edge business cards and make your own calling cards. Ask a clerk at any office supply store to help you find the cards; they'll understand what you want. The package contains 8½-by-11-inch sheets of heavyweight card stock, as well as detailed instructions for finding a business card template on your computer or downloading a template from the Internet. Follow the instructions to design and print your cards. Be creative! Print cards with your name and telephone number (address, too, if you'd like). Add a graphic or make up a slogan, such as "Nana to three," "World's greatest gardener," or "Apple pies are my specialty." Keep a supply of cards in your wallet, and the next time you swap phone numbers, do it with class!

ROUGHING IT

Above and Beyond the Call of Etiquette

In times past, strict standards of courtesy demanded that people be civil to friends who invited them to share their summer house, no matter what the circumstances, as explained by Emily Post in *Etiquette in Society, in Business, in Politics and at Home* (1922): "If you go to stay in a small house in the country, and they give you a bed full of lumps, in a room of mosquitoes and flies, in a chamber over that of a crying baby, under the eaves with a temperature of over a hundred, you *can* the next morning walk to the village, and send yourself a telegram and leave! But though you feel starved, exhausted, wilted, and are mosquito bitten until you resemble a well-developed case of chickenpox or measles, by not so much as a facial muscle must you let the family know that your comfort lacked anything that your happiest imagination could picture—nor must you confide in any one afterwards (having broken bread in the house) how desperately wretched you were."

Give a Great Hostess Gift

What's the best way to show your appreciation for being invited to a terrific party or event? The old standard used to be to call upon the hostess in person to say thank you, as *Godey's Lady's Book* (February 1880) advises: "Calls to return thanks are made upon the hostess within ten days after the festivity." Visiting calls were once an integral part of daily life, and if you can afford the time, they're still a delightful custom. However, with schedules as they are today, it's more the norm to thank a hostess (and/or host) with a simple, thoughtful, and preferably inexpensive gift on the night of the party. The inexpensive part is important, as a pricey gift might embarrass the receivers. The traditional choices for hostess gifts are well known; here are a few twists on the traditions.

Traditional gift. Bouquet of flowers

Gift with a twist. Dried flowers or aromatic dried herbs, either in a bouquet or as a wreath

Traditional gift. Box of candy

Gift with a twist. Boxed exotic fruit, such as baby bananas, Asian pears, mangoes, papayas, or figs

Traditional gift. Bottle of wine

Gift with a twist. Dessert wine, sparkling champagne, or strawberry margarita ingredients—including a basket of strawberries and a bottle of tequila

Traditional gift. A pillar candle

Gift with a twist. An aromatherapy candle tucked into a basket along with bath salts, body lotion, and a loofah.

And for those times when you forget to bring a gift, you always have the option of making that "call to return thanks" or writing a traditional thank-you note. If you want to combine the two approaches, find a beautiful frame that matches your hostess's decor and tape your thank-you note on top of the frame's glass. Deliver it in person (and try to stick with that 10-day guideline).

The Lost Art of Condolence Cards

■ When a dear friend loses a loved one, the first thing we all want to do is comfort this person—but many of us struggle for the right words. What should we say?

One of the best ways to gracefully express what's in your heart is to send a condolence card based on happy memories, says Robin Thompson, director of Etiquette-Network, an etiquette school in Pekin, Illinois. "When someone reads a personal, handwritten note recalling fond memories of the deceased, well, it's just such a thoughtful gesture. You can accomplish so much good with very few words," Robin says. Let's combine Robin's advice with that from a classic template for a condolence letter from *The Ladies' and Gentleman's Model Letter-Writer* (circa 1870). The template suggests emphasizing the positive qualities that you remember about the deceased. Here's an example from that old-time sample template: "She was good in every acceptation of the term: her charities (so unostentatiously dispensed), her cheerful willingness to relieve any real distress, her talents and charms, endeared her to all."

You might begin a condolence letter by briefly expressing your grief over the loss of a valued friend and then quickly move on to a specific happy memory or endearing quality you remember. For example: "While John's passing is very sad and I will surely miss him, his love of children will always make me smile. I remember how he dressed up like a ghost every Halloween and sat on your front stoop, handing out candy and 'scaring' the trick-or-treaters. Every child in the neighborhood wanted to visit the ghost's house! He made the holiday so special for so many." Then simply end your condolence letter with a warm closing. This approach of expressing a cherished memory rather than an aching heart will give the mourner a true reason to smile and will help you comfort yourself, too.

Three Rules for Thank-Yous

Penning a thank-you note is fun and easy for some but a struggle for others. Many people are conditioned to believe that writing is hard, perhaps from reading and hearing decades of sentiments like this one from *Manners and Social Usages* (1887), by Mrs. John Sherwood: "It is impossible to give persons minute directions as to the style of a note, for that must be the outgrowth of years of careful education, training, and good mental powers." Mrs. Sherwood had it wrong! Writing a thank-you note can be easy for anyone. It takes only about 10 minutes to write one, because there's no need to include any news about things like your job, your grandkids, or your outstanding seasonal display of roses, explains Carmen D. Heitz, founder and director of the Etiquette School, in Chicago. "A thank-you card should focus on the gift and the gift giver. Save the rest for another day when you have the time and inclination." Follow these rules for writing excellent short thank-you notes.

1. Visit a proper stationery store and buy either note cards or a stack of pretty postcards. Steer clear of oversized greeting cards or full-size stationery sheets. Also avoid cards inscribed with a traditional "thank you" in script. This sets a very formal tone, and it may not be appropriate for your humorous (yet always tasteful!) note.

2. Write your note out by hand on a card or postcard. A preprinted thank-you card with only your signature says that the gift didn't mean enough to warrant a specific mention. And a thank-you e-mail, unless this is a firmly established mode of communication between two close friends, is also unacceptable.

3. In your first sentence, mention the specific gift and how or why you will enjoy using it. For example, "Thank you so much for the book *1,001 Old-Time Household Hints*. I've always been a history buff, so discovering old-fashioned ways to enjoy life is right up my alley!" Sign off with a warm closing.

CHAPTER 10

Pet Care

A Man's Best Friend Is His Dog (or Cat)

THINK BACK TO YOUR FIRST PET and those wonderful memories. Do you remember that nonstop tail wag or that l-o-n-g purr of contentment? For centuries, we've been on the receiving end of canine kindness, and we've embraced—perhaps even envied—the candid nature of cats. In this chapter, you'll discover great ways to help your pets stay healthy without costly veterinary bills, as well as ways to strengthen that friendship bond you have with dogs and cats. You will benefit from ageless advice designed to help you pamper these pals with a purpose while saving time and effort on caring for your pets.

Natural Remedies for Ailing Pets

WHETHER YOUR PET is a dog or a cat, you sometimes feel helpless when he or she is ailing. Fortunately, our ancestors have passed on many natural remedies using herbs, healthy foods, and plain common sense to help pets bounce back and feel better.

Aloe Soothes Doggy Paws

■ In the good old days, burns were soothed by applying a mixture of castor oil and egg whites, as cited in *Henley's Twentieth Century Book of Formulas, Processes and Trade Secrets* (1912). Today, we know that even dogs can suffer from sunburn, especially when their footpads land on sun-scorched sidewalks during midday walks. If you notice your pet limping or licking her paws, take a look to see if the pads are burned. Then nurse those tender pads with the juice from an aloe vera plant, a remedy recommended by holistic veterinarians. This healing succulent is easy to grow, even for non-gardeners. Keep a pot of it in your home or around your yard. When you need to take the sting out of a burn, just snap off a lower leaf near the center stalk. Remove any spines, and then split the leaf in half lengthwise. Squeeze the juice directly on the burn or wound.

Cologne for Your Dog?

IN VICTORIAN TIMES, flower essences were very popular for making toilet waters for ladies. (See "Blend Your Own Vintage Scent" on page 203.) Some of these same ingredients work on minor skin woes in your dogs. If your dog is suffering from itchy skin not caused by fleas, try this easy-to-make herbal recipe commonly used by holistic veterinarians. Flower essences are readily available at most health food stores and are gentle on your dog's skin.

3 drops of agrimony flower essence
3 drops of beech flower essence
3 drops of walnut flower essence
3 drops of cherry plum flower essence
3 drops of crab apple flower essence

Combine the flower essences in a small plastic spray bottle. Fill the bottle with distilled or spring water. Put on the spray nozzle top, tighten it, and then shake vigorously to mix all the essences well. Twice a day, spritz the itchy spots on your dog. If the itch doesn't go away in a week or so, consult your veterinarian.

Curb Kitty Acne with Epsom Salts

■ Strange but true: Some cats develop what looks like acne under the chin. Fortunately, feline acne is not a medical condition that requires expensive prescriptions to treat successfully, says Lowell Ackerman, D.V.M., a board-certified veterinary dermatologist in Boston. Instead, the way to "cure" feline acne is to rely on a product that has been in households since the 1800s: Epsom salts. "Just sprinkle about half a teaspoon of Epsom salts on a warm, damp washcloth and apply it to your cat's chin for a few minutes a day," says Dr. Ackerman. "It seems to help dry out the area and relieve inflammation."

Oatmeal Eases the Itchies

■ Oatmeal's goodness has never been limited to the breakfast bowl. *The Household Cyclopedia of Practical Receipts and Daily Wants* (1873), by Alexander V. Hamilton, touted the virtues of oatmeal baths to soothe itchy skin in people. Some veterinary dermatologists say an oatmeal bath also can help dogs with minor skin problems that cause them to scratch. However, if the skin condition worsens, be sure to consult your dog's veterinarian.

Easy, Effective Ear Care

■ You may marvel at your dog's hearing ability, but your canine chum relies on you when it comes to keeping those dear ears in tip-top shape. Dawn Logas, D.V.M., a board-certified veterinary dermatologist in Silver Springs, Florida, offers these timeless strategies for monitoring a dog's ears, which exemplify that sometimes the old ways are still the best ways.

Watch for the constant wiggling. Pets generally do not spend a lot of time scratching and fussing with their ears unless there is a problem.

Use the sniff test. A healthy ear should have no odor or discharge. Ears that smell like dirty socks may have a yeast infection. A nauseating odor may indicate a bacterial infection. Note that pets can suffer from a combination of yeast and bacterial infections.

Think pink. The inside of the ears in most breeds should be pink. The skin texture should be smooth and glossy.

There's an old-time method for cleaning your pet's ears that works fine, too. Remove dirt and wax inside the visible part of the ear's interior with cotton balls soaked in a solution of equal parts white vinegar and water. Make sure that you move the cotton ball in an up-and-out direction to avoid pushing debris farther down the ear canal.

If your dog's ears do not appear healthy, consult your veterinarian, as ear infections can become serious.

Garlic Oil Fights Mites

■ Back in 1917, *Everything about Dogs* recommended treating ear mites that irritate dogs' ears with a mixture of sulfur, lime, and water. Fortunately, there's a course of action you can take that is less messy and uses safer ingredients. Crush four garlic cloves and put the crushed garlic in a cup of olive oil in a container. Let the container sit for a day or so. Then skim out the garlic, warm the oil, and put several drops of this mixture into your

OLD-FASHIONED FAVORITES

Make Mites Disappear

WITH HIS UNIQUE BACKGROUND as both a veterinarian and an herbalist, Randy Kidd, D.V.M., Ph.D., relishes spotlighting old-time remedies that stand the test of time when it comes to pet care. "If your pet has ear mites, you can put a drop or two of mineral oil into each ear daily for a week or so, or you can try this herbal treatment," says Dr. Kidd, of McLouth, Kansas. "For success, be persistent and give several treatments a day for a few weeks."

1 to 2 tablespoons fresh or dried mullein flowers (available in health food stores)
Slow cooker (such as a Crock-Pot)
Olive oil

Place the flowers in the cooker and add just enough olive oil to cover. Heat on low for 6 hours. Allow the oil to cool, and then strain out the flowers. Pour the oil into a glass jar. It will keep in the refrigerator for up to 1 month. To use, apply several drops of the oil, warmed to body temperature, to the ear canal. Seek veterinary care if the ear infection does not clear up within 3 weeks.

pet's ears to boot out the itty-bitty white pests. This kitchen remedy is a cheaper alternative to topical medications available through veterinary clinics. "The key is to act quickly, especially if you swab your pet's ears and find what look like coffee grounds, which are a sign of mites," says Arnold Plotnick, D.V.M., a veterinarian in New York City.

Tea Tames Hot Spots

In the past, old veterinary medicine books devoted a lot of attention to dastardly skin conditions like mange, which aren't so common these days. For example, *Everything about Dogs* (1917) offers a remedy using a mix that includes turpentine and oil of tar—but these ingredients definitely aren't recommended today. One skin condition that remains a challenge to cure is hot spots, bare patches on your dog's skin usually triggered by fleas. The dog tries to fight back against the fleas by biting, licking, and scratching the area until it becomes bald, red, and inflamed. To ease discomfort, brew a cup of strong black or green tea. Let the tea cool and then dab it on the hot spots; repeat the treatment daily, say holistic veterinarians. Both of these types of tea contain tannic acid, noted for its drying and healing qualities.

Heat Treatment Relieves Doggy Aches

Heeding the advice of her grandparents, Deb Moore, of Allen, Texas, knows how to keep her aging cocker spaniels, Sassy and Cosmo, feeling comfortable despite bouts of arthritis. "I remember seeing my grandpa sticking a warm water bottle in the bed for his old dog," Deb says. "Especially during the cold weather, I drape a warmed towel over my dogs' hips and massage their bodies using gentle, circular motions to help ease their aches."

Hints for Happier Pill-Taking

Pill-giving has never ranked in the top 10 among pet owners. Even back at the turn of the 20th century, people were turning to experts for advice on how to make the medicine go down easier. *Everything about Dogs* (1917) suggests that you hold your dog's head up, open his mouth with your left hand, and place the pill well down his throat on the base of his tongue. Quickly close his jaws for a few seconds and lightly tap or stroke your fingers against his throat to make him gulp and swallow.

For clever dogs that spit out the pill, you need to go with Plan B instead. Hide the medicine in a piece of cooked hamburger or other tasty meat treat (providing your dog is not so sick that he refuses food). First, fool your dog by giving him a few pieces of meat, one at a time. Then offer him one with the pill tucked discreetly inside. Be sure to follow up with a few more pill-free meat treats so he won't catch on to your medicine-giving game.

Down with Bones

■ In the days before people knew better, they would toss beef and chicken bones to their tail-wagging dogs. But real bones can splinter and harbor germs. Instead of following old and unsafe traditions, treat your dog to sterilized bones sold in pet supply stores, say veterinarians. Even better: Buy hard rubber dog toys that you can stuff with cream cheese, peanut butter, soft pieces of cheddar cheese, or other delicious treats and can wash in your dishwasher.

Plants to Keep Out of Paw's Reach

■ "A dastardly act is to poison a dog, and no punishment is too severe to inflict on the cowardly cur who does it," proclaims *Everything about Dogs* (1917). But what about accidental poisonings? There are hundreds of plants that are potentially poisonous to your pet. Fortunately, these days, if you suspect your pet has eaten something toxic, help can be just a phone call away. Call the ASPCA Animal Poison Control Center at (888) 426-4435, or log on to their Web site: www.apcc.aspca.org.

Jill Richardson, D.V.M., a veterinarian formerly with the ASPCA Animal Poison Control Center and now with Hartz Mountain Corporation, in Secaucus, New Jersey, lists the following as the top 10 houseplants and landscape plants poisonous to pets.

- Autumn crocuses (*Colchicum* spp.)
- Lilies-of-the-valley (*Convallaria* spp.)
- Sago palms (*Cycas* spp.)
- Hyacinths (*Hyacinthus* spp.)
- Tomatoes (*Lycopersicon esculentum*)
- Daffodils (*Narcissus* spp.)
- Oleander (*Nerium oleander*)
- Rhubarbs (*Rheum* spp.)
- Azaleas (*Rhododendron* spp.)
- Japanese yew (*Taxus cuspidata*)

A special warning: Keep your dog away from mushrooms on your walks and hikes in the woods. "Always assume that any mushroom ingested by a dog is toxic and can cause liver failure," says Dr. Richardson. "The problem is that many poisonous mushrooms often grow together with nonpoisonous mushrooms." If you see your dog eating mushrooms, consult your veterinarian as soon as possible.

Special Diet Defeats Diarrhea

■ For those occasional times when diarrhea occurs in dogs, George Waterman of *The Practical Stock Doctor* (1912) recommends a dose of castor oil or a serving of boiled milk mixed with a little flour. Although these remedies may be somewhat effective, a better option for mild cases of diarrhea in pets is to serve them boiled rice and cooked lean ground beef for 2 or 3 days. Mix equal parts of the rice and beef in an amount equivalent to the portion of commercial dried dog food you would normally serve. For example, if your medium-size dog normally eats 2 cups of kibble a day, substitute 1 cup each of rice and ground beef. "Be sure to drain the fat from the cooked beef before serving," says Jill Richardson, D.V.M., a veterinarian in Secaucus, New Jersey, who has relied on this recipe for her own dogs with success.

Gentle Remedies for Constipated Pets

■ Back in the early 1900s, a common solution to cure constipation in cats was to feed the sick kitty a half teaspoon of butter to act as a gentle laxative, as advised by Frances Simpson in *The Book of the Cat* (1903). Butter is high in fat. Castor oil mixed with oatmeal and cooked beef liver was another remedy mentioned by George Waterman in *The Practical Stock Doctor: A Reliable Common-Sense Ready-Reference Book, for the Farmer and Stock Owner* (1912). A better option for relieving constipation in both cats and dogs is additional fiber in the diet. Serve your pets cooked whole-grain pastas or steamed vegetables such as carrots or broccoli. (Always let the foods cool before offering them to your animals.) Another option is to sprinkle a teaspoon of supplemental dietary fiber known as *psyllium* on the pet's regular food two or three times a week.

BIZARRE BUT TRUE

Kippers for Constipated Cats

A POPULAR OLD-TIME REMEDY to cure constipation in cats was to feed the ailing feline a whole kipper (salted or smoked herring), bones and all. Veterinarians today, though, advise against this old remedy, because the small bones in kippers can cause your cat to choke. If you're looking for a safer natural remedy, add about a teaspoon of mineral oil to your cat's food. It acts as a lubricant laxative.

Wheat Biscuits May Not Be Best

■ When it comes to dog biscuits, the ingredients are basically the same as they were 100 years ago. In *Henley's Twentieth Century Book of Formulas, Processes and Trade Secrets* (1912), a section discussing homemade dog biscuits states that each contained mostly wheat flour with about 15 percent being chopped, dried meat scraps. This still holds true today, and that can pose a problem for some dogs. What we know now that people didn't a century ago is dogs can be allergic to wheat. If you've got a new dog or are concerned that your dog has allergies, carefully check ingredient lists on packages of dog biscuits before you buy.

Serve a Warm Meal

■ Older dogs and cats can become finicky about eating, making mealtime stressful for both you and them. To entice

older animals to eat, follow the style of an earlier era, when dogs and cats were fed table scraps and warm dishes like oatmeal. "The warmth unlocks the scent and makes it more pungent and pleasing to an older cat or dog," says Tracy McFarland, D.V.M., a veterinarian who operates a cat practice in Santa Clarita, California. You can gently warm moist foods in a microwave oven for 10 seconds, and even warm up dry food by adding warm water. "You can also add low-salt chicken broth or water-packed tuna juice to the bowl of dry food to make it more appealing," suggests Dr. McFarland.

Healthful Herbs and Foods for Pets

For centuries, people have turned to the healing power of plants to stave off disease. Many holistic-trained veterinarians turn to this green pharmacy to help keep dogs and cats healthy, but they caution pet owners that the worst time to try herbs is when an animal is sick. Medicinal herbs are always more effective when the body's system has prepared itself for them. Work with your veterinarian or knowledgeable herbalist on selecting the right herb in the right form and the right dose for your pet.

Applause for Alfalfa

As a young child living in Pittsfield, Massachusetts, Flo Frum remembers seeing local farmers feeding handfuls of alfalfa to underweight dogs. The dogs seemed to benefit, says Flo, now a retired dollhouse maker living in Oceanside, California. Upon doing some research about alfalfa, Flo discovered that alfalfa was—and is—a good remedy for indigestion in dogs. For best results, use fresh alfalfa or powdered alfalfa in capsules. Consult a holistic veterinarian about the correct dosage for your dog. For a 20- to 40-pound dog, one capsule should be sufficient.

The Wonder Weed

Old-timers cursed—and praised—the dandelion as both a darn weed and a wonderful tonic to cleanse the liver. As it turns out, this weed works just dandy when it comes to treating your pet for allergies, arthritis, constipation, mild pain, or urinary disorders. Just select young leaves and roots from dandelion plants that you know are free of pesticides and other harmful chemical sprays. Allow the leaves and roots to air-dry thoroughly by spreading them on a screen and putting them in a warm, dry place. Chop up the dried plant material and mix about 1

teaspoon into your pet's food at mealtime. *Caution:* Dandelion acts as a diuretic, so make sure you give your dog plenty of bathroom breaks and keep the cat's litter box scooped and filled with fresh litter.

OLD-FASHIONED FAVORITES

Grandma's Aches-Away Stew

A RETIRED high school librarian, Jocelyn Shannon, of Oceanside, California, still enjoys researching old books for ageless ideas. She keeps her checkout cards for area college and city libraries next to her driver's license in her wallet for easy access. Her pursuit of knowledge has paid off for her aging dogs with a recipe she found years ago in an old cookbook. This recipe is believed to ease the aches for people—and dogs—with arthritis. "I wish I could remember the book where I found this recipe, but all I know is that my old dogs seem to move better after chowing down," says Shannon.

- 2 cups barley
- 2 cups brown rice
- 2 cups diced carrots
- 2 cups fresh spinach
- 2 cups chopped beef hearts
- 1 cup lentils
- 1 cup diced celery
- 2 garlic cloves, crushed
- 10 cups water

In a large pot, combine all the ingredients. Bring the mix to a boil on the stovetop, and then reduce the heat to a simmer for 1½ hours. Put a lid on the pot and stir the mix every 15 minutes or so. You may need to add more water. Serve yourself a hearty portion, but allow your dog's serving of stew to cool before giving it to him. Offer your dog the same quantity of the stew as you would of his usual food. You can freeze or refrigerate the leftovers.

Teatime for Fido?

For more than a century, tea sippers around the world have recognized the healthy punch delivered by green tea. Herbalists of then and now tout the antioxidants and vitamins C and E in this popular brew. Share this healthy liquid with your aging dog by pouring a cooled cup of it over his dry kibble as a gravy for an occasional treat, and watch him lap it up.

Catnip: Nature's Calmer

Believe it or not, catnip can *calm* cats and dogs. Catnip has been used for generations as a mild sedative for dogs and cats that are restless, nervous, or having trouble sleeping. Catnip also relieves muscle spasms, diarrhea, gas, and minor respiratory problems. The best way to offer your pet a catnip remedy is to chop up fresh leaves or crumble dried leaves and mix about a teaspoon into your pet's dry or canned food at those times when your pet needs calming (not every day).

Catnip is an "as-needed" herb and should not be regarded in the same way as a multivitamin that you would give your pet daily. Think of it as a natural medicine for your pet that can ease symptoms for specific conditions such as nervousness or gas.

Flea Fixes That Really Work

Fleas have always been a nuisance to pets and pet owners. When you need to send fleas fleeing from your dog or your cat, fight back with these timeless tips, including a daily dose of garlic, homemade flea repellent shampoo and herbal rinse, and more.

Garlic's Goodness

■ Even as a kid, Roger Valentine, D.V.M., now a veterinarian in Santa Monica, California, relied on a fresh clove of garlic a day to make his dog less appetizing to fleas. Now, with his holistic training, Dr. Valentine understands more about the powers of garlic. "Will garlic keep fleas off a dog—or cat? No, but it can make them less appealing," says Dr. Valentine. For chowhounds that gobble up anything, you can just crush the clove and stick it in the food bowl with their meal. For picky eaters, you may need to opt for sprinkling a teaspoon of garlic powder into the dry food and adding some water for gravy.

Pucker Power against Fleas

■ Some homemakers in the late 1800s demonstrated the value of lemon in keeping a fresh-smelling house by reaching for a lemon and squeezing the juice for use in

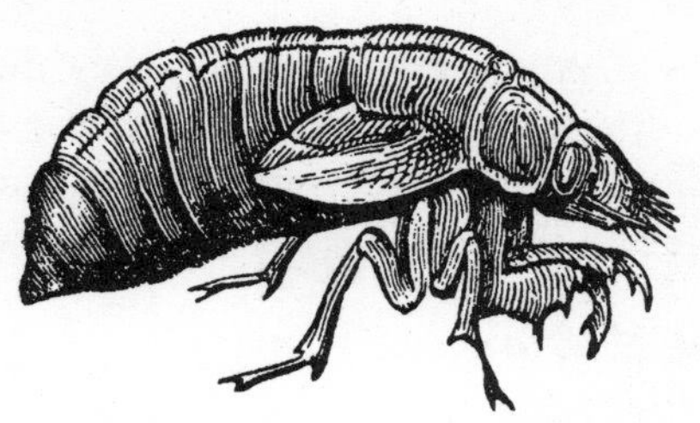

cleaning their sinks, according to *The Household Guide or Domestic Cyclopedia* (1892), by Benjamin Jefferis, M.D., and James Nichols. Turns out that lemons have a repellent effect on fleas and other pests, too. Lemon contains d-limonene, a natural flea-killing substance. Holistic-minded animal herbalists have relied on lemon skin tonic to keep fleas from feasting on their Fidos. To make some, thinly slice a whole lemon, including the peel. Add it to 1 pint of near-boiling water and let it steep overnight. The next day, sponge the cooled liquid onto your dog's skin and let dry. Use this homemade tonic daily for a few days to combat fleas. Say goodbye to your pooch's scratching! Another option for fighting fleas is to wash your dog with pet shampoos that contain d-limonene, a natural extract from citrus fruits that will kill fleas with minimal side effects on dogs. Just be sure not to use this ingredient on cats, because it can be toxic to them.

Essential Ingredients for Flea-Fighting Shampoo

■ "You can make old-fashioned insect-repellent shampoo simply by adding a few drops of essential oil of rosemary, pennyroyal, or eucalyptus to a bottle of natural pet shampoo," says Richard Pitcairn, D.V.M., Ph.D., a holistic-minded veterinarian in practice for more than 45 years. Dr. Pitcairn cautions pet owners to be careful not to apply these oils directly to a dog's skin, because the oils can be too irritating and may cause rashes.

The Newfangled Way to Fight Fleas

■ Back at the turn of the 20th century, one of the few ways to rid a dog of lice, fleas, and ticks was to bathe the animal in a tub of water and carbolic acid soap, according to the *American Woman's Home* (1887). Within days, sometimes even hours, however, the pests were back, and the dogs would resume scratching. Today, most pet owners wouldn't dream of using something that sounds as nasty as carbolic acid to wash their pets, and luckily, they don't have to. Nowadays, veterinarians unleash safe chemical warfare with topical flea and tick medicines that do not harm people or dogs and that need to be administered only once a month. "The chemicals available in the once-a-month topicals are generally safe for people and pets but are really effective against parasites," says Michael Dryden, D.V.M., Ph.D., a parasitology professor at Kansas State University, in Manhattan, Kansas. "Just check with your veterinarian to pick the right one for your pet."

Herbal Rinse Repels Fleas

■ Since Colonial times, people have looked to their herb gardens for all kinds of remedies for common ailments. Picking the right herbs to grow can also keep your pets from scratching up a fuss when summer arrives and fleas are thriving. Here's an easy herbal recipe to fight fleas. In a saucepan, bring 1 pint water to a boil. Add 1 teaspoon dried rosemary or 1 tablespoon fresh rosemary leaves, cover, and steep for 10 minutes. Strain out the herbs and allow the rosemary "tea" to cool to room temperature. Pour this mixture over your dog or cat after her final bath rinse. Rub in and towel dry without further rinsing.

Feline Flea Freedom

■ Even indoor cats are not immune to flea visitors. Pet-friendly herbalists recommend this natural way to discourage fleas from setting up house in your cat's coat. Combine one part each of as many of these herbs as you can find: eucalyptus, rosemary, fennel, yellow dock, wormwood, and rue. Put this mixture in a shaker-top jar (like the one you use for parsley flakes). Apply the herbal flea powder sparingly to your cat's coat by brushing backward with your hand or a comb and sprinkling the herbs into the base of the hairs, especially around the neck, back, and belly. Do this several times a week. Your cat will purr with gratitude. (It won't harm your cat to ingest the powder, so don't be concerned if she licks herself after you apply it.)

Great Grooming and Cleaning Hints

Although we love our pets, we certainly don't adore those balls of fur that skitter across our floors or those hunks of hairball that gum up our carpeting. Face this furry fact: Except for those rare hairless breeds, cats and dogs shed. Tired of doggy odor or matted cat fur? Wish bath time wasn't such a tug of wills? Brush up on your grooming skills with these timeless tips.

Reach for Mother Nature's Brush

■ Professional pet groomers have the luxury of an assortment of brushes and combs at their disposal to address any type of coat in a dog or cat. Your grandparents weren't as fortunate, but whenever their dog or cat came home with a matted coat, they could rely on a "brush" from nature: a pinecone. The good news is that a pinecone still works in a pinch as a makeshift grooming tool to restore your pet's coat to a snarl-free condition.

The Eyes Have Had It

■ Stymied by that dried gunk that likes to adhere to the fur around the eyes of your Persian or Himalayan cat? These breeds, and others with pushed-in faces, tend to produce lots of eye and nasal discharge. Wiping the areas with a cloth doesn't always remove the dried goop. The perfect tool for this job is also an old-fashioned grooming tool for people: a small plastic man's comb with narrowly spaced teeth, suggests Arnold Plotnick, D.V.M., a veterinarian in New York City who specializes in cat care. "I discovered that you can also use a metal flea comb to

clean around the eyes—a tip I wish I could have shared with my grandparents," he says.

Brushing Reduces Burr Buildup

■ Spiny burrs have troubled dogs—domestic and wild—throughout their mutual history. And the best way to help dogs avoid entanglements with nasty burrs during a walk in the wild is an old-fashioned weekly brushing, says veteran

TRASH OR TREASURE

Try This Screen Play

Jill James, of Allen, Texas, always listened to her grandmother's advice to think carefully before throwing anything away. "My grandmother grew up during the Depression and learned clever and unexpected ways to use common items," says Jill, a middle school reading teacher. She shares this gem: When you need to bathe your cat, place an old window screen in the sink or bathtub so that your cat can grip the screen instead of clawing your skin as you lather and rinse her.

dog groomer Susan Sholar, owner of the California School of Dog Grooming, in San Marcos. Daily brushing is even better, because burrs and stickers tend to slide right out of regularly groomed coats.

Even if you do brush your dog regularly, it's a good idea to inspect your dog's coat for burrs after each hike. Pay close attention to the footpads and under the legs, where burrs can hide. It's best to remove burrs from dry fur, though, so let your dog dry out if he's gotten wet. You can remove most burrs by using your fingertips or tweezers in a sliding outward motion. Snip stubborn burrs with thinning scissors.

Solving the Phew Factor

Everyone knows that tomato juice is handy for deskunking a dog, but it's not the only old-time remedy that's effective for reducing the stench of skunk. Some other ingredients to keep on hand in quantity in case of emergency include vanilla extract, apple cider vinegar, and hydrogen peroxide.

Try dousing a skunked dog with about a cup of vanilla extract mixed in a gallon of water, says Hazel Christiansen, a longtime professional groomer and former president of the American Grooming Shop Association, in Lewiston, Idaho. Let the dog soak in the solution for about 10 minutes before applying dog shampoo and rinsing.

For the vinegar remedy, mix 2 parts water with 1 part apple cider vinegar, and set the solution aside (the total amount you'll need to mix depends on the size of your dog). Thoroughly wet your smelly dog's coat with water. Now, work the vinegar solution through the fur. Let the solution sit for about 5 minutes; then rinse thoroughly. Work carefully and be sure the solution doesn't drip into your dog's eyes (it would sting).

If neither of the concoctions above seems to work, here's one last skunk-smell-removing remedy that's been passed on from one generation of dog lovers to the next. Mix 1 quart hydrogen peroxide, ¼ cup baking soda, and 1 teaspoon dish-washing liquid. Apply this mixture in the same way you would the vinegar solution. The quantities listed should make enough deskunking solution for a medium-size dog (30 to 50 pounds), so use less or more as needed for the size of your dog.

Murphy for a Dirty Dog

When it's time to bathe your dog, there's no need to buy special dog shampoo. Just pull out the old-fashioned Murphy Oil Soap. Put your dog into your tub and use Murphy Oil Soap the same way you would use shampoo. Apply it directly to the dog's hair, and add water to lather it up. The soap will rinse out easily with water; be sure you rinse it out thoroughly.

Murphy's works well as a dog shampoo, because the soap is mild to skin and eyes and has a pleasant fragrance that doesn't linger. Your dog's coat will be silky and shiny. It is also the right pH for dogs, and it kills fleas, says Gentry Brann, a spokesperson for Murphy Oil Soap. *Caution:* Citronella, which provides the flea-killing factor in Murphy Oil, is safe for use on dogs but not cats, so don't dunk your cat in a Murphy bath.

Miracles of Mineral Oil

■ Since the 1800s, dog and cat lovers have reached for that bottle of mineral oil or olive oil when their furry friend has shown up on the doorstep brandishing tar or other sticky substances on his tail, footpads, or coat. Apply mineral oil, vegetable shortening, petroleum jelly, or olive oil to the targeted areas, recommends *The Household Guide or Domestic Cyclopedia* (1892), by Benjamin Jefferis, M.D., and James Nichols. Rub the oil into the pet's coat until the sticky substance softens. Then wash with mild soapy water, rinse, and blot dry with a towel. Finish by brushing or combing the coat, being careful not to bear down on the skin. Instead, pull outward to avoid causing a brush burn.

Nature's Scratching Posts

■ A carpeted scratching post to keep the claws of cats honed is a relatively modern invention. In fact, *The Wonderland of Knowledge* (1937) describes how cats, particularly those living primarily outside, kept their claws sharp by tearing on the rough bark of trees. Cats' instincts are still the same as they were in the 1930s, even if they live entirely indoors. So instead of spending a lot of money for a fancy contraption from the pet store, why not bring in a log and designate it as your cat's scratching post? Just inspect it for boring beetles or other insects before you bring it inside.

Paws for Relief

Living in the snowy climate of Conifer, Colorado, lifelong sled dog trainer and racer Margaret Bonham relies on an old family secret, passed on from one generation to the next, to keep snow and ice from clumping between the toes of her huskies. "I just apply a thin layer of aloe or petroleum jelly to their footpads before heading outside when it is cold," says Bonham. "These substances are safe to use, even if your dog licks his feet."

Early Kitty Bathrooms

■ One of the earliest mentions of "indoor plumbing" for cats is found in *Cats: Their Points and Characteristics, with Curiosities of Cat Life* (1920), by W. Gordon Stables, M.D. Dr. Stables wrote of using a "good-sized pan partly filled with dry earth" as a litter box and placing it behind a screen in the hallway. While you probably won't want to dig "dry earth" on a regular basis to supply your cat's litter box, modern-day clump-style litter works in essentially the same way. Veterinarians recommend that you maintain a litter depth of 2 to 3 inches to give your cat ample supply to bury her deposits.

Dental Care Tricks and Techniques

The olden days were not necessarily the good old days for dogs and cats when it came to care of their teeth. A century ago, the notion of doggy toothbrushes was as foreign as the thought of a man walking on the moon. We've taken a major leap in dental care, fortunately, as dogs and cats have become part of the household family. Be sure your vet checks your pet's teeth and gums as part of the annual exam, and try some of these tips for prime dental health.

Meaty Treats for Cleaning Teeth

Your grandmother probably never dreamed of brushing her cat's teeth. After all, cats aren't big fans of anyone fussing in their mouths. Even though cat owners in your grandmother's day didn't realize the benefit, whenever they treated their cats to meat scraps like cooked chunks of beef heart or chicken gizzards, they were actually doing their felines a favor. And this meaty dental treat is still valid, says Roger Valentine, D.V.M., a veterinarian in Santa Monica, California, who specializes in cats. "My favorite thing is to see cats eating fairly large chunks of beef heart. It's tough. They have to chew it up. When they chew it, it massages the gums and keeps the teeth clean," says Dr. Valentine. For dogs, he suggests that you first blanch tough cuts such as stew

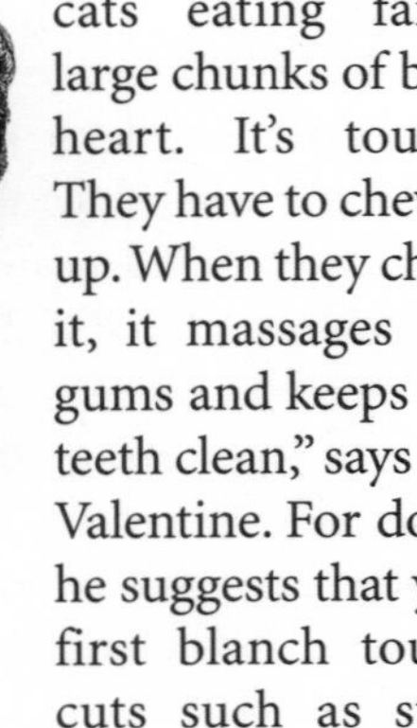

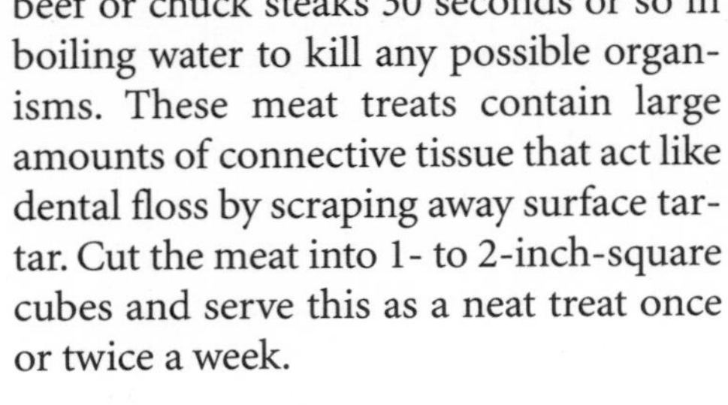

beef or chuck steaks 30 seconds or so in boiling water to kill any possible organisms. These meat treats contain large amounts of connective tissue that act like dental floss by scraping away surface tartar. Cut the meat into 1- to 2-inch-square cubes and serve this as a neat treat once or twice a week.

Danger: Doggy Breath

Most folks a generation or two ago dismissed bad breath from their dogs as a common canine odor. Now, as more veterinarians educate owners about dental care, we know that "doggy breath" often signals gum disease or other health problems. "Offer your dog an 'edible toothbrush,' which you can buy at pet supply stores. Or serve him bits of broccoli stems or raw cauliflower florets as daily treats. This removes surface tartar from his teeth and gets rid of stink-causing plaque," suggests Marty Becker, D.V.M., a veterinarian in Bonners Ferry, Idaho. "Your dog should have kissable breath at any age."

Bits of raw carrot are another great choice, says Patrick Melese, D.V.M., a veterinarian in San Diego. "Carrots are excellent sources of vitamins A and C, plus the chewing action takes away surface tartar. You're keeping your dogs' teeth in good shape in a very inexpensive way."

Down in the Mouth

Nowadays, we can buy pet toothbrushes and other dental products, but old-time pet owners didn't have that choice. They had to rely on natural ways to keep their pets' teeth pearly white. Holistic veterinarians also prefer natural methods, and they recommend serving real bits of tuna for cats—in effect, a "tuna toothbrush." Feed your feline tiny cubes of raw fresh tuna (not tuna flakes from a can) to scrub plaque away. Serve these dental treats no bigger than the size of your thumbnail two or three times a week. Keep a supply in your freezer, and take them out as needed to serve your kitty.

Bark Up a Different Treat

■ Karen Cichocki, a lifetime dog lover from Dyer, Indiana, recalls her grandfather's stories of how he eased the teething time in his puppies. "My grandfather used to smear a little peanut butter on a tree branch and let the pup gnaw away to soothe its gums," says Karen. She has developed her own, safer method for helping puppies survive the trials of teething. She smears peanut butter in a hollow rubber dog toy (sold in most pet supply stores) for her fast-growing canine chums to gnaw.

Help Your Puppy Chill Out

■ Special ice cubes help ease your puppy's teething pain and save you from the pain of chewed-up furnishings. "Puppies like to chew—they need to chew to help bring in their adult teeth," says Flo Frum, who has enjoyed the company of dogs for much of her 80 years. Flo is a retired dollhouse maker in Oceanside, California, and she's raised her share of puppies, including Yorkshire terriers and schnauzers. Flo passes on her ageless advice to all new puppy owners: Fill an ice cube tray about three-quarters full with water and top it off with chicken broth. Allow time for the liquid to freeze, and then give your teething puppy one of these meat-flavored cubes to chew. It will massage her tender gums. "Serve these ice cubes in the kitchen on a floor that's easy to clean. You'll save your living room rugs from being chewed by a teething puppy," says Flo.

PEARLS OF WISDOM

"Heaven goes by favor.
If it went by merit,
you would stay out and
your dog would go in."

MARK TWAIN (1835–1910)

BEST BEHAVIOR AND TRAINING HINTS

EVER SINCE PETS became part of household life, their behavior has been a source of delight—and frustration. Pets don't come with owner's manuals! Your experience of puppy parenting, dog training, and generally coping with your pets can be less hectic and more rewarding when you follow these timeless tips for helping your new puppy adjust, training cats and dogs to obey basic commands, and more.

Perplexed by Puppy Puddles?

■ A century ago, most dogs lived outside with a doghouse or barn for shelter, so dog-bathroom issues were virtually nonexistent. But the beckoning from the backyard to inside homes a few decades ago found that this welcome came with a price: household accidents. A common way to clean up these puddles called for using vinegar and/or ammonia, but thanks to a better understanding of chemical interaction, experts now say that ammonia is actually one of the worst choices for cleaning up a puppy's mess. "Ammonia will actually attract the puppy back to the urine stain," says Patrick Melese, D.V.M., a veterinarian and clinical animal behaviorist in San Diego. Dr. Melese explains that ammonia is so similar to the ingredients in urine that an animal can mistake the smell of ammonia for the odor of urine itself, making it more likely to pee in that spot again. And vinegar acts primarily as a disinfectant, so it only temporarily inhibits the environmental bacteria from producing the odor. Dr. Melese prefers a modern-day solution: cleaning products available in pet supply stores that contain protein enzymes to gobble up the urine and oust the odor. And he offers this final tip: Place the pup's food and water bowls near the targeted spots where you want to avoid repeat accidents. Dogs don't like to eliminate in the same area where they eat.

Ticktock to Snooze Land

It's common for puppies to cry the first night or so in a new home. After all, they miss their mama. To ease their anxiety, try this old-fashioned tip: Place a ticking alarm clock in their bed to help them sleep—along with a hot water bottle. "The ticking of the clock simulates their mom's heartbeat, and the hot water bottle simulates her body warmth," says Alice Moon-Fanelli, Ph.D., a certified applied animal behaviorist at Tufts University, in North Grafton, Massachusetts. "Once the puppy gets used to his new home, you can remove these objects from his bed."

Succeed with Short Lessons

■ Think of your dog in training as a young middle schooler, and you'll realize that his attention span is short. For successful training, you need to make sessions brief and fun—a tip noted in *Cassell's Household Guide* (circa 1880s). In a section devoted to training your dog to understand hunt commands, the authors write, "Neither should he be trained too long at one period, lest he become tired and disgusted." Age-old advice: Limit your doggy tutorials to 5 to 10 minutes for greatest success.

Rein In a Rowdy Dog

■ Back in the late 1800s, the *Delaware County Republican* newspaper reported that lawmakers in Chester, Delaware, had decreed that all dogs within the city limits must wear wire muzzles to prevent any problems. This was bad news for the city's dogs, because a wire muzzle can cut into a dog's face. A newer and much safer option for controlling a pushy dog is the use of a piece of nylon headgear known as a Gen-

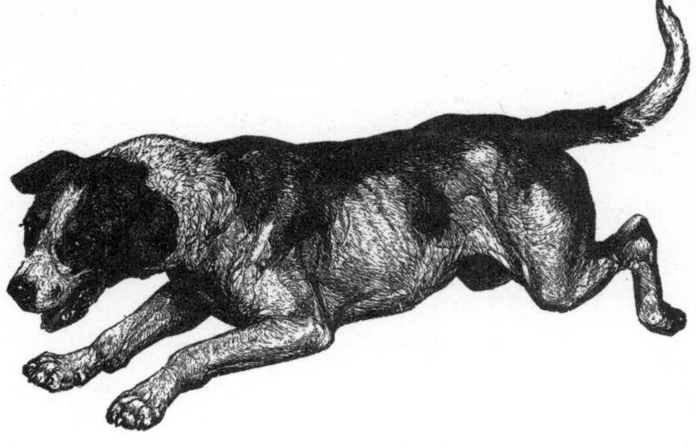

tle Leader, available in major pet supply stores. This product is similar to a horse's bridle, allowing the owner to easily control the head movement of the dog.

Spare the Rod without Spoiling the Dog

▪ Dog trainers of yore relied on whips and physical punishments to force their canines to heed their commands. For example, *Cassell's Household Guide* (circa 1880s) directs dog owners to correct a dog learning to hunt for game by giving "two to half-a-dozen smart cuts with the whip." Reputable animal trainers today shun this approach! Animal behaviorist Alice Moon-Fanelli, Ph.D., of Tufts University, in North Grafton, Massachusetts, says you will achieve greater success and more canine loyalty by using positive reinforcement. Reward and praise the right behavior and ignore or divert unwanted behavior.

"You don't want a dog to cower or become fear-aggressive," warns Dr. Moon-Fanelli. "Instead of bullying your dog into obeying a command, you need to be a benevolent leader who is consistent, clear, and concise with your requests. You'll have a dog willing to learn."

One timeless method: If you have a dog that likes to jump when greeting people, turn your back as the dog approaches. Once the dog sits down, turn around and offer praise and a small treat. Your dog will learn to associate good manners (sitting) with good payoffs (treats).

Train Dogs with Praise

▪ "When you take your dog for a walk, teach him to mind you," advises *Everything about Dogs* (1917). Indeed, for centuries people have trained dogs to heed three basic commands: *come, sit,* and *stay.* These commands remain vital. First and foremost, they can be lifesavers. An obedient dog that responds to *come* rather than trying to chase a car down the street won't be run over. A dog that stays when told will also stay out of potentially hazardous situations. And a dog that sits on cue earns compliments for good manners at the very least.

In training your dog, keep one vintage bit of wisdom from *Everything about Dogs*: "Praise your dog and don't be stingy about it. Encourage him with your words and tone to motivate him so he will be eager to comply. Teach these three commands without force or a bullying tone."

Conquer the Come *Command*

▪ To ensure a reliable recall each and every time you call your dog, do the training in your backyard or another spacious place that doesn't have a lot of distractions, such as other dogs.

Fasten a long clothesline—about 30 or 40 feet—to your dog's collar. Let her sniff and explore ahead of you and then, in an upbeat tone, say her name, followed by the *come* command as you reel her back with the clothesline. Your dog should turn to look at you and then head your way.

When she comes to you, gently grab her collar, hand her a treat without bending over, and take a few strides side by side. Say, "Okay, go play!" and loosen the line again.

This technique encourages your dog to come when called, because she knows she isn't being reprimanded for some doggy misdeed and also that obeying doesn't mean that party time is over.

Sitting Pretty with the Sit *Command*

Does your overly happy dog literally bowl your guests over as they enter your front door? It's up to you to train your dog to greet two-legged visitors with some manners. Try this hands-free method of training your dog to sit on command.

Stash a small treat in your right hand. Slowly glide your hand up and over your dog's head while she is in a standing position. With a positive tone, say her name and the word *sit*. Let gravity be your friend. As you guide the hand up and over your dog's head, she will arch her head back to follow. At some point, she'll sense that she's going to lose her balance, and to prevent that, she'll sit. The second her rump hits the floor, tell her "good sit," and hand over the treat.

Repeat the previous steps four or five times per session. In time, your dog should sit on command with your hand signal, without needing the constant reinforcement of treats.

Hey, Hey, Why Don't You Stay?

Sometimes you need your dog to be in one place—and remain there—until you say otherwise. One example is when you want your dog not to bolt out of the car when you open the car door. Or when the family cat enters the room, and you don't want your dog to give chase. That's where the *stay* command comes in handy.

The first step in teaching your dog to stay is to teach your dog the *watch me* command. You need eye contact and undivided attention from your dog. Say her name and tell her "watch me" as you take a small food treat and move it toward the side of your eye. The goal is to have your dog watch the treat move. When she does, hand over the treat.

Next, command your dog to move into a down or sit position. Wait a second or two before you say "good stay" as you use your hand in a motion like a traffic cop signaling a "stop" to oncoming cars, and then reward with a treat.

As you repeat the sequence, purposely delay the reward to teach your dog that you are requesting that she stay put. With each *stay*, gradually extend the time it takes her to earn a treat from 2 to 5 to 10 seconds and beyond. If your eager dog should get up and move before the designated time, do not give a treat. Initially, aim for a *stay* that lasts 30 seconds to a minute in a quiet, undistracted place in your home or backyard.

Boredom Buster for Kitties

■ Cats have shifted from being mouse-catchers in barns to snoozing on our beds only in the past few decades, so they may find life indoors boring. Cats that don't roam outdoors need a productive way to unleash their energy, or they'll find their own way—such as scratching your couch. "If you invest even 5 or 10 minutes a day playing with your cat, you will benefit by having a cat who is better behaved," says Rolan Tripp, D.V.M., a veterinarian and animal behavior consultant in La Mirada, California. He suggests you toss a Ping-Pong ball in your bathtub for your cat to pounce on. You can also make a homemade toy using a paper grocery bag, an old shoelace, and a small cat toy, such as a mouse. Just cut a hole in the bottom of the bag, place the bag on its side, and fasten the toy to one end of the shoelace. Slip the toy mouse through the hole and along to the opening of the bag. Entice your cat to notice and then stalk the mouse as you reel it into the bag and through the exit hole.

Tricks for Teaching Cats Commands

■ Fifty or 100 years ago, purebred cats spent a lot of time perched on the laps of high-society ladies. Doing any type of trick was unheard-of. Today, we know that cats can perform tricks if they choose to and if they are encouraged. "Cats actually learn at a rate that is faster than some other animals," says Nicholas Dodman, B.V.M.S., veterinarian and director of the Animal Behavior Clinic at Tufts University's School of Veterinary Medicine, in North Grafton, Massachusetts. "Cats who are mentally stimulated are apt to display fewer behavior problems."

Dr. Dodman offers this simple way to teach your cat to come when summoned. Tap a spoon against the side of a can of cat food, the cat bowl, or the kitchen counter at mealtime. Call your cat by her name, saying, "Callie, come." Tap the object a few more times until your cat reaches you. When she arrives, praise her and fill the food bowl.

PEARLS OF WISDOM

"Complete devotion to his master is the dog's dominant trait. He belongs body and soul to his owner. The cat is equally devoted, but in another sense. The cat is never your slave; it is your equal."

The Children's Encyclopedia (1927)

Repeat these steps during mealtime, and your cat will quickly associate those sounds with the pleasure of eating. Don't use the command if you plan to do something that the cat will find unpleasant, such as giving her a pill or putting her in her cat carrier for a trip to the vet's

office. Your goal is to develop trust in your cat so that she'll heed your *come* command, even if she happens to slip out the door and is hiding in fright under the bushes. That way, you'll save both you and your cat from the potential trauma of having her run away from home.

Cats Snooze on the News

An unused wicker basket filled with 4 inches of shredded newspaper makes a fine indoor cat bed, notes cat advocate W. Gordon Stables, M.D., in his book *Cats* (1920). Be sure the basket is in a draft-free spot, Dr. Stables says. His advice is perfectly sound today. Another option, if you don't have a wicker basket on hand, is to place a bath towel on a sturdy shelf for feline napping.

The Better Doghouse

Lucky dogs a century ago were given doghouses to protect themselves against the wind, rain, snow, cold, and heat. Although dogs these days should spend more time indoors and be part of the family, having a doghouse can be handy if you provide one with the right amenities, say animal behaviorists.

If you have a dog that spends a substantial amount of time outdoors in your fenced yard, build a doghouse that is just big enough for your dog to stand up and turn around. This way the animal can better use its body heat to stay warm.

Make sure the doghouse is waterproof, elevated, and lined with straw, cedar shavings, or blankets to provide your dog with protection from Mother Nature's nasty moods. Install a medium-weight or heavyweight clear plastic flap over the opening to keep drafts out and still allow your dog to view the world outside. Choose a piece of plastic that will be heavy enough to resist flapping in the wind, but not so heavy that it will be difficult for the dog to nose in and out of the doghouse.

PART THREE

AN OLD-TIME GARDENER'S GUIDE

GARDENING IS THE MOST POPULAR hobby in the United States, and our passion for plants and gardens has deep roots. Early European settlers brought seeds with them on their voyages across the Atlantic Ocean. After establishing shelter, creating gardens was one of their first tasks. Native Americans taught the settlers about native plants and gardening techniques. Over the centuries, gardening practices and design styles have evolved, but there's still plenty to be learned from the past. Fortunately for us, keeping records is a fundamental part of good gardening. Old-time gardeners and horticulturists often kept extensive records of their gardens and published a wide variety of books, magazines, and journals. The wealth of experience captured in these old-time publications still has plenty to offer today's budding gardeners.

CHAPTER 11

Kitchen Gardening
Reap What You Sow

THE HISTORY OF GARDENING is a history of human survival—gardeners of long ago (and well into the early 20th century) raised food out of necessity, not because they preferred the flavor of homegrown tomatoes to those found in the supermarket! Necessity, of course, is the mother of invention, and gardeners throughout history have proven themselves an inventive bunch. Many of the tools and techniques developed over thousands of years of gardening still have a place in our high-tech world.

Practical Planning Pointers

WE ALL KNOW the essential steps of planning a garden: choosing a good location, laying out our beds to the best advantage, preparing the soil, and deciding where and when to plant each crop. If you skip these steps, you may be sowing yourself a crop of extra weeding, watering, and replanting that could have been avoided. Follow the lead of long-ago gardeners in planning a garden of the right size and shape, planted at the best possible times for a successful harvest.

Don't Dig Up More Than You Can Hoe

■ You may have fond memories of your mother's or grandmother's great big vegetable patch, but don't let nostalgia tempt you to plant a garden that's bigger than you can handle. Old-time gardens tended to be spacious affairs of a quarter-acre or more, but the bigger the garden, the more the work that's required to tend it. It's all too easy to find that the garden of your dreams has grown into the weed patch of your nightmares. Even old-time gardeners found themselves regretting tilling too large a patch of ground, based on the observations of Thomas Bridgeman in *The American Gardener's Assistant* (1869): "If the object be simply to supply one family with vegetables, it is better to appropriate only a small plot of ground to this purpose. It is far better to have a small plot of ground of only a few square rods [about 800 to 1,000 square feet] thoroughly pulverized, well-manured, and properly dressed than one twice as large and all these things . . . only half done. Many persons in the country . . . err greatly in laying out gardens much larger than they cultivate profitably."

By modern standards, even a few square rods is a large garden. What's a reasonable guideline for 21st-century gardeners? If you can spare only short spurts of time to tend your garden during the week plus about 2 hours per weekend, aim to plant a plot of about 100 square feet. This is a reasonable amount of growing space, and what you plant won't end up out of control. As an added benefit, 100 square feet is an easy number to work with when you're calculating the amounts of soil amendments to add to your garden.

Wise Guidelines for Garden Sites

■ Choosing a site for your home orchard (or any other type of garden) is simple when you follow "certain common instructions" set forth in *The Expert Gardener* (1640), including a recommendation for a site protected from "wild beasts . . . in a town or closed orchard where there is not too much shadow, but a sweet ground well muckt [enriched with manure], tilled and turned." If your garden isn't protected by the kind of walls that often surrounded 17th-century villages, consider other options for guarding your crops from those wild beasts. A combination of metal fence posts and 4- to 5-foot-high sturdy plastic mesh or welded-wire fencing works well. Set a

Peaches from the Privy

"I NEVER UNDERSTOOD why my grandparents had a sidewalk that led to the peach tree in their yard, until my mom told me that the tree was planted where the outhouse used to be," says Indiana gardener Michelle Evernham. "The tree was nothing fancy—a seedling that probably grew from one of the pits my grandma tossed out there after a canning session. That old tree produced delicious peaches, but they never tasted quite the same to me after that!"

Four-Square Gardening Still Makes Sense

To lay out a truly functional kitchen garden, follow the example of monastery gardens of medieval Europe. Monastery gardens and other kitchen gardens throughout the ages used a compact arrangement of raised, square-to-rectangular beds. You can lay out a four-square garden right outside your kitchen door, making it convenient to harvest fresh food for every meal. It's easy to plant and tend the small beds from either side without walking on and compacting the soil. Plant the beds with a mixture of herbs, vegetables, and flowers: You'll enjoy gathering fresh bouquets for your table along with fresh food for your meals.

An arrangement of four 5-by-5-foot raised beds with 4-foot-wide paths forming a "plus sign" between the beds makes a tidy, easily managed garden that has plenty of room for growing family favorites. Frame the beds with rot-resistant timbers, such as cedar or recycled plastic lumber. Fill the frames with a mixture of compost and soil dug out from the paths. Put a layer of weed-blocking landscape fabric, cardboard, or several thicknesses of newspaper over the paths, and then "pave" them to suit the style of your garden: wood chips or gravel for a casual look; bricks or interlocking pavers for a more formal appearance.

fence post about every 4 feet around the perimeter of the garden, and be sure to fasten down the fencing at the base—preferably by burying the bottom 6 inches—to keep out burrowing critters. If you're growing fruit trees or blueberries, you may also need to cover individual trees or bushes with bird netting to protect your harvest.

Avoid ground that is infertile, sandy, dry, burned, or salty, *The Expert Gardener* warns, noting that nothing will grow well in such places. If your only choice is less-than-ideal soil, work plenty of compost into it. Finally, make sure there's water available for your garden, advises *The Expert Gardener,* and choose trees that are suited to your climate—all sound advice that works as well today as it did more than 300 years ago.

Plant in Tune with the Moon

Given the moon's prominence in the night sky and its role in some religions, it's no wonder that our ancestors believed the moon had powers over the plants they cultivated for food and shelter. What's news for modern gardeners is that the ancient practice of gardening by the moon may have scientific "roots" that make sense for 21st-century gardens, too.

Gardening by the moon assigns tasks according to the phases of the moon as it waxes (increases from new to full) and then wanes (decreases from full to new). *The Expert Gardener* (1640) set forth "a short instruction very profitable and necessary for all those that delight in gardening, to know the times and seasons when it is good to sow all manner of seeds." This practical guide included the following directives.

- "Cabbages must be sown in February, March, or April, at the waning of the moon, and replanted also in the decrease thereof."
- "Radish must be sown in February, March, or June, in a new moon."
- "Beets must be sown in February or March, in a full moon."
- "Onions and leeks must be sown in February or March, at the waning of the moon."

- "Cucumbers and melons must be sown in February, March, or June, in an old moon."
- "Basil must be sown in March, when the moon is old."

Although scientists have yet to prove that the moon affects plant growth, the moon's gravitational pull on the earth's oceans is well known. And it's possible that the same force that causes the tides also pulls on the water that's held within the soil, making it more available to plants during certain phases of the moon than at others.

To try your hand at the most basic form of moon gardening, simply plan your planting schedule as follows: When the moon is waxing, plant crops that bear above the ground; when the moon is waning, plant root crops.

Consult an almanac or your weather station to tell which phase the moon is in. Keep records of the results of your experiments to determine whether moon gardening makes sense for you and your garden.

Sow the Seeds of Cooperation

"A very good plan, when one wishes a great variety of vegetables and has but a limited amount of room in which to grow them, is to arrange with a neighbor to cooperate in the garden work" and each grow certain crops, explains author Ida Bennett in *The Vegetable Garden* (1908). Her words are even truer today, given the limited size of many of our yards and our other limitations of time, skill, or strength. Chat with your neighbor about what he has the most experience and success growing. Suggest that he plant enough of those crops for both of your families, and offer in turn to "undertake those which he does not grow. This insures a great variety of vegetables at the minimum amount of work and outlay."

This sort of shared effort is especially beneficial for crops that take up lots of garden space, such as sweet corn, and for tomatoes or cucumbers that you want to grow in quantities large enough for canning or freezing. At harvesttime, you can continue your work-saving ways (and increase your overall fun) by holding combined canning sessions at which several neighbors pitch in, assembly-line style, to clean, prepare, and process the fruits of your labors. The old saying that many hands make light work seems especially true of the steamy work of canning, and it's much more pleasurable when you have friends to chat with while you work. At the end of the day, shared cleanup goes more quickly, too, and everyone goes home with a satisfying supply of homegrown food for the coming winter.

Crop Rotation Rules to Grow By

■ Crop rotation may sound complicated, but this age-old practice is such a useful method for thwarting pest and disease problems that it's worth gaining a basic understanding of why crop rotation is important and how to try it in your garden. In *The American Gardener's Assistant* (1869), Thomas Bridgeman offers this reason for crop rotation: "The soil in which some particular vegetables have grown, and into which they have discharged the excretions of their roots, is rendered noxious to the prosperity of plants of the same or allied species, though it be well adapted to the growth ... of other distinct species of vegetables." We now know that the "noxious excretions" described are actually diseases and pests, such as clubroot and carrot weevils, that specifically target crops in a particular family of plants.

In its simplest form, crop rotation is a matter of growing a different crop (one from another plant family) in a garden bed from one season to the next. Here are a few guidelines from *The American Gardener's Assistant* that form the basis of a simplified rotation system.

Alternate between fibrous and fat. "Fibrous-rooted plants may be alternated with tap or tuberous-rooted, and vice versa." For example, follow lettuce, leafy

In Sync with the Stars

GARDENERS of the past who truly took their cues from the moon also believed that the stars (i.e., the signs of the zodiac) affect plant growth. If you'd like to experiment with taking full advantage of the moon's sway over your garden, you'll need to determine what sign the moon is in on a particular day, as well as whether it's waxing or waning. Zodiac signs fall into four categories: water (Pisces, Cancer, and Scorpio), earth (Taurus, Virgo, and Capricorn), air (Aquarius, Gemini, and Libra), and fire (Aries, Leo, and Sagittarius). Plant leafy and aboveground crops when the moon passes through the water signs; plant root crops as it moves through the earth signs. When the moon is in the air and fire signs, don't plant. Instead, spend your time weeding and harvesting. A couple of exceptions to the rules: You can plant herbs in Libra, and the fire signs are considered good for sowing seed crops such as grains and beans (for drying). A good almanac will tell you the moon's position in the zodiac, as well as its phase, for any day of the year.

greens, beans, or peas with turnips, carrots, or beets.

Follow lush leaves with skimpy tops. "Plants which produce luxuriant tops, so as to shade the land, should be succeeded by such as yield small tops or narrow leaves." You can follow this rule by planting carrots, parsley, onions, or garlic where tomatoes or peppers grew the previous year.

Weed one year, not the next. "Those which, during their growth, require the operation of stirring the earth, should precede such as do not require cultivation." Follow sweet corn with cucumbers, melons, or squash.

Trusty Tools Stand the Test of Time

Gardeners have always been a practical bunch, and nowhere is that more evident than in the tools they use the most. While some garden gadgets come and go from one season to the next, the tools that gardeners use almost daily from early spring until fall frosts are those that have stood the test of time.

Dibber. Did you ever use a dibber, also called a *dibble* or *dibbler*? *Gardening for Profit* (1867), by Peter Henderson, known as the great-grandfather of truck farming in America, praises this oddly named device as "a very simple but indispensable tool." The book notes that an experienced planter working with a dibber and an assistant to "drop the plants . . . will plant from 6,000 to 10,000 plants per day." Even if your planting goals are less lofty, you'll find that a dibber speeds the process of making holes for planting seeds, transplants, and bulbs. Ancient gardeners used animal horns and simple pointed sticks as dibbers. Primitive dibbers like these will do the job, or you can choose commercially made dibbers that have curved handles for easy gripping, metal tips that stay sharp and slide easily into the soil, and depth markings to show just how deep you're making each hole.

Scuffle hoe. In *The Vegetable Garden* (1908), author Ida Bennett makes the case for this hoe, which works best when the gardener walks backward while hoeing, thus avoiding the problem of compacting freshly cultivated soil. The scuffle hoe is a back-saver, too, Mrs. Bennett writes: "You can push or pull a scuffle hoe all day without getting a backache," because you'll find it easy to remain standing upright when you use this hoe, rather than bending over to work as you would with a conventional hoe.

Spading fork. The four or five flattened prongs of a spading fork make it a sturdy digging tool, but it's easier to use than a conventional spade. "If it is necessary to spade the garden rather than plow [or till] it, by all means do it with a spading fork," Ida Bennett recommends. "The difference in weight between this and a spade is considerable, so that by its use one saves himself from lifting a good many pounds while digging over the garden. Besides, it is much easier to push into the ground."

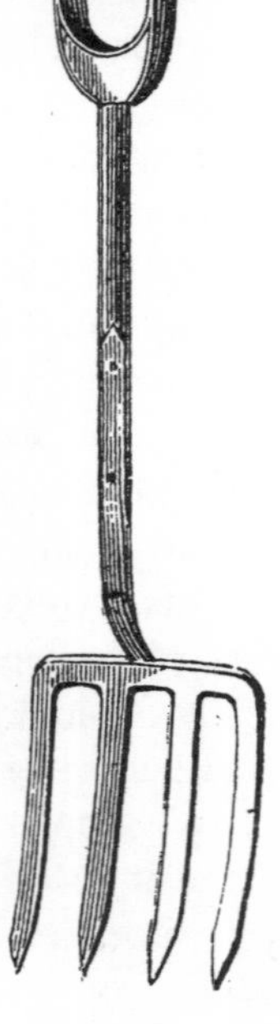

☞ TRASH OR TREASURE ☜

Build Your Own Rain Barrel

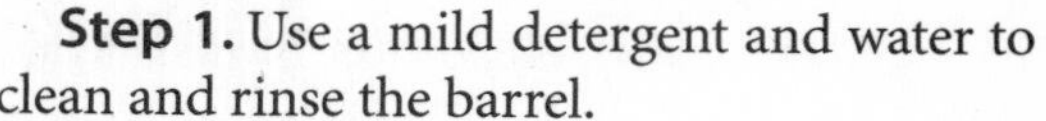

KEEPING YOUR GARDEN well-watered through the summer months is easier when you have a reservoir of spring rain stored in your very own rain barrel. Traditional rain barrels were typically made of wood, but wooden barrels are heavy and expensive, and they eventually decay from exposure to the elements. Pennsylvania organic farmer George DeVault recommends a more practical solution: recycled plastic food barrels. Widely available from markets, restaurants, and food importers, these large plastic barrels are inexpensive, relatively lightweight, and free of toxic chemicals.

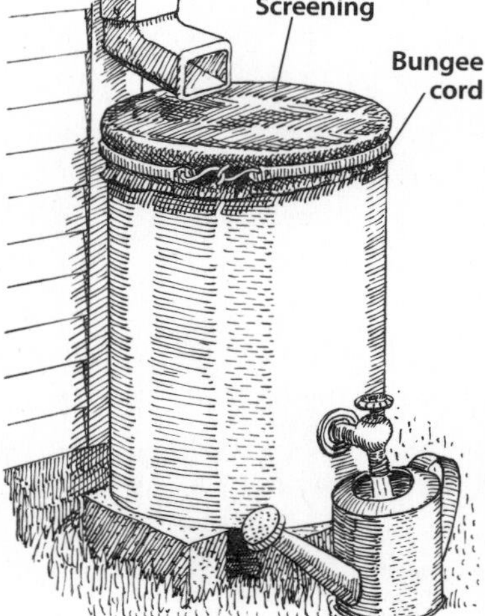

George buys plastic barrels from a local pickle purveyor for less than $20 apiece and converts them for many uses on his family's Pheasant Hill Farm in Vera Cruz, including rain barrels.

You will need:

- 1 large (40- to 55-gallon) plastic food barrel
- Drill with a 3/4-inch spade bit
- 1 outdoor tap
- Plumber's caulk
- Nylon window screen (a piece large enough to fit over the open end of the barrel)
- Bungee cord (long enough to fit tightly around the top of the barrel)
- 2 or 3 cinder blocks

Step 1. Use a mild detergent and water to clean and rinse the barrel.

Step 2. Drill a hole for the tap about 6 inches from the bottom of the barrel.

Step 3. Fit the tap into the hole and caulk it securely. Let the caulk dry for the recommended amount of time before using the barrel.

Step 4. Put the barrel where you want it, setting the barrel on the cinder blocks to allow enough room to position a watering can or bucket under the tap. To collect the most water, place the barrel at the end of a downspout from the eaves of your house or garden shed.

Step 5. Stretch the screening across the top of the barrel and fasten it in place with the bungee cord. This will keep out insects and other critters.

You'll be surprised at how quickly your barrel fills after even a relatively small amount of rain. You can add overflow capacity by making another rain barrel and connecting it to the first one with a length of PVC pipe caulked into both barrels 4 to 6 inches below their tops.

In cold-winter regions, empty your rain barrel and store it indoors before freezing weather arrives. It makes a handy place to store coiled hoses, empty pots, and other seasonal garden equipment through the winter.

Four Rules for Long-Lasting Tools

■ It's tempting to skip tool cleanup when your gardening chores are done—there's always something else that needs your attention. But wise gardeners will heed this advice from the British Ministry of Agriculture's *Allotment & Garden Guide* of January 1945: "A little care is well worth while. Many a tool has had years taken off its useful life by being allowed to rust in a damp shed. No good gardener lets his tools rust, for he knows they take more energy to use when their surfaces are dull." The *Allotment & Garden Guide* offers these rules for maintaining tools in "first-class order."

1. "Never put your garden tools away dirty. Wash off any soil adhering to them and dry them with an old cloth." A strong stream of water from the hose works well for removing soil from tools; if you work over a bucket, you can catch the water for your plants.

2. "Always wipe them over with an oily rag before putting them away." Keep a cloth moistened with vegetable oil or mineral oil in a heavy-duty resealable plastic bag on a hook next to where you store your tools. Wipe the metal parts of your tools with the cloth when you put them away. Refresh the oil on the cloth as needed; when it becomes too soiled from repeated use, either wash it in soapy water or throw it away.

3. "Don't leave them lying about where they may rust or rot."

4. "The best way to keep [tools] in good condition is to use them often."

Soil-Building for Success

Old-time gardeners relied upon readily available materials for building the soil. Ashes, bones, fish, and manure were among the most common fertilizers used to enrich the soil, even after manufactured fertilizers became widely available. Buying a bag of fertilizer is certainly easier, but there's still good sense in the time-honored practice of using materials at hand to improve the soil: Things like grass clippings and fallen leaves are free and full of nutrients that your plants will appreciate just as much as store-bought NPK products.

Compost on the Spot, Shovel Manure Not!

■ Using a simple, on-the-spot composting program to keep your garden's soil rich and ready for spring planting is just as effective as the old-time practice of manuring a garden. In the 1800s and early 1900s, many gardeners could easily transfer manure from the family cow's or horse's stall to the garden. But unless you own livestock or know someone who does, manure is unlikely to play a major role in your garden. Most gardeners today use compost as their forebears used manure, and with equally good results.

To make composting ultra-easy, follow the example of food historian William Woys Weaver, of Devon, Pennsylvania, author of *Heirloom Vegetable Gardening*. William makes movable compost pens out of concrete-reinforcing wire. "I erect them in the beds that need the most soil improvement," William explains. "They stand there over winter and 'cook' during the freezing weather, and in the spring I tip them over and spread rich compost over the beds."

If you do want to try using manure to enrich your garden soil, contact a local stable or a small farm where horses are kept and ask if you can come and carry away some of their (usually ample) supply of manure. Most such places are happy to accommodate courteous gardeners who come at prearranged times and who stay out of the way of stable personnel and riders.

You'll need to create a storage spot on your property where the manure can compost before you apply it to your garden. Fresh manure's high nitrogen content makes it "hot" and likely to burn your plants; it may also introduce microorganisms that are harmful to humans. If you use compost that contains manure, always be sure to wash your harvest thoroughly before taking a bite. Well-rotted manure will be moist and wormy but relatively odorless.

William notes that on-the-spot manure composting works, too, if the timing is right. Gardeners can spread fresh manure over the tops of garden beds in fall—the manure will decompose right where it's needed. In 1793, Thomas Jefferson acknowledged the benefits of this approach when he recommended a heavy winter application of manure to the gardens at Monticello to resolve pest problems that were damaging the crops: "When earth is rich it bids defiance to droughts [and] yields in abundance . . . I suspect that the insects which have harassed you have been encouraged by the feebleness of your plants; and that has been produced by the lean [infertile] state of the soil."

Give Heavy Feeders Their Due

The vegetable crops known as *heavy feeders* practically demand extra servings of fertilizers to be productive. It pays to focus your limited resources—whether the plant food or the time to apply it—on these crops. In *The American Gardener's Assistant* (1869), Thomas Bridgeman maintains that "it is of primary importance that those vegetables be provided for which most need manure. Good, rich manure is indispensably necessary for the production of broccoli, cauliflower, cabbage, lettuce, spinach, onions, radishes, and salads in general." Even if applying manure is not a part of your usual soil-building routine, you can follow Mr. Bridgeman's advice. To substitute for the manuring he recommends, build your garden soil with ample amounts of

ROUGHING IT

Grinding Bones to Feed Your Bed

A BONE GRINDER was a common garden tool in Victorian times. Avid gardeners ground up the bones of slaughtered animals to make phosphorus-rich bonemeal for their plants. Some gardeners preferred to grind fresh bones, often with bits of meat still clinging to them, while others burned the bones first and then pounded them into a fine powder before working them into the soil. It makes the price of a bag of bonemeal seem quite reasonable, doesn't it?

finished compost, and side-dress the crops listed above, as well as other leafy greens, once midway through the growing season with a nitrogen-rich organic fertilizer, such as bloodmeal or fish meal. If you do have access to manure, use it to supercharge your compost pile, rather than applying fresh manure to plants. (See "Compost on the Spot, Shovel Manure Not!" on page 266 for more information about using manure as a soil amendment.)

Grow Comfrey for Your Compost

Another terrific source of nutrients for boosting compost quality is comfrey. The long, thick roots of common comfrey (*Symphytum officinale*), a healing herb cultivated as far back as 400 B.C., travel deep into the soil to bring up nutrients. Those nutrient-mining roots, along with vigorous production of long, hairy leaves, make comfrey a superior green manure for the compost pile, says Pennsylvania organic gardener Nancy Ondra.

Nancy says that her comfrey-enriched compost makes her gardens shine, and the plant grows so quickly that there's always extra available to add to her compost bin. In fact, Nancy recommends planting comfrey in a bed all its own, where you can keep it in check and where it won't overtake less-aggressive garden plants. Your comfrey bed should be surrounded by lawn (where mowing will limit its spread) or border a paved area.

Old-time gardeners also used comfrey leaves as a mulch over potato hills and believed that the nutrients leached into the soil and gave the growing tubers a boost. Herbalists use extracts from comfrey's nutrient-rich leaves and its fleshy roots to heal minor wounds, burns, and bruises. The plant is rich in allantoin, a common ingredient in many skin care products. While comfrey has a long history of use in healing, it is a suspected carcinogen and is not recommended for internal use.

Tips for Planting Success

Planting is truly the fun part of gardening, but it can also be nerve-racking: A late frost or hungry birds can wipe out an entire crop. Old-time gardeners used a combination of lore, know-how, favorite tools, and luck to get their gardens off to a good start—much as today's gardeners do!

Sow When the Weather Is Right

Long before 24-hour weather channels, 5-day forecasts, and personal digital assistants, gardeners used significant days on the calendar to determine when they'd sow certain crops. You've probably heard the best-known of these pithy directives: Plant potatoes (or peas) on St. Patrick's Day (March 17). However, even in the 1800s, gardening experts questioned the wisdom of these planting proverbs. "Some gardeners . . . recommend certain fixed days for sowing and planting particular kinds of seed; I think it necessary to guard my readers against being misled. The failure of crops may be often attributed to the observance of certain days for sowing," notes Thomas Bridgeman in *The American Gardener's Assistant* (1869). A better approach is to watch the weather patterns and trends in a particular season to determine when to plant. And modern gardeners can use several tools not available to old-timers to determine when conditions are right for planting. A soil thermometer (available from mail-order garden supply companies) reveals whether the ground is warm enough for planting. And a minimum-maximum thermometer will tell you how low temperatures are falling at night, as well as how high they go during the day. And then tune in your local weather forecast, just to be safe!

Sow by Soil Temperature

WHAT SOIL TEMPERATURE RANGES are best for planting? When the soil is below 45°F, it's still too cold for most seeds to germinate. At soil temperatures of 45° to 60°F, you can sow beets, carrots, lettuce, parsley, peas, radishes, and spinach. When the soil temperature rises to 65° to 80°F, it's safe to plant beans, corn, cucumbers, melons, and squash.

Mulch More, Work Less

■ Spread the mulch and spare the spade, urged beloved American gardener Ruth Stout (1884–1980). A vocal advocate of working less and enjoying life more, Mrs. Stout wrote several books and articles describing her method of mulching her garden year-round with a thick layer of hay or straw. Mrs. Stout explained that she fell into her "lazy" way of gardening after several years of tending a large garden in the conventional way. After a few successful experiments in which she merely sowed her seeds by pulling back the previous fall's mulch, Mrs. Stout was on her way, and she tended her garden well into her 80s. She often stated that she had no use for a separate compost pile and reported no problems with pests or weeds in her garden.

To follow Mrs. Stout's lazy example, layer about 8 inches of mulch on your garden beds each spring. When it's time to plant, simply pull back the mulch and sow your seeds. After the seeds sprout, push the mulch closer to the seedlings to hold in moisture and prevent weeds from sprouting.

Electrify a Hotbed

"The construction and care of the hotbed is so simple and . . . so inexpensive as to be within the reach of the gardener whose little plot of land comprises but a few square yards of ground," says Ida Bennett in *The Vegetable Garden* (1908). One hundred years later, her words still ring true. A hotbed is a great place to start warm-season crops early, without the hassles of setting up a seed-starting area indoors. Like a coldframe, a hotbed is a rectangular box, open to the soil at the bottom, with a light-admitting cover that's typically slanted to catch as much sunlight as possible and to allow rainwater to run off. Unlike a coldframe, a hotbed includes a source of heat. Old-time gardeners had to use manure, which was messy and smelly. Today, we can install an electric cable, which is much neater and never has to be replenished. You can start tomatoes, peppers, melons, and other heat-loving crops in a hotbed well before the time when they may be planted outdoors without protection.

Use old storm windows or window sash as covers for a hotbed—the size of the sash determines the size of the hotbed. Transparent acrylic, fiberglass, or heavy-duty polyethylene film fastened to a wooden frame will also serve well as a cover. Use recycled lumber, scrap lumber, bricks, or cinder blocks for constructing the sides of the hotbed. Choose what you have available, or buy those materials you can afford.

The secret to success is to dig out a foundation hole about 1 foot deep. In

A coldframe heated by a buried heating cable is a modern equivalent of an old-time hotbed. Be sure to set up the frame on a well-drained site close to an exterior electrical outlet.

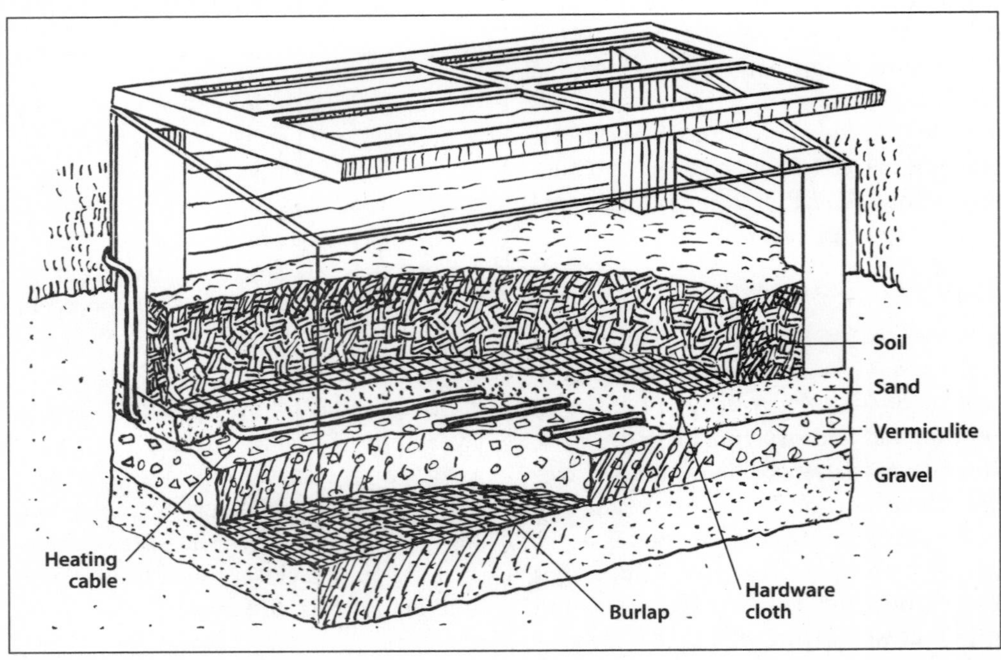

this foundation, you'll sandwich the heating cable between a base of gravel and vermiculite, and a topping of sand (if you'll be sowing seeds in containers) or soil (if you want to start seedlings directly in the hotbed).

A hotbed can be ideal for seed starting when the soil temperature is 70° to 75°F. Monitor the air temperature inside the frame, too, particularly on mild, sunny days. When the air in the frame warms to about 70°F, prop open the cover a bit to avoid cooking your young plants; cool-season crops such as cabbage and broccoli will do better if the daytime air temperature stays closer to 60° to 65°F. Be sure to close the cover again before nightfall.

Put Your Best Foot Forward

■ Seeds germinate poorly in dry soil, but improving germination during dry conditions is as easy as walking through your garden—right down the newly planted rows, in fact. New Jersey vegetable farmer Peter Henderson verified this in *The Use of the Feet in Sowing and Planting* (1880), when he presented the findings of a successful experiment he had conducted on his farm: "On July 2nd of 1874, I sowed twelve rows of sweet corn and twelve rows of beets, treading in, after sowing, every alternate row of each. In both cases, those trod in came up in four days, while those unfirmed remained twelve days before starting, and would not then have germinated had not rain fallen, for the soil was as dry as dust when the seeds were sown."

The report notes that seeds that were "trodden in" grew well and matured to marketable condition by fall, while the rows that weren't firmed languished and

ROUGHING IT

Heating a Hotbed with Manure

GARDENERS of bygone days didn't have electric heating cables at their disposal; their heat source of choice for a hotbed was manure. If you have an ample supply of manure—preferably fresh horse or chicken—you can heat your hotbed the old-fashioned way and save the cost of heating cables and electricity. But heating with manure requires considerably more finesse, as this description from Liberty Hyde Bailey's *Principles of Vegetable-Gardening* (1901) indicates:

"The amount of manure which is to be used will depend (1) upon its quality, (2) the season in which the hotbed is made, (3) the kind of plants to be grown, (4) the skill of the operator in managing the bed. Careless watering, by means of which the manure is kept soaked, will stop the heat in any hotbed. The earlier the bed is made, the larger should be the quantity of manure. Hotbeds which are supposed to hold for two months should have about 2½ feet of manure, as a rule. This is the maximum. For a light hotbed to be used late in the season, 6 or 8 inches may be sufficient."

For best heating results, fresh horse manure mixed with straw bedding was piled, compacted, and allowed to heat up; then turned, repiled, and compacted until it again began to emit heat. Then the manure was packed into a layer about 12 inches deep over gravel at the bottom of an 18- to 30-inch-deep pit. A 4- to 6-inch layer of soil covered the manure; after a few days (during which the soil temperature might exceed 100°F) seeds could be sown in the soil.

did not reach maturity. This old-time method still makes sense today, confirms Pennsylvania organic farmer George DeVault, who treads over the seeds he sows on his family's Pheasant Hill Farm in Vera Cruz. "It really does make a difference when the soil is dry at planting time," George says. However, don't try this technique when the soil is wet, he advises.

PEARLS OF WISDOM

"Don't sow seed when soil sticks to boots."

BRITISH MINISTRY OF AGRICULTURE, *Allotment & Garden Guide* (MARCH 1945)

Merits of the Wheel-Hoe

"The wheel-hoe is the handiest tool in the garden," writes Ida Bennett in her 1908 guide, *The Vegetable Garden*. If you have a substantial garden of ¼ acre (about 100 feet by 100 feet) or more, a wheel-hoe can take the place of several tools and save you a great deal of backbreaking work and uncomfortable bending. While the wheel-hoes of Mrs. Bennett's day "cost anywhere from $3.50 up," she deemed them well worth the purchase price, as were attachments such as plows, rakes, cultivators, hoes, and seed-sowing tools. Of the latter, she said, "It saves one from getting down on his knees, or doubling up like a jack-knife, when sowing the seed. Plus, when you sow seed with a wheel-hoe, you can control the thickness of seeding, and thus use your seed more efficiently." A modern wheel-hoe commands a more substantial price ($150 to $250) than its counterparts of 100 years ago, but gardeners with a large plot to sow and weed may find it worth the price.

WARDING OFF PESTS AND PROBLEMS

THERE'S NOTHING more heartbreaking than finding a whole row of tender transplants mowed down by cutworms, or more maddening than catching crows in the act of tugging out your newly sprouted sweet corn. Old-time gardeners faced pest problems, too, and had a knack for coming up with clever, and sometimes curious, ways to deal with them.

Birds Don't Cotton to Simple Seedling Protectors

To protect your seeds and seedlings from hungry birds, stretch a strand or two of black cotton thread or fine wire just above soil (or seedling) level along each row, fastening it to a stake at each end of the row. Birds venturing into the garden to snack on seedlings will run into the thread before they see it and be frightened away, noted the British Ministry of Agriculture's *Allotment & Garden Guide* for March 1945.

Washington state gardener Sally Roth takes a sturdier stance in protecting newly planted rows of corn and peas, laying a board over the rows immediately after seeding. Sally says she doesn't remove the board until several days later, when the pale, sun-starved seedlings have emerged, but reports that they quickly recover from their days in the dark.

☞ OLD-TIME ODDITIES ☜

Potato "Hawk"

GARDENERS and farmers today use plastic owl figurines, reflective tape, and even cannons that emit loud blasts of noise to scare birds away. These methods might have seemed as odd to old-time gardeners as some of their bird-scare techniques sound to us. For example, here's a variation on the traditional scarecrow described by Alvin Chase, M.D., in *Dr. Chase's Recipes* (circa 1870). This scare device is meant to protect gardens and fields "subject to the inroads of small birds and even chickens." The author claimed that he could decorate a large potato with long goose or turkey feathers to make a successful bird scare. "The maker can exercise his imitative skill in sticking the feathers into the potato so that they resemble the spread tail and wings of a hawk. It is astonishing what a ferocious looking bird of prey can be constructed from the above simple material. It only remains to hang the object from a tall, bent pole, and the wind will do the rest. The bird will make swoops and dashes in the most threatening manner. Even the most inquisitive of venerable hens have been known to hurry rapidly from its dangerous vicinity, while to small birds it carries unmixed dismay."

Although the realistic appearance of the potato "hawk" may have some effect in scaring away potential garden raiders, chances are good that the author's mounting method deserves a good amount of the credit. Irregular and unpredictable movement keeps pest birds (and other varmints) too nervous to enter the garden long after they've grown accustomed to the still-as-a-statue plastic owl perched on the fence post.

To deter crows, which the author felt would be unmoved by the postures of the potato hawk, Dr. Chase recommends the following approach: "String a few kernels of corn on long horsehairs, and place them about the corn fields. The crows will swallow some of them and make such a noise of alarm as to drive the others away . . . This is said to rid the field of them for the season. It is easily tried."

Plant "Buddies" for Your Crops

Companion planting is a time-honored, if not always scientifically proven, technique for combining certain plants with others to protect them from pests or to otherwise enhance their growth. Garden lore includes an almost endless supply of "recipes" for supposedly beneficial plant combinations, and research by scientists and gardeners indicates that many companion planting arrangements really work. Here are some of the ways that companion plants help your garden.

Caught in a trap. Trap crops draw pests away from their target. Nasturtiums planted near apple trees will lure woolly aphids away from the fruit trees. (Trap crops are typically destroyed once they've attracted pests.)

Repelled by smell. Fragrant herbs repel pests or confuse them by masking the scent of their preferred foods. Mint, for example, helps to deter cabbage pests.

Beaten by beneficials. Companion plants provide food, breeding sites, and/or shelter for beneficial insects. Broad, flat flower heads made up of many small blossoms (like those of dill or yarrow) attract tiny parasitic wasps; these wasps' larvae parasitize many species of pest caterpillars.

Some combinations work simply because the plants seem to "cooperate" as they grow, as in the traditional "Three Sisters" arrangement used by Native Americans. In this combination, corn provides a stalk for the beans to vine upward, the beans help fix nitrogen in the soil for the corn, and squash vines growing below the corn help to block out weeds and keep the soil moist.

10 Companion Planting Combos

Here's a list of traditional companion planting recommendations to experiment with in your own garden. Keep notes from year to year to record which ones work for you.

1. Pop in some onions among your cucumber vines to repel pests.

2. Plant leeks close to carrots to repel the carrot (rust) fly.

3. Pair basil with tomatoes to control tomato hornworms. (The basil seems to prosper in this arrangement, as well.)

4. Use a border of onions, chives, or garlic around your garden to protect more-palatable plants from hungry rabbits.

5. Sow radishes around cucumbers to repel cucumber beetles.

6. Plant tansy among raspberries and blackberries to enhance their growth. Tansy is also reported to repel Japanese beetles—an added benefit for the berries.

7. Grow thyme with eggplant, potatoes, and tomatoes.

8. Try including sage with cabbages, carrots, strawberries, and tomatoes—sage is said to enhance the growth of these crops.

9. Sow a border of aromatic French marigolds around your kitchen garden to deter a variety of insects, as well as rabbits, and also to repel nematodes in the soil.

10. Set out pots of catnip to help protect eggplant from flea beetles. (Be careful about planting catnip in the ground in your vegetable garden, as it can spread widely. It'll be fine if you plant it inside a root barrier.)

Piggy Pest Patrol Protects Fruit Trees

Keeping hogs in the orchard is helpful in reducing the populations of two major orchard pests—plum curculios and codling moths—according to S. W. Peek in *The Nursery and the Orchard: A Practical Treatise on Fruit Culture* (1885). In both cases, by eating fallen fruit, the pigs also gobble up the immature pests (grubs and caterpillars) within the fruit, preventing them from maturing.

Plum curculios are brown weevils that leave crescent-shaped scars on the fruit they attack. Severely damaged fruit may drop prematurely. Plum curculios infest apples, blueberries, cherries, peaches, pears, plums, and quinces throughout North America. Codling moths do their damage as brown-headed caterpillars that tunnel into apples and pears.

If you grow tree fruits and don't have helpful hogs for pest patrol, you may have to stoop, literally, to other measures. In his book, Mr. Peek also describes these practical and swine-free solutions to help fruit tree owners put a stop to damage from plum curculios and codling moths.

Plum curculio. "Perhaps the best results are obtained by jarring the trees and destroying the insects and stung fruit that fall. By giving a quick, sharp blow to the tree with a mallet . . . many of the insects will fall and can be caught on a sheet spread under the tree." To avoid injuring the tree, cushion the trunk before striking it with the mallet, the author suggests, adding that the best times to try this technique are early in the morning or just before nightfall. Tie an old blanket folded into several layers around the trunk to pad it against injury from the mallet; an old pillow would also make a suitable cushion.

Codling moth. "It is very important to wash and clean the bark of the trees in early spring, and to see that no cocoons are left in the crevices or under the scales of the bark." Removing loose bark from the trunk and limbs in spring and destroying any cocoons you find is a fairly effective method of ridding your trees of this pest before the growing season begins. Brush the bark of each tree in a top-to-bottom motion, using a stiff-bristled broom or scrub brush. Work carefully to avoid damaging the thin bark.

☞ BIZARRE BUT TRUE ☜

The "Oily" Shovel Gets the Worm?

THE GERMANS who settled in Pennsylvania in the 1700s were experienced gardeners who brought many of their folk customs from Europe to their new homes in America. The Germans called the last Tuesday before Lent "Faschtnacht Day" and observed it by preparing and eating faschtnachts, doughnutlike rectangular pastries deep-fried in lard. One of the many traditions associated with Faschtnacht Day was a belief that the lard in which the faschtnachts were prepared had healing properties. Greasing your shovel with faschtnacht lard before digging the garden was thought to protect your vegetables from pests.

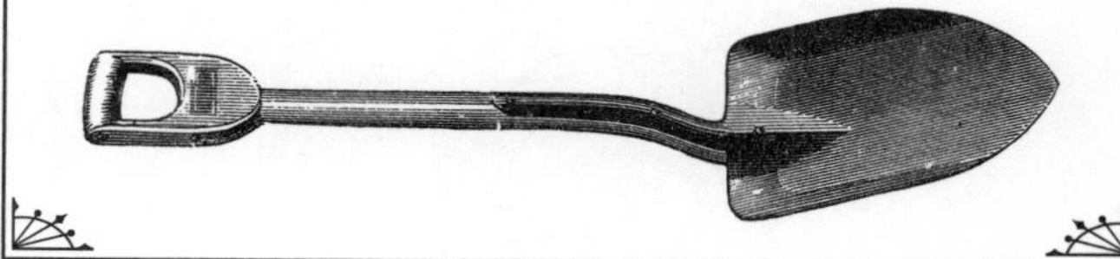

Custom Tips for a Better Harvest

While gardeners of long ago depended upon their gardens for their very survival, they also took pride in coming up with ingenious ways to increase their yields and improve their crops. Read on to discover their best ideas (plus a few newfangled techniques) for no-fuss growing of crops from peas to potatoes, preventing blossom-end rot of tomatoes, fast-and-easy berry picking, and cultivating a "combo" fruit tree.

Gather String Beans Early and Often

■ "To be at their best, string beans should always be gathered when young and tender," advises *The New Garden Encyclopedia: A Complete Practical and Convenient Guide to Every Detail of Gardening* (1945). "When they are picked at frequent intervals, the bearing season is prolonged." These harvesting guidelines for beans are still reliable. Pick beans when they're no thicker than a pencil and before the seeds within the pods begin to show as visible bumps. It's notoriously difficult to spot thin young green-podded string beans like this among the green leaves and stems of bush bean plants. But there's a simple solution for easy harvesting: Grow yellow-podded varieties (also called *wax beans*), such as 'Indy Gold', 'Pencil Pod', or 'Roc d'Or', or purple-podded varieties, such as 'Purple Queen' or 'Royal Burgundy'.

Premium Pickle Pointers

■ If you've been letting your cucumber (and melon) vines sprawl unsupported on the ground, heed this old-time advice about the advantages of trellising. You'll be buying poultry netting and setting up trellises in no time. "Where ground is at a premium and one only desires to grow sufficient fruit for the private table, very satisfactory results may be obtained by growing the melons and cucumbers on netting," writes Ida Bennett in *The Vegetable Garden* (1908). "I do not think the vines produce so freely as on the ground, but the fruit matures quite as well," she continues, noting that the fruits stayed much cleaner when grown off the ground and were much easier to harvest. "There is no labor . . . so trying as that of gathering pickles; the difficulty of getting about among the vines and the stooping position necessary to their gathering make it exceedingly wearisome."

Plastic mesh fencing, sold at home and garden centers, is lightweight and easy to cut to the size you need for your pickle patch. Support it with inexpensive metal fence posts, which usually have built-in "clips" to attach the fencing to. This makes a sturdy trellis that is easy to install and can be used for several seasons. If you're trellising melons, be prepared to give the fruits a little extra support as they mature: A sling made of recycled nylon hosiery works especially

well, and the melons don't seem to mind the runs!

Here's another tidbit from Ida Bennett for gardeners intent on turning their cukes into pickles: "When wanted for pickles, the cucumbers should be gathered as soon as they are large enough. It is better not to gather both pickles and cucumbers for the table from the same vine," because allowing some cucumbers to grow large enough for table use decreases the production of younger fruits for pickling. "Often, however, there will be enough pickles overlooked in gathering to supply an average family with cucumbers for the table. It is always best to gather the tiny pickles first."

When growing cucumbers specifically for making pickles, you'll enjoy best results by choosing varieties developed for pickling. Some good ones to look for include 'Alibi', 'County Fair', and 'National Pickling'.

Fall Mulch Keeps Carrots Coming

"The house cellar is likely to be one of the poorest places in which to store vegetables, particularly if it contains a heater for the residence. In such case it is likely to be too warm and too dry," observed Liberty Hyde Bailey in his 1901 book, *The Principles of Vegetable-Gardening.* This is still true for most modern homes, but don't let that stop you from enjoying fresh carrots well past the time when you've put the rest of your garden to bed. The trick is to store your carrots right in the garden, a technique that even gardeners in northern states can execute successfully. The secret is topping your crop with a thick layer of mulch in fall before the ground freezes, says Pennsylvania gardener Joanna Poncavage. Start when the weather has cooled but before hard frosts arrive, and mulch your carrots with a thick layer of dry leaves or straw, allowing the tops to show above the mulch. Once the tops are killed by the cold, pile on the covers, topping the area with 8 to 10 inches of hay or straw and covering that with a sheet of heavy plastic weighted down with rocks or boards. Joanna says that bags of leaves or bales of straw make good covers, too, and are easy to move aside when you want to dig up some carrots. If snow (another excellent insulator) is likely to hide your cozily mulched carrots from you, add a tall

PEARLS OF WISDOM

"Plant thick and thin quick is the rule for vegetables and flowers in rows. Start thinning when quite young."

Richardson Wright,
The Gardener's Bed-Book (1929)

OLD-TIME HUMOR

Just What the Doctor Ordered

IN *THE VEGETABLE GARDEN* (1908), author Ida Bennett recounts the story of "a mother who took her anemic daughter to a famous physician noted for his bluffness and brevity." After a brief examination, the doctor offered only the directive "claret" before dismissing the patient and her mother with a wave of his hand.

After a month or so, the mother returned with her now-blooming daughter. "At the physician's nod of approval, the mother . . . explained that she 'gave them to her three times a day, cooked and raw.'

" 'Raw?!' exclaimed the physician in amazement." After some discussion, he determined that his instruction to give the girl *claret* had been understood as *carrots,* "and that they had been liberally supplied with the result of a perfect recovery."

marker to help you find your crop below the drifts.

North of USDA Plant Hardiness Zone 6, this thick-mulch approach may not provide enough protection to prevent your carrots from freezing in the deep cold of January and February. Instead of leaving your carrot crop in the ground, dig up all the roots in fall and trim the tops back to 1 inch. Pack whole, uncut carrots in containers of moist sand and store them in a spot, such as a garage, that will stay just above the freezing mark throughout the winter.

Prepare for Spring Peas in Fall

■ Fall is the time to get a head start on your early-spring planting of peas, advises Ida Bennett in *The Vegetable Garden* (1908). Along with your other fall garden tasks, take the time to dig a 10- to 12-inch-deep trench where you want to sow your spring peas. Fill the trench with 8 to 10 inches of compost or well-rotted manure, topped with enough soil to plant your peas in (2 to 3 inches). Frosts and freezes will keep the ground "loose and mellow," Mrs. Bennett explains, and "as soon as the ground has dried sufficiently in the spring, the seed may be gotten into the ground."

Mulch Makes Peas, Potatoes Extra Easy

■ Grow a stellar crop of bush peas by following the lazy example of no-work-gardening advocate Ruth Stout. In the 1950s, she began publicizing her unorthodox (and highly successful) method of keeping her garden under an 8-inch mulch of hay or straw year-round. For bush-type peas, she advised using that thick mulch layer to support the plants so they don't flop over onto the ground and rot. Pull back the mulch to plant the pea seeds, Mrs. Stout instructed, pressing them directly into the soil. When the peas are up and growing, pull the mulch closer to the plants to prevent weeds from sprouting; as the plants grow taller, pull additional mulch up around them for support. She reported that her technique kept the peas clean and easy to pick.

For potatoes, Mrs. Stout would lay the seed potatoes on last year's mulch and cover them with a foot or so of loose hay. Harvesting involved no digging at all; Mrs. Stout simply pulled back the mulch and removed as many potatoes as she needed, then tucked the plants back in until next time.

Start with Certified Seed Potatoes

■ It's tempting to plant those sprouted, shriveled potatoes left in the bottom of the bag you bought at the store. But you're not likely to harvest a satisfactory crop from such a poor start. "No amount of manure or cultivation will make up for the initial disadvantage of poor seed," advises the January 1945 issue of the British Ministry of Agriculture's *Allotment & Garden Guide*. Instead of planting potatoes saved from a previous year's crop, the guide directs, "get good seed carrying a 'Health' certificate, issued by one of the Agriculture Departments." You can follow this same advice to grow successful crops of potatoes. Reputable garden centers and mail-order companies sell certified, disease-free seed potatoes.

The *Allotment & Garden Guide* also offers this advice: "You can work out the quantity [of seed potatoes] you will need fairly easily if you remember that seed potatoes usually average 5 or 6 tubers to the pound, and that a convenient distance to plant early varieties is a foot apart; other varieties 15 inches apart." Each potato plant will produce about 4 pounds of potatoes. So if you want to grow 40 pounds of potatoes, you'll need to buy 2 to 3 pounds of seed potatoes and plant them in a 10- to 15-foot row in your garden.

OLD-FASHIONED FAVORITES

Rhubarb: The Season's First "Fruit"

"Rhubarb was always the first fruit we had each spring," recalls Mary Ann Rusk, of Logansport, Indiana. When she was growing up on a farm in rural Indiana, the only out-of-season fruits that routinely appeared on the table were preserves and canned fruits from the season before. "When spring came and the rhubarb was finally big enough to harvest, it was a real treat. My sister used to eat the stalks raw, but they were too tart for me. Our mother usually made sauce out of the first rhubarb we picked."

4 cups rhubarb, diced into 1-inch pieces
2 tablespoons tapioca
1 cup sugar
Red food coloring (optional)

Put the cut pieces of rhubarb into a 2-quart pan with just a little water and cook over low heat until it softens. Soak the tapioca in ¼ cup water and add it to the rhubarb with the sugar. Stir to combine and continue cooking until the sauce is fairly smooth. Add a few drops of red food coloring, if desired.

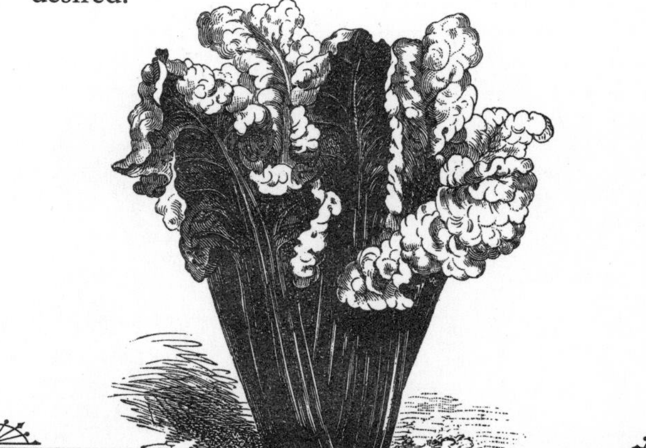

Pointers for Perfect Heirloom Tomatoes

■ Enjoy the finest flavors of yesteryear by planting heirloom crops, especially heirloom tomatoes, which are available in an incredible range of delectable flavors. Be forewarned, though, that most heirloom tomatoes grow on sprawling, unruly vines that can be a real headache in a small or moderate-size garden. To keep the plants in check—and off the ground, where their luscious fruits are in danger of rotting—you need a combination of pruning and support, says organic farmer Don DeVault.

On his family's Pheasant Hill Farm in Vera Cruz, Pennsylvania, Don grows more than 30 different kinds of tomatoes, including several heirloom varieties. For the heirlooms, in particular, pruning out suckers (nonfruiting sideshoots) is critical, he says. "Once a plant gets too big and starts falling on the ground, you run into trouble with rot and pest problems like slugs."

Weave heirloom tomato branches in and out through a twine trellis to keep them upright.

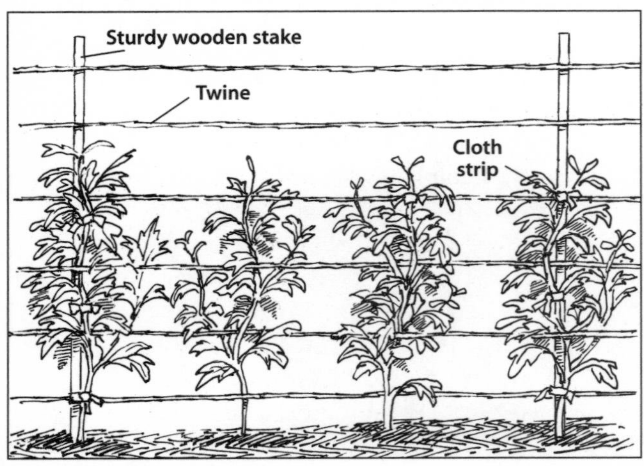

Because his tomatoes are destined for market, Don grows them in the cozy confines of a poly-covered hoophouse and "stakes" the plants with sturdy twine that is suspended from the support structure of the hoophouse. For heirloom tomatoes in the garden, he recommends "basket-weave" staking. In this system, you set out stakes at every third plant and string lengths of sturdy twine between the stakes. Tie the plants immediately next to a stake directly to that stake, and for the plants in between, weave the vines through the lengths of twine.

Don counts the big pinkish purple fruits of 'Brandywine' tomatoes among his favorite heirlooms, and says he also likes the petite, pretty, and slightly fuzzy 'Garden Peach' tomatoes. "Because heirlooms are so fragile when they're dead-ripe, we always pick them a day or two early," he adds. The tomatoes still have great flavor, Don notes, and gathering them a little sooner prevents the heartbreak of finding a formerly promising tomato that's been attacked at the peak of perfection by pests.

Crushed Shells Make Egg-cellent Tomatoes

■ Protect your tomatoes from the ravages of blossom-end rot (those dark, sunken circles that disfigure the bottoms of otherwise lovely ripe fruits) and make like an old-time gardener by recycling leftover eggshells. Pennsylvania gardener Mike McGrath, host of the nationally syndicated National Public Radio program *You Bet Your Garden,* swears by crushed eggshells to help him grow superior tomatoes. The calcium from the shells improves the flavor of the fruits,

Mike explains, and helps protect them from blossom-end rot, the dreaded result of widely varying soil moisture during the growing season.

Mike recommends collecting as many shells as you can, letting them air-dry for about a day, and then crushing them and adding about a dozen's worth to each planting hole. If you have extra shells, he adds, sprinkle them on the soil around the base of your plants to create a sharp, scratchy barrier against hungry slugs.

Dry Herbs at the Right Time

■ Dried basil, mint, and other herbs help pep up wintertime cooking, so save some of your bounty if you can't use it all fresh. To get the best flavor from dried herbs, it's important to harvest the fresh leaves for drying at the correct point in the growing season, notes *The Cooking School Text Book; and Housekeepers' Guide to Cookery and Kitchen Management* (1879). The book's author, Juliet Corson, recommends the following:

- Parsley and tarragon: Harvest in June and July, just before flowering.
- Mint: Harvest in June and July.
- Thyme, summer savory, and sweet marjoram: Harvest in July and August.
- Basil and sage: Harvest in August and September.

Bear in mind that the cookbook was written for New York City (Zones 5 and 6), so you may need to adjust the timing for your location. To determine your hardiness zone, visit www.usna.usda.gov, click on Gardens & Horticulture, and scroll down to USDA Plant Hardiness Zone Map.

Tender herbs in the mint family—basil, tarragon, lemon balm, and the mints—have high moisture content and will mold if not dried quickly, says Libby Hull, an extension agent with the Clemson University Cooperative Extension Service, in Lexington, South Carolina. Try hanging small bunches of them upside down to dry indoors in a cool, dry place such as a closet (large amounts will mold). If you're worried about them dropping leaves, suspend each bunch inside a paper bag ventilated with tears or punched holes. Close the top with a rubber band and place where air currents will circulate through the bag.

Once the herbs are dry, "their flavor is best preserved by keeping them in air-tight tin cans, or in tightly corked glass bottles," according to Juliet Corson.

Save Thyme in a Bottle

■ While dried herbs are readily available year-round on supermarket shelves, these little green "flecks" don't always deliver the flavor that fresh herbs offer. In *The Virginia House-Wife* (1831), Mary Randolph describes her method for preserving the flavor of thyme, noting that it is "greatly preferable to the dried thyme commonly used during the season when it cannot be obtained in a fresh state."

Gather thyme when it is in full perfection, Mrs. Randolph advises, and pick the leaves from the stalks. Place a large handful of leaves in a jar and pour a quart of vinegar or brandy over them; then cover tightly. The next day, remove the thyme and discard it. Replace it with a fresh handful. Repeat this for a third day; then strain and bottle the liquid and seal it securely.

Mint flavor may be preserved in the same way, but care must be taken to avoid leaving either herb to steep for more than 24 hours, lest a bitter flavor develop. Use the flavored vinegar in salad dressings, sauces, soups, and marinades.

Quick Drying Keeps Parsley Green

■ Consult *Mary at the Farm* (1915), by Edith Thomas, for a technique for drying parsley that will preserve the herb's bright green color: Wash the parsley in cold water and shake off any excess. While it's still moist, place it on baking sheets and dry it quickly in a very hot oven (about 400°F). Watch carefully, as it scorches easily. When dried, store the parsley in airtight containers.

If you have a food dehydrator, you don't have to worry about scorching your parsley. Drying parsley in a dehydrator preserves color and flavor nicely. If you've wished for a food dehydrator but didn't think it worth the price, ask a gardening friend or two if they want to be your dehydration partners. By dividing the purchase price, you'll be able to afford a bigger (more efficient) unit, and you and your co-owners can all enjoy the benefits of drying your own herbs, fruits, and vegetables.

☞ BIZARRE BUT TRUE ☜

Prescription for Sprouting Parsley Seeds

FROM Dr. Daniel Schmidt's German family medicine book of 1829, by way of the Landis Valley Museum, in Lancaster, Pennsylvania, comes "Uncle John's Receipt Number 87" for preparing parsley seeds for planting: "Parsley seed soaked in Whiskey for 24 hours, then sowed in a composition of 2 parts wood ashes 1 part earth and sprinkled with rainwater will sprout and grow in 15 minutes."

In fact, it is difficult to sprout parsley seeds, which are coated with a compound that inhibits germination. But don't use whiskey for soaking parsley seeds. Instead try soaking parsley seeds overnight in warm water before sowing. Some gardeners also report success by freezing parsley seeds overnight in water-filled ice cube trays and planting the seeds, ice cubes and all!

Rope Your Berries

■ A simple rope trick makes berry picking a breeze, reports Indiana gardener Michelle Evernham. "Instead of carrying your bucket, you tie its handle to a length of cord around your waist, so you can use both hands to pick," Michelle explains. "I carry my bucket that way whenever I go berry picking."

Michelle learned this trick as a child, when her family made special excursions to a farm to pick blueberries. They wanted to make the most of the trip—and minimize the time spent in the hot sun. Her family's rope trick helped each berry picker work as efficiently as possible. If you don't have a suitable piece of cord, use the strap of a fanny pack instead. The pack also provides a place to stow a water bottle, sunscreen, insect repellent, and other handy items.

Grow an Orchard—On One Tree!

"There is really no reason why our lawn trees should not, at least in part, be made up of fruit trees," observes Edward Powell in *The Orchard and Fruit Garden* (1914). Today's gardeners can still grow fruit trees on a small lawn, thanks to the availability of dwarf varieties. You can even grow your own "combo" apple, cherry, peach, or pear tree, with two or three varieties of fruit grafted onto one tree. "Just develop a fruit tree with a few main branches, as you would normally do," explains New York State garden writer and lecturer Lee Reich, author of *Uncommon Fruits for Every Garden*. "Then whip-graft a different variety onto each of those branches, keeping in mind that only the same species or closely related species are compatible for grafting. For example, you can't graft an apple onto peach rootstock, but apricot and peach are cross-compatible."

Supplies, including rootstocks and scion wood (the part you graft onto the rootstock), are available from mail-order fruit nurseries. Many offer combination trees that are already grafted, too.

Whip grafting is done in late winter to early spring, before growth begins. It works best when the scion and the rootstock branch are close to the same diameter, preferably between ¼ and ½ inch.

You will need:

- Scion wood
- Rootstock
- A small, very sharp knife
- Rubber bands, grafting tape, or electrical tape
- Grafting wax or pruning sealant

Step 1. Choose your scion from 1-year-old wood of the desired size and cut a 1- to 1½-foot piece diagonally at the bottom (the end that will be nearest the rootstock). Make a perpendicular cut across the top end.

Step 2. Prepare the branch of the rootstock that will receive the scion by making a diagonal, sloping cut about 1½ to 2 inches long. Make the cut in one smooth motion, so the cut surface is smooth.

Step 3. Fit the sloping cuts of the scion and rootstock together. The areas directly beneath the bark on each piece need to match up in order for the graft to take.

Step 4. Wrap the graft with a wide rubber band, grafting tape, or electrical tape, starting on the stock and working upward onto the scion. Cover the graft union and its wrapping with grafting wax or pruning sealant.

Step 5. Keep an eye on the graft in the following days to make sure that it remains sealed against moisture loss. Knock off any sprouts that begin growing on the stock below the graft. Once the scion begins growing, carefully cut away the wrapping around the graft to prevent girdling.

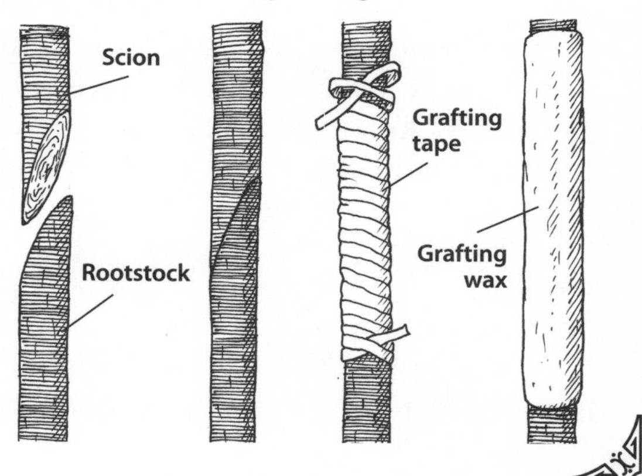

Old-Time Fruits for Flavor and Beauty

■ Rediscover fruit flavors enjoyed by America's earliest inhabitants and enhance your landscape with productive, attractive plants, suggests New York State garden writer and lecturer Lee Reich, author of *Uncommon Fruits for Every Garden*. Native fruit-bearing trees and shrubs can fit neatly into your yard, where they'll produce tasty results—often with a minimal amount of care. Here are three of Lee's favorites.

Juneberries. The flavor of Juneberries (*Amelanchier* spp.) is sweet, with the richness of a sweet cherry and a hint of almond. Juneberries are native across North America, and they range in size from low shrubs to medium-size trees; the plants are easy to grow. In early spring, Juneberries bear loads of delicate white flowers; the summer-ripening fruits resemble blueberries; and in fall, the foliage turns purple, orange, and yellow. Birds enjoy Juneberries, too, Lee warns, so be prepared to shield the plants with a net when the fruits begin to ripen.

Mulberries. Sometimes maligned for their weedy ways and their purple, staining fruits, mulberries (*Morus* spp.) are "among the best-flavored of all fruits," Lee says. Mulberries include our native red mulberry (*M. rubra*) and Asian natives white mulberry (*M. alba*) and black mulberry (*M. nigra*), as well as hybrids of red and white mulberries. The large shrubs or medium-to-large trees produce sweet blackberrylike fruits that may be white, lavender, dark red, or deep purple-black. Mulberries thrive in full sun with ample growing space. Plant mulberry plants with 15 feet of "elbow room" on all sides, and site them away from walkways to avoid tracking purple juice indoors and onto carpets, Lee advises. Mulberry trees usually produce enough fruit to satisfy both people and birds.

Pawpaw. For tropical flavor far north of the equator, try the pawpaw (*Asimina triloba*), a cold-hardy member of a family of otherwise tropical fruits. A small tree with long, droopy leaves, pawpaw produces potato-shaped fruits that ripen to a greenish yellow marked with brown. The custardlike flesh has hints of banana, vanilla, and mango; the seeds are not edible. Pawpaw trees have long taproots and are difficult to transplant; for best results, choose container-grown trees, or plant seeds where you wish the trees to grow. Young trees prefer shade, but fruit production is best in sunny locations. A few varieties of pawpaw are self-fertile, but most need cross-pollination to set fruit. These trees send up suckers and will slowly form a small grove, but you can keep them in check by mowing around them, says Lee.

CHAPTER 12

Flower Gardening
April Showers Bring May Flowers

Flower gardening has changed dramatically in the past 200 years, but in many ways, gardeners have stayed the same. We still invest lots of time and energy in deciding what to plant, how to lay out our garden beds, and what our plants need to look their best. We worry about the weather, fight weeds and pests, and develop strong opinions about which flowers are the prettiest, whether annuals are easier to care for than perennials, and how to design garden beds for long-lasting beauty. In this chapter, you'll find great ideas for tending flower gardens and using and growing annuals, perennials, bulbs, and roses. Plus, you'll catch the feeling of old-time garden designs with ideas for a Victorian carpet bed, a fern basket, a rootery, and more.

Maintaining Gardens at Their Best

Garden styles and trendy plants come and go, but good flower gardening practices have always involved the same basic chores—caring for the soil, cultivating, watering, propagating, and watching out for pests. Read on for great ideas for low-care edgings, best tools for every task, wise ways to water, and plenty of other old-time garden wisdom.

Gravel Bed for a Sturdy Edge

■ Plastic or PVC edgings maintain a clean line at the boundary of garden beds, but these edgings aren't foolproof. What to do when you knock the edging loose by hitting it with your lawn mower, or when frost heaving pushes the edging out of place? A solution to a similar problem faced by 19th-century gardeners may help you deal with uncooperative edging materials.

Gardeners of the 1800s often used clay tiles as an edging. The tiles were either brick size or 8 by 8 inches (and 1 to 2 inches thick). Gardeners would stand the tiles on edge and sink them 4 inches into the soil, creating an edging 4 inches high. But Jane Webb Loudon notes in *Instructions in Gardening for Ladies* (1838) that these edgings would get "out of place, and have a ragged and temporary appearance." The solution was to set the tiles in "concealed brickwork," lodging them solidly in a foundation that could resist that expansion and contraction of the soil.

You can apply this idea by digging a 4-inch-deep, 2-inch-wide trench along the route where you want to install plastic or PVC edging. Place the edging in the trench so that it protrudes slightly above the soil surface. Then fill the trench on both sides of the edging with fine gravel to 1 inch below the soil surface. Gravel has air spaces between the pieces, creating a buffer that resists heaving and stabilizes the edging against blows. Fill the top inch of the trench with soil (this is important to prevent gravel pieces from being kicked up by your lawn mower).

OLD-FASHIONED FAVORITES

An Herbal Edging Option

FLOWERING ANNUALS and perennials aren't the only choice for edging a garden bed. Among her favorites for edging, Jane Webb Loudon, author of *Instructions in Gardening for Ladies* (1838), included parsley, probably referring to curly-leaf parsley. Flat-leaf, or Italian, parsley will serve well as an edging plant, too.

Put an Edge on Garden Edgings

■ According to *The New Garden Encyclopedia: A Complete Practical and Convenient Guide to Every Detail of Gardening* (1945), "neat, well-kept edgings enhance the garden's appearance and simplify its care." Today's garden designers and landscapers would agree with this advice. The encyclopedia advises using annuals that will tolerate clipping, such as sweet alyssum (*Lobularia maritima*), edging lobelia (*Lobelia erinus*), common ageratum (*Ageratum houstonianum*), and wishbone flowers (*Torenia* spp.), next to a path or along the edge of a bed. Low-growing perennials such as evergreen candytuft (*Iberis sempervirens*), rock cresses (*Arabis* spp.), moss phlox (*Phlox subulata*), pinks (*Dianthus* spp.), and violets are good choices, too.

No matter what plants you choose, however, there will still be some maintenance involved, because weeds will pop up between your plants, and some plants may try to grow out of bounds. To make edging maintenance simpler, garden designer Sharon Webber, of Buffalo, New York, an educator for Cornell Cooperative Extension, recommends that you dig a V-shaped trench at least 4 inches across at soil level around the garden bed. According to Sharon, this is especially helpful where the beds are bordered by lawn, because turfgrass can vigorously spread into well-prepared garden beds. "The V-shaped trench is a lot simpler to maintain than landscape fabric, pavers, or rocks. It never requires the Weed Wacker, and it decreases the risk of lawn-mowing disasters, such as mowing over flowering plants because the difference between turf and flowers wasn't clear," Sharon says.

A Simple Edger

■ "You don't have to purchase an edging tool to make a clean edge around a garden bed or along a sidewalk," says Master Gardener Carl Walter, of Hamburg, New York. Carl passes along this tip from the members of the Men's Garden Club of Hamburg, which has been sharing the wisdom of its members since the 1940s: "Just sharpen the edge of a wide putty knife and edge with it."

The Most Helpful Hoe

■ Choosing the hoe best adapted to the task at hand will save you plenty of time and effort in the garden. *The New Garden Encyclopedia* (1945) offers these insights on hoes and their uses.

Common garden hoe. The thin, sharp blade of this hoe works well for heavy weed chopping and for weeding in heavy or compacted soil.

Warren hoe. This heart-shaped hoe with pointed shoulders is useful for opening furrows for seeds or for nipping out weeds among closely planted flowers or crops.

Onion hoe. Wide and shallow, an onion hoe is a good tool for shallowly scraping the soil surface for light cultivation or to dislodge weed seedlings.

Bayonet hoe. Rather like a trowel, this hoe has a narrow blade that is well-designed for thinning seedlings planted in rows.

Grubbing hoe. This heavy hoe has an axlike blade on one side for chopping roots, and a hoe-shaped blade on the other side for slicing through hard soil.

Scuffle hoe. Also called a *push hoe,* a scuffle hoe has a multiedged blade that cuts weeds and loosens soil on both the push and pull strokes.

Bare-Bones Tool List

■ If you find yourself spending too much on fancy gardening tools and gadgets, consider this advice from *The Home Garden* magazine (May 1943), which boils down the list of essential tools for gardeners to the bare minimum:

- Large three-pronged iron fork with a short handle to loosen the ground and uproot weeds
- Rake
- Hoe
- Trowel
- Spade
- Watering can with a large nozzle and fine sprinkler

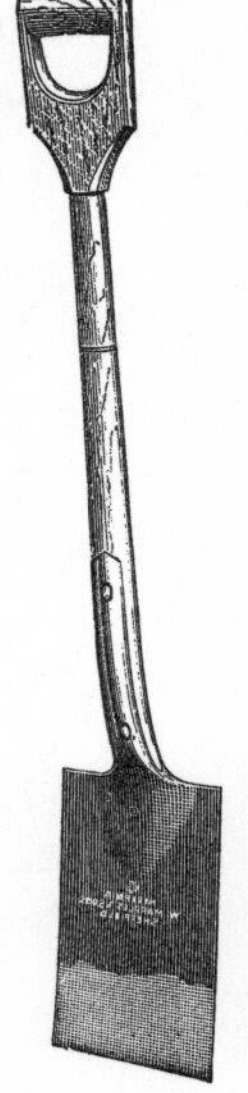

Three Old-Time Tool Rules

Many gardeners have learned from someone older and wiser through the centuries, and some of the best advice involves tools.

1. "Do not throw down your hoe with the blade upwards." —Jane Webb Loudon, *Instructions in Gardening for Ladies* (1838)

2. "Check [in February] to see if the gardener has sharpened all edge tools." —Richardson Wright, *The Gardener's Bed-Book* (1929)

3. "Only a fool leaves the rake tines up." —Harry Harper, gardener from Eden, New York (1952)

Carpet for Comfort

An old piece of carpeting cushions your knees when you kneel in the garden to plant or weed, writes Louisa Johnson in *Every Woman Her Own Flower Gardener: A Handy Manual of Flower Gardening for Ladies* (1858). "If your knees are not accustomed to that position, humor them by placing an empty raisin or soap box upon the carpet, and sit upon that—and if a cushion would also be agreeable, cover a small pillow with some dark chintz, and place that on the box. Now you will have a luxurious seat, and can garden without a sense of pain." Modern gardeners may find it easier to procure a 5-gallon plastic bucket for a seat rather than a raisin or soap box.

Also, you may want to buy a foam kneeling pad, which is easier to carry and store than a piece of carpet. Instead, use the carpet to cover a pathway and block weeds. Cover the carpet with an organic mulch. If the carpet is made of natural fiber, such as wool or cotton, it will decompose and return organic matter to the soil over time.

Three Transplanting Rules from Grandpa Harper

Harry Harper grew perennials from the 1940s until 1965 in a windy spot in Eden, New York, where the climate can be tough on new transplants. His rules for transplanting—shared by his granddaughter, garden writer Sally Cunningham, of East Aurora, New York—can help you succeed with new perennials wherever you live. Here are Grandpa Harper's transplanting rules.

1. Avoid transplanting in the heat of the day, and never expose the roots of transplants to the sun or wind. Transplants tend to lose moisture faster than the roots can replace it, because the roots don't function optimally immediately after transplanting.

2. Put transplants in a little "bathtub." Set transplants just a little lower than the soil surface, in a basinlike depression, making a rim of soil to hold in extra water. Do this on a permanent basis for those perennials and shrubs that require moist soil.

3. Use a shovel to check soil moisture near new transplants. Never judge soil moisture by the appearance of the soil surface. If the soil is dry at a depth of 2 or 3 inches next to a recent transplant, the plants need water, even if the soil surface appears moist.

"People love to credit some gardeners with a magical green thumb," Sally says, "but I don't believe in it. That's what everybody attributed to my grandpa Harper. But there was no magical gift at all . . . He knew what he was doing and why, and he taught me to think about things from the plant's point of view, and to notice their needs."

Deliver the Drink Slowly

"Little drippings of water are bad for all plants, for such a method of watering only destroys the surface looseness," states *Garden Guide, The Amateur Gardeners' Handbook* (1946). This may be true, but what's more critical is that shallow watering leads plants to form shallow roots, leaving them more vulnerable to moisture stress during dry periods. The wise course is to water your flowerbeds and other landscape plantings slowly for a prolonged period, rather than all at once. But if you have a lot of plants or beds to water, this approach isn't easy. "Almost nobody will stand over a plant, holding a hose or water wand, long enough to water deeply," says Rochelle Smith, a landscape instructor at Niagara County Community College, in Sanborn, New York. "Most people dampen the top of the soil and move on. If you can, install landscape irrigation for precious plantings, or use drip hoses. The slow way is really the *only* way."

To deliver water the right way, take a tip from former times and give each plant its own water source that provides a slow drip. One way to do this is to poke a few tiny holes in the bottom of a container and place it next to the plant. In earlier times, the container might have been a leaky pail, leather sack, or tin can. Today, plastic gallon jugs are an obvious choice. (In the case of tree plantings or large beds, you can even use a 20- or 30-gallon plastic garbage can.)

BIZARRE BUT TRUE

Old-Time Gardening Garb

A FAR CRY from blue jeans and clogs, clothing for gardening was somewhat different in 1873, judging by *Every Woman Her Own Flower Gardener:* "Of course flounces, puffs and furbelows, with their accompanying upper skirts, are not suitable for such occupations," writes author Louisa Johnson. "A dark chintz skirt is the best, for it can go into the washtub when it is in need of cleansing. A woolen bathing dress makes an excellent garden costume—for skirts are always in the way. If it is admissible on the beach, where wealth and fashion do congregate, why not in the garden, surrounding one's house? A large shade hat, and a pair of kid gloves are indispensable. Rubber gloves are often recommended, but are far too clumsy for the finger."

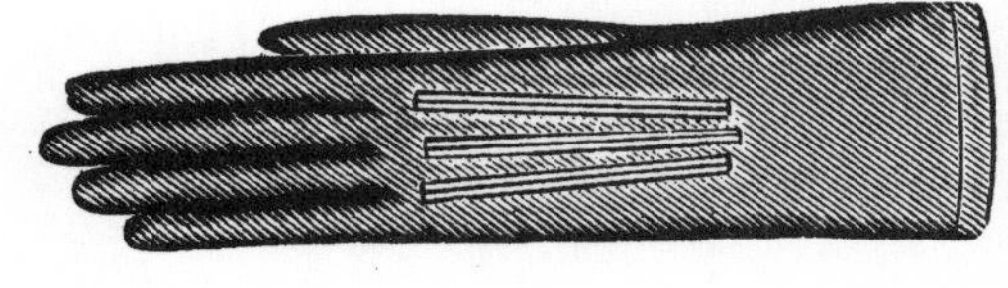

Experiment with the container you've chosen. Start with one tiny hole that allows water to escape drip by drip, and time how long it takes for the container to become empty. Add more holes as needed until you reach about the ideal release rate of 1 gallon of water per hour.

Old-Time Watering Wisdom

The next time you need to conserve water in the garden—whether it's due to drought, a dried-up well, or high water bills—follow in the footsteps of old-time gardeners as they went about watering

Water Gently, Water Well

A HIDDEN POT that serves as a watering reservoir can save the day in several garden situations. Tuck a cork into the drainage hole of a clay pot, and the pot becomes a water reservoir that releases moisture very slowly through the porous walls of the pot, notes *The New Garden Encyclopedia* (1945). This trick is especially helpful in the following situations.

- Tender seedlings have just emerged in a bed, and watering with a hose could disturb the soil and unseat the seedlings.
- Plants that need regular watering are planted in a location that tends to be dry, such as under the canopy of a large tree.
- You have to be away from home for a few days, and you're worried that your container plants won't be able to last without water.

You may need to experiment to see how large a pot, or how many pots, you need to put in place to deliver the right amount of water. And if water seems to drain too slowly with the drainage holes blocked, try removing the corks.

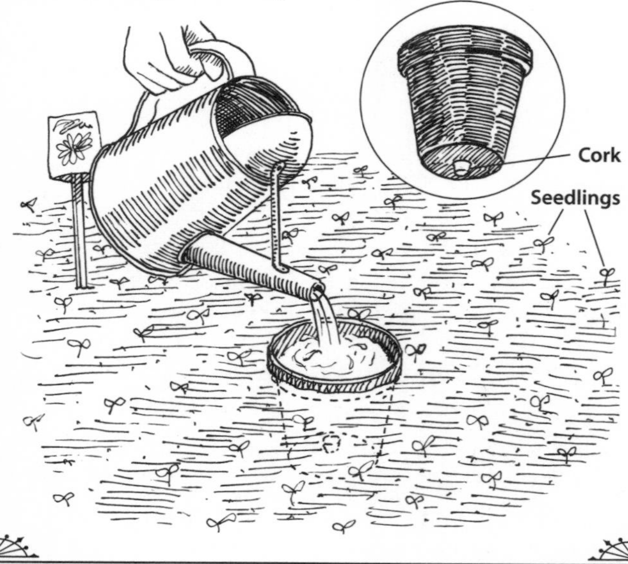

their gardens. After all, they didn't have the luxury of automatic sprinklers, multisetting spray nozzles, and irrigation systems. Since watering was no easy task, they found ways to water as efficiently as possible.

Collect the rain. Put rain barrels (large garbage cans will do) at the corners of buildings to collect rainfall from the downspouts. (Prevent mosquito larvae from developing by using the water every few days or covering the barrels tightly between rainfalls.)

Also, line up buckets, watering cans, and tubs near the garden to catch every bit of rain you can.

Put a pump in the pond. If you're lucky enough to have a pond on your property, install a small pump and use that water for the garden. Don't try to pump water out of any stream, river, lake, or other public waterway.

Save the cooking water. When you prepare corn on the cob, pasta, or potatoes, don't pour the hot cooking water down the drain. Instead, remove the food with tongs and let the water sit to cool down. Later, dump the water directly from the pot onto a thirsty plant, or save it in a larger container. For example, keep a few buckets on hand, and use a child's wagon or your garden cart to transport the full buckets out to your garden.

Water Wisely—Or Whenever

■ An early edition of *The Old Farmer's Almanack* tells readers, "Water during cooler hours, when evaporation is slower. Early morning is better than evening, because the sunshine during the day dries up moisture which encourages fungal growth and slugs."

These are wise old rules, passed down from the *Almanack's* inception in the days of George Washington, but horticulturists of today note that gardeners may have to allow some exceptions to accommodate modern living. "Whether or not it is the right time of day, water whenever you notice that plants have wilted," says garden designer Peg Giermek of Nature Calls Landscaping, in East Aurora, New York. "Wilting is a sure sign of stress, which weakens the plant. In today's busy lives, sometimes we are lucky to find *any* time to water the garden!"

Deadhead for Better Bloom

▪ Deadheading (removing the spent flowers from plants) can lead to more blooms and stronger plants, something that gardeners knew about even in the 1800s. In *The American Gardener* (1821), William Cobbett explains: "Seed production is a most debilitating process; the plant should therefore be prevented from doing this excessive labor."

Actually, preventing seed production isn't the only goal for the dedicated deadheader. Proper deadheading not only prevents seed formation; it also stimulates the plants to even greater flower production. "Deadhead for tomorrow and next week, not for today," says Carolyn Schaffner, group president of the Western New York Hosta Society, in Buffalo, New York. "Many flowers can be deadheaded to the first or second leaf node, past the expired flower clusters. Often, the next bloom will erupt there, either as a flower on a single stem, as on annual poppies, or as two stems, one on each side of the main stem, as on butterfly bush."

Carolyn advises gardeners to experiment with deadheading different kinds of plants to see how they respond. "The plants teach you as you go along, and you can do no harm: Any deadheading is better than none!"

☞ TRASH OR TREASURE ☜

Rotate Your Hose

AN OLD AUTOMOBILE WHEEL RIM makes a perfect place to coil a garden hose, claims a 1928 edition of *Better Homes and Gardens.* Lay the wheel on the ground and coil the hose around it, or if you're handy with wood and tools, you can construct a simple wooden stand that lets the hose be coiled and uncoiled as the wheel spins. A coat of white or green metal primer will dress up the old wheel for garden use. "We're not so likely to find tire rims these days except in a junkyard, because people reuse them or recycle them as scrap metal," says car aficionado Jim Pavel, of Buffalo, New York. "You're more likely to find a discarded hose reel on trash day or at a yard sale, rather than a tire rim!" Another cast-off item that can be used to stash a hose is a child's wading pool (coil the hose inside the empty pool).

A New Take on Manure Tea

■ "Manure water poured around Spring-blooming perennials will often produce larger flowers," notes Richardson Wright in *The Gardener's Bed-Book: Short and Long Pieces to Be Read in Bed by Those Who Love Husbandry and the Green Growing Things of Earth* (1929). Today, garden experts would use the term *manure tea* instead of *manure water,* and many experts also advise using compost tea instead of manure, due to health concerns about handling animal manure.

Research shows that compost tea offers disease-prevention and disease-fighting benefits as well as a wide range of nutrients. Applying compost tea to your garden also stimulates beneficial soil organisms.

To make compost tea, put a shovelful of finished compost into a burlap (or any cloth) bag and soak it for a few days in a barrel or bucket. Then water plants with this liquid. Since the formula is not exact and all composts differ, experiment at first, and water with a diluted solution until you experience desirable results. It is one of the pleasures for gardeners, old-time or modern, to experience the results when millions of microorganisms begin working for you.

If you're interested in gaining the maximum benefits from compost tea, check garden centers and mail-order suppliers for kits that allow you to make aerated compost tea. The kit includes a pump that continuously forces air through the liquid and compost, which is thought to promote even greater microbial activity in the tea.

A Time to Mulch, a Time to Cultivate

■ Everybody seems to be piling mulch on their gardens these days, but old-time gardeners didn't rely much on mulch. "Many old gardening books describe cultivation as an everyday step in gardening activity," says garden writer Sally Cunningham, of East Aurora, New York. "Cultivation is simply raking or hoeing the soil surface around plants. We tend to mulch intensively instead, but if you don't want to spend a lot of money on fancy mulches, cultivating is an option."

Mulch does have advantages: It keeps the soil surface moist, prevents soil from crusting over or becoming hard, and

OLD-TIME HUMOR

Deadheading for Dummies

In *The Gardener's Bed-Book* (1929), Richardson Wright offers this wry advice about seeking help with deadheading from nongardening visitors. "I keep several pairs of scissors hanging [nearby] and when any citified visitor in August elicits the slightest interest in gardening, I press one of these into her hand with my blessing. Of course, after the first hour, her enthusiasm melts, but by changing visitors every couple of days we manage to keep the annuals tidied."

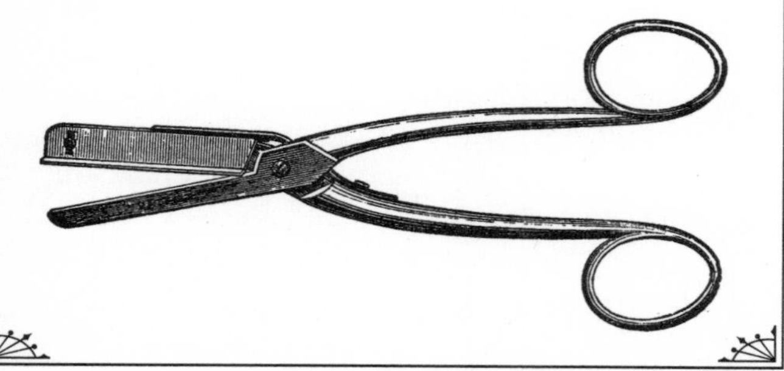

blocks most weeds. The 1946 edition of *Garden Guide, The Amateur Gardeners' Handbook,* noted some special circumstances in which mulch is a good choice: "If you have too many beds to cultivate so often, if you are more than commonly lazy, or if you have to be away from the garden for long periods, cultivation may be abandoned if the beds are mulched with some suitable material." The guide recommended several types of mulch, including moss, buckwheat hulls, grass clippings, sawdust, and tobacco stems, "but a thick coat of manure is better than anything, except that it may be very weedy."

Garden experts today wouldn't recommend using peat moss as mulch, because it actually has a drying effect when used on top of the soil, wicking soil moisture out into the air. And rather than manure, compost is now considered one of the finest mulches.

One time you shouldn't mulch *or* cultivate is when you want to allow a plant, such as cosmos, spider flower (*Cleome hassleriana*), or love-in-a-mist (*Nigella damascena*), to self-sow, Sally says. Mulching will stifle the seedlings, and cultivating may uproot them before you even know they're there. Once seedlings are established (a few inches tall), you may then lightly mulch. In the meantime, hand-pull weeds.

Avoid Fertilizer in August

One time when applying fertilizer might harm your plants is mid- to late summer, according to Richardson Wright in *The Gardener's Bed-Book* (1929): "Excessive fertilizer [in August] causes late fall flowering and continued sappy growth."

Late flowering "depletes the plant's strength" when it needs to be preparing a strong root system for surviving the winter.

PEARLS OF WISDOM

"Weed all borders thoroughly, as a weed caught in time saves nine."

RICHARDSON WRIGHT,
The Gardener's Bed-Book (1929)

Karen Dean Hall, an educator in commercial horticulture for Cornell Cooperative Extension, in western New York State, explains it this way: "When your plants are flagging in the heat of August, it may be tempting to 'green them up' with fertilizer. However, it's not the best time. Fertilizer provided late in the growing season encourages succulent growth, which is weak—likely to be attractive to insects and vulnerable to damage from early freezes. In the heat of summer, the most important thing to do for most plants is to water them deeply to encourage root development." And if you are gardening farther south, where winter comes later, the same principle applies: Stop fertilizing 2 months from your average first-frost date or the start of the cold season for you. All plants benefit from a rest period.

More Roots with Willow Water

■ To increase your odds of success at rooting cuttings, use the willow-water trick, a practice that dates to the Middle Ages, advises Carolyn Schaffner, president of the Western New York Hosta Society, in Buffalo, New York. "Early European settlers in North America found Native Americans gathering bark from willow trees to treat pain, chills, and fever. Around 1828, French and German chemists extracted white willow's active chemical, salicin," Carolyn says. Salicin is a plant growth hormone. "The first report of willow used for growth stimulation came to us later from Grandma Mills, a farmer and descendant of a pioneer to Allegany County, New York. She used the willow branches as divining rods for dowsing, and the bark as a plant growth stimulant." Carolyn says that members of the Hosta Society have used willow water to increase their stock for plant sales. The trick is to use water in which willow branches have soaked.

Cut several stems of willows, particularly in early spring, and bring the stems inside to your kitchen. Using a sharp knife, scrape the bark from the stems. Measure the bark by teaspoons into an old saucepan. Add 1 cup cold water for each 1 to 3 teaspoons bark. Let the bark soak for 2 to 5 hours; then bring the water and bark to a boil. Boil for 20 minutes. Allow the willow water to cool, and then use this water in cups or vases to root the cuttings of annual or perennial flowers, trees, or shrubs.

Some gardeners prefer to dispense with the chore of scraping and boiling the bark. Instead, they put the intact stems in a tub or pail, pour in enough water to cover, and let the stems soak for several days.

TRASH OR TREASURE

Keeping String Straightened Out

To avoid "tangled and annoying knots of string or cord, keep your string ever ready in a homemade container just for the purpose," recommends *The New Garden Encyclopedia* (1945). Follow the example of old-time gardeners and recycle a cardboard food container, such as an ice cream tub or an oatmeal canister, for housing your garden twine. Clean and dry the container as needed and punch a hole in the lid. Feed the loose end of a ball of twine up through the hole, put the ball in the container, and push the lid into place. Then when you need strings to mark a straight line or guide the morning glories, you are ready to go, with no messy tangles to untangle.

Horsetail for Fighting Fungus

WHEN A FUNGAL DISEASE such as powdery mildew troubles your roses or phlox, try a traditional concoction made out of horsetail (*Equisetum* spp.). Some gardeners consider horsetail one of the worst weeds in the world, because removing it involves perpetual digging or smothering efforts. But horsetail contains silica, and silica fights fungal diseases. At the very least, there is some satisfaction in chopping the weed to bits, and you may find some improvement in the situation. You can make a fungicidal spray from boiled horsetail plants. When you work with horsetail and horsetail solution, always wear protective gloves.

You will need:

Shovel
Horsetail plants
Baking sheet (optional)
Cast-off cooking pot
Cheesecloth or fine strainer
Hand-pump sprayer

Step 1. Dig up (with the whole root system) the horsetail plants infesting your garden. Reserve some and dry them by laying them on a table or baking sheet for a day or two in a sheltered location.

Step 2. Add ⅛ cup dried horsetail to ½ gallon water in a pot that is no longer used for cooking, and boil it for about 30 minutes.

Step 3. Remove from the heat and allow to steep for 1 day.

Step 4. Filter the solution through the cheesecloth or strainer into the sprayer. (If you have a very large area to do, you will need to make more solution and use a larger sprayer.)

Step 5. Test-spray a small area of each of the various mildew- or black-spot-prone plants in your garden and wait a day or two to observe any reaction. If the plants withstand the test spray, follow up by spraying them thoroughly, including the undersides of the leaves, with the solution every 2 weeks in spring, from the time the plants first leaf out until about midsummer.

Horsetail spray is reported to be effective against black spot on roses and against powdery mildew, which is common on roses, phlox, bee balm, and many other plants, especially during humid conditions. *Caution:* Even if you find horsetail spray effective, don't encourage horsetail to grow, because of its invasive nature. Instead, combine your disease-fighting efforts with your efforts to keep horsetail under control.

Hints for Hiring Help

■ Finding good garden and landscaping help has always been a tough task. "Every man, who can dig and hoe and rake, calls himself a Gardener as soon as he lands here from England. These (persons) are generally called handy men . . . But as to the art of gardening they generally know nothing of it," writes William Cobbett in *The American Gardener* (1821).

Today, many people call themselves landscapers even though they have little or no expertise. Many states have no standards regulating who can sell landscaping or gardening services. Kim Decker, a perennial grower in western New York, calls it "the Red Truck Syndrome." "Don't automatically accept the lowest bid for work on your home landscape or garden . . . Just because a person has a truck doesn't mean he or she knows plants," Kim says.

To find a good landscaper or professional gardener, follow these tips from Sharon Webber, of Buffalo, New York, an extension educator and former president of the Western New York Nursery and Landscape Association.

■ Ask for certification or credentials (standards vary by state, so learn the standards in your area). This isn't a guarantee of competency, but it indicates at least a minimum qualification—showing that the person has genuine knowledge and/or training in landscaping, rather than just claiming the name *landscaper.*

■ Look for gardens you like in your area and ask the property owners whether they hired a professional landscaper or garden designer. "Whether they did it themselves or hired a pro, they will be flattered you like it," says Sharon. "Just a note in the mailbox might get you great advice."

■ Ask at a garden center or nursery you admire whom they recommend for gardening work. Be specific about your needs: Do you want someone to plant a perennial border, an annual garden, or an all-shrub landscape?

■ When you interview a landscaper or gardener, before you describe your vision, ask him or her for pictures and lists of plants they have used recently. Even if you aren't a plant expert, this will give you an idea of the candidate's range of styles and variety in the plant palette. What you want to avoid is hiring a "professional" who provides cookie-cutter designs with the same old plants—especially if you are looking for a personalized landscape that includes perennials.

ANNUALS IN STYLE

ANNUALS REACHED a peak of popularity during the Victorian era of "carpet-bedding" or "bedding-out." Many annuals that the Victorians loved are trendy again in the early 21st century, even though our style of planting them has changed. But there's still a lot we can learn from old-time gardeners about when to plant pansies, how to propagate zonal geraniums, and more.

Two Old-Time Annuals

■ Although it's fun to try the latest releases of flowering annuals in your garden, it pays to use some old reliable favorites, too. Here are recommendations from *The American Gardener* (1821) and *The Gardener's Bed-Book* (1929) on growing two old-fashioned favorites, with some modern-day improvements thrown in.

Stock. Common stock (*Matthiola incana*) is usually sold and grown as an annual, but it's actually a biennial or short-lived perennial, sometimes called *10-week stock,* referring to the time required from seed to flower. Colors are purple, red, white, and scarlet, with a choice of gray-green or sea-green leaves. To care for common stock, sink potted plants into the soil in your garden and allow them to grow there until November; then lift them to overwinter. Nineteenth-century gardeners overwintered stock plants indoors, but because our modern homes are generally much warmer than theirs were, we need a different strategy. Store stock—or any semihardy biennial or perennial—in containers in a cool basement, an enclosed sunporch, or a garage with a window. Be sure the plants do not freeze. Replant them outdoors when danger of frost has passed. And if you are tempted by new cultivars as they come on the market, remember that while hybrids offer a desirable feature—such as larger or double flowers—they may not offer the lovely scent of the original.

Sweet peas. In the early 1800s, there were many annual sweet peas (*Lathyrus odoratus*) in a variety of colors. Growing sweet peas is similar to growing common garden peas, and pea sticks are one type of support you can use to prevent them from flopping over. Pea sticks, also called *pea brush,* are sturdy sticks 2 to 4 feet long that have some branching or forked twigs. Collect these as part of your spring yard cleanup or pruning sessions. Sweet peas have been hybridized today, and recent improvements include cultivars that are somewhat heat-tolerant. Newer cultivars also produce larger flowers, and some dwarf types may not need support from pea sticks. Keep in mind, though, that some improved cultivars are not fragrant.

Plant Pansies in Fall

Gardeners in cold-winter areas can enjoy annual flowers in early spring, well before the weather is warm enough for planting tender annuals like marigolds and zinnias. The secret is to plant winter-hardy pansies in fall. Way back in 1821, William Cobbett described these plants, which he called "heart's-ease," in *The American Gardener:* "A beautiful little annual, which has great varieties. It may be sown in the fall, without any care about covering the ground, but it must not come up in this country, till spring." The plant acquired the name *heart's-ease* because it flowers in purple, white, and yellow. In the Victorian language of flowers, these colors all referred to sentiments that would *ease the hearts* of separated lovers. (For more, see "Speak in the Language of Flowers" on page 132.)

Whatever you call this charming annual, plant out bedding plants in early fall in most parts of the Northeast and upper Midwest (Zone 5 or colder). The plants will shrivel up during the winter, but will make a successful comeback from their roots the following spring.

OLD-FASHIONED FAVORITES

Ode to the Sweet Pea

ALTHOUGH it's unconventional to receive gardening advice in the form of a poem, this ode to sweet peas from *Garden Guide, The Amateur Gardeners' Handbook* (1946)—penned by an unknown author—offers some practical tips for growing sweet peas.

Peas along the border, Peas upon the lawn,
Peas against an eastern wall to welcome
in the dawn.
Peas among the Roses, Peas behind the Pinks;
Peas to catch the western glow when
evening sunlight sinks.
Peas upheld with Chestnut,
Peas held up with Ash;
Peas asprawl on Hazel spray,
Peas on Larchen Brash.
Peas on still unyielding wire,
Peas tied up with string;
Peas upon the trellis work
where Rambler Roses
swing.
Oh! Merry, merry, merry,
are the gay Sweet Peas;
Plant them when and how you will;
it's certain they will please."

Making More Zonal Geraniums

A tried-and-true technique for propagating zonal geraniums (*Pelargonium × hortorum*) is still the best way to make more of these old-fashioned—and modern—favorites. Even in commercial greenhouses, taking cuttings is the preferred method for propagating zonal geraniums to guarantee plants that are true to type. Follow the advice from *The New Garden Encyclopedia* (1945) to multiply zonal geraniums by rooting cuttings. The best time to propagate zonal geraniums is in early spring, if you have overwintered a favorite plant indoors, or anytime your plants are becoming leggy.

To get started, fill several pots with lightweight potting soil (such as a peat-perlite mix), and put the pots in a plastic flat. Water the pots until the mix is thoroughly moist. Use sharp scissors or clippers to take 3- to 4-inch-long cuttings from the ends of leggy zonal geranium stems. Remove all but the top pair of leaves from each cutting. Insert one cutting into each pot. If desired, cover each cutting with an upturned jelly jar. Place the cuttings where the roots will stay warm (use a heating mat if it's a cold time of year), but don't let the tops overheat. Avoid locations that get direct sun. If excessive moisture accumulates in the jar or the air becomes very warm (over 80°F), lift the glass off from time to time. When several new leaves have formed and the little plants are rooted firmly, remove the jars, and gradually harden off the cuttings before moving the pots outdoors. You can replant the cuttings into larger pots or into garden beds as desired.

Try Bedding-Out the 21st-Century Way

Thanks to new types of fast-spreading annuals, you can create a flowering carpet of color like the kind Victorian gardeners specialized in creating—but with a lot less labor and expense. This style of gardening, called *carpet-bedding* or *bedding-out,* uses bold picture designs, such as clocks, fleurs-de-lis, birds, or family crests. Victorian gardeners sometimes planted hundreds of closely spaced plants to create one of these gardens. You can get the same effect, but with much less planting effort, by using spreading annuals such as Wave Series petunias. Your design will be most effective if you keep it simple.

To start, decide on the overall size and shape of your garden bed, and trace it on graph paper. Within that outline, draw the simple design of your choice. Divide the design into sections, and determine the number of square feet that each section takes up.

Next, prepare your site by removing weeds and enriching the soil with lots of organic matter, such as compost or well-aged manure. Go to a garden center to choose plants (see "Carpet-Bedding Favorites" on page 300 for suggestions). As you're figuring how many plants to buy, keep in mind that you'll want to space plants fairly closely and have a few extra plants left over as fillers in case any plants die out.

Back at home, use a hose, rope, or flour to mark the design. Plant your bed, working section by section. Water and weed your new garden regularly for the first few weeks. Cut or pinch off flower buds for the first weeks, too, in order to increase fullness and encourage plant growth. Throughout the season, pinch or trim plants as needed to prevent them from rambling outside their sections.

To re-create a Victorian carpet-bedding garden, you might develop a design based on a symbol, such as a fleur-de-lis or an animal, or create an abstract design.

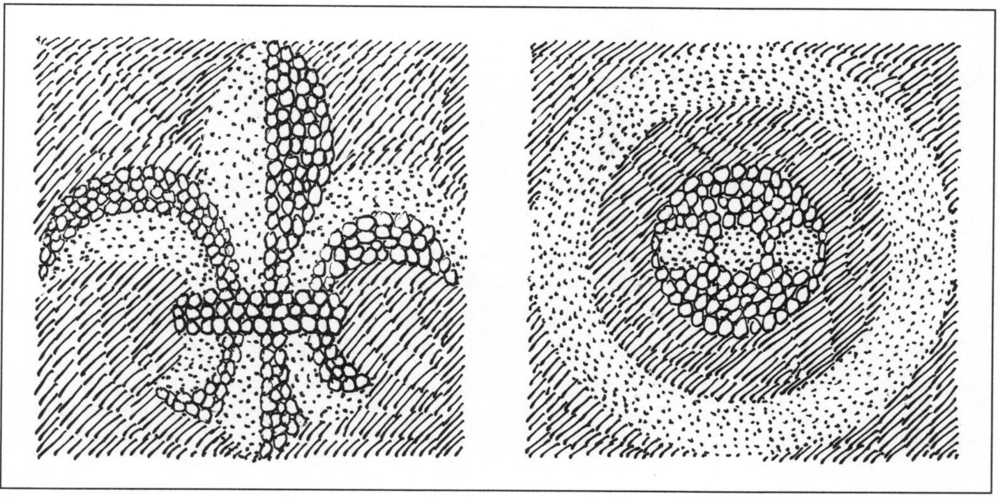

Carpet-Bedding Favorites

VICTORIANS PREFERRED bold colors in their garden beds, such as electric blues, reds, and golds. You can choose annuals or perennials, but remember that your goal is to achieve solid blocks of color. Foliage plants such as coleus and caladiums work well, too. Old-time carpet-bedding gardens almost always used sun-loving plants.

TRIED-AND-TRUE FAVORITES	
Common ageratum (*Ageratum houstonianum*)	Also called common flossflower, this annual has blue, pink, or mauve flowers and is nice for edgings.
Basket-of-gold (*Aurinia saxatilis*)	A perennial with thick clumps of bright yellow flowers, it blooms in midspring to early summer.
Celosias, cockscombs (*Celosia* spp.)	Their shiny leaves and brightly colored flowers with interesting texture make these upright annuals striking in any garden.
Edging lobelia (*Lobelia erinus*)	This bushy, trailing annual is covered with tiny blue, purple, pink, or white flowers.
Sweet alyssum (*Lobularia maritima*)	A familiar low-growing annual, sweet alyssum is available in white-, mauve-, or lilac-flowering varieties.
Sages (*Salvia* spp.)	Sages, both bushy perennials and tender perennials, produce spikes of blue, purple, red, or white flowers.
Garden verbenas (*Verbena × hybrida*)	Annual verbenas come in a variety of plant forms, with clusters of sweet-smelling tubular flowers in many colors.
Zinnias (*Zinnia* spp. and cvs.)	Tall or dwarf annuals with daisylike flowers in many colors; many modern cultivars are mildew-resistant

MODERN FAVORITES	
Flowering kale (*Brassica oleracea acephala*)	This hybridized form of the garden vegetable undergoes dramatic color changes in fall.
New Guinea impatiens (*Impatiens* New Guinea Group)	This hybrid annual bears large flowers in bold colors. It tolerates a variety of light conditions and prefers to be kept well-watered.
Sweet potato vine (*Ipomoea batatas*)	The attraction of this fast-spreading tender perennial lies in its bright lime green, maroon, or variegated foliage.
Petunias (*Petunia × hybrida*)	You will find this popular annual with flowers in a rainbow of colors. Groundcover types such as the Wave Series spread 3 feet or more.
Dusty miller (*Senecio cineraria*)	Its fuzzy silvery leaves have made dusty miller a longtime garden staple. It sometimes survives over winter.
Coleus (*Solenostemon scutellarioides*)	This annual is now available in hundreds of improved cultivars, sporting an amazing variety of foliage colors and color combinations.
Bacopa (*Sutera cordata*)	These hanging-basket or container annuals also spread well when planted in garden beds. They produce a heavy bloom of small mauve, pink, violet, red, or white flowers.

Practical Perennial Pointers

PERENNIALS have nearly always been garden favorites, thanks to their wonderful habit of returning each spring—with proper care and a little luck. Choices in America were limited in the early 1800s, but by the latter part of the century, plant collectors were traipsing all over the world to feed the Victorian collecting craze. Check out some suggestions from times past for choosing great perennials and keeping them at their best.

New Isn't Necessarily Best

■ Heed these wise words from *The Home Garden* magazine (February 1943): "Possibly you are like most amateur gardeners—you like to have something to show your garden friends that they do not have. But this desire may lead you into many disappointing experiences if the plants you grow are not selected as to their adaptability. Just because a variety is new is no reason for its being good. In fact many of our oldest perennials are among the best, but are almost rare in home gardens."

The magazine offers recommendations for "older perennials" worth growing. Sure enough, these are wonderful plants to grow, even 60 years hence!

Astilbes. These perennials need steady soil moisture, best supplied by a highly organic compost-rich soil. Astilbes (*Astilbe* spp. and hybrids) do best in cool-summer climates and need shade in hot-summer areas, especially in the late afternoon. White-flowered astilbes are the true old-fashioned form, but any of the hundreds of pastel-colored cultivars available today still provide the feeling of an old-fashioned woodland garden.

Black snakeroot. A shade-tolerant native American plant, black snakeroot (*Cimicifuga racemosa*) was somewhat overlooked as a garden perennial in the 1940s, and the same could be said today. If you have a large shady perennial garden, though, black snakeroot will offer shrublike form and dazzling white flower spikes in late summer.

Globeflowers. Globeflowers (*Trollius* spp.) prefer ample moisture, even boggy sites; they thrive on north sides of buildings. *The Home Garden* recommends *T. ledebourii* (now *T. chinensis*) 'Golden Queen'.

Goat's beard. Another native American plant, goat's beard (*Aruncus dioicus,* also called *A. sylvester*) has been a regular part of shade gardens for decades, perhaps because it is able to survive in many types of soils.

Heucheras. Old-time gardeners called this perennial *coral bells,* a name that's still a familiar synonym for heucheras

(*Heuchera* spp. and cvs.) today. Many varieties that were new in the 1940s remain available, including 'Pink Delight' and 'Queen of Hearts'. For a new twist, though, choose among the hundreds of hybrid cultivars developed by heuchera hybridizers.

Phlox. New varieties of garden phlox (*Phlox paniculata*) and Carolina phlox (*P. carolina*) beat out old ones because they tend to have greater resistance to powdery mildew. Do not let them go to seed, because seedlings do not come true and may be weedy.

Purple coneflower. The sun-loving purple coneflower (*Echinacea purpurea*) is easy to grow. An old variety, 'The King', is still available, but improved hybrids such as 'Magnum' have larger flowers.

Torch lilies. Gardeners sometimes overwintered older varieties of torch lilies (*Kniphofia* spp. and hybrids) in a coldframe, but today there are many hardy cultivars, ranging in height from 18 to 48 inches.

Ferreting Out Fragrant Plants

A WORD TO THE WISE SHOPPER in search of fragrant plants: In old-time gardening books or catalogs, plant descriptions referring to fragrance were dependable, but today you need to ask questions or read the fine print when you buy seeds or plants. The more hybridized a plant is, the less likely it is to retain its scent. For instance, many of the newer pinks (*Dianthus* cvs.) sport two-toned patterns and larger flowers, but their flowers are not fragrant. Also, rose growers will gladly tell you about the loss of fragrance in some of the long-blooming landscape-type shrub roses. When in doubt, choose a plant described as a species plant or heirloom plant, or choose one without a cultivar name shown.

Watch Out for Late Arrivals

"Take care, in your early cultivation, not to disturb the roots of *Platycodon* [*grandiflorus*] (balloon-flower)" or other perennials that emerge late in spring, warns Richardson Wright in *The Gardener's Bed-Book* (1929). Other slow-to-emerge perennials include butterfly weed (*Asclepias tuberosa*) and leadwort (*Ceratostigma plumbaginoides*).

To avoid losing these great plants by accidentally cutting into the roots and crowns when you dig and plant early in the season, use an attention-getting place marker, says cut-flower grower Roxanne McCoy, owner of Lilies of the Field, in West Falls, New York. "Use Popsicle sticks, shirt collar stays, golf tees, whatever it will take to tell you 'don't dig here.' I do the same for bulbs, too."

How to Grow a Peony

Peonies have been popular in America for more than 200 years. In 1821, William Cobbett wrote in *The American Gardener*, "[The peony] is a perennial flower that may be raised from seed for offsets. A grand flower for shrubberies. Each flower is usually as big as a tea-cup." Yet today many homeowners hesitate to buy peonies, thinking that they are difficult to stake or hearing that they fail to flower.

Take this advice about the basic needs of peonies, provided by the American Peony Society in *The Home Garden* magazine (June 1943).

Plan for sunshine. The location should have full sun, now and in the future. You should look overhead to ensure that new trees will not grow to block the sunlight in coming years.

Enrich the soil. Peonies are known as one of the longest-lasting perennials, and 30- or 40-year-old plants are not uncommon. So it makes sense to heed the traditional recommendation to prepare peony beds thoroughly. First, remove the top foot of soil from the bed and set it aside. Then, loosen the remaining soil with your fork, to at least a 2-foot depth. Replace the set-aside soil. If your soil is sandy or in poor condition, turn in a lot of compost—a bushel basketful per peony if you can procure that much, or 4 to 6 inches spread evenly over an entire peony bed. A heavy soil is preferable to a light soil; clay loam is excellent.

Set plants properly. Place the plants at least 3 feet apart with the crowns buried 3 inches below the surface. If the crowns are covered too deeply, the plants will not flower freely. If they're planted too shallowly, the winter frosts will heave them from the soil.

Don't change your mind. Although it's easy to dig and transplant some perennials from place to place in your yard, that's not true of peonies. If you move them, be prepared to wait 2 to 3 years for them to begin blooming again.

Continue to cultivate. When the plants have finished blooming, do not neglect cultivation, since they must make good growth and mature their foliage, or the following year's bloom will suffer.

Groom in autumn. Before winter, cut the stalks off a few inches above soil level.

Feed the soil. In the 1940s, the American Peony Society recommended enriching beds with "bonemeal, hardwood ashes, and sheep manure every year or two." But today, a better choice is compost. Wood ashes may include toxic residues and can also increase soil alkalinity. Sheep manure may be hard for most gardeners to come by. Bonemeal is fine to add if you choose (although some modern research questions the nutritional value of bonemeal, because the product is now being heat-treated). Rich compost will supply a balance of nutrients and will not have any harmful effect on soil pH.

Give the Gift of Irises Carefully

■ Beginning gardeners are often grateful for any plant that survives, but smart gardeners learn that some plants just are not worthy of propagating. According to Richardson Wright in *The Gardener's Bed-Book* (1929), "The birth control of poor Iris is a worthy crusade of any gardener." The author tells us to resist the urge to give other people clumps of common plants such as his "poor Iris" and instead burn them.

In modern times in the Northeast, gardener Kathy Guest Shadrack, of East Aurora, New York, who has spent years as an officer of iris societies, says, "I would never consider irises 'common,' but make sure you are sharing one that will reward the receiver with bloom."

To increase the blooms of irises, after the blooming time each year (late spring or early summer, depending on where you live), dig the clump and discard any rhizomes that are soft or have no leaves. Then look closely at the rhizomes for bloom stalk scars—the flat place on top of one end of each rhizome—which have already produced blooms and will not bloom again. Set these aside; then go through the rhizomes that remain, and select some large, firm rhizomes, which will be sure to bloom at the next opportunity. "Irises are a pass-along plant, and a wonderful memento from a cherished auntie or a good green friend," Kathy says.

Staking in Time Saves Perennial Problems

■ Procrastinating about staking perennials seems to be a bad habit with a long history. As far back as 1929, Richardson Wright, author of *The Gardener's Bed-Book,* urged gardeners to stake in a timely way, specifying May 10 as the date to "stake Peonies before the buds begin to swell and for larger bloom take off small side buds," and May 19 as a time to "begin to stake Dephiniums, Gladioli, and other perennials." While the precise dates for staking vary depending on where you live, the general rule to stake early is always a good one to follow. You might even take a page from the *Bed-Book* and mark your calendar ahead of time with reminders that it's time to stake those perennials that otherwise will flop over, becoming a garden eyesore rather than a garden highlight.

Mark your calendar with a reminder to prune during March if you'll have perennials you need to stake. Why? Because small-diameter prunings from shrubs and trees are handy as pea brush for staking. Simply set the prunings in a pile (perhaps near your compost pile) for a few weeks, and they'll be right at hand when it's time to set up stakes in late April and May. Push the prunings cut-end-first into the ground around perennials that will grow up as tall, bushy masses. The foliage will hide the prunings, and the brush will provide support for the leafy and flowering stems of the perennials.

Never Toss a Basket

■ Bushel and half-bushel baskets were household items in the early 20th century, when most families had home gar-

dens and needed to harvest and carry fruits and vegetables. Even after the bottoms of the baskets rotted or broke, resourceful gardeners found a use for the remaining basket frames. "I remember bottomless baskets as a real treasure for staking floppy flowers, such as peonies," says Sally Cunningham, a garden writer from East Aurora, New York. "The color was inconspicuous, soon covered by other plants in the border, and the height was right to prop many midsize perennials. Even now I watch for them among gardening throw-aways or at yard sales."

Truckin' Your Plants

■ "The commonest mistake made by inexperienced persons packing flowers for traveling," writes A. J. MacSelf in *The Woman's Treasury for Home and Garden* (1939), "is that of leaving the blooms far too loose in the box. A great deal more damage will be done if flowers have sufficient room to move about a little, and so hit each other and the sides of the box, than if they are packed so firmly that no amount of shaking can disturb them."

To make sure your plants are "packed firmly," all you need are some cardboard boxes and plastic garment bags or clear plastic garbage bags. Dry-cleaning bags are adequate, but they rip easily. Before moving day, count the plants you plan to move and decide how many bags and boxes you will need. (The boxes are for groups of smaller plants, and also for larger plants potted in breakable containers.)

If a plant is potted in a breakable container, start by setting the plant in a box large enough to allow 2 inches of extra space on all sides of the pot. Fill the open space with foam peanuts or crumpled newspaper. If you have a hot-air popcorn popper, you can also pop a few batches of popcorn and use that to fill the space (no salt or butter, please). The advantage of popcorn is that when your journey to your new home is complete, you can use it to start your compost pile! If you put more than one plant in a box, check the weight as you work to make sure the boxes won't be too heavy.

Once the box is packed, set the box into a bag (open end up). Plants that are in plastic pots don't need to be boxed—you can put them directly into bags. Use twist ties to close the bags.

Stick with Subtle Staking

When you stake perennials that tend to flop, don't make the stakes conspicuous. As *Garden Guide, The Amateur Gardeners' Handbook* (1946), instructs, "Paint the stake green and tie with green cord or raffia, but do not use an old mop handle nor tie with brilliant calico."

Wild Ones in the Shrubs

■ Keeping aggressive perennials in their place is not a new garden problem, and this advice from *Garden Guide, The Amateur Gardeners' Handbook* (1946), will still work well in your garden: "Know their habits . . . and put those that are wild and aggressive only among the shrubbery."

Beware the Plume Poppy

PLUME POPPY (*Macleaya cordata*) is an old-fashioned tall (10 feet) perennial that readily self-seeds and sprawls. As a backdrop, it is spectacular, but take note of this warning from *The Gardener's Bed-Book* (1929), by Richardson Wright: "Resolve that, unless you can afford an extra gardener to watch it, you'll never let Plume Poppy . . . loose in your garden."

The first step in following this advice is to learn which perennials are likely to take over and overwhelm a garden—preferably before you plant them! Then, if there are aggressive perennials that you find highly appealing and want to grow, create a territory in your yard especially for them, where they can do no harm to your tamer flowering plants.

Contemporary garden writer Sally Cunningham, of East Aurora, New York, suggests that zealous spreaders need an area farther from your house and, if possible, in a more naturalized setting. They should be bounded by a fence, driveway, or other barrier to prevent them from escaping into neighbors' yards or into nature. This works well for perennials that form huge clumps rapidly or spread by runners or rhizomes, as well as any plant that propagates wantonly by seed. Sally also notes that this garden needs a different style of maintenance than other beds: "Tending this garden area will be a matter of yanking out whole sections from time to time to keep the clumps somewhat balanced. The good thing about a bed of wild spreaders is that most normal 'weeds' won't have a chance!" Sally includes the following perennials in her top list of rapid spreaders.

- Mugwort (*Artemisia vulgaris*)
- Shasta daisy (*Leucanthemum* × *superbum,* also called *Chrysanthemum* × *superbum*)
- Loosestrifes (*Lysimachia* spp.)
- Plume poppies (*Macleaya* spp.)
- Bee balm (*Monarda didyma*)
- Obedient plant (*Physostegia virginiana*)
- Black-eyed Susans (*Rudbeckia* spp.)

Beautiful Bulbs

Bulbs are a reliable choice for adding splashes of bright color to flowerbeds in spring and summer. Old-time gardeners loved bulbs, too, and you can benefit from their advice on bulb planting depth, protecting bulbs over winter in a "plunging bed," and growing gladioli, dahlias, and other traditional favorite bulbs.

Size Up Soil before Setting Bulbs

▪ When planting bulbs, a rule of thumb that's been repeated through the ages is to plant bulbs at a depth of about three times the height of the bulb itself. *Garden Guide, The Amateur Gardeners' Handbook* (1946), fine-tunes this advice: "In lighter, sandier soils, plant deeper; in medium soils plant by the rule, and in heavier soils plant a little shallower (perhaps twice the height of the bulb)." Why the differences? Bulbs have to work twice as hard—perhaps too hard—to push their foliage through heavy, compacted clay, whereas the rise through sand is easy. Also, in a winter freeze-thaw cycle, a bulb can more easily be heaved out of sandy soil, so deeper planting offers better protection. And it's smart to place bulbs a bit farther down in sandy soil because the soil drains so quickly, and farther down is where the moisture is.

Protect Bulbs in a Plunging Bed

▪ Extra bulbs need never go to waste. So if you bought more bulbs for fall planting than you can handle, or if snow arrives early, or if you encounter an end-of-season bulb sale that you can't resist, try preserving them in a "plunging bed." First, pot up all of the bulbs just as you would for forcing, with the bulb partially emerging from the soil an inch from the top of the pot. Plastic would be a wiser choice than clay in this case, because clay pots will absorb moisture and crack from the pressure of freezing-thawing action.

Then make your plunging bed, following the directions from Master Gardener Carl Walter, of Hamburg, New York, who remembers his uncle describing a "plunging bed" used when he worked for a bulb grower in Rochester. (In cold-winter regions such as New England and northern New York State, place this plunging bed on the eastern or sheltered side of your house or garage.)

"First, you dig a pit at least four times the depth of the pots for the bulbs [2 to 3 feet]," Carl says. "Then, place coarse ashes or loose soil on the bottom of the pit,

Plant Petite Bulbs First

Plant bulbs as early in the fall as possible, especially small bulbs such as grape hyacinths or glory-of-the-snow (*Chionodoxa luciliae*), advises *Garden Guide, The Amateur Gardeners' Handbook* (1946). However, it is acceptable "to go to December for the more vigorous, larger varieties." So when you're in a rush and out of time to plant all the bulbs you bought at that great bulb sale, put the smallest ones in the soil first, and save the larger ones for your next planting session.

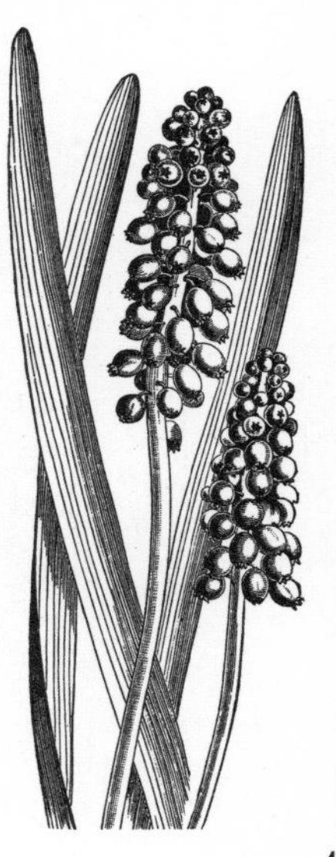

about the depth of one pot, to ensure drainage. Set the potted bulbs on this layer, and place an empty pot upside down over each pot. Then cover the whole trench with fine ashes or soil and leave them until spring." When you dig out the pots in spring, new shoots will have formed (protected by the inverted pot), and they will soon green up when they see some light. Refill the plunging bed with the soil you removed from it the preceding season. Cover it with mulch or plant some annuals there if the site is suitable. It will be easy to dig out the soil again when the time rolls around to protect your bulbs.

Glad to Grow Glads

■ Gladioli have fallen somewhat out of favor today because of their close association with funeral parlor flower arrangements, says Scott Kunst, editor of *Old House Journal* and an expert on old bulbs and historic gardens. Yet gladioli were among the favorite bulbs of Victorian gardeners in England and America. Follow this advice from old-time horticulturists for growing gladioli successfully.

Seek top-quality bulbs. Select corms (bulblike structures) that are very firm. Some local garden centers offer gladiolus corms, but since they are not as popular as they once were, you may need to shop from mail-order suppliers (for listings, see Resources on page 349).

Prepare a nice bed. Prepare the planting bed by loosening the soil, mixing in aged compost, and adding a high-phosphate fertilizer labeled for bulbs, in the amount recommended on the package. (If you think the soil has been frequently amended in the past, it is always advisable to get a soil nutrient test through an extension office or a commercial source.) Organic growers often add rock phosphate every 3 or 4 years to maintain the available phosphorus content. This is done by broadcasting a light sprinkling of the product over the soil surface. Aged compost is always a good soil amendment and may account for up to one-third of a soil mix.

Set the depth right. Plant corms 5 to 9 inches deep (on the shallow side if the soil is heavy clay; deeper in light or sandy soil). Deep planting is especially helpful for gladioli, because the plants are top-heavy, and planting deeply provides some support. Deep planting also keeps the corms cooler and moister, conditions they require for best growth.

Set up a support system. Install stakes or plant supports early in the season, since these plants tend to flop. Propping methods include sticking pea brush into the soil among the plants, setting up stakes and twine along rows of gladioli, and planting sturdy flowers such as marigolds, calendulas, zinnias, pinks, or sedum in front of the glads. Tomato cages or 12-inch wire fencing may also be used to prop glads.

Water with care. Gladioli need lots of water, so don't let the soil crust over around your glads, or precious water will run off instead of soaking in. Don't water from overhead with a hose, as this will compact the soil surface. To maximize water penetration around glads, mulch the soil at the base of the plants, and use a watering wand to introduce water gently at soil level.

Multiply Your Wealth

▪ If you live in a cold-winter area, don't spend precious dollars buying new gladiolus bulbs each year. Instead try this technique for lifting and storing the bulbs over winter from *The Gardener's Bed-Book* (1921). According to the author, Richardson Wright, you can preserve—and even increase—your supply of glads by taking advantage of their prolific nature. "Gladiolus [are] investments. Like picking up money in the street is the increase of the Gladiolus. And one of these early April days . . . I sit amid the heaps [of bulb corms] and count my gold . . . And each year . . . the Gladiolus patch grows bigger . . . For each bulb is a seasoned, gilt-edged investment . . . Would that my banker could accept it for collateral!"

Lift your bulbs in fall, break off the new corms on the side of the main bulbs, and store them all in sawdust in a cool place. Plant in spring—both large and small bulbs—and stagger the plantings over several weeks in late spring to increase the bloom period.

Helping Glads Survive the Winter

GLADIOLI ARE usually not hardy in Zone 5 or colder, so put some corms in storage indoors over winter. After the plants flower, let them dry for about 3 weeks—don't water the plants during this period. When the foliage has died down, lift the corms and separate the new corms from the old. (Unlike other types of bulbs, the old corms of gladioli will not resprout from year to year, but they produce new corms each season that grow and flower the following year.) Set the corms in a warm, dry place. Once the corms are dry, brush off any soil still clinging to them, and store them in a container filled with peat moss or sawdust at about 50°F. Since some gladioli will overwinter successfully even in Zone 5, leave at least a few corms in place in the garden. You may be pleasantly surprised.

Support Opportunities for Gladioli

▪ According to *Garden Guide, The Amateur Gardeners' Handbook* (1946), the advantage of gladioli is that they require minimal space but give maximum effect. They grow well among shrubs—try planting them in front of and between shrubs if there is some open space. Remember that these bulbs do need at least 6 hours of sun daily. While they will do fine placed beside a shrub or support so that they get half a day of direct sun, they should not be so close to the shrub that they are *under* its branches.

You can also include gladioli in vegetable gardens, taking advantage of the plant supports that you've installed for your vegetable crops. Plant glads in a straight row on the eastern, southern, or western side of a row of caged tomatoes, or along a fence where climbing peas or beans are growing. If you have a raised vegetable bed, plant the gladioli around the outside edge of the bed, where the bed will support them. Or line them up next to sturdy plants such as brussels sprouts, cabbages, broccoli, or bush beans.

Force Bulbs for Winter Color

Plan ahead this fall to give yourself a treat in late winter—pots of daffodils, tulips, or hyacinths blooming inside the house. The process, called *forcing*, is easy to do, although exact timing is difficult. In *The Gardener's Bed-Book* (1929), Richardson Wright notes, "There is more good luck than marksmanship in this game."

To prepare bulbs for late-winter bloom, pot them up in late fall in plastic or clay pots. Although pots that are slightly wider than deep are best, bulbs are tolerant of many variables, and any pots with drainage holes will do. Use a light potting soil, such as one of the commercial mixes labeled for growing bulbs. Fill the pots to 1 to 2 inches from the rims with the mix. Place the bulbs in the pots, close together and only partially covered by the mix—the top half of the bulbs should be above soil level. Store the pots in an area that can be kept about 40°F for about 2 months. (The time varies according to the type of bulb.) An attached garage, an unheated area of the cellar, or a refrigerator can all serve for this chilling period.

After the chilling period, bring the pots into an area with indirect light and temperatures between 55° and 65°F, and begin to water regularly to stimulate growth. Once the shoots begin to turn green, provide direct sunlight or bright daylight, or supplement with artificial lighting. To prolong flowering, keep the potted bulbs cool, ideally 55°F, at night. (Daytime temperatures may be warmer, but any flowering plants or bulbs last longer if you maintain your home on the cool side.) Here are instructions from *The Gardener's Bed-Book* for forcing bulbs as gifts or for decorating your house for holidays or special events: "Prepare 3 times as many pots as you need for the event and stagger the times you start them." Thus if the average time for a narcissus or tulip to bloom is 6 weeks from the time you bring it in from cold storage, bring some in at 8 weeks and some at 7, 6, 5, and 4 weeks.

If you don't have an unheated area or enough extra refrigerator space for chilling the potted bulbs, take this advice from cut-flower grower Roxanne McCoy, owner of Lilies of the Field, in West Falls, New York: "Pot up bulbs for forcing in plastic pots in late fall or early winter. Layer different bulbs in the same pot if you wish," Roxanne explains. "Then put the pots outside, right against the foundation of your house, with one foot of mulch such as chopped leaves, wood mulch, sawdust, or straw on top. Bring them inside about six weeks before the date when you want the bulbs to be in bloom."

Frost Protection for Foxtail Lilies

Foxtail lilies (*Eremurus* spp.) produce spectacular flowers in early summer, but they can be challenging to grow in areas that have unpredictable spring frosts, says cut-flower grower Roxanne McCoy. "They are winter-hardy but not spring-frost-hardy," Roxanne says. But don't shy away from growing foxtail lilies. Follow these old-time methods (plus one modern method) for preventing late-frost damage.

Mulch them with ashes. "A mound of wood ashes drawn over the crown or a watertight box filled with dry leaves will give winter protection," notes *The New Garden Encyclopedia* (1945). The idea is to provide a layer of protection to buffer the plants from exposure to changing temperatures and to slow them down from emerging too early.

Today, however, we know that wood ashes can raise soil pH. That could be good for foxtail lilies, because they do like alkaline soil. However, adding wood ashes repeatedly to the soil can drive the pH too high for any plants to grow well. So if you mulch your foxtail lilies, alternate between leaves and ashes from year to year. And if you're in doubt about how the ashes are affecting your soil, take a soil test. Test kits are available from Cooperative Extension offices in most states, or check at a local garden center.

Just use pine boughs. *Garden Guide, The Amateur Gardeners' Handbook* (1946), recommends covering the beds with homemade mats, made by weaving twine or cord with straw or reeds—but also notes that pine boughs are a simpler choice, if available. Roxanne McCoy concurs and uses the pine bough method: "Since I grow a lot of foxtail lilies, I don't mulch my foxtail lilies until after Christmas, when there are a lot of discarded holiday trees along the roadside," says Roxanne. Roxanne gathers a few trees, which gives her a plentiful supply of evergreen boughs for mulching. "They provide just the right amount of buffer, with air space so that the young plants aren't smothered in spring," she says. One tree should supply more than enough boughs to mulch your patch of foxtail lilies.

Let Foxtail Lilies Stand Tall

THE FLOWERS of foxtail lilies bloom atop stems that can reach as tall as 8 feet, but unless you provide support, those tall stems may blow flat on a windy day. To keep your lilies standing tall, plant them among sturdy shrubs or surround them with cages or a stakes-and-twine support frame early in the season, instructs *The New Garden Encyclopedia* (1945). The foliage will hide these supports as the season progresses.

Bring Back Old-Time Bulb Beauties

■ Thanks to collectors of heirloom bulbs, two popular old-time tender bulbs are widely available today. These bulbs are easy to grow in pots, just as they were over a century ago.

Tuberoses. These fragrant, long-blooming beauties were grown in Williamsburg in 1730, when they were common in most gardens. You will probably have to order tuberoses (*Polianthes tuberosa*) by mail and grow them in pots in order to bring them inside for overwintering. One unusual aspect of growing tuberoses is that you don't replant the "mother bulb" from year to year, as you do with tulips and gladioli. Instead, you discard the large bulbs and replant the small offsets or bulblets. Or you can let the commercial growers do the work for you (they grow their plants from seed) and buy tuberoses already potted and ready to bloom each year.

Rain lilies. Though not as widely available as tuberoses, rain lilies (*Zephyranthes candida*) would probably be more popular if they were hardier. As it is, these native South American bulbs are grown mostly in the Southeast, forming short, attractive clumps of pastel lily-shaped flowers. In colder climates, they make attractive indoor plants in a bright window or under artificial lights. The plant has the nickname *storm lily* because it tends to flower in cloudy weather.

Best Locations for Lilies

■ Lilies offer spectacular summer flowers, but should you plant them in your perennial garden or in a shrub border? *Garden Guide, The Amateur Gardeners' Handbook* (1946), offers ways to use lilies in both settings.

◆ "The wild yellow or Canada [*Lilium canadense*], the Turkscap [*L. superbum*], and the yellow speciosum [Japanese] or Henryi [Henry] succeed admirably in beds of Rhododendrons."

◆ "The Goldband . . . [*L. auratum*] should be planted among shrubs so that the roots are continually shaded, and where a fair degree of moisture is maintained."

◆ "The Coral . . . [*L. pumilum*] [is] excellent planted among ferns, which furnish an excellent landscape effect besides."

◆ "The Madonna [*L. candidum*] grows nicely by itself and is most useful for clumps under pergolas or as edging for walks . . . Superb combined with *Delphinium* or *Aconitum*."

Get More Lilies Free

■ When transplanting or lifting lilies to fertilize or store them, look for the little scales or bulblets on the sides of the larger bulbs. These are baby lilies waiting to grow. If you want to increase your lilies and your budget is limited, do what gardeners did in the early part of the 20th century and coddle these babies into becoming full-size lily plants. Gently remove the scales from the bulbs. Plant the little bulblets in a holding bed of rich soil in a partly shaded location. Plant the bulblets about ½ inch deep, spaced a few inches apart. Water them regularly and control weeds for the first two seasons, and you should be rewarded by an abundance of lilies—at the right price.

Disbud for Bigger Dahlias

■ If you want bigger dahlias (or apples or roses), apply this theory from old-time experts: There are only so many nutrients and so much water to go around, so if you want a big flower or fruit, you'd better limit how many share it all. The practice of snipping off some buds to stimulate production of large flowers or fruit is called *disbudding.*

The Home Garden magazine (May 1943) recommends leaving the terminal (tallest) bud on each dahlia plant and removing the side buds. This will produce a tall plant with a large flower, and you may need to fasten the tall stem to a stake as it grows. For smaller-flowered dahlia varieties, where you want more flowers on a bushier plant, remove the terminal buds and leave the side buds.

Rediscover an "Old Friend" for Dahlias

■ A great plant combination from the late 1800s still packs a punch today: bright dahlias surrounded by perilla (*Perilla frutescens*), a dramatic purple foliage plant that has recently made a comeback. Perilla was popular in Victorian times because of its generous tendency to self-seed and provide contrasts in bedding-plant schemes. But for years it was out of fashion, and gardeners from the 1930s to the 1980s might have known perilla only as a hand-me-down plant. Now you'll find perilla for sale at garden centers among trendy "new" tropicals or annuals, especially those that promote container gardening.

To re-create this old-time combination with class, plant dahlias at the back of a border with a line of perilla in front of them. In front of the perilla, try a row of scarlet or white zonal geraniums or gold-leaved feverfew (*Tanacetum parthenium*) or another yellow foliage plant. Edge this planting with verbena.

To give the old combo a new twist, plant it in a large container or planter on your patio or deck, or place it as a focal point in the garden. (Note that dahlias develop large root systems, so you need a large, deep planter. This is not a window-

Dahlias Need Room to Reproduce

EVEN IN THE 1930S, expert gardeners understood the importance of spacing dahlia tubers properly. Given well-drained soil and sufficient space, one dahlia tuber can produce 5 to 15 tubers in just one season, notes *The New Garden Encyclopedia* (1945). "This shows the gross feeding capacity of the plant, whose rootlets shoot out from the tubers in all directions." What is the proper spacing for dahlias? Depending on their height, you should plant individual tubers 2 to 3 feet apart, the tallest dahlias requiring the wider spacing.

Give Dahlias a Private Pantry

DAHLIAS NEED lots of nutrients for best bloom. "To grow an extensive root system and large plant in a short time," advises *The Home Garden* magazine (May 1943), "you may want to provide fertilizer on an individual plant basis. To do this, dig the planting hole several inches deeper than the plant itself requires. [Dahlia roots should be set 4 to 5 inches below the soil surface, so in this example dig the hole about 8 inches deep.] Then add a shovel full of aged manure and a handful of bone meal into each hole. Cover the fertilizer with 3 inches of soil."

The New Garden Encyclopedia (1945) also offers instructions for planting dahlias.

You will need:

- 6- to 7-foot-long wooden or bamboo stakes, one for each dahlia tuber
- Dahlia tubers
- Soft materials for ties (such as strips of cloth, pipe cleaners, or pieces of panty hose)

Step 1. Pound a stake 18 inches into the soil next to the spot where you plan to plant a dahlia.

Step 2. Dig a hole 6 inches deep next to the stake.

Step 3. Lay a dahlia tuber flat on the soil, with the new growth or sprout end nearest the stake.

Step 4. Cover the tuber with a couple of inches of soil.

Step 5. As the plant emerges, add soil gradually, so that 2 to 3 inches of the sprout shows above soil level at all times. Continue until the hole is filled to ground level.

Step 6. As the stem continues to push upward, tie it to the stake loosely every 9 to 12 inches, using soft materials that will not cut the stem.

■ *The Home Garden* magazine also recommends fertilizing dahlias in midsummer. Spray with fish emulsion or seaweed extract.

box or hanging-basket planting!) Simply plant one central dahlia in a pot 2½ to 3 feet in diameter, with three to five perilla plants in a ring around it. If you'd like, embellish this container planting with trailing plants such as licorice plant (*Helichrysum petiolare*).

Simple Paper Plant Ties

■ Dahlias and heavy-flowered perennials look their best when you discreetly tie the tall flower stems to sturdy stakes. Some gardeners buy Velcro fasteners or other commercial plant ties, but you can save yourself the bother of a trip to the garden center for these supplies by using old-fashioned paper and wire. *The New Garden Encyclopedia* (1945) explains how: Simply fold a 4- to 6-inch-wide strip of green or neutral-colored construction paper or other heavy paper (such as butcher paper) in half lengthwise and put a piece of copper or stainless steel wire down the center. Use a glue stick or household glue to seal the folded edges of the paper together. Twist the paper around the wire to form a sturdy plant tie. Another advantage of making homemade ties is that you can fashion them at any length you need.

Growing Sensational Roses

Few flowering plants excite such strong opinions and passionate feelings as roses. Inspirations for poets through the centuries, roses are the symbol of romantic love. Whether you're a rose aficionado or a novice rose grower, you'll find great ideas for all-natural rose care in the following tips from rose growers of days gone by.

Natural Secrets for Feeding Roses

■ Despite what you may have been told, it is *not* necessary to use synthetic fertilizers for great roses. Instead, try these tricks cited in *Garden Guide, The Amateur Gardeners' Handbook* (1946).

Sawdust scheme. A prizewinning rose grower from Sacramento, California, recommended adding great volumes of compost and mulch on top of the soil every year. This grower layered on several inches of sawdust and shavings around her roses. To overcome the tendency of woody mulches to use up soil nitrogen, "just add handfuls of cottonseed meal under the mulch to replace the Nitrogen it uses to decay." As a final touch, spray the foliage with a liquid seaweed solution.

Hairy help. Try stirring cuttings of human hair into the soil near roses for a natural nitrogen boost. (You can ask to collect hair clippings from a local barbershop.)

Seed supplement. Another rose grower recommended putting a handful of seedpods in the soil near each plant, as they provide "concentrated food energy." You can collect seeds from any perennial or tree, as long as they're not weedy plants. Cover the seeds with soil or mulch to prevent them from sprouting.

More favorites. Other popular rosebush amendments mentioned in *Garden Guide, The Amateur Gardeners' Handbook,* include banana peels, coffee grounds, guano (bat manure), and bonemeal. In all of these cases, bury the products a few inches below the soil surface, for easier decomposition and to avoid any interest from passing animals that might be curious. However, be careful not to disturb the plant roots.

Time the Rose Hip Harvest Right

■ Rose hips can be a valuable source of vitamin C, but only if you harvest them at the right time, notes George Graves in *Medicinal Plants* (1900). The author specifically cited the "agreeable acid taste" of the common dog rose (*Rosa canina*), but his harvesting advice applies to all shrub roses that produce hips. Ideal harvesting time is the month of

September (in Zone 7 and north), before frost. The hips will persist on the plants through winter (and many songbirds love to eat them), but after frosts strike, the hips lose much of their acidity, and thus their vitamin content.

To make rose hip tea, pick the hips in fall, cut them into pieces, and dry them on a screen or tray covered with a clean cloth, in an attic or somewhere the temperature remains above 70°F for a week or two. Bring to a boil 1 tablespoon dried hips in 1½ cups water, and then steep for 15 minutes to make one vitamin-rich cup of tea.

Time-Tested Rose Care Tips

■ Way back in 1821, author William Cobbett of *The American Gardener* offered these useful tips for rose growers, which are still sound advice today.

Propagate by suckers. Most shrub roses and climbers propagate easily from suckers that sprout near old stems during the summer. Dig up these suckers in fall, and replant them where you would like them to grow. "In the spring they are cut to the ground, and in the next year they *blow* [bloom]." In climates with severe winters (Zone 5 and north), revise this process by root-pruning (severing the sucker from the parent plant) in fall, and then leaving the sucker in place over winter; transplant in spring.

Don't try this technique with hybrid roses that are grafted onto a rootstock. For these roses, remove all growth that emerges below the bud graft.

Pamper the roots. Remember that roses can't produce healthy foliage and beautiful blooms unless the soil is excellent. To give them a good start, seek out well-drained soil. Roses can grow in a variety of soils, including clay soil, as long as they don't suffer from wet feet. When you prepare a planting site for roses, work plenty of well-aged compost into the bed. (A good goal is for one-third of the planting area to be aged compost mixed into the parent soil.)

Prune for prettiness. Except when they are trained against walls or over bowers, roses "should be kept cut down low for, when they get long stems and limbs they, like peach trees, not only look ugly but bear few flowers, and those very mean ones." Prune your roses to 12 inches or shorter, and remove all dead or weak wood, "without leaving any ugly stubs." Most pruning instructors recommend making pruning cuts above a bud that faces outward, in the direction you would desire for future growth. Make the cut at an angle, parallel to the direction the bud is pointing.

OLD-TIME HUMOR

Are You a Gardening "Crank"?

If you have ever watched passionate plant collectors at a plant auction or gone shopping with one (or *been* one), you know how obsessive a plant person can be. With tongue in cheek, *Garden Guide, The Amateur Gardeners' Handbook* (1946), describes the phenomenon: "First we become interested in a particular flower because of a shape or color or thrifty habit we admire . . . Our interest broadens when we get a great many varieties of the same . . . Finally we are even interested in its botanical relatives. It is then that we become 'cranks.' "

Brickbats for Better Drainage

Roses must have "a steady drainage of surplus moisture away from their roots," instructs *Garden Guide, The Amateur Gardeners' Handbook* (1946)—and the same may be said of many other garden flowers. According to the guide, you can improve drainage by adding several inches of drainage material, such as "rough cinders, cobble stones, or brickbats" in the bottom of the beds, with an outlet into tile drains. (*Brickbats* is an old-time term for broken pieces of bricks.) If you are short on brickbats, you can make a rose bed on a base of gravel or drainage tiles. (If you plan to install several large beds or a whole home landscape, you'll probably need professional help and suitable equipment, such as a backhoe.)

Even to install a single bed of this type, you will have to be a strong digger. Dig out your planned planting area from 18 to 24 inches deep, and then dig a trench at least 3 feet deep that will channel subsurface water away from the planting bed. Put drainage tiles in the trench, and then backfill the trench with soil. Spread grass seed or mulch over this back-filled area. In the bottom of the planting area, first spread out a 4- to 6-inch layer of coarse gravel. Fill the bed with a compost-rich soil mixture, and continue adding the soil-compost mixture to at least 6 inches above soil level (this is necessary because the bed will settle over time). A planting bed with a drainage outlet is also good for Mediterranean or desert plants, which also require excellent drainage. For these tough plants, use a leaner soil mixture than you would for roses.

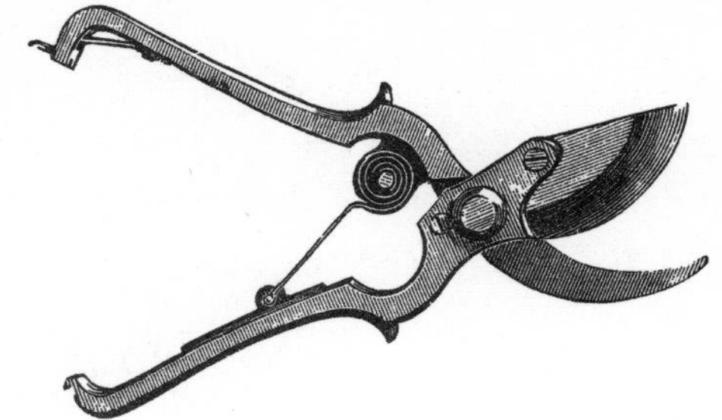

Pruning Produces Big Blossoms

Pruning roses in spring offers two big benefits, says *Garden Guide, The Amateur Gardeners' Handbook* (1946): bigger flowers and better-behaved plants. Pruning limits the number of flower buds, and "the fewer blooms that are produced, the better they are." The book also notes, "Of course, anyone who is satisfied with thin rags of color instead of real Roses does not need to prune."

Rosarian Steve Ruback, of Snyder, New York, teaches gardening classes and has grown more than 250 roses around his home. Steve stresses that incorrect pruning, especially where the climate is cold, can be fatal. "Timing is everything. Don't prune them all the way down in the fall or go at it too soon in the spring," Steve says. "The roses will die back from wherever you make the cut, and if you do it in the fall, the roses will die right back to the ground during a hard winter. The old adage 'Prune roses when forsythias bloom' is a good rule of thumb for most parts of the country, because those plants blossom when the soil has warmed enough that there will probably not be a severe killing frost."

How to prune is a fine art, according to many rosarians, and it varies according to the type of rose—shrub, hybrid

TRASH OR TREASURE

Join the Rootery Club

IT'S TRAGIC WHEN a strong windstorm uproots a tree or blows down large branches, but you can turn that tragedy into a creative gardening opportunity. Steal an idea from English gardens of the 1800s and make a rootery (also called a *stumpery*). The idea is to use roots or stumps as a design feature of a garden (English gardeners used them instead of rocks), accented by woodland plants, such as ferns or vines.

Start your rootery by building a soil mound, perhaps at the edge of a woodland or naturalized area. The size of the mound depends on how many stumps or roots you have to work with. A typical mound would be oval or kidney-shaped, 10 feet long, 4 to 5 feet wide, and 1 to 2 feet tall. (If you have subsoil or fill soil available, you can use it for the base of the mound, but be sure to provide 1 foot of topsoil or a compost-and-soil mixture on top of it.

Place the tree parts—stumps, roots, or large branches—on top of and partway into the soil. They should lie sideways, as if fallen in place, and be partially submerged, so that they look as if they have been there awhile.

Look for pockets or curves in which to plant ferns or other woodland plants, such as bergenias, corydalis, and bleeding hearts (*Dicentra* spp.). For additional garden appeal, add moss, rocks, and trailing vines, such as ivy or clematis, which thrives with its roots in the shade as long as it can climb into the sunlight.

tea, climber, and more. For any kind of rose, the knowledge starts with understanding *why* you are pruning—to maintain an attractive shape, increase flower size, minimize disease due to overcrowding and poor air circulation, or get a large climber or shrub under control. Once that is established, you will have a better idea where to make the cuts. Steve explains further, "People are overly concerned about the commonly quoted rule about cutting above a five-leafed branchlet, at an angle pointing in the direction you want the next branch to grow. This is done to increase flowering after a rose has bloomed. It does increase flowers, but frankly the shrub doesn't care if you make a cut right there, or at what angle you cut it. The important thing is to prune it to remove old flowers, and let some air and sunlight in."

Decorative Design Ideas

GARDENERS in bygone days worked just as hard as we do to create beautiful gardens that are unique and original. Those gardeners knew that what makes a garden distinctive is not just what you plant but how you combine plants and select garden ornaments and art to highlight your gardens. Peruse these garden design tips from our 18th- and 19th-century predecessors, and you may find inspiration for a "new" garden style.

Discover the Benefits of Island Planting

■ Some advice from *The Encyclopedia of Gardening* (1850) may help you decide where to locate garden beds in your landscape. The predictable choice is to dig beds along the foundation of your house or at the perimeter of your property. But the encyclopedia instead calls "grouping on turf" the most elegant approach to plantings. We would call this planting an *island bed,* which is a bed located in the midst of a lawn area. Island beds of mixed shrubs and perennials are highly versatile, and with an island bed, you can choose the site that has exactly the type of sun exposure you want. The encyclopedia points out an additional advantage of island beds: As your perennials mature and produce larger clumps, you can easily dig, divide, and enlarge the bed simply by "appropriating a part of the turf"—that is to say, convert more lawn at the edges of the island into garden. As your garden grows, you'll enjoy even more flowering pleasure, while slowly but surely reducing your mowing chores over time.

Plant a Poetry Garden

■ Victorian gardeners excelled at developing theme gardens using plants named in poems or plays written by Shakespeare, Chaucer, and other well-known writers. For example, a Shakespeare garden could include hellebores, columbines, daffodils, violets, tulips, poppies, black-eyed Susans, and, of course, roses. If you're not a fan of these poets, you could take a modern approach to this Victorian gardening custom by taking inspiration from contemporary literature that your family enjoys, such as the Tolkien trilogy or the Harry Potter books. Challenge the readers in your family to find plants named in those books, and design a garden using them.

Try a Topiary

■ To complement a flower garden, try adding a topiary nearby. Topiary is pruning or carving shrubs into shapes, such as pyramids, spirals, birds, and other animals. This horticultural art form is centuries old but is still popular today, especially in formal garden settings. Boxwood and yew are common choices for topiary, but holly and hemlock also adapt well to this art form.

If you aspire to be the Edward Scissorhands of your neighborhood, practice first on expendable shrubs that are not in prime locations on your lawn.

OLD-FASHIONED FAVORITES

Flowers as Hedges

WHILE ALL GARDENS look beautiful when they have a wall or hedge as a backdrop, there is not always room for formal shrub hedges. Instead, try the dooryard garden look, which was fashionable in the early part of the 1900s. Back up your flower garden with a row of tall flowers or flowering vines on a trellis. Good choices include love-lies-bleeding (*Amaranthus caudatus*), hollyhock (*Alcea rosea*), or a row of climbing sweet peas on a trellis.

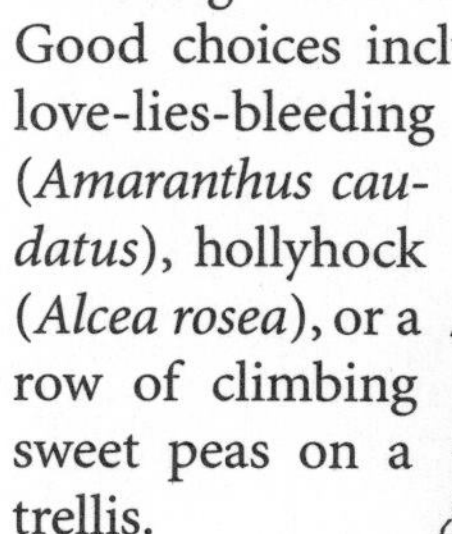

An ideal opportunity would be to prune deciduous or evergreen trees or shrubs growing in a nearby field—after asking the owner's permission, of course. If you're practicing on a deciduous shrub, clip in late spring after the plant has leafed out. (This is an exception to general rules for pruning many kinds of deciduous shrubs, which are usually pruned in late winter or early spring, when the shrubs are dormant.)

☞ TRASH OR TREASURE ☜

Never Lose the Name Game

How many times have you thought you would remember a plant name—and then gone blank? Labeling the plants in your garden is important, but commercial plastic plant labels get lost or broken and are too expensive.

Don't give up, though. Take a tip from frugal gardeners of the past, and make your own plant labels from everyday items

Aluminum pie tins. Cut a tin up into long strips. Use a large nail or a ballpoint pen to mark the letters (as indentations in the soft aluminum) of the plant name.

Discarded metal venetian blinds. Cut the slats into the lengths you need. Mark these with a nail or pen, as you would a pie tin.

Tongue depressors. You wouldn't want to recycle used tongue depressors for the purpose, but you can buy a package inexpensively at a drugstore or medical supply outlet. These make sturdy, long-lasting labels. Mark the names clearly with a pencil.

White detergent or bleach bottles. Cut them into strips, and write the plant names on the strips with a permanent marker.

After practice, when you're ready to tackle topiary in your own yard, start with a shrub or tree that has already sustained some damage, advises second-generation nurseryman Skip Murray, of Orchard Park, New York. Try to find a shrub in your yard that has a broken limb, or that has a poor shape or poor growth habit. "The trick," says Skip, "is to see the shape that's suggested in the shrub, rather than forcing it into some other form." Start with a plant of the height you desire. Observe where the growth is thick and where it's thin. Using your pruners, start trimming, working to exaggerate whatever shape seems to suggest itself—perhaps a ball or a spiral or a pyramid. For example, you might want to make the thin part thinner, and clip the thick parts at the ends very lightly to maintain the thickness. It may take a couple of years, pruning several times a year, to create the shape you want. And after that, you'll need to prune as needed to maintain the shape.

"Topiaries were high-maintenance novelties in the old days, when there were hired gardeners on estates, and even more so now, because nobody has as much free time as they want for pastimes like gardening," Skip says. He recommends that people choose slow-growing shrubs for topiary and that they keep in mind that topiary is not easy. "Topiary may be fun," says Skip, "but don't start practicing in the front yard."

If you'd like to take an easier and more modern approach to creating topiary, check at your local garden center for topiary frames that you can set over a shrub and use as a guide to pruning the shrub to shape.

Make a Setting Fit for Ferns

▪ Ferns can add a classic 19th-century feeling to a home landscape, even if you have a contemporary home. An old-fashioned edging accentuates the effect, and an easy one to try is a Victorian fern "basket," which is actually a raised bed created by weaving grapevines through a framework of rustic sticks.

You'll have plenty of choices of ferns for a fern basket. Most ferns require moist soil, good drainage, and protection from direct sunlight. Soil pH should be neutral to slightly acid (6.2 to 6.9). See "Ferns for a Fern Basket" on page 322 for suggestions.

You'll need to prepare a planting mix to fill your fern basket, rather than using regular garden soil. *The New Garden Encyclopedia* (1945) recommends that gardeners prepare a mix of equal parts leaf mold, garden loam or topsoil, coarse sand, and peat moss for growing ferns. This mix should work well as a simulation of the natural soil in which many ferns thrive.

To make a bed that's about 5 to 8 feet in diameter, you will need 75 to 100 feet of grapevines and 15 to 25 sticks. Choose sticks at least ½ inch in diameter and 15 to 18 inches long. Soak the grapevines in a tub until they're easy to bend and shape. While they soak, map out the shape of the bed (use a rope or flour), and use a mallet to pound in the sticks. Leave about 1 foot of each stick protruding above soil level. Weaving the grapevines through the sticks takes awhile, but you'll probably find it an enjoyable task. You can use natural-colored twine to tie the ends of the vines to the sticks, but it's not necessary.

When the basket is complete, fill it halfway with the soil mix, and plant the ferns. Place small rocks and pieces of tree roots among the foliage or next to the basket. Keep in mind that Victorian gardeners didn't try to re-create nature in their garden designs, but rather they used natural elements to decorate and enhance their plantings.

Use grapevines to weave a Victorian fern basket, where you'll plant a grouping of ferns accented with rocks and logs.

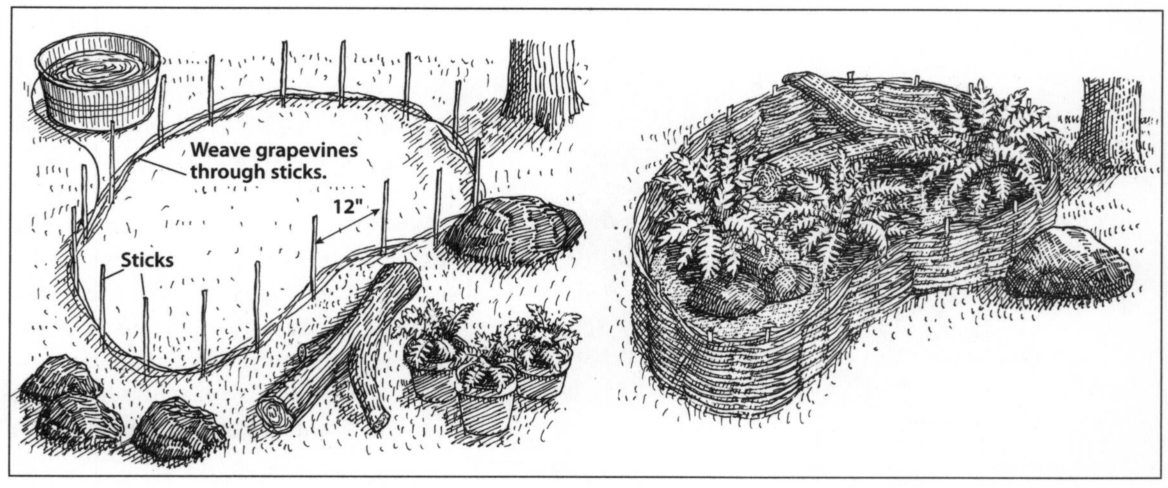

Build a Victorian Rockery

Rocky soil doesn't have to ruin your gardening plans. In fact, you can turn a pile of rocks into a highlight of your garden by following the fashion of 1890 and turning those darn rocks into a rockery. Victorian gardeners piled up large, irregular stones in a sort of mini-mountain, and then planted alpine and miniature plants in the nooks and crannies around the rocks.

Ferns for a Fern Basket

THE FOLLOWING FERNS are good choices for a fern basket, or for most garden beds. *Caution:* Many ferns are endangered or threatened, so buy ferns from a reputable nursery rather than digging them from the wild.

- Hart's tongue fern (*Asplenium bulbiferum*)
- Lady fern (*Athyrium filix-femina*)
- Sensitive fern (*Onoclea sensibilis*)
- Cinnamon fern (*Osmunda cinnamomea*)
- Christmas fern (*Polystichum acrostichoides*)
- New York fern (*Thelypteris noveboracensis*)
- Marsh fern (*T. palustris*)

For your first attempt at a rockery, don't build the pile higher than chest height. You'll need between 30 and 50 rocks of fairly uniform size, as well as a couple of 5-gallon buckets filled with gravel or small stones. Have some topsoil and compost available too.

Pile the rocks pyramid-style, with the outside slopes no steeper than 45 degrees, so that rocks will not roll off the pile. *Caution:* Working with rocks can result in injuries. Always wear gloves and sturdy shoes. Don't pull out rocks from underneath other rocks in a pile, or you may end up with smashed fingers. Lift a rock only if you can do so without strain; otherwise, enlist a helper. When you lift rocks, keep your back straight and your weight centered, and lift with your legs.

When you're pleased with the looks of your rockery, create some planting pockets among the rocks. Mix equal parts topsoil and compost together. Wear gloves, and pack the mixture into the crevices between rocks. Overfill the spaces, because much of the mixture will settle or be washed away during the first rains.

Plant into the soil-filled crevices, placing the roots far back into the crevices. Choose small, drought-tolerant plants such as ajugas, sea thrift (*Armeria maritima*), basket-of-gold (*Aurinia saxatilis*), creeping baby's-breath (*Gypsophila repens*), dwarf junipers, creeping phlox (*Phlox stolonifera*), and hens-and-chicks (*Sempervivum tectorum*). Set the plants about 2 inches more deeply than you would in a ground-level planting, so that just the tops of the plants show.

Next, place a sprinkler or watering wand at the top of the pile and turn on the water supply (to simulate rain). Let the water run for 30 minutes. Much of the soil mix will wash away during this watering.

Turn off the water and repack soil mix around the roots of the plants. If you notice places where soil has washed out leaving roots exposed, move the plants to locations where there is a deeper or larger nook or crevice instead. Spread gravel or small stones over the soil mix around the plants to help hold down the soil.

Water the rockery regularly for the first few weeks or during a dry season, especially when you see any plants beginning to wilt. The rockery will probably need more frequent watering than an in-ground garden because of the small volume of soil and because the rocks will retain and reflect heat.

The Art of Garden Art

▪ Victorian gardens burst with ornamentation—the more gazing balls, sculpture, vases, arbors, and furniture that could be crammed into a space, the better. Some gardeners today also like this style, and if it suits you—go for it! But if you'd prefer to use garden art lightly in the landscape, or if your budget sets the limit on how much artwork you can use, follow these guidelines for adding garden art to a home landscape in moderation.

Find points where paths disappear. Stand at one end of a path or walkway in your yard, and focus on the point where the path curves out of sight or seems to disappear from view. Place one garden treasure right there, so it's visible from the beginning of the path. It could be a bench, fountain, statue, or trellis. The art object will lure visitors down the path to see it. Conversely, if your home landscape already has a natural focal point (such as a fountain), style a garden path to lead toward it.

Suit the ornament's size to the setting. If you have a path that is more than 75 to 100 feet long, you might choose a 5-foot urn or statue, or put a dramatic container planting on a platform at eye level. If the path is short, perhaps 25 feet, a smaller, more delicate ornament—such as a 24-inch gazing ball or 12-inch fairy figure—will be enough to attract the viewer.

Look up. Use vertical space—tree limbs, trellises, ladders, porch railings, or walls—as a framework for art. Hang a glass candleholder or birdhouse from a tree limb. Suspend a decorative hanging basket from a tree or from the porch roofline. Most often, people first see your home and garden from a distance, and features that are up high stand out more than those at ground level.

Include surprises. Place an ornament or interesting feature (birdbath, gargoyle, statue, or urn) around a corner of your house, or partially obscured by a plant, where a visitor will encounter it unexpectedly. You'll know you've succeeded if visitors exclaim, "Ahhh!" or "Oh, look!" when they spy the artwork. In an old-time garden, gardeners might have chosen a Greek statue, fairy, or Buddha figure for this purpose. You can do the same, or follow your own sense of whimsy. You might choose seashells in honor of a favorite trip, a copper dragonfly, or a rustic child's chair.

Smother That Smell

If your garden is downwind from a highway, an industrial plant, a lake or bay, manure piles, or anything else that smells unpleasant at times, apply the old-time tactic of planting fragrant plants to mask bad smells. Even if scented flowers can't completely make up for the vile odors, at least your nose gets a break once in a while!

Try planting the fragrant plants listed below in your garden and in containers. "But don't just stick them in the middle of the garden," says garden writer Sally Cunningham, of East Aurora, New York. "Put them upwind—so the breeze passes over them on its way to you—and as close to nose level as possible. Try planting fragrant plants in a window box, next to your deck, close to your deck chair, or along the edge of the path to your garage."

PLANT NAME	DESCRIPTION	COMMENTS
Artemisias (*Artemisia* spp.)	Perennial herbs; foliage has a sharp mintlike or pungent scent	Fragrance reputed to repel some insects (*Caution:* Some species spread aggressively.)
Sweet William (*Dianthus barbatus*)	Biennial with fragrant flowers; usually grown as a self-sowing annual	Old-fashioned 'Excelsior' has sweetly scented flower clusters
Cottage pink (*D. plumarius*)	Hardy perennial; grassy foliage and spicy-smelling flowers	Place beside a path for close-up appreciation of the delicate flowers
Heliotrope (*Heliotropium arborescens*)	Annual with highly fragrant flowers; richly sweet scents of vanilla or cherries	Also called *cherry pie*
Lavenders (*Lavandula* spp.)	Popular perennial herbs with silvery foliage and upright flowerstalks	Some species only marginally hardy
Common stock (*Matthiola incana*)	Annual; flowers have distinctive spicy fragrance	Grows best in cool-summer areas, or during cool months in hot climates
Mints (*Mentha* spp.)	Vigorous perennial herbs with square stems; foliage scents include chocolate, apple, orange, and more	Plant in pots or in sunken containers in a garden bed
Nicotianas (*Nicotiana* spp. and hybrids)	Annuals related to the tobacco plant (*N. tabacum*); sweetly scented flowers	Also called *flowering tobacco;* some hybrid cultivars are scentless; choose cultivars described as fragrant
Scented geraniums (*Pelargonium* spp.)	Scented foliage; wide range of choices including lemon, rose, and coconut; flowers usually insignificant	Foliage scents reputed to repel many kinds of insect pests
Garden phlox (*Phlox paniculata*)	Popular perennial with upright stems topped with clusters of sweetly scented flowers	Fragrance carries significant distances; plants can suffer from powdery mildew, especially in shady conditions
Sages (*Salvia* spp.)	Annuals and perennials with very fragrant foliage	Some types culinary; others strictly ornamental

Be Sensibly Stylish

▪ The Victorian era was famous for lavish gardening, both in scale and style. The effects could be wonderful, but sometimes the mistakes were also on a grand scale. Many gardeners today are equally exuberant about ornamentation and lack restraint, or just need some guiding principles. Master Gardener Babbidean Huber, of Amherst, New York, an officer of the New York State Federated Garden Clubs, recommends some practical guidelines to avoid going overboard with garden ornaments.

Try the blinders test. "One focal point within the line of sight in any one bed or plant grouping is enough," Babbidean says. "To judge this, put blinders on. Face the flowerbed or planting area, and place your hands on either side of your eyes to block off peripheral vision. Look straight at the garden area or scene. Within that frame, pick an opening among the plants—preferably just off-center—for your art object."

Stick with one style. "Choose one style, one theme, and related colors and materials. A copper dragonfly won't be compatible with a brightly painted ladder and a china fairy, for example," Babbidean says. "But it would create a pleasing scene to have a copper dragonfly and a couple of other copper pieces in the same garden area. If your choice is a painted ladder, then the other ornaments you choose should also be made of wood and painted in similar colors, with a similar decorative style. If it's primitive or childlike, stick with that feeling; if it is lacquered or delicately detailed, stick with that."

Easy Disguise for Old-Time Containers

▪ Plastic and fiberglass containers for patio gardens are very convenient, but they don't always harmonize well with historic or old-fashioned homes. For a more authentic feel, you can easily disguise containers to look like natural-fiber

The Proper Birdhouse

A BIRDHOUSE IS a lovely accent piece for an ornamental garden, but don't be disappointed if an ornate birdhouse doesn't attract any tenants. *Barns, Sheds and Outbuildings* (1881) explains why this is so. "It is a mistake to have bird houses too showy and too much exposed. Most birds naturally choose a retired place for their nests, and slip into them quietly, that no enemy may discover where they live . . . An old hat, with a hole for a door, tacked by the rim against a shed will be occupied by birds sooner than a showy bird house." Indeed, Charles Kennedy, of the South Alabama Birding Association, says at least one species, the house wren, will readily nest in "a box, tin can, apron pocket, or almost anything else that resembles a nest cavity." Make sure the house is in a site sheltered from wind and rain, such as under the eaves of a roof, Charles adds.

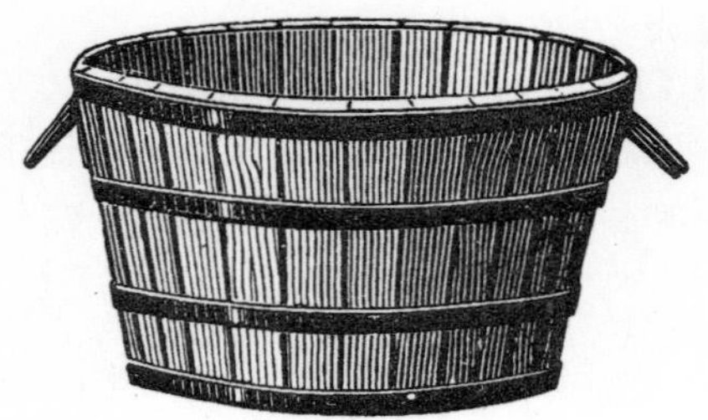

baskets—once used for everything from carrying babies and seeding the garden to harvesting food. The trick is to wrap containers with grapevines or flexible twigs and saplings, such as those of willows and shrubby dogwoods.

Start by soaking the branches in hot water or steaming them in a colander over a large pot of boiling water, such as a spaghetti pot. Soak or steam them until they bend easily. Next, select a container. You can use a plastic pot, an old wooden salad bowl, a fruit crate, or even a heavy cardboard box. Then start wrapping. If you have selected a wooden or cardboard container, you can use a staple gun to fasten the vines or twigs to the container, since it won't crack if you staple into it. To fasten twigs to plastic pots, use a hot glue gun to cover a section of the pot with a generous amount of glue, and then press the twigs into place.

Fill your rustic planters with old-fashioned favorites such as caladiums, upright dracaenas, ferns, impatiens, ivies, and ivy geraniums (*Pelargonium peltatum* hybrids). Remember that most plants require good drainage and do not tolerate standing in water, so you must provide a drainage hole in your container or use it as a cachepot (outer container) and plant into clay pots. If you use a cardboard container or a basket that could rot, line the bottom with a clay saucer.

CHAPTER 13

HOUSEPLANTS
Cultivate the Garden Within

GARDENING HAS A VENERABLE HISTORY, but growing houseplants is a comparatively recent pastime. In Colonial times, glass was scarce and expensive; consequently, windows were small and few. Storm windows were unknown, and if anyone ventured to overwinter precious flowers, they were likely to freeze on the windowsills. By the late 1800s, bay windows in Victorian houses provided ample sunlight, but houseplants struggled in the gaslit, chilly parlors of the day. Pioneering windowsill gardeners persevered and grew many kinds of houseplants. Even though our challenges are different ones, we can still benefit from some of the lessons they learned—sometimes the hard way.

HELPFUL HOUSEPLANT HINTS

EVEN THOUGH they're protected from drought, storms, and frost, houseplants don't necessarily have life easy. These plants have to put up with unnatural conditions, such as low humidity, low light, and our sometimes hit-and-miss care. We can try to replace what's missing from their rain forest or riverbank homes, but finally it will be the tough plants, carefully chosen, that survive best.

Houseplants Need Hardening Off

■ Moving houseplants outdoors for the summer can be good for the plants, but only if they make the transition gently.

Just like vegetable and flower seedlings started indoors, houseplants need to go through a hardening-off process. In *The Gardener's Bed-Book: Short and Long Pieces to Be Read in Bed by Those Who Love Green Growing Things* (1929), Richardson Wright recommends this procedure: "If a warm day comes with rain, set the houseplants out of doors for a few hours." Then bring them indoors overnight. Continue this process for a few weeks, until outdoor temperatures are favorable both during the day and at night. Making a gradual transition is important, says garden writer Sally Cunningham, of East Aurora, New York. Plants can suffer from sunburn due to the sudden increase in light, because even the brightest lighting in most homes is much dimmer than outdoor light. Another problem for houseplants set outside too early in spring is nighttime temperature changes, says Sally. "Drops of over 15 degrees, or temperatures below 55°F, are too much for most houseplants to tolerate until they have hardened off."

Don't Overheat the Houseplants

■ If you think you're providing everything right for your houseplants—correct light, watering, soil mix, and fertilization—but they seem unhealthy, the problem might be heat. An overheated house will cause houseplants, as well as people, to suffer. To keep your houseplants healthy, follow these guidelines from *The Home Garden* magazine (January 1943): "Many plants, [such as] the succulents, grape ivy and philodendron, will tolerate living-room heat of 72 to 75[°F], but will be in better health if daytime heat is near 65 with a drop to 55 or 60 at night . . . In the greenhouse the florist grows the Jerusalem Cherry, the Christmas Pepper, and the Persian Cyclamen [*Cyclamen persicum*] at 50 to 52[°F]. He finds Kalanchoe has a richer coloring at this low temperature than at 60, while the Christmas Begonia, azaleas and primroses prefer 60."

Since most of us don't have the luxury of owning a greenhouse, we have to help our houseplants survive in temperatures that are too warm for many of them. Use the following list to figure out why your houseplants aren't doing well, and which plants you should bother keeping.

Citrus family plants. Citrus plants grow well in sunny situations in the house, but thrive best if they are allowed to go slightly dry in the winter and are kept below 60°F but always above 50°F.

Cyclamens. When temperatures are above 61°F, cyclamens will droop severely, but they do very well in bright, humid conditions at temperatures from 50° to 60°F.

Gloxinias. While the tuber is sprouting, gloxinias do best at 70° to 80°F, and they tolerate equally warm temperatures once they are growing. High humidity is essential for these.

Jerusalem cherries and Christmas peppers. Both of these members of the nightshade family accept average house temperatures. Jerusalem cherries (*Solanum pseudocapsicum*) are poisonous; Christmas peppers (*Capsicum annuum* var. *annuum*) are edible, but the little peppers are extremely hot.

Kalanchoes. Try rooting cuttings of kalanchoes in a warm location (to 75°F) when you are rooting cuttings. These plants will do well outdoors during the summer. In winter, keep them at 45° to 60°F with limited water, to stimulate vigorous blooming.

Poinsettias. These holiday favorites should not be exposed to drafts or sudden temperature changes. Poinsettias prefer nighttime temperatures under 60°F and will last the longest if daytime temperatures are below 68°F.

Flowering begonias. Also called *angelwing begonias, Rieger begonias,* and *wax begonias,* these plants grow well at moderate temperatures (50° to 60°F at night; up to 75°F by day).

Finally, before you toss out any of these plants because they aren't getting that needed temperature range, remember that around your house there are many microclimates—little areas with their own specific airflows and temperatures. Use a thermometer and experiment: You might find that the kalanchoe and cyclamen that are drooping over in their current home perk right up in a new spot just a few feet away.

☞ BIZARRE BUT TRUE ☜

Just Don't Sleep with Them

MODERN RESEARCH shows that the presence of indoor plants can improve the quality of indoor air, but in the late 1800s, people wouldn't have believed it. *Window Gardening: Devoted Specially to the Culture of Flowers and Ornamental Plants, for Indoor Use and Parlor Decoration* (1878) includes this advice to readers: "Strong scented plants are injurious to have in the room at night. The Tuberose, Hyacinth, and Jessamine are too sweet and should not be patronized by invalids."

Wash but Don't Boil

▪ "Palms in the house appear to enjoy a monthly bath of soap and water," reports *The Gardener's Bed-Book* (1929), by Richardson Wright. That is true for most houseplants, which all benefit from having dust removed from their leaves and their stomata (pores in the leaves) opened up. The correct method of bathing your plants depends on the season and the size of the plant. In mild weather, once the temperature outside is above 55°F, move your plants outside onto the deck or lawn and attach a watering wand to your hose to use like a showerhead. If the plant is too big to take outside, spread plastic sheeting around its base and spray its leaves thoroughly with a handheld spray bottle of warm water. If you suspect insect infestations, spraying with a solution of ½ teaspoon dish-washing liquid in a quart bottle of water will help in most cases. Small

Wait for Water to Warm Up

HOUSEPLANTS that hail from the tropics or deserts need warmth to flourish. This practical advice from *Houseplants and Their Care* (1887), by Hugo Mulertt, will help keep your plants healthy. "Water cold from the well or pump is not suitable for plants. Rainwater is best. The best rule in all cases is to use water warm to the hands." Simply fill buckets and allow them to sit indoors overnight. This also allows chlorine in the water, which may cause brown leaf tips, to evaporate as the water warms to room temperature.

plants are easy to wash indoors or out. You can place them in the sink and wash them with warm water—or share your shower with them!

When you are bathing the plants, take care not to boil them. This advice comes from Gerry Murray Sr., owner of Murray Brothers Nursery, in Orchard Park, New York. Gerry warns that outdoor hoses that shut off at the nozzle can be full of very hot water after the sun has been shining on them for a few hours. "When hosing down any plant or even watering the soil around their roots, be sure to run the hose awhile—enough time to run all the hot water out," Gerry says. "Feel it with your hands. If it's too hot for you, the plants will get a scalding!"

Keep Drips Off Fuzzy Leaves

■ Houseplants with glossy, waxy leaves, such as camellias or jade plants, thrive when you water them with abandon. Showering is a great way to rinse dusty leaves. But not so with fuzzy-leaved plants, such as African violets and rex begonias. In *Houseplants and Their Care: A Manual for Every Home of Taste* (1887), Hugo Mulertt advises, "The novice may generally find it true that the plants with soft, porous, and hairy leaves should be very cautiously wetted overhead." This is because droplets cling to fuzzy leaves. When the sun shines through the water droplets, it can scorch the leaves, leaving them prone to discoloration and rot. So remember: If they are fuzzy-leaved, water the soil and not the leaves.

Wet Feet Hurt

■ Watering mistakes kill plants sooner than nearly any other factor, and letting plants sit in standing water is one of the common ones. J. P. Casey, author of *Treatise on the Culture and Growth of Different Sorts of Flower Roots, and of Green House Plants Kept in Rooms* (1821), notes: "All green house plants . . . must be constantly supplied with water, which should be always applied on the tops of the pots, and from no consideration whatever should any be suffered to remain in the water-pans under the pots, particularly in the winter season."

Garden writer Sally Cunningham, of East Aurora, New York, says that most gardeners who grow houseplants learn quickly to water carefully. "But I see a common mistake when the plants go out for the summer. A lot of gardeners still keep the plants in saucers, to protect their deck or patio from stains. Then when the rains come, they forget to dump the saucers. Plants that did well all winter indoors suddenly are suffering from soggy soil, oxygen deprivation, and root-rot diseases. So remove those saucers or dump water after it rains!"

Repotting Rules from a "Crock-Boy"

In *The Home Garden* magazine (1943), expert plantsman Montague Free recalls his job as a "crock-boy," cleaning and soaking pots, which he held for 2 years before he was allowed to actually repot a plant. With 40 years of subsequent experience raising container plants, Mr. Free offered this advice about repotting plants to *Home Garden* readers.

When is more important than how. The best time to replant houseplants is at the end of their natural rest period—usually late winter. But for potted plants that you'll eventually plant outdoors in the garden, repot whenever the roots begin to overcrowd the pot.

Proper pot prep matters. Clean pots with mild soap and water. Soak clay pots in water for at least 10 minutes to saturate the clay. (In the case of plastic, it is not necessary.) Choose a pot size that permits about 1 inch of new soil between the root ball and the pot edge.

Protecting roots is important. When it's time to remove a plant from its current pot, place the fingers of one hand across the surface of the pot, turn the pot and plant upside down, and tap the pot gently against a table or other hard object to dislodge the rootball. This step is "*not* done by holding the pot with one hand and yanking at the plant with the other," Mr. Free writes.

Settling into the new pot. Scrape away loose surface soil and any dead or tightly wound roots. Place a little soil in the new pot, enough that the plant will sit at the same level as it was previously, with the soil level 1 inch below the rim of the pot. Tamp down that soil with your fingers and gently tap the pot on the table or floor, to remove air spaces. Then set the plant in place and add more soil, filling in the sides and continuing the tamping as you work. Some people use a "potting stick" for this purpose—anything that will pack the soil firmly. (Potting sticks could be tongue depressors, wooden spoons, ice cream scoops—anything with a large flat or rounded surface that will firm in the soil.) Finally, once again tap the pot on the table surface to jar the soil into settling.

Watering in the roots. Soak the soil thoroughly with a fine spray, in the case of a little pot. Use a watering can to wet larger pots. Then let the plant dry thoroughly before the next watering.

The top-dressing alternative. Sometimes you won't want to replant all of your houseplants in larger pots—because of lack of space or to economize. Fortunately, there's a great way to boost soil nutrients without repotting. Mr. Free recommended removing some of the surface soil and adding "some loam and aged manure with bone meal added." A modern alternative is to add some compost in place of the removed soil. However, if the plant is so potbound that you can't loosen and remove any surface soil, then the plant is beyond top-dressing and it's truly time to repot.

Bigger Is Not Always Better

■ When times are tight, people may buy clothing for their children that is a size too large so the clothing will last longer. That's probably not very comfortable for the kids, and having a container that's too large isn't so good for houseplants, either. "Regarding the size of pots," writes Hugo Mulertt in *Houseplants and Their Care* (1887), "amateurs use too large pots for their plants. Always bear in mind that not the quantity but the quality of the soil is what grows the plants, if otherwise properly cared for, to perfection." When you repot a houseplant, the general rule is to increase the size of the pot by 1 inch in diameter; 2 inches if the plant's current pot is 15 inches in diameter or more.

Propagate Rex Begonias from Leaves

REX BEGONIAS HAVE a lot going for them: Their foliage sports rich, jewel-like colors and a metallic sheen; they will bloom indoors; and they're also cold-tolerant, surviving near-freezing temperatures. But as you might imagine, these exotic beauties can be costly. Take a tip from *Houseplants and How to Grow Them* (1909), by Parker Barnes, for propagating several new plants from a single rex begonia leaf.

You will need:

- Mature leaves
- Cutting board
- Sharp knife, such as an X-Acto knife
- Plant saucer or tray filled with damp sand
- Toothpicks

Step 1. Place a mature leaf upside down on a cutting board and use the knife to make a cut across the veins of the leaf.

Step 2. Place the leaf right side up on damp sand, pin it down with toothpicks which have been bent in two, and shade it. At each cut in the leaf's vein a new plant will be formed. One good place to put the leaves while the new plants form is on a windowsill that's shaded by sheer curtains.

Step 3: "As soon as they have made a couple of small leaves, separate the young plants from the old leaf and pot them off in a sandy soil with lots of leaf mould [compost] in it."

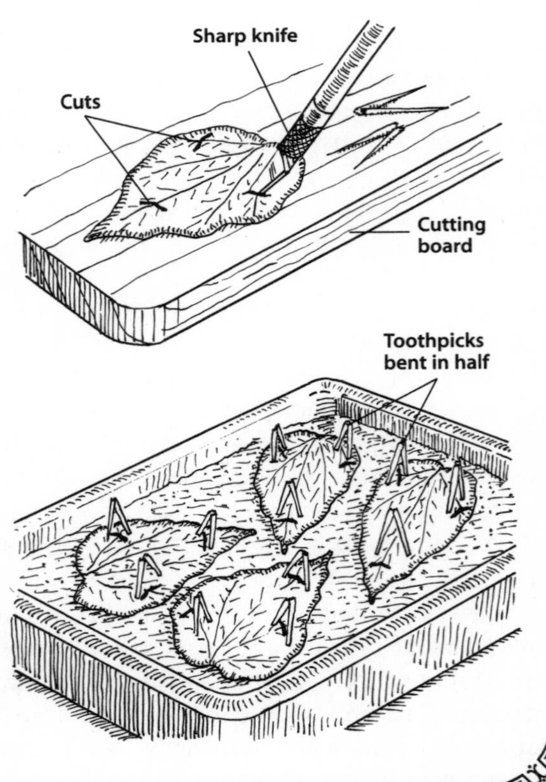

Lessons in Lighting

Providing supplemental lighting for houseplants was quite a mystery in the first half of the 20th century. *The New Garden Encyclopedia* (1945) notes: "Artificial light is helpful to supplement daylight in greenhouses, and recent experiments tend to show that with the right size and type of bulbs used, electric light will help greatly in promoting the health and growth of plants that would soon die without it."

If you're new to growing houseplants, you may also be wondering how to provide artificial lighting for your plants. There's a wealth of supplemental lighting alternatives available. And as our ingenuity about setting up lights increases, we continue to push the limits of what plants we can grow indoors. Keep these guidelines in mind as you work on setting up lights for indoor plants.

Lighting for foliage plants. The least demanding foliage plants, such as philodendrons and ivies, need only 4 to 6 hours of artificial light daily. Many gardeners use a simple light setup consisting of two 48-inch, 40-watt daylight or white fluorescent tubes. Foliage plants can survive without this extra light. But if your house has limited natural light, you'll see a noticeable difference if you give your foliage plants a lighting boost. They'll thrive as never before.

Lighting for tropicals. Ordinary daylight from windows is not enough for most tropicals, such as zebra plant (*Aphelandra squarossa*), a dramatic dark green plant with bright white veins from Brazil, or *Cordyline terminalis* from the East Indies, a plant with strong red striations or broad bands in the leaves. When you are guessing how much light a plant needs, take your cues from its leaf color, as well as its place of origin and its exposure to the bright light in its native environment. Plants with strong red or lots of white in the leaves often need the most light. Tropical plants need 12 to 16 hours of light daily, with some daily exposure to intense light in order to produce flowers. The traditional indoor light setup of

Lighting Logistics

SUSPEND LIGHT FIXTURES for indoor plants above the plants on a table, plant rack, or shelves. The fixtures usually have attached chains, which allow you to adjust the height according to your plants' height and preferences. You can buy lights specifically labeled for plant lighting, but many successful home gardeners propagate and care for all their indoor plants using the less-expensive tubes labeled *cool* or *warm* white lights. Just buy one of each. Adjust the lights according to the plants you're growing. For example, African violets do best when the pot rim is about 11 inches from the tubes, with the darkest-colored violets nearest the center, and whites or pinks toward the outer ends, where light is weaker. Gloxinia (*Sinningia speciosa*), bulbs, and miniature roses do well when the foliage is about 8 inches from the tubes. Long, willowy stems and scanty blossoms are a sign that plants need more light. Bleached foliage means that plants are receiving too much light.

two 48-inch, 40-watt fluorescent tubes isn't enough. Four tubes, however, provide light equivalent to that of a sunny outdoor garden, and a four-tube setup is the best choice for tropicals. A combination of warm white and cool white tubes is sufficient.

Taking the Bite Out of Frostbite

■ Before the days of reliable central heating, one skill worth cultivating was that of reviving houseplants that had endured a winter frost overnight on a cold windowsill. And if you keep plants on an unheated porch during the winter or wait until the last minute to bring your summering houseplants in from the patio in autumn, you can still benefit from the advice of Hugo Mulertt in *Houseplants and Their Care* (1887): "If [frost damage] happens, don't get discouraged. Take the frozen plants tenderly and dip them into cold water (or if the plant is too large for that, sprinkle it for a minute or two) then place them in complete darkness, and in three days at the most you will find them fresh as ever." There's no guarantee that this technique will work for every plant, every time, but it's worth trying.

Picking the Right Plants

It's just as important to match plants to the proper site indoors as it is outdoors. Old-time gardeners figured out decades ago that they needed indoor plants that could tolerate cold, drafty conditions during the winter. Since most modern homes provide a different balance of light and temperature than 19th-century houses did, it takes some careful thought to match old-time favorite houseplants to your site. Here's an overview of popular houseplants of yesterday and today, with ideas old and new on how to choose plants and locations wisely.

Get the Light Right

■ In many parts of the Northern Hemisphere, it's a challenge to provide enough light for plants—and ourselves, too—during the winter. But it's a matter of life or death for some plants, so you need to know which plants can survive in the light conditions your house offers. *The Home Garden* magazine (January 1943) suggests these basic guidelines for growing houseplants. "All plants require a fully *light* location. Some flowering subjects must also have sunlight." The magazine cites these specific light needs of familiar houseplants.

Cyclamens. Morning sunlight is fine for cyclamens, but not hot afternoon sun.

Foliage plants. Most foliage plants thrive on indirect light alone, but many are "exuberantly lovely if some full hours of sun reach them."

Poinsettias. A bright location is best, but watch for sunscald (yellow spots) on leaves if strong sun is filtered through clear glass (which sometimes increases the intensity).

Wax begonias and African violets. Place these away from direct sun; northern windows are good.

Zonal geraniums (*Pelargonium* × *hortorum*). Provide the sunniest southeastern exposure available.

Castoffs for Cachepots

A houseplant may remain in the same container for decades, so that plant and container seem to become an inseparable combination. Plants such as Christmas cactus, peperomias, and some ferns rarely need repotting and may increase in pot size only once or twice in 25 years. In these cases, the outer container—also called a *cachepot* or *jardiniere*—in which you hide the inner plastic or clay pot becomes just as important decoratively as the plant itself. You can buy cachepots at the garden center or have fun ferreting out unusual cast-off containers for your houseplants.

Audrey Segebarth, of Eden, New York, now in her 80s, has a few houseplants that she's been tending for her entire adult life—the plants are more than 70 years old! Audrey has always enjoyed turning household items into houseplant containers, and she has even broken some of the standard rules—such as planting houseplants directly in the cachepots, even if they don't have drainage holes. According to Audrey, the secret is to water sparingly and never, ever apply so much water that all the air spaces in the soil reservoir become flooded. Just in case, she puts a layer of potsherds in the bottom of all her pots to add a little room for extra water to drain.

OLD-FASHIONED FAVORITES

Old Favorites for Low Light

SECLUDED INTERIOR CORNERS of rooms can be much brighter and more welcoming when they include plants. Fortunately, some time-tested favorites will grow well in these low-light exposures. Just keep in mind that even these houseplants will benefit from the occasional shift to a location that offers more light.

- Chinese evergreens (*Aglaeonema* spp. and cvs.)
- Cast-iron plant (*Aspidistra elatior*)
- Dracaenas (*Dracaena fragrans* and *D. marginata*)
- Philodendrons (*Philodendron* spp.)
- Snake plant (*Sansevieria trifasciata*)
- Peace lily (*Spathiphyllum* hybrids)

Here are some of Audrey's favorite plant-and-planter combinations.

- A 75-year-old Christmas cactus is planted directly in a china washbowl, part of a bedroom wash set. It sits in an upstairs hall of Audrey's 150-year-old farmhouse (which stays cool in winter, typically around 60°F at night). The plant flowers annually, and Audrey gives it very little water. "I water it about once a month in the winter," she says, "and not much more in summer."

◆ A very old shamrock resides in a chamber pot, which Audrey's late husband, Jack Segebarth, remembered was called a "growler." Of course, the chamber pot was thoroughly cleaned before the shamrock was planted.

◆ A copper boiler, once used to boil clothes, now holds bromeliads. The pot is nearly 3 feet long, fairly narrow, and 18 inches tall, and the plants are in terracotta pots set inside, propped up so that the tops of the inside pots are just below the level of the container.

◆ Other antiques that Audrey has converted to houseplant containers include pickle crocks, umbrella stands (some have just the right circumference to suspend a 1-gallon pot), cast iron Dutch ovens, teapots, and cooking pots of all kinds.

Houseplants for Food Fanciers

MANY GARDENERS have experimented with raising houseplants started from seeds or other parts of plants bought at the grocery store, such as avocado pits and grapefruit seeds. Here are a couple of unusual houseplant ideas in this vein from *A Garden in the House* (1939), by Helen Van Pelt Wilson.

Horseradish greens. "Cut off the top of a horseradish, and set it in a dish to which a little water is added time to time, and all winter long one handsome arrow-shaped leaf after another will unfold."

Leafy lentils. "Lentils make house plants as well as soup! Place them in a saucer with enough water to moisten them thoroughly without allowing them to float. Just add a little at a time to see how much they will take up. Keep the saucer on a window sill and you will be promptly delighted with a whole miniature forest of sturdy shoots."

Ferns: The Challenge Continues

■ Ferns are symbolic of the Victorian parlor, where the fern stand was ubiquitous. In books, the plants are lush and green, but in reality, most people remember the crispy, dried fronds—and it may even be worse today. That's because the fern's worst enemy is dry heat, typical of our homes in winter. In *Houseplants and Their Care* (1887), Hugo Mulertt cautions that "a dry atmosphere is just as detrimental to the growth of ferns as a dry soil." The writer also notes that ferns are "very impatient of standing water, but need a good deal of moisture." For those reasons, ferns were often grown inside a plant case (terrarium) in a thick layer of damp sand or moss, which kept the air and soil moist.

The Home Garden magazine (February 1943) advises readers to water carefully, directing the water near the outer rim of the pot, but not letting it settle into the crown of the plant. Also, to maximize the benefits of daily watering, once a week the plant might be set in a pan of water for just an hour while it soaks up all it can. *The Home Garden* recommended bird's-nest fern (*Asplenium nidus*) or holly ferns (*Cyrtomium* spp.) as easier than Boston fern, especially without a terrarium. Rabbit's foot fern (*Davallia fejeensis*) is also tolerant of hot, dry atmospheres and is a good substitute for the popular maidenhair ferns (*Adiantum* spp.), which require intense humidity. If you want to grow a maidenhair fern indoors, plant it in a terrarium (see "Try a Terrarium" on page 345).

Brighten the House with Verbena

■ Verbena fills outdoor flowerbeds with colorful blooms, but it's long been a favorite indoor flowering plant, as well. *Treatise on the Culture and Growth of Different Sorts of Flower Roots* (1821), by J. P. Casey, refers to verbena as "sweet vervain" and describes it as a "beautiful plant for rooms, particularly in the summer." However, "it loses its leaves generally about December, when many people throw it away thinking it is dead; but, if it can be cut back rather short, and shifted into a larger pot, in good rich mould [use one part potting soil and one part compost], as soon as the leaves fall off, it will form a fine green plant, and retain its leaves after till next winter."

Today, growers produce a wide range of hybrid verbenas, some highly scented and all profusely flowering. Peruvian verbena (*Verbena peruviana*) is sometimes recommended as a houseplant, and many others may be suitable. Like many verbenas, Peruvian verbena requires strong indoor light (bright window or supplemental lighting), generous watering in summer and lighter watering in winter, and winter temperatures no lower than 45°F.

Forcing Easter Lilies

■ It's a simple treat to pick up a potted Easter lily in bloom at the grocery store or garden center, but for an indoor gardening challenge, try forcing Easter lilies into bloom the way old-time gardeners did. In *Treatise on the Culture and Growth of Different Sorts of Flower Roots* (1821), writer J. P. Casey describes the process of potting up Easter lilies from the garden for forcing, noting that "large bunches [are] planted in large pots, in which they will thrive remarkably well. The best time for taking them up is in January or February. Keep them in a warm room in a sunny window; constantly supply them

with water, and they will blossom very fine." This technique still works, and digging the plants in January is fine for mild-winter areas. However, if you live in a region where the ground freezes solid in late winter, you can pot lily bulbs in fall and store the pots in a cold, but not freezing, place (such as an unheated porch or garage). Come January, bring the pots into your house and treat them as described above.

Understand the Potted Azalea

The secret to success with potted azaleas is to fertilize them the first summer after bloom, according to *The Home Gar-*

Out with the Old, In with the New

Some houseplant growers succeed at bringing out the best in nearly everything and getting even the toughest plants to reflower. But experts have often recommended that we learn when to let go. According to A. J. MacSelf in *The Woman's Treasury for Home and Garden* (1939), it's particularly difficult to keep flowering or berry-producing plants—such as florist's cyclamens, winter-flowering begonias, azaleas, hydrangeas, flowering peppers (*Capsicum annuum* var. *annuum*), or Jerusalem cherries (*Solanum pseudocapsicum*)—producing "fruit" indoors. They need more light than is available in the brightest of windows.

In the *Pocket Book of Flower Gardening* (1937), author Montague Free states a firm opinion about what to do with such plants: "Growing plants in the home offers an outlet for such enthusiasts, and I, for one, am in favor of it—if conducted with a modicum of sanity. Too many people become sentimental about their houseplants and just because a particular specimen was a gift from Aunt Amelia they continue to give it houseroom long after it has lost its beauty. [Spent houseplants] should be relegated to the rubbish pile just as soon as they become unsightly!"

With the availability of contemporary lighting supplies, that discouraging pronouncement may no longer be true, and many people do keep cyclamens and other challenging beauties going. Still, we might question what is worth the effort. Rochelle Smith, instructor of the "interior-scaping" course at Niagara County Community College, in Sanborn, New York, says, "When there are so many cool plants that look wonderful in the house, why take up space dragging an old cyclamen back to life? Besides, the local growers work so hard just to make a living. For heaven's sake, compost it and buy a new cyclamen next season!"

den magazine (December 1943). All too often, potted azaleas are in glorious bloom when we buy them, but we struggle to get them to rebloom—or even survive—the following season. When you follow *The Home Garden*'s advice, choose seaweed extract or fish emulsion fertilizer, and apply it according to label instructions. As fall approaches, bring the plant inside and position it in a cold, sunny window—ideally where the temperature stays above 45°F but rarely goes above 60°F. The idea is to give the azalea the equivalent of winter conditions in the southern United States. Water weekly, and by spring you should see buds and blooms appearing. If your house is particularly warm and dry, you may see leaves dropping. This is a sign that you need to water more often. *The Home Garden* suggests watering under an open faucet, tilting the plant at an angle and letting a slow stream of water saturate the soil. To prevent the soil from being washed out, place your hand over the mouth of the pot, with your fingers around the plant.

Savoring the New Treasures

■ As gardeners have learned which fine old favorite plants, such as scented geraniums, are worth bringing inside for the winter, it's well worth our time today to find out which of the stunning new plants in the contemporary plant scene survive and thrive in our homes. Horticulturist Jeff Leyonmark, of Lockwood's Greenhouses, in Hamburg, New York, is known for creating lavish garden and container displays. He often teaches groups about using the newest annuals and tender perennials. Jeff recommends the following plants—some new discoveries and some new cultivars of old friends—for outdoor excitement in summer and indoor satisfaction in winter.

Clivia. Sometimes called *Kafir lily,* clivia (*Clivia miniata*) is related to amaryllis and provides dramatic deep orange bloom in winter. During the summer growing season, water and fertilize with a balanced organic houseplant fertilizer once a month, and then decrease water and stop fertilizing in fall to stimulate bloom. Cool night temperatures are important during this period. Clivia tolerates dry indoor air, making it an indestructible container plant.

Chinese evergreen. *Aglaonema* is a long-enduring houseplant that tolerates low light and dry conditions, but it was often considered dull by our forebears. Today's new cultivars, such as 'Snowcap' and 'Golden Bay', provide exciting foliage choices.

Coleus. Innumerable color combinations have helped coleus (*Solenostemon scutellarioides*) leap into prominence as a garden plant and houseplant. There are types for sun as well as partial shade. They are easy to propagate from cuttings and prefer regular moisture and increased humidity at house temperatures. (Set them on trays of pebbles filled with water.)

Philodendrons. With many forms and color variations, philodendrons prefer lots of water in spring and summer and lean conditions in fall and winter (a cool room, low water, no fertilizer). Variegated 'Brazil' is spectacular, says Jeff, as is the shimmering green 'Moonlight'. Some new entries, such as 'Prince of Orange' and 'Black Cardinal', take their names from the foliage colors. These plants actually prefer indoor light to a greenhouse situation, where the bright light fades their foliage.

Plectranthus. This old favorite has never looked better, with new cultivars expanding the selection beyond the tried-and-true Swedish ivy (*Plectranthus australis*). Try the brilliant chartreuse *P. forsteri* 'Marginatus' (also sold as *P. coleoides* 'Marginatus') or *P. hilliardiae* for stunning tubular, candelabra-shaped lavender flowers. These plants perform best in bright but filtered indoor light (no direct sunlight).

Pothos. Widely available are gold- or silver-colored cultivars and new patterns or hues, such as the aptly named, extremely vibrant 'Neon'. Grow them as you would philodendrons.

Passionflowers. Thanks to extensive hybridizing at the Missouri Botanical Garden and other locations, passionflowers (*Passiflora*) now are hardier, flower more profusely, and produce larger blossoms. Indoors, they like a sunny or partially sunny window, moist air, and even moisture. Teresa Buchanan, an associate of Jeff Leyonmark at Lockwood's Greenhouses, recommends new cultivars such as 'Star of Clevedon' (white), 'Lady Margaret' or 'Ruby Glow' (red), and 'Purple Haze' or 'Elizabeth' (purple). "And don't miss 'Jeanette'," says Teresa. "It has deeply cut, silvery blue leaves and profuse violet-banded flowers."

Plants with a Future

"Whether the handsome Easter gift plants from the florist have at our windows a prolonged present, a real future—or only a past—depends on the nature of the plant and also on the nature of the owner," notes *The Home Garden* magazine (April 1943). Here's how the magazine explains the care of gardenias and hydrangeas—two favorite Easter plants—with some modern tips to boot.

Gardenias. In spite of a reputation as tricky even for florists, gardenias (*Gardenia jasminoides*) are "amenable for the amateur" if you achieve the right temperatures: no lower than 55°F at night and 60°F in the daytime (and never higher than 70°F). The warmer the temperature, the more likely the mealybug will attack. Marge Vogel, of Eden, New York, has kept a large gardenia going for 15 years, with the basic approach of "benign neglect," Marge says. "Or on a positive note, moderation in all things—as in never too much water, never too warm, and therefore never too dry." Marge rarely provides fertilizer and has repotted only twice, yet her gardenia blooms and smells as sweet as it did when it came from the florist long ago.

Gardenias also prefer morning sun, and it's helpful to syringe the foliage daily, or at least weekly, and place them on a tray of pebbles to increase humidity. Let gardenias dry between waterings, and once a week set them in a pail of water up to an inch below the pot rim. Once the water has absorbed to the soil surface, remove the pot from the pail. Water amply during active growth periods whenever the soil surface is slightly dry. During the summer, move them to a porch or plunge them in a sheltered garden bed.

Hydrangeas. Living conditions for hydrangeas should be similar to those for gardenias, but you should also prune back the tops to two pairs of leaves after the plant flowers. When roots fill the pot, replant, preferably after flowering. In September, put them in a cold place (unheated room) with very little water. The leaves will all drop. Then in January, introduce the plant gradually to a little more heat, some water, some fertilizer, and eventually full sunlight. You can plant your hydrangeas outdoors permanently in the garden or leave them potted and repeat the same operation next season.

Alpine Strawberries Inside

■ Take a tip from *New York Times* garden writer Dorothy Bovee Jones, and try alpine strawberries as a houseplant. As Dorothy Jones wrote in 1946, "In the house these plants are . . . infrequently seen, but as easy to grow and as decorative as they are in the garden. Flowers and fruit appear all winter . . . The bright red, green, and white colors are cheery when skies outside are gray."

Please, Not Those Again!

EVEN IN 1869, homemakers had whimsy, as evident in this idea from *The American Woman's Home*, by Catharine Beecher and Harriet Beecher Stowe: "A sponge, kept wet by daily immersion, can be filled with flax seed and suspended by a cord, when it will ere long be covered with verdure and afterward with flowers." (Next thing you know, they will be shaping them into animals and marketing them as "pets" on television at holiday time!)

To succeed with alpine strawberries indoors, either in a strawberry pot or a regular planter, pot up the plants in September in fine rich soil (contemporary bagged houseplant potting soil will do). Place them in a south window, and keep them evenly moist.

Grown in this way, these plants will produce a couple of berries per plant at a time—delightful on a salad or dessert—and add some color during the winter months. And if you wish to fertilize the plants with a balanced houseplant fertilizer monthly, there will be many more berries at one time.

Stylizing the Windowsill Planting

Houseplants aren't just plants that you care for inside your house; they're part of your decorating scheme. And just as styles of furniture, floors, and wall coverings have changed over time, so has the range of houseplants and containers. If you have a period home, use the guidelines in the following tips to create houseplant displays with a Colonial, Victorian, or other historical flair. Indoor plants arranged in special settings, such as a terrarium, miniature garden scene, and fern ball, can highlight such displays.

Plants for Colonial Style

■ In general, Americans of the 1700s seldom grew houseplants, but there were exceptions—botanists, eccentrics, and collectors attempting to propagate and grow plants they had brought with them to the New World. Most commonly, people grew only those indoor plants with a purpose, such as herbs or plants with a strong, pleasant fragrance (to cover up less-pleasant odors). Today's owners of Colonial homes don't have to limit themselves to these plants, of course. But if you'd like to reserve one window for plants of the Colonial era, set up a display that includes rosemary, parsley, chives, thyme, and scented geraniums.

Wild Look for Rustic Homes

■ Bringing the outdoors in seems like a modern concept, but even in the 1800s, nature lovers knew that some shade-loving woodland plants, as well as some garden flowers, were equally at home on windowsills. In *The American Woman's Home* (1869), Catharine Beecher and Harriet Beecher Stowe describe their indoor plants: "We present a plain kind of window ornamented with a variety of rural adornings . . . In the hanging baskets are ferns that flourish in the deep woods, and around the window is the ivy, running from two boxes; and in case the window has some sun, a nasturtium may spread its bright blossoms among the leaves."

It's easy to re-create this type of rustic, woodsy look today with a combination of native and nonnative plants that are readily available at garden centers. For spots with poor light, choose English ivy (*Hedera helix*) or holly ferns (*Cyrtomium* spp.), maidenhair ferns (*Adiantum* spp.), or Boston fern (*Nephrolepsis exaltata*). When you shop for nasturtiums for a sunny window, look for 'Alaska', which has orange flowers and cream-and-green variegated leaves; 'Cream', with flowers that live up to its name; 'Mahogany', which sports deep red flowers; or orange-flowered 'Vesuvius'.

Victorian Vines and Flowers

■ When most of us imagine Victorian decor, we think of lavish, intricate, and complicated designs and furnishings. The same was true in plant selection. *The New Garden Encyclopedia* (1945) remembers the period as one in which "brilliant colors, and profuse forms were as popular as ruffled lace curtains." You can re-create this look using ferns and plants with lush variegated foliage on a windowsill, with multiple vines twining around lace curtains. Coleus, begonias, and caladiums will fit right in—in fact, no plant will be too exotic.

Accent Plants for Art Deco Homes

■ When your decorating style is Art Deco, your cue in choosing houseplants will be the fabrics of the 1920s and the bright colors of dishware and American pottery—McCoy or Hall vases or pots and Fiestaware, for example. If the fabrics of your sofa or chair coverings, pillows, and curtains depict vines, ferns, or palms, try to find houseplants in a style to match, such as dracaenas, small palms, or a banana tree. Some houseplants that might beautifully reflect the Fiestaware, McCoy, or Hall pottery include coleus (with the advantage of today's many hybrids in dark red, cheerful coral, creamy yellow, and even lime green) and amaryllis (*Hippeastrum*), with its strong clear colors.

Houseplants for War-Era Homes

■ Decorating trends in the 1940s and 1950s were a sharp departure from the flair and fullness of the Victorian and Art Deco periods. *The New Garden Encyclopedia* (1945) declares, "Modern taste favors simple, even severe lines, and smaller plant subjects. Glass shelves offer real opportunities." The look should be uncluttered. A classic window of this era might have plaid curtains with a boxy valance and plants with clean lines, such as cacti, a Christmas cactus, a snake plant, and a rectangular terrarium.

Artful Vines

■ For an artful effect without the price tag of artwork, decorate with trailing plants and vines, suggests *The Home Garden* magazine (June 1943). If you have a sunny window (southern exposure), you can easily grow asparagus fern, grape ivy, and philodendron. Others that will thrive: "if the temperature usually [is kept] below 70 degrees . . . English ivy, large and small-leaved, and wandering Jew (*Tradescantia fluminensis*) and its relative, *Zebrina pendula.*"

While Victorian gardeners often trained the vines around window curtains, you may want to try these tricks instead: Stretch a small net over the window, twine nylon fishing line around small nails hammered into the wall, or stretch fishing line from a curtain rod to stakes anchored in the vine's pot.

You might use the type of net called *pea netting, deer netting,* or *bird netting,* or perhaps even the kind sometimes sold for stuffed-animal hammocks in children's bedrooms. Simply stretch such netting over the curtain rod or hooks at the upper corners of the window (perhaps hooks already there for curtain rods). If you are using single fishing line, drape it in vertical lines from the curtain rod or hooks down to the pot containing your climbing plants. With just a little training and placement of the tendrils as your vine grows, you will have a lovely green "living window curtain."

She Plants Seashells

TURN A VACATION SOUVENIR into a planter, as described in *Window Gardening* (1878): Start with "a pretty little idea of a sea shell, fitted to a rustic frame." The seashell would be stuffed with compost or moss, and a small fern planted inside. To take this project a step further, you can suspend the planted shell in a window or on a wall by wrapping it with wire and then fashioning a box of rough twigs (or driftwood) into which you can slip the shell. The frame will disguise the wire. If you don't want to hang your planter, use the frame to keep it steady on a tabletop. Or, suggests *Window Gardening*, settle the planted seashell (no wiring needed) into a "nest of twigs."

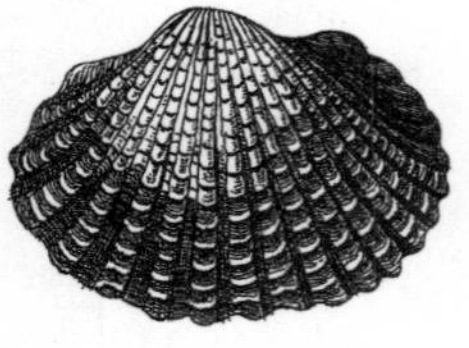

An Indoor Jungle

Take a page from history and create an indoor jungle from simple ivy cuttings. Catharine Beecher and Harriet Beecher Stowe describe the effect in *The American Woman's Home* (1869): "A beautiful ornament for a room with a picture is Geranium ivy. Slips of this will start without roots in bottles of water. Slide the bottle behind the picture, and the ivy will seem to come from fairyland and hang its verdure in all manner of pretty curves around the picture. It may then be trained to travel toward other ivy and thus aid in forming a green cornice along the ceiling. We have seen some rooms that had an ivy cornice around the whole, giving the air of a leafy bower."

Using a bottle set on a table below a picture will work fine, says garden writer Sally Cunningham, of East Aurora, New York, or you can try a small flower holder attached to a suction cup. Such holders are often sold at flower shows, garden shops, or botanical gàrden gift shops. Affix the flower holder to the wall behind a picture frame, stick in a piece of ivy, and let the vine trail around the frame and over the picture. Grown in water, ivy will last a long time, as long as you check that the water in the tube has not been used or evaporated. Once a month, or whenever the plant looks pale or chlorotic (deficient in nitrogen), add a drop or two of fertilizer such as fish emulsion.

Try a Terrarium

ONE WAY TO GROW moisture-loving plants indoors, even in a dry apartment, is to plant them in a terrarium. The terrarium was invented in 1829 by the British botanist Dr. Nathaniel Bagshaw Ward. Early terrariums were small and simple, but it didn't take long for them to evolve into ornate miniature greenhouses where diminutive landscapes flourished, protected from the dry heat and coal fumes of Victorian parlors. These little greenhouses, called *Wardian cases*, were the perfect indoor settings for displaying ferns, small orchids, and African violets. Reproduction Wardian cases are available from specialty suppliers, but when you make a terrarium yourself, you can create one just the right size to fit a windowsill in your house. All you need is a clear glass container with an opening big enough to allow you to insert small plants, such as a brandy snifter, a covered aquarium, or even an old-fashioned candy jar. For most plants, standard houseplant potting mixes will do.

You will need:

- Activated charcoal (sold at aquarium shops)
- Clear glass or plastic container
- 1 quart potting soil suitable for the type of plant you have selected
- Wooden chopstick
- Long-handled spoon
- Three or more small plants (see "Venerable Terrarium Plants" on page 347)
- Decorative gravel or moss
- Small decorative rocks and driftwood
- Long-handled artist's paintbrush
- Plastic wrap (optional)

Step 1. To provide drainage and keep the soil fresh-smelling, put a ½-inch-deep layer of activated charcoal on the bottom of the container. Top the charcoal with enough potting soil to fill the container one-third full.

Step 2. Using the chopstick and long-handled spoon, dig small holes, and plant each plant in the container's soil.

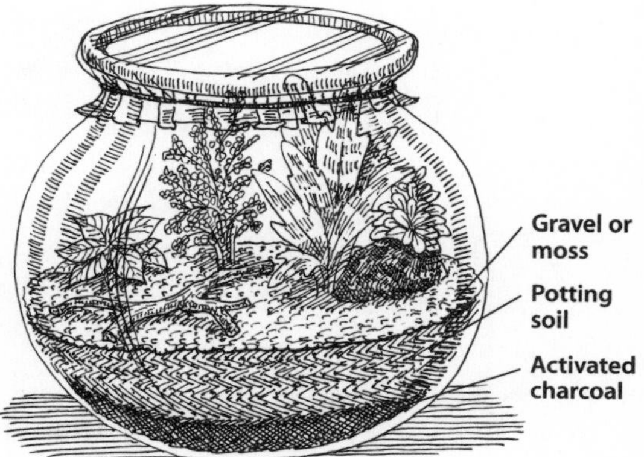

Step 3. Cover the surface of the soil with either gravel or moss, and set in rocks or small pieces of driftwood as decorations. Use the paintbrush to dust away any soil that clings to the walls of the container. Moisten the soil with water, using a mister or a very diffused spray from a watering wand.

Step 4. If the container has a lid, put the lid in place. Otherwise, seal the opening with plastic wrap.

■ Your terrarium can house a desert landscape of miniature cacti, a ferny woodland dell, or a diminutive cloud forest for miniature orchids. There are soil mixes designed for the needs of cacti, ferns, and orchids.

It's a Small World

■ Creating picturesque scenes featuring miniature plants is an indoor gardening hobby that's as charming now as it was when it first came to popularity in the Victorian era. An article from *The Home Garden* magazine (January 1943) explains how. First, you'll need to set up a Wardian case or terrarium (as described in "Try a Terrarium" on page 345). The soil in the terrarium "may be shaped into terrace-like contours or left level, as taste dictates." With the help of florists or plant specialists, choose small plants with similar cultural preferences (moisture-loving woodland plants *or* cacti and succulents, for instance, but not all of them together). Use taller plants to represent miniature trees, and spreading plants to represent fields. Place the plants in the terrarium in order from largest to smallest, and then add miniature figurines of people and animals as you please.

Once your small world is assembled, after the first light watering, it will need almost no care. Put a lid on it, watch, and enjoy. If the glass mists, there is too much humidity, and you need only lift the lid for a few hours. If the misting is constant, prop the lid open on a regular basis.

Here are some plants that will work well for creating a miniature landscape.

- Miniature English ivies (*Hedera helix,* dwarf cvs.)
- Peperomias (*Peperomia* spp.)
- Tiny primroses (*Primula marginata* or *P. vulgaris,* dwarf cvs.)
- Small ferns, including *Pteris cretica* 'Albo-lineata' or *P. ensiformis* 'Evergemiensis'
- Strawberry begonia (*Saxifraga stolonifera*)
- Peacock moss (*Selaginella uncinata*)
- Bird's-foot violet (*Viola pedata*)

Fashion a Fern Ball

■ In Victorian conservatories, ferns were not only grown at ground and table level but also suspended from the ceiling as fern baskets or fern balls. Fern baskets, which remained popular to varying degrees through the 1940s, were made of coconut shells, or of wire or wood lined with moss. According to *The New Garden Encyclopedia* (1945), these were "especially good for ferns with creeping roots,

OLD-FASHIONED FAVORITES

Venerable Terrarium Plants

WHETHER YOU'RE GROWING PLANTS in a goldfish bowl, a terrarium, or a historic Wardian case, remember that the increased humidity in these enclosed containers—wonderful for ferns—is terrible for some other plants (African violets, for instance).

To replicate a Victorian terrarium, include some of the following plants suggested in *Garden Guide: The Amateur Gardeners' Handbook* (1946).

PLANT NAME	DESCRIPTION	COMMENTS
Croton (*Codiaeum variegatum* var. *pictum*)	Leathery-leaved plant with bright foliage colors, including pinks, reds, and oranges	Rarely survives in the house without extra humidity; prefers regular watering in winter and abundant watering in summer; strong light
Corn plant (*Dracaena fragrans* var. *massangeana* or *victoriae*, or *D. deremensis* 'Warneckei')	Sword-shaped, upright or drooping leaves that grow in a spiral from the plant stem	Requires high humidity; thrives in bright indoor locations; the lightest leaves require the most light
Creeping fig (*Ficus pumila*)	Small-leaved, dark green plant that climbs easily, clinging to surfaces with ivylike roots	Drops leaves in dry air and does not recover well afterward; tolerates moderate light indoors
Fittonia (*Fittonia verschaffeltii*, including miniature varieties such as *F. verschaffeltii argyroneura* 'Minima')	Perennial herbaceous plant with bright green leaves crisscrossed by white veins	Needs to be cut back often to prevent stems from growing overly long, especially in low light; requires high humidity, generous watering, and moderate to strong indoor lighting
Prayer plant (*Maranta leuconeura* and *M. leuconeura* var. *kerchoveana*)	Delicate foliage with patterning that resembles a fish spine	Prefers diffused light to direct sunlight; water sparingly in winter, generously in summer

like maidenhair." Fern balls, which fell out of fashion after the Victorian period, were made of wire frames lined with sphagnum moss and wound with the rhizomes of hare's foot fern—thick, hairy, and pliable when wet. The roots penetrate the sphagnum, which holds water for a long time. Fern fronds emerge all over the ball. Some were shaped into animals or other forms, as novelties or to amaze the visitor.

Find a source for hare's foot fern (*Davallia fejeensis*), also called *lacy paw* (usually available where ferns or tropical foliage plants are sold). This fern grows well indoors or in a cool greenhouse, producing foot-long fronds. Fashion a ball-shaped frame out of wire. You can use chicken wire, tomato cage wire, or any wire mesh with holes at least an inch in size that can be bent into an approximate ball shape. Before you fasten the ball closed, stuff a clump of sphagnum moss into the center. Use fine wire or the cut ends of the mesh to fasten the ball. Poke more sphagnum moss through the mesh, as much as it can hold, and then soak the ball thoroughly.

Gently insert the roots of the hare's foot fern, using florist's pins to push and hold the fronds in the sphagnum. In order to ensure evenly distributed growth while the roots are taking hold, you will need to set the ball in a tray in a bright location (diffused light) for a few weeks. Turn the ball occasionally to encourage even growth. Once the roots have become entangled in the sphagnum, suspend the ball from a hook on the ceiling or protruding from a wall.

Resources

Supplies and Equipment for Homes, Health, Body Care, and Pets

Aubrey Organics
4419 N. Manhattan Ave.
Tampa, FL 33614
Phone: (800) 282-7394
Fax: (813) 876-8166
Web site: www.aubrey-organics.com

Aveda
4000 Pheasant Ridge Dr.
Blaine, MN 55449
Phone: (800) 644-4831
Web site: www.aveda.com

Bachman's
6010 Lyndale Ave.
Minneapolis, MN 55419
Phone: (866) 222-4626
Web site: www.bachmans.com
Oxalis plants (shamrocks)

The Bark Canoe Store
2317 W. Fairview Ave.
Spokane, WA 99205
Phone: (509) 327-7902
Web site: www.barkcanoe.com
Birch bark for toy canoes

Berea College Crafts
CPO 2145
Berea, KY 40404
Phone: (800) 347-3892
E-mail: contact@bereacollegecrafts.com
Web site: http://bereacc.site.yahoo.net
Heirloom-quality traditional crafts made by Berea College artisans and their students

Better Botanicals
335 Victory Dr.
Herndon, VA 20170
Phone: (888) 224-3727
Fax: (703) 481-7459
Web site: www.betterbotanicals.com

Broomshop.com
PO Box 1182
Grants Pass, OR 97528
Phone: (541) 474-3575
Web site: www.broomshop.com
Handcrafted brooms

California Antilles Trading
3735 Adams Ave.
San Diego, CA 92116
Phone: (619) 283-4834
E-mail: sales@calantilles.com
Web site: www.calantilles.com
Bay rum aftershave

Chef's Catalog
PO Box 650589
Dallas, TX 75265-0589
Phone: (800) 884-2433
Web site: www.chefscatalog.com

Cooking.com
2850 Ocean Park Blvd., Suite 310
Santa Monica, CA 90405
Phone: (800) 663-8810
Web site: www.cooking.com

GoodHumans
343 Soquel Ave., PMB #327
Santa Cruz, CA 95062
Phone: (866) 420-4208
Web site: www.goodhumans.com
Environmentally responsible home and personal care products

Jack's Country Store
PO Box 710
Ocean Park, WA 98640-0710
Phone: (888) 665-4989
E-mail: service@jackscountrystore.com
Web site: www.jackscountrystore.com

Japanese Style
16159 320th St.
New Prague, MN 56071
Phone: (877) 226-4387
Web site: www.japanesegifts.com
Paper parasols

The Jersey Jerry Broomsquire
911 Larkspur Pl. S
Mount Laurel, NJ 08054-4960
Phone: (856) 222-0713
E-mail: Moyerbase@aol.com
Web site: www.broomcrafters.com
Handmade brooms

Jewish Bazaar
9501 Mary Knoll Rd.
Rockville, MD 20850
Phone: (888) 738-6486
Fax: (301) 315-2665
Web site: www.jewishbazaar.com
Dreidels

Kitchenemporium.com
32A Friendship St.
Westerly, RI 02891
Phone: (888) 858-7920
Web site: www.kitchenemporium.com

Lehman's
One Lehman Circle
PO Box 321
Kidron, OH 44636
Phone: (877) 438-5346
Fax: (888) 780-4975
Web site: www.lehmans.com
Fireplace cranes and a variety of other home products

Master Garden Products
3223 C St. NE, #1
Auburn, WA 98002
Phone: (800) 574-7248
Web site:
www.mastergardenproducts.com
Barrel chairs; also a variety of garden furniture and garden structures

Petguys.com
3535 Hollis St., Building B
Oakland, CA 94608
Phone: (800) 360-4144
Web site: www.petguys.com

Restoration Hardware
15 Koch Rd., Suite J
Corte Madera, CA 94925
Phone: (800) 910-9836
Web site: www.restorationhardware.com

Soaps Gone Buy
1085 College Rd.
Eldorado, IL 62930
Phone: (877) 796-9498
Web site: www.soapsgonebuy.com
Fels-Naptha soap, washing soda, castile soap

Thayers Natural Pharmaceuticals
PO Box 56
Westport, CT 06881-0056
Phone: (203) 226-0940
Fax: (203) 227-8183
E-mail: Hthayerco@aol.com
Web site: www.thayers.com
Slippery elm lozenges and other natural remedies

Uncle Harry's Natural Products
6975 176th Ave. NE, #360
Redmond, WA 98052
Phone: (425) 558-4251
Fax: (425) 895-9391
Web site: www.uncleharrys.com

The Vermont Country Store
PO Box 6999
Rutland, VT 05702-6999
Phone: (802) 362-8460
Fax: (802) 362-0285
Web site:
www.vermontcountrystore.com
Soap savers, feather dusters, and a wide range of other old-fashioned equipment and supplies for the home

Vermont Crafts Council
PO Box 938
Montpelier, VT 05601
Phone: (802) 223-3380
E-mail: vt1crafts@aol.com
Web site: www.vermontcrafts.com
Listings of artisans of floorcloths and other crafts

Weleda
1 Closter Rd.
Palisades, NY 10964
Phone: (800) 241-1030
Web site: www.weleda.com
Natural personal care products

Plants, Seeds, and Gardening Supplies

Baker Creek Heirloom Seeds
2278 Baker Creek Rd.
Mansfield, MO 65704
Phone: (417) 924-8917
Web site: www.rareseeds.com

Bay Laurel Nursery
2500 El Camino Real
Atascadero, CA 93422
Phone: (800) 847-6473
Web site: www.baylaurelnursery.com
"Combo" fruit trees (multiple kinds of fruit trees grafted onto one rootstock)

Bluestone Perennials
7211 Middle Ridge Rd.
Madison, OH 44057
Phone/fax: (800) 852-5243
Web site: www.bluestoneperennials.com

W. Atlee Burpee & Co.
300 Park Ave.
Warminster, PA 18974
Phone: (800) 888-1447
Web site: www.burpee.com

Edible Landscaping
361 Spirit Ridge Ln.
Afton, VA 22920
Phone: (434) 361-9134
Web site: www.eat-it.com
Native fruits

Emery's Garden
2829 164th St. SW
Lynnwood, WA 98037
Phone: (425) 743-4555
Web site: www.emerysgarden.com

Gardener's Supply Co.
128 Intervale Rd.
Burlington, VT 05401
Phone: (888) 833-1412
Web site: www.gardeners.com

Gurney's Seed & Nursery Co.
PO Box 4178
Greendale, IN 47025-4178
Phone: (513) 354-1491
Web site: www.gurneys.com

Heirloom Seeds
PO Box 245
West Elizabeth, PA 15088-0245
Phone: (412) 384-0852
Web site: www.heirloomseeds.com

Johnny's Selected Seeds
955 Benton Ave.
Winslow, ME 04901
Phone: (207) 861-3999
Fax: (800) 738-6314
E-mail: homegarden@johnnyseeds.com
Web site: www.johnnyseeds.com

Klehm's Song Sparrow Perennial Farm
13101 E. Rye Rd.
Avalon, WI 53505
Phone: (800) 553-3715
Fax: (608) 883-2257
Web site: www.songsparrow.com

Logee's Greenhouses Ltd.
141 North St.
Danielson, CT 06239
Phone: (888) 330-8038
Fax: (973) 237-9043
E-mail: logee-info@logees.com
Web site: www.logees.com
Tropical and subtropical plants

Niche Gardens
1111 Dawson Rd.
Chapel Hill, NC 27516
Phone: (919) 967-0078
Fax: (919) 967-4026
Web site: www.nichegardens.com

Peaceful Valley Farm Supply
PO Box 2209
Grass Valley, CA 95945
Phone: (888) 784-1722
Web site: www.groworganic.com

Pinetree Garden Seeds
PO Box 300
New Gloucester, ME 04260
Phone: (207) 926-3400
Web site: www.superseeds.com

Prohoe
204 S. Munden Ave.
PO Box 87
Munden, KS 66959
Web site: http://web.inetba.com/prohoe/
Scuffle hoes

Raintree Nursery
391 Butts Rd.
Morton, WA 98356
Phone: (360) 496-6400
Web site: www.raintreenursery.com

Seed Savers Exchange
3076 N. Winn Rd.
Decorah, IA 52101
Phone: (563) 382-5990
Web site: www.seedsavers.org
Heirloom seeds

Sheridan Gardens Nursery
8714 Glenoaks Blvd.
Sun Valley, CA 91352
Phone: (818) 767-8890
Web site: www.sheridangardens.com

Stokes Tropicals
4806 E. Old Spanish Trail
Jeanerette, LA 70544
Phone: (866) 478-2502
Email: info@stokestropicals.com
Web site: www.stokestropicals.com

Thomas Jefferson Center for Historic Plants
Monticello
PO Box 316
Charlottesville, VA 2290
Phone: (800) 243-1743
Web site: http://store.yahoo.com/monticellostore/

Thompson & Morgan
PO Box 1308
Jackson, NJ 08527
Phone: (800) 274-7333
Fax: (888) 466-4769
Web site: www.thompson-morgan.com

Valley Oak Tool Co.
PO Box 1225
Chico, CA 95927
Phone: (530) 342-6188
Web site: www.valleyoaktool.com

Wayside Gardens
1 Garden Ln.
Hodges, SC 29695
Phone: (800) 213-0379
Web site: www.waysidegardens.com

Recommended Reading

Cebenko, Jill Jesiolowski, and Deborah L. Martin, eds. *Insect, Disease and Weed I.D. Guide.* Emmaus, PA: Rodale Inc., 2001

Editors, *The Old Farmer's Almanac. Ben Franklin's Almanac of Wit, Wisdom, and Practical Advice.* Emmaus, PA: Rodale Inc., 2003

Heinrichs, Jay, et al. *Home Remedies from the Country Doctor.* Emmaus, PA: Rodale Inc., 1999

Lukkens, Miriam. *Mrs. Dunwoody's Excellent Instructions for Housekeeping.* New York: Warner Books, 2004

Martin, Deborah L., editor. *1,001 Ingenious Gardening Ideas.* Emmaus, PA: Rodale Inc., 1999

Martin, Tovah. *Once upon a Windowsill: A History of Indoor Plants.* Portland, OR: Timber Press, 1988

McGrath, Mike. *You Bet Your Tomatoes!* Emmaus, PA: Rodale Inc., 2002

Mendelson, Cheryl. *Home Comforts.* New York: Scribner, 1999

Proulx, Earl, and the editors of *Yankee* magazine. *Yankee Magazine's Vinegar, Duct Tape, Milk Jugs and More.* Emmaus, PA: Rodale Inc., 1999

Reich, Lee A. *Uncommon Fruits for Every Garden*. Portland, OR: Timber Press, 2004

Weaver, William Woys. *Heirloom Vegetable Gardening*. New York: Henry Holt, 1997

INDEX

Underscored page references indicate boxed text and tables. **Boldface** references indicate illustrations.

C

M

N

R

S

Z